Tax
Exempt
Organizations

Recent Titles from QUORUM BOOKS

Tax Exempt Organizations

E. C. LASHBROOKE, JR.

Q

Quorum Books

Westport, Connecticut · London, England

Library of Congress Cataloging in Publication Data

Lashbrooke, E. C.
  Tax exempt organizations.

  Bibliography: p.
  Includes index.
    1. Corporations, Nonprofit—Taxation—United States. 2. Charitable uses, trusts, and
  foundations—Taxation—United States. 3. Corporations, Nonprofit—United States. 4. Charitable
  uses, trusts, and foundations—United States. I. Title.
  KF6449.L37   1985   343.7306'6   84-22253
  ISBN 0-89930-083-9 (lib. bdg.)   347.30366

Library of Congress Catalog Card Number: 84-22253
ISBN: 0-89930-083-9

First published in 1985 by Quorum Books

Greenwood Press
A division of Congressional Information Service, Inc.
88 Post Road West, Westport, Connecticut 06881

Printed in the United States of America

10 9 8 7 6 5 4 3 2 1

To my wife, Meg, whose enthusiastic support has made the difference.

Contents

Tables

Preface

This work grew out of the frustration felt when attempting to do research in the area of tax exempt organizations. Considering the huge sums of money passing through the plethora of nonprofit organizations in the United States, the literature is rather sparse and diffuse. Although the subject of nonprofit, tax exempt organizations is multidisciplined, integrated works are virtually nonexistent. The tax materials generally are compiled as a separate body of law. When they are incorporated in other works, the tax materials appear to be superficial and mysterious. Moreover, tax exemption materials seem to be limited to section 501(c)(3) charitable organizations while little attention is given to the other subparagraphs of section 501(c). (For the complete text of IRC Section 501, see the Appendix at the end of this volume.)

This book presents detailed and meaningful tax materials and organizational law in chronological order, beginning with conception and proceeding through the different stages in the life of a nonprofit, tax exempt organization. While detailed, the tax materials represent general principles, guidelines, and directions rather than a reproduction of the myriad revenue rulings, revenue procedures, letter rulings, general counsels' memoranda, and other sources of minutia concerning tax exempt organizations. Intended to be a reference guide for foundation managers and practitioners who deal with nonprofit, tax exempt organizations, this book also may be adapted for use as a textbook in a basic course in nonprofit, tax exempt organizations or an advanced tax course in tax exempt organizations.

It is customary at this point to give recognition to those persons whose contributions assisted in the completion of the book. To that end I would like to thank my secretary, Cathy Burch, who spent many long hours typing and retyping the manuscript.

Tax
Exempt
Organizations

1

Definition and Characteristics of a Tax Exempt Organization

Tax exempt organizations are essential elements of American society. It is almost inconceivable that any member of our society is not a member of or associated with a tax exempt organization. Tax exempt organizations have become such an integral part of our society and lives that they are hardly discernible. Indeed, in a random sample of households in the New Haven, Connecticut, Standard Metropolitan Statistical Area (SMSA) a majority of the respondents failed to identify five local nonprofit organizations as such.[1]

Few individuals are aware of the vast number and relative sizes of tax exempt organizations. For example, there are approximately 135,700,000 persons in the United States who are members of over 331,000 religious congregations.[2] The *1983 World Almanac* lists almost 1,200 associations and societies.[3] Typical membership figures are AFL-CIO, 15,000,000;[4] Boy Scouts of America, 4,355,723;[5] and Knights of Columbus, 1,359,000.[6]

It is generally believed that the history of the tax exempt status granted to individuals can be traced back to the Statute of Charitable Uses in 1601.[7] However, the earliest written record proclaiming tax exempt status for an organization appears to be in the Old Testament.[8] Whatever the historical source of tax exempt status for an organization may be, tax exempt status has been accorded to certain organizations since the beginning of this Republic.

Prior to the enactment of the Revenue Act of 1894,[9] certain charitable organizations were exempt from taxation by omission. The absence of any specific tax exemption is easily understood in light of the history of United States revenue law. Until the burden of fighting a civil war was imposed on the federal government, federal revenue was derived primarily from customs duties and excise taxes. The first federal income tax was imposed in 1862 and repealed in 1872. No specific exemptions were contained in the law, but since the tax was imposed

economically on only about 1 percent of the population, it is not hard to understand why charitable organizations were tax exempt by omission.

Express tax exemptions for "corporations, companies or associations organized and conducted solely for charitable, religious, or educational purposes"
first appeared in section 32 of the Revenue Act of 1894.[10] Congress imposed a
tax only on "corporations, companies, or associations doing business for profit."[11] This first modern federal income tax act was challenged immediately. The
United States Supreme Court in *Pollack v. Farmers Loan & Trust Co.*[12] declared
that the rental income tax portion of the act was unconstitutional because the
direct tax was not apportioned among the states according to population.[13]
Because the 1894 act was not severable, the entire act, including the tax exemptions, failed. The tax exempt status accorded organizations having charitable,
religious, or educational purposes has appeared in every subsequent revenue act
and has been embodied since 1954 in I.R.C.§ 501(c) (3).

Since the original revenue act, tax exempt status has been extended to include
other types of organizations. In 1909, it was extended to labor, agricultural, and
horticultural organizations.[14] Mutual cemetery companies, business leagues,
chambers of commerce, social welfare organizations, and scientific organizations were added in 1913.[15] Social clubs, land banks, and organizations associated with farming and title holding companies, public utilities, and state instrumentalities gained favorable tax exempt status in 1916.[16] The Revenue Act of
1918 included a society for the prevention of cruelty to animals and children.[17]
Community chest funds and foundations joined the list in 1921.[18] The Tax
Reform Act of 1976[19] rounded out the list by including organizations which
foster national and international sports competition,[20] homeowner associations
including elected condominium management and residential real estate management associations,[21] and fishing associations.[22]

Many attempts have been made to explain the underlying rationale for tax
exemption or to find the common thread running through the patchwork of the
tax exempt organization pattern, if indeed it is a pattern. One rationale for the tax
exemption accorded to certain organizations is that their classification as nonprofit or not-for-profit[23] organizations is not accidental. Business ventures are
organized for profit, and the tax code is a set of rules whereby the gains or profits
generated by businesses are determined and taxed. Nonprofit organizations do
not generate profits in the business sense, and accounting principles are not
easily adaptable to nonprofit operations.[24] This rationale was articulated by
Congress in 1909 when it exempted from taxation organizations that could not
reasonably be expected to generate any meaningful income.[25]

Later, Congress based the tax exemption on a public welfare theory, the theory
being that tax exempt organizations perform services that the government would
otherwise have to provide in their absence; therefore, any loss of revenue resulting from the tax exemptions is more than offset by shifting the financial burden
for providing those services from the federal treasury to tax exempt organiza-

tions.[26] The tax exemptions encourage the private sector to actively engage in activities generally regarded as fundamental or socially desirable, and thereby to promote the general welfare.[27]

The recent popularity of economic analysis of law has prompted the development of a failure of contract theory to explain the existence of nonprofit organizations.[28] Under this theory, the nonprofit form of organization results from inadequate contractual devices to guarantee that the services desired by contributors or patrons of nonprofit organizations will actually be performed. The failure of ordinary contractual devices is inherent either in the nature of the desired services or the circumstances under which they are to be provided, because ordinary contractual devices assume a profit motive for the person providing the services. The contractual failure is cured by a nonprofit organization, because no part of the net earnings may inure to the benefit of any private shareholder or individual, which is the pivotal requirement for tax exempt status under I.R.C. § 501 (c) (3). Admittedly, the theory does not hold up when applied to other nonprofit organizations such as social clubs and other consumer cooperatives.[29] Contributors, patrons, or consumers of nonprofit organizations are said to believe them to be more trustworthy and reliable than for-profit organizations and prefer to have nonprofits provide the service.[30] This theory has been attacked as not being in touch with reality.[31] It has been pointed out that the three basic assumptions on which the economic theory of contract failure is based are not true.[32] However, the theory does provide fodder for academic debate.

While different rationales for tax exempt or nonprofit status abound, no one of them is sufficient justification for the whole spectrum of tax exemptions that Congress has granted. In short, the potpourri of moral, political, historical, and pragmatic considerations propounded accounts for the congressional decisions to grant tax exempt status to certain organizations.

The defining characteristic of a nonprofit organization is the prohibition against distributing any part of the net earnings to persons who are private shareholders, officers, directors, or members of the organization. The prohibition is against distribution of the net earnings only. Reasonable salaries or compensation may be paid by nonprofit organizations to any person who provides services or capital to the nonprofit organization regardless of that person's relationship to the organization.

This prohibition against distributing net earnings is found in the Model Nonprofit Corporation Act and nonprofit corporation acts of the states.[33] If the nonprofit organization is a charitable trust, the distribution prohibition is imposed by the law of trusts.[34] An unincorporated nonprofit association, other than a trust, does not have externally imposed law prohibiting distribution of the net earnings, but the distribution prohibition is a requirement to obtain tax exempt status.[35]

The common thread in all nonprofit organizations is that the net earnings must be devoted to the purpose for which the nonprofit organization was formed; tax exempt status depends on it. The purposes for which a nonprofit organization may be formed are many and are discussed in detail in Chapter 2, *infra*. Indeed, some nonprofit corporation acts and the Model Nonprofit Corporation Act provide for incorporation for any lawful purpose[36] which seems to prohibit only those purposes that are criminal or against public policy. Consequently, there is no characteristic purpose. Moreover, the nonprofit corporation statutes allow incorporation for many more purposes than the Internal Revenue Code allows for tax exempt status, but even within I.R.C. § 501(c) there is no characteristic purpose. Nor is there a characteristic form of organization.

The most popular organizational form of nonprofit organizations is the nonprofit corporation, although other forms are permissible: charitable trusts, unincorporated associations such as labor unions, and private foundations. However, no tax exemption may be granted to an individual or partnership unless the partnership is treated as a corporation for tax purposes.[37]

Other than the prohibition against distribution of net earnings, the only common characteristic of nonprofit organizations seems to be that they are not organized and operated for the benefit of investors seeking a return on their capital. The intended beneficiaries may be the members of the nonprofit organization or third-party beneficiaries. But regardless of whom or what segment of society the nonprofit organization is organized and operated to benefit, the organization must be organized and operated exclusively for tax exempt purposes to obtain and maintain tax exempt status under I.R.C. § 501(c)(3).[38] However, see the discussion in Chapter 4, *infra,* regarding unrelated business income and activities which serve both an exempt and nonexempt purpose.

Not all nonprofit organizations qualify as tax exempt organizations. Section 501(c)(3) organizations and other section 501(c) organizations which prohibit distribution of net earnings generally are nonprofit organizations in the traditional sense that nonprofit status is only granted for certain enumerated purposes.[39] In the expanded sense of a nonprofit corporation, which may be incorporated for any lawful purpose,[40] all tax exempt organizations are a subset of the category of nonprofit organizations.

Tax exempt status is not automatically bestowed on a nonprofit organization by virtue of its existence. Tax exempt status must be applied for and approved by the Internal Revenue Service. Moreover, tax exempt status must be maintained by careful and strict compliance with the Internal Revenue Code and treasury regulations. The goal of this book is to provide the reader with information necessary to organize and qualify a nonprofit organization for tax exempt status and to maintain that status once it is obtained.

NOTES

1. Permut, *Consumer Perceptions of Nonprofit Enterprise: A Comment on Hansmann,* 90 Yale L. J. 1623, 1626–28 (1981).

2. *1983 World Almanac* 352–53.

3. *Id.* at 338–51.

4. *Id.* at 338.

5. *Id.* at 339.

6. *Id.* at 344.

7. 43 Eliz. I. ch. 4 (1601).

8. *Ezra* 7:24, "also we certify you, that touching any of the priests and Levites, singers, porters, Nethinim, or Ministers of this House of God, it shall not be lawful to impose toll, tribute, or customs upon them."

9. 28 Stat. 509 (1894).

10. Ch. 349, § 32, 28 Stat. 556 (1894).

11. *Id.*

12. 157 U.S. 429, 583 (1895).

13. U.S. Const., Art. I, § 2, cl. 3.

14. Corporation Excise Tax of 1909, § 38, 36 Stat. 112, 113.

15. Revenue Act of 1913, § II, para. G(a), 38 Stat. 114, 172.

16. Revenue Act of 1916, § 11(a), 39 Stat. 756, 766–67.

17. Section 231(6), 40 Stat. 1057, 1076.

18. Revenue Act of 1921, § 231(6), 42 Stat. 227, 253.

19. Pub. L. No. 94-455, 90 Stat. 1730.

20. *Id.* § 1313.

21. *Id.* § 2101.

22. *Id.* § 2113.

23. Although some commentators draw a distinction between these two terms, as used here they are synonymous.

24. *See,* Bittker & Rahdert, *The Exemption of Nonprofit Organizations from Federal Income Taxation,* 85 Yale L. J. 299, 307–14 (1976).

25. Corporation Excise Tax Act of 1909, § 38, 36 Stat. 112, 113.

26. H. R. Rep. No. 1860, 75th Cong., 3d Sess., 1939–1 (Part II) C. B. 742.

27. *Id.*

28. *See,* Hansmann, *The Role of Nonprofit Enterprise,* 89 Yale L. J. 835 (1980) and Hansmann, *Reforming Nonprofit Corporation Law,* 129 U. Pa. L. R. 497 (1981).

29. Hansmann, *Reforming Nonprofit Corporation Law,* 129 U. Pa. L. R. 497, 582 (1981).

30. *Id.* at 504–8.

31. *See,* Permut, *Consumer Perceptions of Nonprofit Enterprise: A Comment on Hansmann,* 90 Yale L. J. 1623 (1981).

32. *Id.* at 1626–29.

33. ALI-ABA Model Nonprofit Corporation Act, § 2(c) (1964); *e.g.,* Fla. Stat. § 617.01(2); Ill. Rev. Stat. 163a1, § 2(c); N.Y. Not-for-Profit Corporation Law § 102(5) (McKinney); Tex. Rev. Civ. Stat. Ann. art. 1396–1.02(3) (Vernon).

34. *See,* A. Scott, *Law of Trusts,* § 348 (3d ed. 1967).

35. I.R.C. § 501(c).

36. ALI-ABA Model Nonprofit Corporation Act, § 4 alternative (1964); *e.g.,* Fla. Stat. § 617.01(1); Tex. Rev. Civ. Stat. Ann. art. 1396–2.01.

37. Treas. Reg. § 301.7701–2. An unincorporated association or partnership which more closely resembles a corporation than not will be treated as a corporation for tax

purposes. The regulation is written in such a manner that a partnership created in a jurisdiction which adopted the Uniform Partnership Act in substance will not be treated as a corporation for tax purposes.

38. Treas. Reg. § 1.501(c)(3)-1(d)(iii).

39. ALI-ABA Model Nonprofit Corporation Act, § 4 (1964); Ill. Rev. Stat. 163a3, § 4; N.Y. Not-for-Profit Corporation Law § 201.

40. *See,* note 36, *supra.*

2

Organizers

Virtually any adult person can organize a nonprofit, tax exempt organization regardless of the form of the organization. Organizer, as used in this chapter, means any juridical person who organizes a nonprofit association regardless of form. Organizer includes a settlor or grantor, promoter, and incorporator.

CHARITABLE TRUSTS

A charitable trust may be created by any person who has the capacity to make the particular transfer in question. There are five different ways to create a charitable trust.

A person who has the capacity to transfer property *inter vivos* may declare himself trustee of property for charitable purposes.[1] Capacity to transfer property beneficially generally is lacking only in infants and the insane. Creation of a charitable trust by *inter vivos* transfer in trust requires the capacity to transfer property beneficially by way of gift or sale.[2]

Creation of a charitable trust by will requires testamentary capacity.[3] Testamentary capacity requires that a person attain a statutorily specified age, generally that of majority, and be of sound mind. A person is of sound mind if he understands in a general way (1) the nature and extent of his property, (2) the persons who are the natural objects of his bounty, and (3) the disposition he is making of his property, and understands the relationship among those three things.[4] A person may have testamentary capacity even though he lacks capacity to contract or transfer property *inter vivos*.

A person who holds either a general or special power of appointment may create a charitable trust.[5] If the donee of the power of appointment has the capacity to transfer property beneficially to a person, he has the capacity to transfer the property in trust.[6] Some states require that the donee of the power of appointment have the capacity to transfer property, but generally a donee of a power of appointment may exercise it even though he individually lacks capacity to transfer property *inter vivos* or make a will.[7]

A charitable trust may be created by a promise made by one person to another whose rights are to be held in trust for charitable purposes.[8] The capacity required here is that of contract. If the promise is a binding contract, a charitable trust is created. Incapacity to contract generally occurs as a result of infancy or insanity.

FOUNDATIONS

Requirements and qualifications of organizers of foundations depend on the form of organization of the foundation. An unincorporated foundation is a charitable trust. If the foundation is incorporated, then the statutory provisions dealing with organizing and incorporating a nonprofit corporation apply.

NONPROFIT CORPORATION

An organizer of a nonprofit corporation may or may not be an incorporator or member of the corporation after incorporation. For purposes of this section an organizer who is a promoter in the business corporation sense will be so designated, and an organizer who is merely an incorporator will be so designated.

Promoters

Qualifications

There is no real difference between a promoter of a business corporation and a promoter of a nonprofit corporation. A promoter is the moving force behind the creation of a corporation. The promoter is the person with the idea who interests others in the idea and solicits their contribution to the effort. The promoter starts the wheels of incorporation in motion and sees the project through to incorporation at which time his function ceases to exist.

Promoters and promoters' activities generally are not the subject of legislation.[9] Most of the law dealing with promoters is of case law origin. Promoters are subject to certain fiduciary duties and liabilities with respect to their activities, but no qualifications are imposed other than the implicit capacity to contract.

Duties and Liabilities

A promoter owes obligations to other promoters jointly engaged, the nonexistent corporation, and future shareholders or members of the corporation.

Promoters are joint venturers.[10] A joint venture is generally considered to be a partnership for limited purposes short of the conduct of an ongoing business.[11] It should be noted that some commentators argue that a joint venture is a business form apart from that of partnership.[12] Nonetheless, a business purpose is required for a joint venture. As joint venturers they are partners and hence agents of each other.[13] Each has the power within the limits of the joint venture agreement to contractually bind the other joint venturers.[14] Likewise, the joint venturers are liable for torts committed by one of them within the scope of the joint venture.[15] The joint venturers are jointly and severally liable to third parties in both contract and tort.[16]

The lack of a business purpose would seem to disqualify the activity of nonprofit corporation promoters as a joint venture or partnership. Even so, liability among the promoters *inter se* and to third parties would be determined under the contractual agreement, express or implied, which established the joint venture. In some states, tort liability exists for joint enterprise without regard to the existence of business purpose.[17]

Joint venturers are in a fiduciary relationship similar to that of partners.[18] That relationship is characterized by Judge Cardozo's now-famous words: "Not honesty alone but the punctilio of an honor the most sensitive, is then the standard of behavior."[19] Breach of that fiduciary duty is actionable in equity by the other joint venturers.

A promoter cannot be an agent for a nonexistent corporate principal prior to incorporation.[20] The liability of a promoter for any agreement entered into before incorporation depends on the type of agreement in question.

The first kind of agreement is an offer contingent upon formation of the corporation or acceptance by the newly formed corporation. This type of agreement is not a contract at all but a revocable offer. The promoter has neither enforceable rights nor liabilities under the agreement. If the proposed corporation is not formed or refuses to accept the offer, if not revoked, then no contract is ever formed. This type of agreement must be carefully worded because courts are reluctant to find that the parties did not intend to create immediate, legally enforceable rights.[21] While a promoter has no liability under the agreement, the promoter may be liable for misrepresentations or breach of warranty arising out of the agreement.[22]

Another type of agreement is a contract between a promoter and third party whereby the promoter promises to form the corporation and use his best efforts to have the newly formed corporation accept the irrevocable offer given in exchange for the promoter's promise. The promoter is personally liable for failing to form the corporation or not using his best efforts to get an acceptance of the offer in addition to potential liability for misrepresentation or breach of warranty. If the proposed corporation is not formed or refuses the offer, if formed, no contract exists between the corporation and the third party, and the corporation has no liabilities or rights under the promoter's contract. If the offer is accepted by the newly formed corporation, the corporation is bound by the terms of the contract between it and the third party, and the promoter's obligations and liabilities under his contract are extinguished except for misrepresentation or breach of warranty.

A contract between a third party and a promoter on behalf of a proposed corporation is binding on the promoter as principal unless otherwise qualified.[23] If the proposed corporation is not formed or does nothing with respect to the contract, the promoter remains liable. Moreover, even if the corporation is formed and ratifies or adopts the contract or becomes the assignee of the promoter, the promoter remains personally liable on the contract in addition to liability for misrepresentation or breach of warranty. Only in case of a novation in which the corporation is substituted for the promoter is the promoter released from liability. In the event of breach of the contract by the corporation where the promoter remains personally liable, the promoter has a cause of action against the corporation based on either *quantum meruit* or reliance and estoppel against the corporation to deny liability.

However, before a contract or act of a promoter is adopted or ratified, the promoter must make full disclosure.[24] Promoters owe a fiduciary duty to the newly formed corporation which consists of good faith, fair dealing, and full disclosure.[25] If the board of directors of the newly formed corporation is an independent board, then full disclosure to the board is sufficient to satisfy the obligation of full disclosure.[26] But if the board of directors is not independent, full disclosure must be made to the shareholders or membership.[27] There is a split of authority as to whether full disclosure extends to the group of shareholders or membership existent at the time of ratification or adoption or whether it extends to contemplated shareholders or members.[28]

The corporation either in its own stead or by shareholder derivative suit may bring a cause of action against the promoters for breach of fiduciary duty. The typical suit is for disgorgement of secret profits made by the promoters at the expense of the corporation.[29]

Promoters owe fiduciary duties to potential shareholders or members. Separate from any corporate cause of action are claims of fraud against the promoters in connection with the sale of stock or membership subscription, the primary claim being one of misrepresentation or omission of a material fact in connection with the sale of stock or membership subscription.[30] Courts have held that there is no material difference in fiduciary duty owed to potential shareholders or members or liability to be imposed between a promoter of a business corporation and a promoter of a nonprofit corporation.[31]

Control Agreements

In nonmembership nonprofit corporations, the corporation is controlled by the board of directors or trustees. The organizers are in a position to appoint themselves to such positions and control the nonprofit corporation. Preincorporation agreements to perpetuate control are not uncommon in business corporations and without doubt could be utilized in nonprofit corporations.[32] The agreement is not binding on the corporation, but as long as the organizers control the board of directors or trustees, it will be effective.

In membership nonprofit corporations, such an agreement will not survive the initial board of directors or trustees unless the organizers control the membership vote or unless membership inertia allows the control agreement to continue. Control of the membership vote is allowed in certain states by statutes that authorize voting control agreements.[33]

Compensation

Generally, anyone who performs services in connection with the formation of a corporation expects to receive compensation for such services. The preincorporation contract for the services provided is with the promoter because the corporation is nonexistent. The promoter remains personally liable until the corporation is formed and assumes responsibility for the contracts by acceptance of the offer, ratification, adoption, assignment, or novation.[34] A third party may recover against a corporation that accepts the benefits of the services without formal action assuming that responsibility is based on *quantum meruit*.

Compensation for promoters of business corporations is expected and generally received. Compensation must be fair and reasonable, and full disclosure must be made. Promoters of nonprofit corporations are under the same duties of fair dealing and full disclosure as are promoters of business corporations. Compensation for services rendered does not violate the antidistribution of net profit rule for nonprofit corporations. Determining the value of such services is the most difficult step in the process.

Incorporators

Incorporators, technically, are persons who sign the original articles of incorporation. They derive their status strictly from the corporation statutes. Qualifications are expressly set out in the appropriate state statute (see Table 1).

The qualifications for an incorporator of a nonprofit corporation are *de minimis* under the laws of the several states. Most states have separate nonprofit corporation acts, but a few merely insert nonprofit corporation provisions into their business corporation act in which case the business corporation act controls many aspects of nonprofit corporation law.[35]

The number of incorporators required to sign the original articles of incorporation varies from state to state. Thirty-one states require only one incorporator. Of the remaining states three require two incorporators; thirteen require three incorporators; three require five incorporators; and one requires a majority of the members to consent to incorporation.

Twenty-one states restrict incorporators to natural persons. The remainder use

Table 1
Incorporators

State	Person	Natural	Partnership	Profit Corp	NFP Corp	United States	State	Age	1	2	3	4	5	Other	Remarks
Alabama		x						19			x				§ 10-3-22
Alaska		x						19			x				§ 10.20.146
Arizona	x							C	x						§ 10-1028
Arkansas		x						21	x						For Profit Act § 64-501
California	x								x						§ 5120
Colorado	x								x						§ 7-21-101
Connecticut	x								x						§ 33-426
Delaware	x								x						For Profit Act tit. 8, § 101
District of Columbia	x							21			x				§ 29-1029
Florida		x	x	x					x						§ 617.013
Georgia	x	x		x	x			19	x						§ 22-2701
Hawaii	x					x					x				Corp. Act § 416-20
Idaho		x	x						x						§ 30-1-53
Illinois		x			x			21			x				§ 163a27
Indiana		x	x						x						§ 23-7-1.1-16
Iowa		x					x	M	x						§ 504.1
Kansas														x	§ 17-701 requires majority of members to consent
Kentucky	x								x						§ 273.343
Louisiana	x							C	x						R.S.12:202
Maine	x								x						13-B § 401
Maryland		x						18	x						§ 2-101
Massachusetts	x							18	x						C.180 § 3
Michigan	x								x						§ 450-2201
Minnesota		x						M	x						§ 317.07
Mississippi		x					x	M			x				§ 79-11-1
Missouri		x			x			18			x				§ 355-040
Montana	x								x						§ 35-2-201
Nebraska	x									x					§ 21-1927
Nevada							x				x				§ 81.010
New Hampshire		x						M						x	§ 292:1
New Jersey	x													x	§ 15:1-1
New Mexico	x			x	x				x						§ 53-8-30
New York		x						18	x						N-PCL § 401
North Carolina		x						18	x						§ 55A-6
North Dakota	x								x						§ 10-28-28
Ohio	x								x						§ 1702.04(A)
Oklahoma		x						C			x				18 § 853
Oregon		x	x	x	x			18	x						§ 61.305
Pennsylvania		x		x	x			M	x						15 § 7312
Rhode Island		x						M						x	§ 7-6-3
South Carolina										x					officers or agents of organization

Table 1 (continued)
Incorporators

State	Person					Citizen		Age	Number						Remarks
	Person	Natural	Partnership	Profit Corp	NFP Corp	United States	State		1	2	3	4	5	Other	
South Carolina (continued)															§ 33-31-20
South Dakota		x						M		x					§ 47-22-5
Tennessee		x							x						§ 48-201
Texas		x				2		18		x					Art. 1396-3.01(A)
Utah		x						21		x					§ 16-10-48
Vermont		x				1		M	x						tit. 11, § 2401
Virginia	x							21							§ 13.1-230
Washington		x	x	x					x						Gov't. body or agency can organize § 24.06.020
West Virginia		x	x						x						§ 31-1-26
Wisconsin		x						18	x						§ 181.30
Wyoming	x								x						§ 17-6-101

C – power to contract
M – age of majority

a broader definition of juridical person. Of the states that allow any person to be an incorporator, some specifically include in the definition persons such as domestic and foreign corporations, nonprofit corporations, partnerships, and associations.

Capacity to contract is a requirement. Capacity to contract is only specified by four states but is implicit in the age requirements for natural persons and in the nature of other juridical persons. Capacity to contract in a natural person is a function of age unless the person is otherwise incapacitated by insanity or incompetence. Ages between eighteen and twenty-one years of age or majority are specified by twenty-three states.

Only nine states have a residency or citizenship qualification. Two states require United States citizenship while the other seven require a minimum number of the incorporators to be residents of the state of incorporation.

UNINCORPORATED ASSOCIATIONS OTHER THAN TRUSTS

Any group of persons having a common purpose or goal may form an unincorporated nonprofit association. Typical examples are political committees, religious communes, sports clubs, fraternal orders, patriotic societies, trade associations, and labor unions. An unincorporated nonprofit association is not a partnership because a partnership is defined as an association of two or more persons to carry on a business for profit.[36]

Unincorporated nonprofit associations generally are not treated by statute. New Jersey has the most complete statutory regulation; however, its primary purpose is to provide unincorporated associations with some of the attributes of a juridical person, primarily that of the right to sue and be sued in the name of the unincorporated association.[37] A few other states have provisions that deal with a particular type of unincorporated association.[38] There are no qualifications for being an organizer of such an association other than what may generally be required to contract or transfer property.

NOTES

1. A. Scott, *Law of Trusts,* § 18 (3d ed. 1967).

2. *Id.* § 19.

3. *Id.* § 20.

4. T. Atkinson, *Handbook of the Law of Wills and Other Principles of Succession, including Intestacy and Administration of Decedent's Estates,* 232 (2d ed. 1953).

5. *See* note 1, *supra,* § 21.

6. *Id.*

7. *Id.*

8. *Id.* § 22.

9. *But see,* N.C. Bus. Corp. Act § 55–53 and Fla. stat. §§ 718.503, 718.302, 718.301 (1977).

10. H. Henn & J. Alexander, *Laws of Corporations,* 238–39 (3d ed. 1983).

11. *Id.* at 105–6.

12. Jaeger, *Partnership v. Joint Venture,* 37 Notre Dame Law. 138 (1961); Taubman, *What Constitutes a Joint Venture,* 41 Corn. L.Q. 640 (1956).

13. Uniform Partnership Act § 9.

14. *Id.*

15. Uniform Partnership Act §§ 13, 14.

16. Uniform Partnership Act § 15.

17. *Pierson v. Edstrom,* 286 Minn. 164, 174 N.W. 2d 712 (1970).

18. *See* note 10, *supra,* at 107.

19. *Meinhard v. Salmon,* 249 N.Y. 458, 464, 164 N.E. 545, 546 (1928).

20. Restatement (Second) of Agency § 326 (1958).

21. R. Stevens, *Handbook on the Law of Private Corporations,* 210–13 (2d ed. 1949). *See* Note, *Preincorporation Agreements,* 11 Sw. L.J. 509 (1957); Restatement (Second) of Agency § 328 (1958).

22. *See* note 10, *supra* at 250.

23. Restatement (Second) of Agency § 326 (1958).

24. *See* note 10, at 239–40.

25. *Id.*

26. *Id.* at 240.

27. *Id.*

28. *Old Dominion Copper Mining & Smelting Co. v. Bigelow,* 188 Mass. 315, 74 N.E. 653 (1905); *Old Dominion Copper Mining & Smelting Co. v. Lewisohn,* 210 U.S. 206 (1908). These two cases arose out of the same transactions; however, the outcomes were different as a result of different theories being applied by the two different courts.

29. *Id.*

30. *McCandless v. Furlaud,* 296 U.S. 140 (1935), *rehearing denied,* 296 U.S. 664 (1936).

31. *Post v. U.S.,* 407 F.2d 319, 328–30 (C.A.D.C. 1969), *cert. denied,* 393 U.S. 1092 (1969); *Riviera Condominium Apts v. Weinberger,* 231 S.2d 850 (Fla. App. 1970); *Fountainview Assn. Inc. v. Bell,* 203 S.2d 657 (Fla. App. 1967).

32. H. Oleck, *Nonprofit Corporations, Organizations, and Associations,* 211 (4th ed. 1980).

33. N.Y. N-P-CL § 619 (1970); Calif. Corp. Code § 5240(b)(3).

34. *See* discussion, *supra* at *12–16.*

35. *See, e.g.,* Ark. Stat. Ann. § 64-501; Del. Code Ann., tit. 8, § 101; Idaho Code § 30-1-53.

36. Uniform Partnership Act § 6.

37. N.J. Stat. Ann. §§ 64-1 to 64-6 (West).

38. *See, e.g.,* N.Y. Gen. Ass'ns and N.Y. Consol. Laws., ch. 29 (McKinney Supp. 1978–79).

3

Tax Exempt Purposes

Section 501 of the Internal Revenue Code is the keystone of the statutory system. For an organization to have tax exempt status, it must fit within one of the categories of I.R.C. §§ 401(a), 501(c), or 501(d).[1] These sections describe the purposes for which a tax exempt organization may be formed. Tax exempt purposes described in the code are not coterminous with the purposes for which nonprofit organizations may be formed under state law today. In the formative years of the federal income tax the distinction was between profit and nonprofit.[2] As the federal tax law developed, the present-day categories were gradually incorporated, and the distinction between profit and nonprofit blurred into the concept of tax exempt status.[3]

Many states still explicitly limit the purposes for which a nonprofit corporation may be formed. These statutory provisions generally resemble I.R.C. § 501(c) and typically limit the purposes to charitable, educational, literary, and others that are similar.[4] The modern trend is to allow incorporation of a nonprofit corporation "for any lawful purpose."[5]

Charitable trusts must be formed for charitable purposes within the common law meaning of the word "charitable." According to the Treasury Regulations and the United States Supreme Court, the common law meaning of charitable is incorporated in I.R.C. § 501(c).[6]

The following are recognized as tax exempt purposes for organizations:

1. A trust created or organized in the United States which forms part of a stock bonus, pension, or profit sharing plan of an employer for the exclusive benefit of his employees and their beneficiaries[7]

2. Instrumentalities of the United States organized by act of Congress and tax exempt by such act[8]

18

3. Corporations organized for the exclusive purpose of holding title to property for other tax exempt organizations[9]

4. Corporations and any community chest, fund, or foundation organized for religious, charitable, scientific, testing for public safety, literary, or educational purposes, or to foster national or international amateur sports competition, or for the prevention of cruelty to children or animals[10]

5. Civic leagues or organizations organized to promote social welfare[11]

6. Local employee associations[12]

7. Labor, agricultural, or horticultural associations[13]

8. Nonprofit business leagues, chambers of commerce, real estate boards, boards of trade, or professional football leagues[14]

9. Social clubs operated for pleasure, recreation, and other nonprofit purposes[15]

10. Fraternal beneficiary societies, orders, or associations operating under the lodge system which provide insurance benefits to members[16]

11. Voluntary employees' beneficiary associations which provide insurance benefits to members[17]

12. Domestic fraternal societies, orders, or associations which do not provide insurance benefits to members[18]

13. Local teacher retirement fund associations[19]

14. Local benevolent life insurance associations[20]

15. Cemetery companies formed exclusively for the disposal of bodies of deceased members by burial or cremation[21]

16. Certain nonstock credit unions and certain mutual nonstock associations[22]

17. Certain mutual insurance companies or associations[23]

18. Organizations of farmers' coops or their members to finance their crops[24]

19. Trusts formed as part of a plan to provide supplemental unemployment compensation benefits[25]

20. Certain trusts created before June 25, 1959, as part of a pension plan to provide nondiscrimination benefits[26]

21. A post or organization of past or present members of the armed forces of the United States, or an auxiliary unit or society of, or a trust or foundation for such post or organization[27]

22. Trusts formed to provide qualified group legal services under a plan[28]

23. Trusts for the payment of black lung benefits[29]

24. Trusts created for payment of certain withdrawal liabilities of pension plans[30]

25. Certain associations of present or past members of the armed forces created before 1880 for the purpose of providing insurance and other benefits to veterans and their dependents[31]

26. Certain religious and apostolic associations[32]

UNITED STATES INSTRUMENTALITIES

Instrumentalities of the United States which are created by act of Congress and are exempted from federal taxes by Congress under that act are tax exempt organizations.[33] The following is a partial list of such instrumentalities:

1. Commodity Credit Corporation
2. Farmers Home Corporation
3. Federal Credit Unions
4. Federal Crop Insurance Corporation
5. Federal Deposit Insurance Corporation
6. Federal Farm Mortgage Corporation
7. Federal Home Loan Banks
8. Federal National Mortgage Association
9. Federal Land Banks
10. Federal Reserve Banks
11. Federal Intermediate Credit Banks
12. Federal Savings & Loan Insurance Corporation
13. National Farm Loan Association
14. Home Owners' Loan Corporation
15. Central Bank for Cooperatives
16. Production Credit Associations
17. Banks for Cooperatives
18. Reconstruction Finance Corporation
19. Public Housing Administration
20. War Finance Corporation
21. National Insurance Development Fund
22. U.S. Railway Association Federal Financing Bank
23. Central Liquidity Facility

HOLDING COMPANIES

Corporations that are organized for the exclusive purpose of holding title to property, collecting the income from that property, and transmitting the entire amount less expenses to another tax exempt organization are exempt from federal income taxation.[34] The corporation must be organized exclusively as a holding company and may not conduct any other business activities other than holding title and collecting income.

A corporation that rents the real property to which it holds title to the general public and that remits the income less expenses to a tax exempt organization is exempt.[35] Carrying on a business activity results in a denial of tax exempt status. A university cooperative bookstore which sold books and various supplies was held not to be an exempt organization.[36] To be detrimental an activity carried on by the holding company must constitute a trade or business. For example, the purchase of oil and gas production payments from properties with borrowed funds without acquiring ownership of working interests is not a trade or business and does not preclude the tax exemption.[37] The incorporation and operation of a subsidiary which is a tax exempt title-holding company organized for the exclusive purpose of holding title to property, collecting the income from the property, and turning over the income, less expenses, to the parent corporation is not the conduct of a trade or business which will destroy the tax exemption of the parent.[38]

The income from the property, less expenses, must be remitted to another tax exempt organization. Retention of income in a reserve fund is not permissible.[39] Moreover, all of the income, less expenses, must go to tax exempt organizations. Any disposition of income to private recipients results in loss or denial of tax exempt status.[40] The tax exempt status of the holding company will be terminated when one of the recipient organizations ceases to qualify for a tax exemption.[41] However, a tax exempt holding corporation may retain part of the income collected to apply to indebtedness on the property to which it holds title, in which event the income will be treated as if it had been turned over to the tax exempt parent and later used to make a capital contribution to the holding company which in turn applied the contribution to the indebtedness.[42]

It is not necessary that the corporation be expressly incorporated as a tax exempt organization, provided its planned purpose and operations establish its exempt purpose.[43] But a corporation which was organized and operated as a business cannot subsequently be transformed into a tax exempt organization.[44]

501(c)(3) ORGANIZATIONS

Corporations, and any community chest, fund, or foundation, organized and operated exclusively for religious, literary, or educational purposes, or to foster national or international amateur sports competition, or for the prevention of cruelty to children or animals may be accorded tax exempt status.[45]

Religious

An organization formed exclusively for religious purposes may be tax exempt under section 501(c)(3). The wording of that section has been the subject of considerable controversy. The purposes generally set out in section 501(c)(3) are charitable purposes within the common law definition of the word charitable.[46]

Nonetheless, the enumeration of purposes in section 501(c)(3), while seemingly redundant, have been given independent significance. At the same time, neither the code nor the Treasury Regulations contain a definition of "religious purpose." Doubtless, the reluctance to promulgate such a definition is related to first amendment constitutional issues and sensitive political considerations. Likewise, I.R.C. § 170(c)(2)(B) which defines the term "charitable contribution" as a gift to an organization exclusively organized and operated for religious purposes contains no definition of religious purpose nor do the regulations promulgated pursuant to that section. On the other hand, courts have given an expansive definition to the term "religious organization" regardless of the organization's professed tenets and practices.[47] Denials of tax exempt status to religious organizations are primarily on grounds other than its religious purpose.

While an organization formed for religious purposes is broader than the organization and operation of a church, the regulations do contain a definition of the term "church." A church includes a religious order or religious organization that is an integral part of a church and is engaged in carrying out the functions of the church which includes the ministration of sacredotal duties and the conduct of religious services.[48] What constitutes the conduct of religious worship or the ministration of sacredotal functions depends on the tenets and practices of the religious body which constitutes the church.[49] Former commissioner Jerome Kurtz of the Internal Revenue Service expanded the definition of church as provided in the regulations.[50] The IRS will examine the following characteristics to determine whether or not a particular organization is a church:

1. A distinct legal existence
2. A recognized creed and form of worship
3. A definite and distinct ecclesiastical government
4. A formal code of doctrine and discipline
5. A distinct religious history
6. A membership not associated with any church or denomination
7. A complete organization of ordained ministers ministering to their congregations
8. Ordained ministers selected after completing prescribed courses of study
9. A literature of its own
10. Established places of worship
11. Regular congregations
12. Regular religious services
13. Sunday schools for the religious instruction of the young
14. Schools for the preparation of its ministers[51]

The Internal Revenue Service states, however, that controlling weight cannot be given to any single factor and that the determination of whether or not the organization is a church must be made case by case.[52]

Without doubt, a church qualifies as a religious organization; however, the definition of church is not illuminating with respect to the general classification of organizations formed for a religious purpose.

The courts and the Internal Revenue Service have been reluctant to question stated religious purposes regardless of the extreme position taken by the adherents thereto. An examination of the case law clearly establishes this fact. The reluctance of the courts and the Internal Revenue Service to define religious purpose does not prevent the Service nor the courts from finding that the organization is not tax exempt on other grounds however.[53]

Apart from churches, the parameters of religious purposes for which tax exempt status may be granted are best defined by examining past administrative decisions. Publication of a newspaper primarily devoted to church and religious matters is a sufficient religious purpose to qualify for exemption.[54] Compilation of genealogical data for members of a religious group to perform religious ordinances is a religious purpose.[55] Supervision of the preparation and inspection of food products prepared commercially to insure that they satisfy dietary standards of a particular religious sect is religious purpose.[56] Establishment of low-cost temporary housing and related services for missionary families on furlough or reassignment in the United States from abroad is an acceptable religious purpose.[57] Operation of a weekend religious retreat facility open to diverse Christian denominations for recreational purposes during free time qualifies as a religious purpose.[58]

Charitable

All categories of organizations exempt under section 501(c)(3) must be charitable in its common law meaning.[59] In that respect, the ordering of the categories in section 501(c)(3) seems convoluted. The specific enumeration of charitable purpose as the second purpose for which an organization may be tax exempt under section 501(c)(3) must give to it a meaning other than the general definition of common law charity. Although Congress has not defined charitable as used in section 501(c)(3), the Internal Revenue Service has.[60] "Charitable" as that term is used in section 501(c)(3) is not to be construed as limited by the separate enumeration of the other categories in that section.[61] The term charitable as used in the regulations includes not only the traditional meaning of the term, which is relief for the poor, the distressed, or the underprivileged, but it also includes activities that benefit the community and lessen the burden of government.[62] Since the charitable exemption is justified on the basis of the conferral of a public benefit, the charitable purpose must demonstrably serve and be in harmony with the public interest.

Relief for the Poor, Distressed, or Underprivileged

The traditional form of charity and indeed the one most recognized by the public is relief for the poor, distressed, or underprivileged. But the activities of charitable organizations go far beyond providing food, clothing, and shelter to these people. The scope of the charitable exemption can be seen from a sampler of purposes which have been ruled tax exempt by the Internal Revenue Service.

A nonexhaustive list follows: operation of a day-care center;[63] rehabilitation of convicts and ex-prisoners;[64] provision of low-cost legal services to the indigent based on ability to pay;[65] furnishing funds for bail or fees to a commercial bail bondsman for indigent criminal defendants;[66] closed-circuit radio broadcasts of noncommercial broadcasts directed to the special concerns of the elderly in nursing homes;[67] provision of employment placement services, counseling services on health, housing, finances, education, and employment to the elderly;[68] provision of vacations at a rural rest home, home delivery of meals at cost and low-cost bus transportation;[69] provision of instruction and guidance to low-income families to build their own homes;[70] conducting a low-income housing program;[71] provision of information on public housing regulations to public housing tenants;[72] education of the public with respect to the desirability of the availability of nondiscriminatory housing;[73] activities designed to lessen neighborhood tensions, eliminate prejudice and discrimination, and combat community deterioration; [74] provision of emergency and rescue services to disaster victims;[75] provision of assistance to needy families in developing countries;[76] provision of technical and material assistance for self-help projects designed to improve living conditions;[77] provision of vocational training to unemployed and underemployed persons;[78] furnishing low-income individuals who have financial problems with information on personal money management and assistance;[79] assistance to widows and orphans of firemen and policemen killed in the line of duty;[80] and marketing the needlework and cooking of needy women.[81]

Advancement of Religion

An organization that might not otherwise be tax exempt under section 501(c)(3) for religious purposes may acquire tax exempt status if it is organized exclusively for the charitable purpose of the advancement of religion.[82] However, the category of advancement of religion within charitable purpose is not particularly useful to religious organizations. Given the reluctance of Congress, the Internal Revenue Service, and the courts to delve into the meaning of religious purpose and, consequently, the broad latitude given to the term religious purpose, if an organization cannot qualify for tax exempt status for being organized for religious purposes, it will not qualify as a charitable organization for the advancement of religion.

Advancement of Education or Science

Although exemption for an educational purpose is stated separately in section 501(c)(3), the regulations include advancement of education or science within the definition of charitable purpose.[83] Advancement of education or science does not suffer from the infirmity under which the category of advancement of religion seems to operate. The courts and the Internal Revenue Service have been more specific with respect to the definition of the terms "educational" and "scientific." In general, advancement of education or science incorporates activities that do not involve the establishment and maintenance of schools, colleges and universities, libraries, or museums nor the carrying on of research in institutes or laboratories.[84] One must be cautious of trying to obtain tax exempt status as a charitable organization if the organization otherwise would fail the test of being organized for an educational or scientific purpose.

Examples of charitable purposes for which organizations have been granted tax exempt status on the basis of advancement of education or science are providing scholarships and grants to enable needy individuals to continue work in the creative arts;[85] accrediting activities including preparation of standards and identification of schools and colleges conforming to those standards;[86] operating a hospitality center for foreign visitors and students;[87] granting assistance to needy and worthy students;[88] awarding scholarships for scholastic ability without regard to financial need;[89] maintaining a training table for members and coaches of a university's athletic teams;[90] selecting and enrolling students and faculty at foreign universities;[91] providing housing for college students;[92] providing work experience to high school graduates and college students in selected trades and professions;[93] giving assistance in using computers provided to colleges and universities;[94] providing financial aid and low-cost investment and endowment management services;[95] publishing a law review;[96] operating a university alumni association;[97] promoting interscholastic high school competition;[98] providing low-interest student loans;[99] recruiting college students for government internship programs;[100] surveying, preparing, and distributing abstracts of medical and scientific literature;[101] and supporting research and anthropology by casting reproductions of anthropological specimens for sale to scholars.[102]

Erection or Maintenance of Public Buildings, Monuments, or Works

Few tax exempt organizations are created for the purpose of erecting or maintaining public buildings, monuments, or works. These functions are generally performed by governments or governmental agencies. One organization created to construct and maintain a building for the exclusive purpose of housing and servicing exempt member agencies of a community chest agency was ruled tax exempt by the Internal Revenue Service.[103]

Other activities held to be charitable by having as a purpose the erection or maintenance of public buildings, monuments, or works include sharing in the upkeep of public buildings, such as museums, city halls, correctional centers, and police and fire department structures;[104] helping to keep the public transportation system in operation;[105] establishing needed public parking facilities in congested downtown business districts;[106] encouraging municipal programs of beautification through tree planting;[107] and improving lakes and rivers for recreational use.[108]

Lessening the Burdens of Government

The erection or maintenance of public buildings, monuments, or works is a tangible way of lessening the burdens of government. Less tangible ways of lessening the burden of government fall into this category of charitable purposes. Examples of activities that qualify as charitable purposes by lessening the burden of government are carrying on research in the regional problems of municipal governments, such as water and air pollution, waste disposal, water supply, and transportation;[109] assisting municipal police and fire departments to better serve in emergency or disaster situations, by helping to finance rewards for use by the police;[110] establishing and maintaining a volunteer fire department;[111] providing food and drink to police and fire department personnel at the scene;[112] or assisting the victims of fire, flood, or other disaster by providing free emergency rescue and other emergency services;[113] developing programs to inform the public about traffic safety;[114] and establishing safety standards for products used on pleasure boats.[115]

Lessening the burdens of government must result in a public benefit, and organizations must be careful to avoid any inurement to the benefit of private individuals.

Promotion of Social Welfare

Organizations created to promote the social welfare by lessening neighborhood tensions, eliminating prejudice and discrimination, defending human and civil rights secured by law, and combating community deterioration and juvenile delinquency are tax exempt.[116] Such an organization need not limit its purpose to one of the above enumerated purposes. Any combination of them is permissible. Nor is the list intended to be inclusive. Any activity that promotes the social welfare by furthering the happiness or general well-being of the community at large qualifies as a charitable purpose. Purchasing land in an economically depressed community and converting it into an industrial park to provide employment opportunities to low-income residents of the area is a charitable purpose promoting the social welfare by lessening neighborhood tensions.[117] Elimination or reduction of prejudice and discrimination against various groups such as women, racial minorities, and homosexuals falls within the category of charitable purpose for the elimination of prejudice and discrimination.[118] Providing public housing tenant groups with information on public housing laws and regulations fits into the categories of defending human and civil rights secured by law, elimination of prejudice and discrimination, lessening neighborhood tension, and combating community deterioration and juvenile delinquency.[119] Combating community deterioration and juvenile delinquency includes activities such as providing interest-free home repair loans to low-income home owners in deteriorated urban neighborhoods and informing residents of above-average districts of ways of arresting housing deterioration in their neighborhoods.[120]

Promoting the social welfare also includes activities such as helping to recycle solid waste;[121] helping to combat air and water pollution or to protect the natural environment;[122] preserving a lake as a public recreational facility or as a sanctuary for wild birds and animals;[123] maintaining the operation of public transportation;[124] relieving parking congestion;[125] promoting the arts by encouraging struggling but promising young artists through scholarship aid;[126] presenting awards for conspicuous citizens' support;[127] sponsoring stock theatre and summer concerts and further appreciation of art, music, and theatre;[128] establishing and operating a repertory theatre;[129] and actually producing and putting on plays, concerts, and public exhibits of unknown but promising artists.[130]

Other Charitable Purposes

Charitable purpose is an expandable category and includes such other charitable purposes as operating an abortion clinic;[131] operating a vasectomy clinic;[132] operating a legal assistance program;[133] operating a public interest law firm;[134] creating community development corporations with programs of financial assistance to private businesses in economically depressed areas;[135] providing computer program services for donations of human organs for transplant.[136] In reality these categories of other charitable purposes fall within the category of promotion of the social welfare; social welfare is understood not to be limited merely to aiding the poor or disadvantaged but to include virtually any service rendered to the community at large or to lessen the burdens of government.

Educational

As defined in the Treasury Regulations the term "educational" relates to the instruction or training of the individual for the purpose of improving or developing his capabilities or the instruction of the public on subjects useful to the individual and beneficial to the community.[137]

The purpose is educational even though it may advocate a particular position or viewpoint, provided it presents a sufficiently full and fair exposition of the pertinent facts so that an individual or the public may form an independent opinion or conclusion.[138] Conversely, an organization does not serve an educational purpose if its principal function is merely to present unsupported opinion.

The Treasury Regulations provide four examples of educational organizations: (1) a school whether it be primary, secondary, college, professional, or trade school which has a regularly scheduled curriculum, a regular faculty, and a regularly enrolled student body in attendance at a place where the educational activities are regularly carried on; (2) an organization which presents public discussion groups, forums, panels, lectures, or other similar programs which may be on radio or television; (3) an organization which has a course of instruction presented by correspondence or by television or radio; and (4) museums, zoos, planetariums, symphony orchestras, and other similar organizations.[139]

Providing care for children away from their homes so that individuals may be gainfully employed was included within the meaning of educational purpose by the Tax Reform Act of 1984 which added a new section 501(k) to the Internal Revenue Code.

Instruction of the Individual

Educational purposes for the instruction of the individual include providing financial and other aid to scholars which may be in the form of scholarships, or student loans whether given to attend school or to conduct research and regardless of whether based on scholastic merit or need, provided that an interest rate charged on a student loan or security required must not suggest an ordinary commercial transaction;[140] providing assistance in the form of scholarship, housing, and books to students selected on the basis of superior scholarship performance and demonstrated financial need;[141] recruiting and securing employment for college students in local governmental organizations;[142] assisting law students in securing employment with exempt public interest law firms and legal aid societies and supplementing their salaries;[143] operating a university book and supply store;[144] operating a university cafeteria for the convenience of students and faculty;[145] establishing a law review under the control of a law school faculty to train law students in legal research and writing;[146] establishing a high school athletic association to promote interscholastic competition on a high level;[147] creating a university founded, faculty controlled organization to give business students securities management experience;[148] and establishing a national honor society to recognize scholastic achievement, leadership ability, and school service.[149]

Organizations whose primary function or purpose is educational rather than incidental may be tax exempt, for example, an honor fraternity whose members are selected for scholastic achievement rather than for social compatibility and whose activities are primarily educationally centered and not merely incidental[150] or an alumni association whose social and recreational activities are merely incidental and whose basic purpose is to advance the interest of the university such as raising funds for building programs, establishing scholarships, making awards to outstanding alumni, and publishing an alumni magazine.[151] However, organizations which have as their principal activity or purpose persuading students of outstanding athletic ability to attend a particular university or operating a college fraternity or sorority whose primary activity is social or recreational are not organized and operated exclusively for educational purposes and are denied tax exemption.[152]

Organizations that conduct study courses or seminars designed to improve the business or professional capabilities of employees of banking institutions, practicing physicians, or attorneys or that provide apprenticeships or on-the-job training for students may be granted tax exempt status on the basis of an educational purpose, provided the principal purpose is not running a private business for profit or advancing the interests of individual members of the organization.[153] Such organizations, however, may be granted tax exempt status under another subsection of section 501(c).

Educational activities do not have to be carried out in a school setting. Vocational training programs may be accorded tax exempt status. Examples of such programs are the retraining of recently released prisoners and parolees;[154] education of immigrants seeking to become citizens;[155] courses for sports and racing enthusiasts;[156] workshops to train budding young artists;[157] workshops to provide opportunity for display and sale of works of young artists;[158] programs for study and research;[159] facilities to provide travel study;[160] and tutoring and psychotherapy for children and adolescents with learning and emotional disabilities.[161]

Instruction of the General Public

Activities that constitute instruction of the public include those services considered useful to the individual and beneficial to the community such as health and other personal services, community improvement, and encouragement or engagement in nonpartisan analysis, study, or research which will be made available to the public and is not related to the conduct of a business for profit.

Health and other personal services which have been considered useful to the individual and beneficial to the community include marriage counseling;[162] counseling women on a particular method of painless childbirth;[163] resolving unwanted pregnancies, including methods of lawful abortion;[164] counseling men on voluntary sterilization;[165] and counseling the public on the effects of controlling the overuse of mind-affecting drugs.[166]

Activities that promote community improvement which have been held to be tax exempt include training citizens in urban beautification through planting trees;[167] control of trash and solid waste materials;[168] programs on better land use;[169] programs to lessen neighborhood, racial, and ethnic tensions, community deterioration, and juvenile delinquency;[170] efforts to provide more open political campaigns;[171] programs to provide healthier programming on television and radio;[172] programs to provide a more effective court or parole system;[173] programs which promote a wider appreciation of the arts, music, or theatre;[174] establishment of a repertory theatre;[175] fostering community appreciation of music and drama by sponsoring professional presentations;[176] promoting appreciation of harmony singing;[177] promoting or sponsoring jazz as an American art form;[178] operating a dance school;[179] encouraging young artists through grants and awards;[180] displaying and selling the works of young artists; and instruction in gardening and presentation of garden shows.

Education of the public through encouraging or engaging in nonpartisan analysis, study, or research includes delving into the causes and cures of physical and mental disorders;[181] extracting from scientific and medical literature information on current developments;[182] inquiring into the critical problems of municipalities of a particular region, including water and air pollution, transportation, and waste disposal;[183] collecting and collating speeches, interviews, and comments on a political campaign after the election as an historical event;[184] manufacturing high-quality cost reproductions of anthropological specimens to facilitate research into human evolution.[185]

Other activities that constitute instruction of the general public which have been ruled tax exempt are establishment of self-help projects to improve living conditions in foreign countries;[186] ownership and operation by a local bar association of a law library limited to use by attorneys, judges, law students, and their designees;[187] operation of a county public library;[188] promotion and direction of interscholastic high school competition;[189] and operation of a sports museum, including items of interest in particular sports and sponsorship of activities concerning the history of sports.[190]

Education of the public need not be carried out through direct contact with an individual or groups of individuals but may be effected through indirect contact by way of radio, television, or the press.

Scientific

A scientific purpose has been recognized as being tax exempt under section 501(c)(3) since 1913; however, the regulations only date back to 1959.[191] Moreover, the regulation is preoccupied with only one form of scientific activity. Research that is the subject of the regulation does not constitute a definition of scientific, which is a much broader classification. A scientific purpose seems to be inexorably entwined with educational and charitable purposes. Whatever the scientific purpose, it must be carried on in the public interest, which requires that the results of the research be made available to the public on a nondiscriminatory basis or that the research be performed for a local, state, or federal governmental agency or that the research be directed toward benefiting the public.[192]

For research to be scientific it must be carried on to advance a scientific purpose. The determination of whether the scientific purpose is tax exempt within the meaning of section 501(c)(3) is not dependent on whether the research is classified as "fundamental" or "basic" as opposed to "applied" or "practical."[193] Scientific research does not include activities ordinarily conducted incident to commercial or industrial operations.

Examples of scientific research which the regulations consider to be directed toward benefiting the public and, therefore, to be regarded as carried on in the public interest are (1) scientific research that aids in the scientific education of college or university students; (2) scientific research of which the results are published in a treatise, thesis, trade publication, or in any form that is available to the interested public; (3) scientific research directed toward discovering a cure for a disease; or (4) scientific research designed to benefit a community or geographical area by attracting new industry or by encouraging the development or retention of industry in the community or area, regardless of whether the sponsors of the research have retained ownership rights in patents, processes, or formulae resulting from such research.[194]

The Internal Revenue Service has denied tax exempt status to bar associations and medical societies on the grounds that the scientific purpose is outweighed by purposes whose primary thrust is the promotion and protection of the practice of the particular profession.[195] Where the dominant activity is carrying on research, the professional society may be granted tax exempt status under the scientific purpose category. For example, a heating and air conditioning engineers' professional society was granted tax exempt status.[196] Likewise, an organization which consisted of nonprofit operators of regional health data collection programs whose basic purpose was the study and improvement of health care and not the establishment of professional standards or regulation of the industry was granted tax exempt status.[197]

Literary

Organizations which espouse a literary purpose are generally considered under the educational purpose criterion of section 501(c)(3) rather than as a separate category even though it exists in the statute as such.

Testing for Public Safety

Testing for public safety includes organizations whose purpose is the testing of consumer products such as electrical products for fire safety hazards[198] or pleasure boats for safety in their general use by the public.[199] Testing for public safety was added as a tax exempt purpose to section 501(c)(3) as a congressional override of the decision by the Seventh Circuit Court of Appeals in *Underwriters Laboratory, Inc. v. Commissioner.*[200] The court had decided that Underwriters Laboratory could not be tax exempt under the scientific purpose category because the testing was primarily for the benefit of private business and only incidentally for the benefit of the public.[201] Testing for public safety does not really fit into the category of charitable.

Prevention of Cruelty to Children and Animals

While the distinction should be drawn between an organization whose purpose is the prevention of cruelty to children and one whose purpose is the prevention of cruelty to animals, the types of organizations granted tax exempt status under this purpose are rather obvious.

Organizations granted tax exempt status whose purpose is prevention of cruelty to children include an organization formed and operated to prevent children from working in hazardous trades and occupations in violation of state law;[202] a day nursery for children of working parents;[203] an educational day-care center operated in conjunction with an industrial company that enrolled children on the basis of family's financial need and the child's need for care and development;[204] an organization formed to provide educational day care for children from six months to three years of age in which custodial services provided were merely incidental to the corporation's educational purpose.[205]

Organizations granted tax exempt status whose purpose is prevention of cruelty to animals include an organization developing a sanctuary for wild birds and animals for education of the public;[206] organizations formed to promote humane treatment of laboratory animals by carrying on a program for accreditation of animal care facilities that supply, keep, and care for animals used in medical or scientific research;[207] and an organization formed to prevent overbreeding of dogs and cats by providing funds to pet owners who wish to have their pets spayed or neutered, but who could not afford the cost of the operation.[208]

Fostering of Sports Competition

The Tax Reform Act of 1976[209] amended section 501(c)(3) to provide for the exemption of organizations whose primary purpose is the fostering of national or international sports competition. That part of the Tax Reform Act of 1976 which prohibited providing athletic facilities or equipment was modified by section 286, Tax Equity and Fiscal Responsibility Act of 1982.[210] A qualified amateur sports organization which is organized and operated exclusively to foster national or international amateur sports competition and which primarily conducts national or international competition in sports or supports and develops amateur athletes for national or international competition in sports may provide athletic facilities or equipment.[211]

CIVIC LEAGUES AND SOCIAL WELFARE ORGANIZATIONS

Civic leagues or organizations which are not organized or operated for profit and are operated exclusively for the promotion of social welfare may be tax exempt. An organization is operated exclusively for the promotion of social welfare if its primary activity is promoting the common good and general welfare of the people of the community in some way.[212] The organization must be operated primarily to bring about civic betterment and social improvement.[213]

Section 501(c)(4) was enacted to provide tax exempt status for civic organizations which otherwise qualify as charitable organizations under section 501(c)(3) except that they are action organizations. An action organization devotes a substantial part of its activities to attempting to influence legislation by propaganda or otherwise participates or intervenes, directly or indirectly, in any political campaign on behalf of or in opposition to any candidate for public office or can only attain its primary objectives or goals by legislation or defeat of proposed legislation and advocates or campaigns for those objectives or goals.[214] A social welfare organization which otherwise qualifies under section 501(c)(3) may qualify under section 501(c)(4) even if it is an action organization, except that direct or indirect participation in a political campaign will result in denial or loss of tax exempt status.[215] Section 501(c)(4) is not available to social clubs whose primary activity is for the benefit, pleasure, or recreation of its members. Such social clubs must otherwise qualify under section 501(c)(6). A nonprofit organization may be exempt under both sections 501(c)(3) and 501(c)(4) as in the case of a volunteer fire company which provided fire protection and ambulance and rescue services to the community and qualified as both a charitable organization and a social welfare organization.[216]

Organizations with the following purposes have qualified for tax exempt status as social welfare organizations: operation of an annual football bowl game with profits distributed to civic enterprises;[217] cooperation with parent-teacher associations for the purpose of selecting a student insurer;[218] building and operation of a stadium for the use of a school district;[219] rehabilitation of overage unemployed persons and minimization of prejudice against the elderly;[220] provision of low-cost housing to low-income groups;[221] provision of facilities for firearms practice and instruction to the community in safe handling and proper care of weapons;[222] organization and maintenance of an amateur baseball association which consisted of baseball teams having college-age amateur players;[223] operation of a ''drag strip'' for the purpose of alleviating lawless activities of juveniles who raced high-powered automobiles on public streets;[224] aid and promotion of the Area Redevelopment Act;[225] provision of loans to business entities for the purpose of inducing them to locate in a depressed area for the alleviation of unemployment;[226] development of dignified and simple funeral services and registration of members' burial wishes;[227] conduct of various youth and community benefit programs by the Junior Chamber of Commerce;[228] provision of consumer credit counseling services to the general public;[229] improvement of the water supply of a community;[230] organization of a garden club for the purpose of promoting horticultural subjects and area beautification;[231] operation of a roller skating rink for the use of residents of a particular county which charged nominal dues and admission to defray operating expenses;[232] stimulation of interest of community youth in organized sports;[233] conduct of an annual festival which centered around regional customs and traditions;[234] promotion and regulation of amateur sports;[235] creation of an organization for the preservation and beautification of public areas in a city block which benefits the community as a whole;[236] an organization which contracts with a private security firm to provide the community with security patrols assisted by guard dogs and works to improve public services, housing, and residential parking, publishes a community newspaper distributed free of charge to all community residents, and sponsors a community basketball league, holiday programs, and meetings of community residents;[237] process and review of consumer complaints concerning products and services provided by business establishments to encourage resolution of the problem, recommending fair solutions and informing parties of appropriate judicial or administrative bodies for the resolution of disputes if nonlegal resolution is not possible;[238] provision of bus transportation to isolated areas of a community not served by the existing municipal bus system;[239] provision of bus service between a suburban community and major development centers in a metropolitan area during rush hours when regular bus service was inadequate;[240] development and encouragement of interest in painting, sculpture, and other art forms through the conduct of a noncommercial community art show;[241] operation of an airport on land owned by a municipality that supervises the overall operation which is used by the general public and key local businesses essential to the economy of a four-county rural area that has no other airport facilities;[242] prevention of spills within a city port area and the development of containment and cleanup programs made available to the community at large;[243] representation of public interest at legislative and administrative hearings on tax matters;[244] stimulation of participation in politics through seminars, workshops, and distribution of publications;[245] education of the public on abortions, promotion of the rights of unborn children, and support of legislative and constitutional changes to restrict women's access to abortions;[246] provision of a television reception service other than closed circuit in which the signals were made available to the community at large;[247] promotion of legal rights of tenants in a particular community and occasional initiation of litigation to contest the validity of legislation adversely affecting the tenants;[248] and maintenance and operation of a volunteer fire department for the benefit of the community.[249]

A local association of employees may be granted tax exempt status if the membership of the association is limited to the employees of a designated person or persons in a particular municipality and the net earnings of the association are devoted exclusively to charitable, educational, or recreational purposes.[250] The terms "charitable" and "educational" have the same meaning in section 501(c)(4) as they do in section 501(c)(3). The association is local if its business activities are confined to a particular community, place, or district regardless of political subdivision.[251] Retired employees who were members of the association as of the time they retired may continue as employee members.[252] The net earnings of a local association of employees must be exclusively devoted to charitable, educational, or recreational purposes; otherwise, the tax exemption will be denied as in the cases of a local employees' association formed for the purpose of paying lump sum retirement benefits to eligible members or death benefits to their survivors as the net profits inured to the benefit of the members or their survivors[253] and a local association whose major activity consisted of providing sickness, medical, and death benefits to its members and their relations rather than devoting the net profits exclusively to charitable, educational, or recreational purposes.[254] However, an association of employees which was organized for recreational purposes and supplemented its income from dues by operation of a service station selling oil and gasoline to the member employer was granted tax exempt status on the grounds that the profits from the operation of the service station were a form of employer subsidy to the organization.[255] To qualify for tax exempt status as a local association of employees, the associations must conduct the types of services for members that Congress contemplated in enacting the predecessor of section 501(c)(4) in 1924.

LABOR, AGRICULTURAL, AND HORTICULTURAL ORGANIZATIONS

Labor, agricultural, and horticultural organizations established for the purpose of bettering the conditions of those engaged in labor and agricultural pursuits, the improvement of the grade of their products, and the development of greater efficiency in those occupations may be granted tax exempt status.

Labor organizations having the following purposes have been ruled tax exempt: operation of a "labor temple" by a union-owned corporation which contained meeting places, offices, and recreational facilities;[256] provision of strike and lock-out benefits to members of a labor union;[257] publication of a labor newspaper for union members;[258] payment of law enforcement officers' legal defense in actions brought against them in connection with official duties;[259] improvement of city school teachers' professional abilities and securement of better salaries and working conditions, sponsor of seminars and courses for members, participation in teacher conventions, collective bargaining and grievance process, and provision of information to members through regular meetings

and newsletters;[260] acting as collective bargaining agent for a nurses' association;[261] the establishment of standards for the employment of apprentices;[262]
operation of a dispatch hall to allocate work assignments among labor union
members;[263] establishment of a trust under a collective bargaining agreement
that is funded and administered by employees for the purpose of compensating a
multiemployer steward engaged in dispute settlement, complaint investigation,
and compliance throughout the whole industry under the union's direct control;[264] operation of an apprenticeship and training committee formed by a union
and the employers' association in connection with a collective bargaining agreement for the conduct of educational classes and programs concerning the trade to
ensure conformity with national codes on quality of work for industry and also to
provide for the selection and supervision of the training of apprentices;[265] and
the operation by a labor union at the request of the Bureau of Indian Affairs of an
apprentice training program for American Indians in skilled trades.[266]

Agricultural and horticultural organizations have been granted tax exemption
for the following purposes: operation of a rodeo by a farm center to encourage
agriculture;[267] encouragement of better methods of raising fur-bearing animals;[268] publication of a register on Welsh ponies for the purpose of improving
the breed;[269] the education of the public in soil science through soil tests and
reports;[270] improvement of a breed of dairy and beef cattle;[271] operation of a
garden club to create better conditions for persons in horticultural pursuits;[272]
improvement of milk production by processing individual farmer's milk production records;[273] improvement of milk production by weighing and testing milk of
members' cows and providing statistical information based on tests available to
members, nonmembers, and governmental agencies;[274] enhancement and improvement of the agricultural way of life in a particular state by farmers
wives;[275] encouragement of better and more economical methods of fish farming
and promotion of interest of persons engaged in raising fish as a cash crop on
farms;[276] negotiation with processors for price to be paid to growers and producers of a particular agricultural commodity;[277] and promotion of more effective agricultural control through pest management scouts who periodically inspect member's fields, identify and count agricultural pests, and compile data on
agricultural pest infestation.[278] Agricultural organizations include not only fish
farms but also organizations whose purpose is the improvement or promotion of
fishing or related occupations.[279]

NONPROFIT BUSINESS LEAGUES, CHAMBERS OF
COMMERCE, REAL ESTATE BOARDS, BOARDS OF
TRADE, OR PROFESSIONAL FOOTBALL LEAGUES

The Treasury Regulations define business league as an association of persons
having some common business interest which promotes the common interest of

the members rather than individual persons.[280] An organization whose purpose is to engage in a regular business for profit whether conducted on a cooperative basis or not is not a business league.[281] Further, an organization which furnishes information to prospective investors is not a business league because it does not further any common business interest.[282] Moreover, a stock or commodity exchange is not a business league, chamber of commerce, or board of trade for purposes of tax exempt status under section 501(c)(6).[283]

Organizations formed for the following purposes have been accorded tax exempt status: promoting business in a particular industry and advertising primarily for the benefit of the industry as a whole;[284] educating the public on credit buying;[285] regulating auction sales of agricultural commodities;[286] serving common interest of members engaged in manufacture and use of refractories;[287] promoting industry and bringing trade to an area;[288] performing functions required by an insurance commissioner;[289] conducting fire patrol and salvaging corps;[290] operating a bid registry in a particular industry to encourage fair bidding practices;[291] investigating and prosecuting criminal, fraudulent, and unethical conduct of lawyers, doctors, and laymen in matters of casualty claims against insurance companies;[292] operating woodworking machinery and equipment shows;[293] promoting the sale and use of a processed agricultural product;[294] promoting a cooperative method of doing business;[295] informing the public of the benefits of plywood and advertising its trademark to ensure safe plywood through quality control;[296] holding luncheon meetings devoted to discussion, review, and consideration of various problems of a particular industry;[297] investigating, analyzing, compiling, disseminating, and making recommendations to a government agency with respect to the establishment, revision, and change of rates, tariffs, rules, regulations, and practices in the industry;[298] licensing small loan companies formed under state law and furnishing information to members on consumer borrowing to cut back excessive loans;[299] verifying advertising claims of publications selling advertising space and making reports available to members of the advertising industry in general;[300] devising and administering written examinations to doctors in medical specialties and issuing certificates of completion to successful candidates;[301] operating peer review boards of physicians in a state to establish and maintain standards of quality, quantity, and reasonableness of cost of medical services;[302] and paying claims against insolvent fire and casualty insurance companies pursuant to state law.[303]

SOCIAL CLUBS

A social club is defined in the regulations as a club organized and operated exclusively for pleasure, recreation, and other nonprofitable purposes and extends to social and recreational clubs supported solely by membership fees, dues, and assessments or by raising revenue through the use of club facilities or in connection with club activities.[304] The pleasure, recreation, or other nonprofitable activity need not be legal under local law.[305]

Automobile clubs have been denied tax exempt status by the Internal Revenue Service as a result of the commercial nature of the services rendered to members.[306] A garden club formed for the purpose of promoting the common interest in gardening was granted tax exempt status.[307] A gem and mineral club formed for the purpose of increasing the proficiency of the members in their hobby was granted tax exempt status.[308] Tax exempt status was also granted to a chapter home of university students;[309] a political club consisting of members interested in affairs of the political party;[310] a homeowners' club exclusively devoted to and granting automatic membership to homeowners in a particular housing development;[311] a college fraternity chapter house which served as a center for social activities;[312] and a club that protects and promotes a particular breed of dog not used as a farm animal.[313]

FRATERNAL BENEFICIARY SOCIETIES, ORDERS OR ASSOCIATIONS OPERATING UNDER THE LODGE SYSTEM WHICH PROVIDE INSURANCE BENEFITS TO MEMBERS

To qualify for tax exempt status under section 501(c)(8) a fraternal beneficiary society must be operated under the lodge system or for the exclusive benefit of members of a fraternal beneficiary society operated under the lodge system, and it must have an established system for payment to its members or their dependents of life, sick, accident, or other benefits. Benefits may be direct benefits paid by the organization or provided under a life, health, or accident insurance policy. The benefits may be cash or noncash benefits such as clinical care services by visiting nurses or transportation furnished to obtain medical care. A benefit is similar to a life, health, or accident benefit if it is intended to safeguard or improve the health of a member or a member's dependents or if it protects against a contingency that interrupts or impairs a member's earning power. Qualification requires both a lodge system and an established benefit system. A lodge system is a form of organization that is made up of local branches which are chartered by a parent organization and are largely self-governing.[314] It is immaterial whether the lodge system fraternal benefits or the benefit system predominates as long as both are present.[315] A mutual benefit burial system operated for the benefit of members of a church is not an exempt fraternal society.[316] An organized church is not a fraternity although the burial association might qualify for tax exempt status as a cemetery company.[317] A local association which aided its members in time of sickness or death without a lodge system is not a fraternal lodge but may be tax exempt as a social welfare organization.[318] A fraternal benefit society itself must provide for the payment of life, sick, accident or other benefits to its members and may not arrange with insurance companies to provide optional insurance to its members to qualify under section 501(c)(8).[319] However, a fraternal beneficiary society will not lose its tax exempt status under section 501(c)(8) by participating in a state-sponsored reinsurance pool that protects participating insurers from excessive losses on major medical health and accident insurance since participation was primarily for the benefit of members and any benefit derived by other reinsurers was incidental.[320]

VOLUNTARY EMPLOYEES' BENEFICIARY ASSOCIATIONS WHICH PROVIDE INSURANCE BENEFITS TO MEMBERS

A voluntary employees' association whose primary purpose is to provide for the payment of life, sick, accident or other benefits to its members or their dependents or designated beneficiaries is tax exempt under section 501(c)(9). Substantially all of the operations of the association must further the purpose of providing benefits to its members or their dependents or designated beneficiaries.[321] Benefits may be direct benefits paid by the organization or provided under a life, health, or accident insurance policy. The benefits may be cash or noncash benefits such as clinical care services by visiting nurses or transportation furnished to obtain medical care. A benefit is similar to a life, health, or accident benefit if it is intended to safeguard or improve the health of a member or a member's dependents or if it protects against a contingency that interrupts or impairs a member's earning power. The association may still be a voluntary association even if membership is mandatory, provided that no detriment to the individual is caused or membership is required by a collective bargaining agreement or labor union.[322] An "employee" is an individual who is considered to be an employee for employment tax purposes under subtitle C of the Internal Revenue Code or is considered to be an employee for purposes of a collective bargaining agreement whether or not the individual would qualify as an employee under common law rules.[323] Employee includes a surviving spouse and dependents and retired, laid-off, or disabled employees.[324] All employees of the association must share a common employment-related bond.[325]

The benefits to be provided to the membership of the association include life, health, accident, and disability insurance or other benefits to improve health and protect against interruptions in earning capacity.[326] Other benefits include such items as payments for vacations, recreational activities, child-care facilities, educational, and legal service.[327] Nonqualified benefits include annuities or pensions on retirement, stock bonuses, profit sharing plans, and other deferred compensation plans that are not based on unanticipated events but rather computed on the basis of passage of time.[328]

DOMESTIC FRATERNAL SOCIETIES, ORDERS, OR ASSOCIATIONS THAT DO NOT PROVIDE INSURANCE BENEFITS TO MEMBERS

To qualify for tax exemption under section 501(c)(10) the organization must be a fraternal beneficiary society, order, or association otherwise qualified under section 501(c)(8) except that it does not provide insurance benefits to its members. In addition, the fraternal beneficiary society must devote its net earnings exclusively to religious, charitable, scientific, literary, educational, and fraternal purposes.[329] National college fraternities and other organizations qualified under section 501(c)(7) are not qualified organizations under section 501(c)(10).[330]

A domestic fraternal beneficiary society of farmers operating under the lodge system that did not provide insurance benefits to its members but arranged with insurance companies to provide optional insurance to its members and devoted its net earnings exclusively to religious, charitable, scientific, literary, educational, and fraternal purposes was qualified for tax exempt status under section 501(c)(10).[331] A domestic fraternal society operating under the lodge system which did not provide insurance benefits to its members but whose purpose was the exploration of and philosophy behind a method of attempting to divine the future and devoted its net income to providing instruction on the use of the method, maintaining a reference library, and supplying information on the method of divining the future to the public at large was tax exempt under section 501(c)(10).[332]

LOCAL TEACHER RETIREMENT FUND ASSOCIATIONS

A teacher's retirement fund association which is purely local in character and whose income is derived from public taxation, assessments on teachers' salaries, and income from investments is tax exempt under section 501(c)(11). There are no reported cases nor Treasury Regulations promulgated pursuant to this provision.

LOCAL BENEVOLENT LIFE INSURANCE ASSOCIATIONS, MUTUAL DITCH OR IRRIGATION COMPANIES, MUTUAL OR COOPERATIVE TELEPHONE COMPANIES, OR LIKE ORGANIZATIONS

Tax exempt status is extended only to benevolent life insurance associations and organizations like them if they are of purely local character which is defined in the regulations to mean having business activities which are confined to a particular community or district regardless of political subdivision.[333] A community or district which is coextensive with a state is not purely local.[334] Further, benevolent life insurance associations and organizations like them must be operated on a cooperative or mutual basis.[335] The phrase "of a purely local character" applies only to benevolent life insurance associations and organizations like them but not to the other organizations specified in this subsection.[336]

Organizations which are "like" benevolent life insurance associations are a cooperative which operated a nonprofit two-way radio system for members;[337] a mutual benefit company formed by owners of waterfront property to contract with the United States to prevent riverbank erosion;[338] a cooperative association which furnished light and water to its members;[339] a mutual water company;[340] and a cooperative association that furnished cable television service to its membership which included individuals and rural school districts.[341] Organizations which are not considered to be like a benevolent life insurance association are an automobile club;[342] a cooperative that provided financing for customers' purchases and installation of electrical, water, and plumbing systems from rural electrical cooperatives which constituted its membership;[343] a cooperative housing organization operated for the personal benefit of tenant-owner members;[344] and a nonprofit organization created to purchase land to be leased to members and to construct improvements for their benefit.[345]

CEMETERY COMPANIES AND CREMATORIA

Section 501(c)(13) provides a tax exemption for three categories of cemetery companies. Mutual cemetery companies owned and operated exclusively for the benefit of their members are tax exempt provided the owners hold their lots for bona fide burial purposes and not for resale. The cemetery company need not be operated for a public purpose. In fact, a mutual cemetery company may limit its membership to a particular class of individuals, such as the members of a particular family.[346] Moreover, a mutual cemetery company may engage in charitable activities such as burial of paupers.[347]

The second category of tax exempt cemetery company under section 501(c)(13) is nonprofit cemetery companies and crematoria. The same rules that apply to mutual cemetery companies owned and operated exclusively for the benefit of their members apply to a nonprofit mutual cemetery company.

The third category is a corporation whose sole purpose of incorporation is to bury or cremate bodies and other limited activities necessarily incident to that purpose. The establishment and operation of a mortuary is an activity not necessarily incident to the operation of the cemetery company and will disqualify its tax exempt status;[348] however, the sale of monuments, markers, vaults, and flowers solely for use in the cemetery—the profits of which are used for maintenance of the cemetery[349] or the operation of a crematorium[350]—does not disqualify the tax exempt status.

CREDIT UNIONS AND MUTUAL INSURANCE FUNDS

Mutual nonprofit, nonstock credit unions and mutual insurance funds are tax exempt organizations.[351] Credit unions, other than federal credit unions exempt under section 501(c)(1) are tax exempt if they are nonprofit, nonstock organizations organized and operated for mutual purposes. Mutual nonprofit, nonstock corporations or associations organized before September 1, 1957, to provide reserve funds for and insurance of shares or deposits in domestic building and loan associations, mutual nonprofit, nonstock cooperative banks, or mutual savings banks not having capital stock represented by shares are tax exempt; however, this exemption is only for tax years beginning after 1959 if the organization was created after September 1, 1951. Mutual nonprofit corporations or associations organized before September 1, 1957, which provide reserve funds for domestic building and loan associations, mutual nonprofit, nonstock cooperative banks, or mutual savings banks not having capital stock represented by shares are tax exempt, provided at least 85 percent of the income is attributable to providing such reserve funds and to investments.

A state-chartered credit union may qualify for tax exempt status if it is formed and operated under state law governing formation of credit unions and operated as a nonprofit organization for the mutual benefit of its members under federal law.[352] A credit union formed by individuals at a military base in a foreign country which meets all of the territorial requirements of the federal credit union act is a credit union for purposes of the tax exemption.[353] An insurer of accounts of shareholders of member savings and loan associations is not eligible for tax exempt status.[354]

MUTUAL INSURANCE COMPANIES OR ASSOCIATIONS

Mutual insurance companies or associations other than life or marine (including interinsurers and reciprocal underwriters) may be tax exempt, provided the gross amount received during any taxable year from gross investment income and from premiums (including deposits and assessments) does not exceed $150,000.[355] Gross investment income includes interest (including tax exempt interest and partially tax exempt interest), dividends, rents and royalties, and gross income from any trade or business (other than an insurance business) carried on by the company or association or by a partnership of which the company or association is a partner.[356]

A mutual insurance company must exhibit at least the following characteristics: (1) the right of policyholders to be members to the exclusion of others and the right of members to choose management; (2) sole business purpose to supply insurance substantially at cost; (3) the right of members to a return of premiums in excess of amounts needed to cover losses and expenses; and (4) a common equitable ownership of assets by members.[357] The sale of insurance to nonmembers disqualifies the organization from tax exempt status.[358]

CROP FINANCING ORGANIZATIONS

A corporation organized by a farmers' cooperative marketing or purchasing association or its members to finance ordinary crop operations of the members or other producers may be tax exempt if the marketing or purchasing association is exempt under section 521 and the financing corporation is operated in conjunction with the marketing or purchasing association.[359]

Treasury Regulations section 1.521-1 as it relates to a surplus or reserve and to capital stock applies to corporations tax exempt under section 501(c)(16).

A crop financing corporation may have capital stock if the dividend rate of that stock is fixed in an amount not greater than 8 percent per annum or the legal rate of interest in the state of incorporation, whichever is greater, and if substantially all the stock, other than nonvoting preferred stock, is owned by the association or its members.[360] A crop financing corporation may accumulate and maintain a reserve required by state law or a reasonable reserve for any necessary purpose.[361]

SUPPLEMENTAL UNEMPLOYMENT TRUST

Tax exempt status may be granted to a trust which forms part of a plan to provide supplemental unemployment compensation benefit payments.[362] To qualify for tax exempt status, the trust must be part of a plan whereby the trust corpus or income cannot be used prior to the satisfaction of all liabilities under the plan to provide supplemental unemployment compensation benefits. The benefits must be payable to employees under a classification which does not discriminate in favor of officers, shareholders, persons whose principal duties consist of supervising other employees, or highly compensated employees, and the benefits do not discriminate in favor of officers, shareholders, supervisors, or highly compensated employees. The plan is not discriminatory if the benefits provided under the plan are directly related to total compensation or to the regular or basic rate of compensation of employees covered by the plan.

Supplemental unemployment compensation benefits are paid to an employee as a result of involuntary separation from employment, temporarily or permanently, due to a reduction in force, discontinuance of a plan or operation or similar conditions and include sick and accident benefits subordinate to the benefits paid to the employee as a result of involuntary separation. Sick and accident benefits do not include death or retirement benefits. A supplemental unemployment compensation trust may be tax exempt as a supplemental unemployment benefit trust under section 501(c)(17) or as a voluntary employees' beneficiary association under section 501(c)(9).

CERTAIN FUNDED PENSION TRUSTS

Section 501(c)(18) applies to trusts created before June 25, 1959, which form part of a pension plan to provide payments of benefits to employees out of a fund created solely from contributions of employees.

No part of the corpus of the trust or income from the corpus of the trust may be used for or diverted to any purpose other than providing benefits under the plan until all liabilities with respect to employees under the plan have been satisfied. The plan must not discriminate in favor of officers, shareholders, supervisors, or highly compensated employees with respect to eligibility or amount of benefits, provided that a plan is not discriminatory merely because the benefits received under the plan bear a uniform relationship to the total compensation or basic or regular rate of compensation of the covered employees.

VETERANS' ORGANIZATIONS

Section 501(c)(19) provides for a tax exemption for a post or organization of past or present members of the armed forces of the United States, or an auxiliary unit or society of, or a trust or foundation for, any such post or organization. The post or organization must have been organized in the United States or its possessions. The membership must consist of at least 75 percent war veterans, and at least 97.5 percent of the members must be war veterans, present or former members of the armed forces, cadets, or spouses, widows, or widowers of past or present members of the armed forces of the United States or cadets.[363]

Treasury Regulations section 1.501(c)(19)-1 imposes an exempt purpose requirement on veterans' organizations. Permissible exempt purposes are to promote the social welfare of the community as defined in section 501(c)(4); to assist disabled and needy war veterans and members of the United States armed forces and their dependents, and widows and orphans of deceased veterans; to provide entertainment, care, and assistance to hospitalized veterans or members of the United States armed forces; to carry on programs to perpetuate the memory of deceased veterans and members of the United States armed forces and to comfort their survivors; to conduct programs for religious, charitable, scientific, literary, or educational purposes; to sponsor or participate in activities of a patriotic nature; to provide insurance benefits for their members or the dependents of the members or both; to provide social and recreational activities for the members.

For purposes of section 501(c)(19) "war veteran" is a person who served in the armed forces of the United States during a period of war "including the

Korean and Vietnam conflicts.''[364] Dates of periods of war are contained in 38 U.S.C. § 101.

GROUP LEGAL SERVICES

Tax exemption may be granted to an organization or trust whose exclusive function is to perform part of a qualified group legal services plan within the meaning of section 120.[365]

BLACK LUNG TRUSTS

A domestic trust may be tax exempt if the exclusive purpose of the trust is to satisfy, in whole or in part, the liability of a contributing member other than an insurance company for or with respect to claims for compensation for disability or death resulting from eneumoconiosis under Black Lung Acts, to pay premiums for insurance exclusively covering such liability, and to pay administrative and other incidental expenses of the trust in connection with its operation and processing of claims under the Black Lung Act.[366] Black Lung Acts mean part C of title IV of the Federal Mine Safety and Health Act of 1977 and any state law providing compensation for disability or death due to eneumoconiosis. The purpose of section 501(c)(21) is to facilitate and ensure long-term financing of black lung benefits by coal mine operators.

WITHDRAWAL LIABILITY FUNDS

Sponsors of multiemployer plans may create and operate a tax exempt domestic trust created or organized in writing exclusively to pay unattributable withdrawal liabilities, liabilities excused under the *de minimis* or the twenty-year cap rule of sections 4208, 4209, 4219, and 4225 or the Employee Retirement Income Security Act of 1974 (ERISA) and to pay reasonable and necessary administrative expenses in connection with the establishment and operation of the trust and processing of claims against it.[367]

VETERANS' ASSOCIATIONS ORGANIZED BEFORE 1880

In addition to war veterans' organizations exempt from taxation under section 501(c)(19), certain veterans' associations organized before 1880 are also granted tax exempt status.[368] To qualify, the war veterans' association membership must consist of more than 75 percent of present or past members of the armed forces and be primarily organized to provide insurance and other benefits to veterans or their dependents.

RELIGIOUS AND APOSTOLIC ORGANIZATIONS

Religious or apostolic associations or corporations having a common or community treasury may be granted tax exempt status, even if the association or corporation engages in business for the common benefit of the members, but only if the individual members include in their gross income their entire pro rata shares of the taxable income of the association or corporation for each taxable year whether that income was distributed or not.[369]

A communal religious organization which does not conduct any business activity of its own but is supported by wages earned by its members from outside employment is not a tax exempt or apostolic organization.[370]

COOPERATIVE HOSPITAL SERVICES ORGANIZATIONS

Section 501(e) provides for tax exemption for certain organizations organized and operated solely to perform, on a centralized basis, services on behalf of a hospital which qualifies for tax exempt status under section 501(c)(3). Qualified services consist of data processing, purchasing, warehousing, billing and collection, food, clinical, industrial engineering, laboratory, printing, communications, record center, and personnel services.[371] The hospital service organization may perform its services for two or more hospitals each of which is (1) tax exempt under the provisions of section 501(c)(3); (2) a constituent part of a section 501(c)(3) organization which if organized and operated as a separate entity would constitute a section 501(c)(3) organization; or (3) an organization owned and operated by the United States, a state, the District of Columbia, or a possession of the United States, or a political subdivision or any agency or instrumentality thereof.

The hospital service organization must be organized and operated on a cooperative basis, and it must allocate or pay within eight and one-half months after the close of its taxable year all net earnings to its patrons prorated on the basis of services performed for them.

COOPERATIVE SERVICE ORGANIZATIONS OF OPERATING EDUCATIONAL ORGANIZATIONS

An organization that is organized and operated solely to hold, commingle, and collectively invest and reinvest the monies contributed to the organization by the members of the organization in stocks and securities will be treated as an organization organized and operated exclusively for charitable purposes if it turns over all income collected from its investments, less expenses, to its members and it is organized and controlled by one or more of its members, and the membership consists solely of tax exempt educational organizations or organizations which normally receive a substantial part of its support from the United States or any state or political subdivision as provided in section 170(b)(1)(A)(ii) or (iv).[372]

NOTES

1. I.R.C. § 501(a).
2. Revenue Act of 1894, 28 Stat. 509.
3. Treas. Reg. § 1.501(a)-1(a)(2).
4. Ill. Ann. Stat. ch. 32, § 16323.
5. ALI-ABA Model Nonprofit Corp. Act, § 4.
6. Treas. Reg. § 1.501(c)(3)-1(d)(2); *Bob Jones University v. U.S.*, 461 U.S. 574 , 103 S.Ct. 2017 (1983).
7. I.R.C. § 401(a).
8. I.R.C. § 501(c)(1).
9. I.R.C. § 501(c)(2).
10. I.R.C. § 501(c)(3).
11. I.R.C. § 501(c)(4).
12. *Id.*
13. I.R.C. § 501(c)(5).
14. I.R.C. § 501(c)(6).
15. I.R.C. § 501(c)(7).
16. I.R.C. § 501(c)(8).
17. I.R.C. § 501(c)(9).
18. I.R.C. § 501(c)(10).
19. I.R.C. § 501(c)(11).
20. I.R.C. § 501(c)(12).
21. I.R.C. § 501(c)(13).
22. I.R.C. § 501(c)(14).
23. I.R.C. § 501(c)(15).
24. I.R.C. § 501(c)(16).
25. I.R.C. § 501(c)(17).
26. I.R.C. § 501(c)(18).
27. I.R.C. § 501(c)(19).
28. I.R.C. § 501(c)(20).
29. I.R.C. § 501(c)(21).
30. I.R.C. § 501(c)(22).
31. I.R.C. § 501(c)(23).
32. I.R.C. § 501(d).
33. I.R.C. § 501(c)(1).
34. I.R.C. § 501(c)(2).
35. Rev. Rul. 81-108, 1981-1 C.B. 327.
36. *Stanford University Book Store*, 83 F.2d 710 (D.C. Cir. 1936).
37. Rev. Rul. 66-295, 1966-2 C.B. 207.
38. Rev. Rul. 76-335, 1976-2 C.B. 141.
39. *Gagne v. Hanover Water Works Co.*, 92 F.2d 659 (1st Cir. 1937).

40. *See, e.g., Banner Bldg. Co., Inc.*, 46 B.T.A. 857 (1942); *Kanawha-Roane Lands, Inc.*, 136 F. Supp. 631 (1955); *Santa Cruz Bldg. Assn. v. U.S.*, 411 F. Supp. 871 (1976).

41. Rev. Rul. 68-371, 1968-2 C.B. 204.

42. Rev. Rul. 77-429, 1977-2 C.B. 189.

43. N.P.E.F. Corp., ¶ 46,100 P-H Memo TC.

44. *Sun-Herald Corp. v. Duggan*, 160 F.2d 475 (2d Cir. 1947).

45. I.R.C. § 501(c)(3).

46. *Bob Jones University v. U.S.*, 461 U.S. 574, 586-88, 103 S.Ct. 2017, 2026 (1983).

47. *See, e.g., Founding Church of Scientology v. U.S.*, 412 F.2d 1197 (Ct. Cl. 1969), *cert. denied*, 397 U.S. 1009 (1970); *Universal Life Church Inc. v. U.S.*, 372 F. Supp. 770 (E.D. Cal. 1974); *Unity School of Christianity*, 4 B.T.A. 61 (1926); *A. A. Allen Revivals, Inc.*, 22 T.C.M. (CCH) 1435 (1963); *Merle E. Parker v. Comm.*, 365 F.2d 792 (8th Cir. 1966).

48. Treas. Reg. § 1.511-2(a)(3)(ii).

49. *A. A. Salkov*, 46 T.C. 190 (1966).

50. Remarks of IRS commissioner Jerome Kurtz, PLI Seventh Biennial Conference on Tax Planning (Jan. 9, 1978), *reprinted in* Fed. Taxes (P-H) ¶ 54,820 (1978).

51. *Id.*

52. *Id.*

53. *E.g.*, Racial discrimination—*Bob Jones University v. U.S.*, 461 U.S. 574, 103 S.Ct. 2017 (1983); Rev. Rul. 71-447, 1971-2 C.B. 230, Rev. Rul. 75-231, 1975-1, C.B. 231; Inurement to private individuals—*Founding Church of Scientology v. U.S.*, 412 F.2d 1197 (Ct. Cl. 1969), *cert. denied*, 397 U.S. 1009 (1970); Prohibited lobbying— *Christian Echoes Nat'l Ministry, Inc. v. U.S.*, 470 F. 2d 849 (10th Cir. 1972), *cert. denied*, 414 U.S. 864 (1973).

54. Rev. Rul. 68-306, 1968-1 C.B. 257.

55. Rev. Rul. 71-580, 1971-2 C.B. 235.

56. Rev. Rul. 74-575, 1974-2 C.B. 161.

57. Rev. Rul. 75-434, 1975-2 C.B. 205.

58. Rev. Rul. 77-430, 1977-2 C.B. 194.

59. *Bob Jones University v. U.S.*, 461 U.S. 574, 586-88, 103 S.Ct. 2017, 2026 (1983).

60. Treas. Reg. § 1.501(c)(3)-1(d)(2).

61. *Id.*

62. *Id.*

63. Rev. Rul. 70-533, 1970-2 C.B. 112; Rev. Rul. 68-166, 1968-1 C.B. 225.

64. Rev. Rul. 70-583, 1970-2 C.B. 114; Rev. Rul. 67-150, 1967-1 C.B. 133.

65. Rev. Rul. 72-559, 1972-2 C.B. 247; Rev. Rul. 69-161, 1969-1 C.B. 149, *amplified by* Rev. Rul. 78-428, 1978-2 C.B. 177.

66. Rev. Rul. 76-21, 1976-1 C.B. 147.

67. Rev. Rul. 77-42, 1977-1 C.B. 142.

68. Rev. Rul. 66-257, 1966-2 C.B. 212; Rev. Rul. 75-198, 1975-1 C.B. 157.

69. Rev. Rul. 75-385, 1975-2 C.B. 205; Rev. Rul. 76-244, 1976-1 C.B. 155; Rev. Rul. 77-246, 1977-2 C.B. 190.

70. Rev. Rul. 67-138, 1967-1 C.B. 129.
71. Rev. Rul. 68-17, 1968-1 C.B. 247.
72. Rev. Rul. 75-283, 1975-2 C.B. 201.
73. Rev. Rul. 67-250, 1967-2 C.B. 182.
74. Rev. Rul. 70-585, 1970-2 C.B. 115.
75. Rev. Rul. 69-174, 1969-1 C.B. 149.
76. Rev. Rul. 68-117, 1968-1 C.B. 251.
77. Rev. Rul. 68-165, 1968-1 C.B. 253.
78. Rev. Rul. 73-128, 1973-1 C.B. 222.
79. Rev. Rul. 69-441, 1969-2 C.B. 115.
80. Rev. Rul. 55-406, 1955-1 C.B. 73.
81. Rev. Rul. 68-167, 1968-1 C.B. 255.
82. Treas. Reg. § 1.501(c)(3)-1(d)(2).
83. *Id.*
84. *See,* Treas. Reg. §§ 1.501(c)(3)-1(d)(3) & (4) for definitions of "educational" and "scientific."
85. Rev. Rul. 66-103, 1966-1 C.B. 134.
86. Rev. Rul. 74-146, 1974-1 C.B. 129.
87. Rev. Rul. 65-191, 1965-2 C.B. 157.
88. Rev. Rul. 64-274, 1964-2 C.B. 141.
89. Rev. Rul. 69-257, 1969-1 C.B. 151.
90. Rev. Rul. 67-291, 1967-2 C.B. 184.
91. Rev. Rul. 69-400, 1969-2 C.B. 114.
92. Rev. Rul. 76-336, 1976-2 C.B. 143.
93. Rev. Rul. 75-284, 1975-2 C.B. 202.
94. Rev. Rul. 74-614, 1974-2 C.B. 164.
95. Rev. Rul. 67-149, 1967-1 C.B. 133; Rev. Rul. 71-529, 1971-2 C.B. 234.
96. Rev. Rul. 63-225, 1963-2 C.B. 210.
97. Rev. Rul. 56-486, 1956-2 C.B. 309.
98. Rev. Rul. 55-587, 1955-2 C.B. 261.
99. Rev. Rul. 63-220, 1963-2 C.B. 208; Rev. Rul. 61-87, 1961-1 C.B. 191.
100. Rev. Rul. 70-584, 1970-2 C.B. 114.
101. Rev. Rul. 66-147, 1966-1 C.B. 137.
102. Rev. Rul. 70-129, 1970-1 C.B. 128.
103. Rev. Rul. 69-572, 1969-2 C.B. 119.
104. Rev. Rul. 70-583, 1970-2 C.B. 114.
105. Rev. Rul. 71-29, 1971-1 C.B. 150.
106. *Monterey Pub. Parking v. U.S.,* 481 F.2d 175 (9th Cir. 1973).
107. Rev. Rul. 68-14, 1968-1 C.B. 243, *distinguished in* Rev. Rul. 75-286, 1975-2 C.B. 210.
108. Rev. Rul. 70-186, 1970-1 C.B. 128.
109. Rev. Rul. 70-79, 1970-1 C.B. 127.
110. Rev. Rul. 74-246, 1974-1 C.B. 130.
111. Rev. Rul. 74-361, 1974-2 C.B. 159.
112. Rev. Rul. 71-99, 1971-1 C.B. 151.
113. Rev. Rul. 69-174, 1969-1 C.B. 149.

114. Rev. Rul. 76-418, 1976-2 C.B. 145.

115. Rev. Rul. 65-61, 1965-1 C.B. 234.

116. Treas. Reg. § 1.501(c)(3)-1(d)(2).

117. Rev. Rul. 76-419, 1976-2 C.B. 146.

118. Rev. Rul. 72-228, 1972-1 C.B. 148; Rev. Rul. 75-285, 1975-2 C.B. 203; Rev. Rul. 78-305, 1978-2 C.B. 172.

119. Rev. Rul. 75-283, 1975-2 C.B. 201.

120. Rev. Rul. 76-408, 1976-2 C.B. 145; Rev. Rul. 67-138, 1967-1 C.B. 129; Rev. Rul. 68-17, 1968-1 C.B. 247.

121. Rev. Rul. 72-560, 1972-2 C.B. 248.

122. Rev. Rul. 76-204, 1976-1 C.B. 152.

123. Rev. Rul. 67-292, 1967-2 C.B. 184.

124. Rev. Rul. 71-29, 1971-1 C.B. 150.

125. *Monterey Pub. Parking Corp. v. U.S.,* 481 F.2d 175 (9th Cir. 1973).

126. Rev. Rul. 66-103, 1966-1 C.B. 134.

127. *Bok v. McCaughn,* 42 F.2d 616 (3d Cir. 1930).

128. Rev. Rul. 64-174, 1964-1 (Part 1) C.B. 183.

129. Rev. Rul. 64-175, 1964-1 (Part 1) C.B. 185.

130. Rev. Rul. 66-178, 1966-1 C.B. 138.

131. Rev. Rul. 73-569, 1973-2 C.B. 178.

132. Rev. Rul. 74-559, 1974-2 C.B. 164.

133. Rev. Rul. 72-559, 1972-2 C.B. 247.

134. Rev. Rul. 75-74, 1975-1 C.B. 152; Rev. Rul. 75-75, 1975-1 C.B. 154; Rev. Rul. 75-76, 1975-1 C.B. 154.

135. Rev. Rul. 74-587, 1974-2 C.B. 162.

136. Rev. Rul. 75-197, 1975-1 C.B. 156.

137. Treas. Reg. § 1.501(c)(3)-1(d)(3)(i).

138. *Id.*

139. Treas. Reg. § 1.501(c)(3)-1(d)(3)(ii).

140. Rev. Rul. 66-103, 1966-1 C.B. 134; Rev. Rul. 69-257, 1969-1 C.B. 151; Rev. Rul. 61-87, 1961-1 C.B. 191.

141. Rev. Rul. 64-274, 1964-2 C.B. 141.

142. Rev. Rul. 70-584, 1970-2 C.B. 114.

143. Rev. Rul. 78-310, 1978-2 C.B. 173.

144. Rev. Rul. 64-274, 1964-2 C.B. 141.

145. *Id.*

146. Rev. Rul. 63-235, 1963-2 C.B. 210.

147. Rev. Rul. 55-587, 1955-2 C.B. 261.

148. Rev. Rul. 68-16, 1968-1 C.B. 246.

149. Rev. Rul. 71-97, 1971-1 C.B. 150.

150. Internal Revenue Service, *Exempt Organizations Handbook* ¶ 754.4(2) (1974).

151. Rev. Rul. 60-143, 1960-1 C.B. 192.

152. Rev. Rul. 56-13, 1956-1 C.B. 198.

153. Rev. Rul. 68-504, 1968-2 C.B. 211; Rev. Rul. 65-298, 1965-2 C.B. 163; Rev. Rul. 76-37, 1976-1 C.B. 149.

154. Rev. Rul. 67-150, 1967-1 C.B. 133; Rev. Rul. 70-583, 1970-2 C.B. 114.
155. Rev. Rul. 76-205, 1976-1 C.B. 154.
156. Rev. Rul. 64-275, 1964-2 C.B. 142.
157. Rev. Rul. 66-103, 1966-1 C.B. 134; Rev. Rul. 67-148, 1967-1 C.B. 132.
158. Rev. Rul. 66-178, 1966-1 C.B. 138.
159. Rev. Rul. 64-195, 1964-2 C.B. 138; Rev. Rul. 67-148, 1967-1 C.B. 132; Rev. Rul. 68-71, 1968-1 C.B. 249.
160. Rev. Rul. 70-534, 1970-2 C.B. 113.
161. Rev. Rul. 77-68, 1977-1 C.B. 142.
162. Rev. Rul. 70-640, 1970-2 C.B. 117.
163. Rev. Rul. 66-255, 1966-2 C.B. 210.
164. Rev. Rul. 73-569, 1973-2 C.B. 178.
165. Rev. Rul. 74-595, 1974-2 C.B. 164.
166. Rev. Rul. 70-590, 1970-2 C.B. 116.
167. Rev. Rul. 68-14, 1968-1 C.B. 243, *distinguished in* Rev. Rul. 75-286, 1975-2 C.B. 210.
168. Rev. Rul. 70-79, 1970-1 C.B. 127; Rev. Rul. 72-560, 1972-2 C.B. 248.
169. Rev. Rul. 67-391, 1967-2 C.B. 190.
170. Treas. Reg. § 1.501(c)(3)-1(d)(2); Rev. Rul. 70-585, 1970-2 C,B. 115.
171. Rev. Rul. 66-258, 1966-2 C.B. 213.
172. Rev. Rul. 64-192, 1964-2 C.B. 136.
173. Rev. Rul. 70-583, 1970-2 C.B. 114.
174. Rev. Rul. 73-45, 1973-1 C.B. 220.
175. Rev. Rul. 64-174, 1964-1 (Part 1) C.B. 183.
176. Rev. Rul. 73-45, 1973-1 C.B. 220.
177. Rev. Rul. 66-46, 1966-1 C.B. 133.
178. Rev. Rul. 65-271, 1965-2 C.B. 161.
179. Rev. Rul. 65-270, 1965-2 C.B. 160.
180. Rev. Rul. 66-103, 1966-1 C.B. 134.
181. Rev. Rul. 67-4, 1967-1 C.B. 121.
182. Rev. Rul. 66-147, 1966-1 C.B. 137.
183. Rev. Rul. 70-79, 1970-1 C.B. 127.
184. Rev. Rul. 70-321, 1970-1 C.B. 129.
185. Rev. Rul. 70-129, 1970-1 C.B. 128.
186. Rev. Rul. 68-165, 1968-1 C.B. 253.
187. Rev. Rul. 75-196, 1975-1 C.B. 155.
188. Rev. Rul. 74-15, 1974-1 C.B. 126.
189. Rev. Rul. 55-587, 1955-2 C.B. 261.
190. Rev. Rul. 68-372, 1968-2 C.B. 205.
191. Treas. Reg. § 1.501(c)(3)-1(f).
192. Treas. Reg. § 1.501(c)(3)-1(d)(5)(iii).
193. Treas. Reg. § 1.501(c)(3)-1(d)(5)(i).
194. Treas. Reg. § 1.501(c)(3)-1(d)(5)(iii)(c).
195. Rev. Rul. 71-504, 1971-2 C.B. 231; Rev. Rul. 71-505, 1971-2 C.B. 232.
196. Rev. Rul. 71-506, 1971-2 C.B. 233.

197. Rev. Rul. 76-455, 1976-2 C.B. 150.

198. Treas. Reg. § 1.501(c)(3)-1(d).

199. Rev. Rul. 65-61, 1965-1 C.B. 234.

200. *Underwriters Laboratory, Inc. v. Comm.*, 135 F.2d 371 (7th Cir. 1943).

201. *Id.*

202. Rev. Rul. 67-151, 1967-1 C.B. 134.

203. Rev. Rul. 68-166, 1968-1 C.B. 255.

204. Rev. Rul. 70-533, 1970-2 C.B. 112.

205. *San Francisco Infant School, Inc.*, 69 T.C. 957 (1978).

206. Rev. Rul. 67-292, 1967-2 C.B. 184.

207. Rev. Rul. 66-359, 1966-2 C.B. 219.

208. Rev. Rul. 74-194, 1974-1 C.B. 129.

209. Pub. L. No. 94-455, 90 Stat. 1520.

210. Pub. L. No. 97-248, 96 Stat. 435.

211. I.R.C. § 501(j).

212. Treas. Reg. § 1.501(c)(4)-1(a)(2).

213. *Id.*

214. Treas. Reg. § 1.501(c)(3)-1(c)(3).

215. Treas. Reg. § 1.501(c)(4)-1(a)(2)(ii).

216. Rev. Rul. 74-361, 1974-2 C.B. 159, *superseding* Rev. Rul. 66-221, 1966-2 C.B. 220, and *clarifying* Rev. Rul. 71-47, 1971-1 C.B. 92.

217. *Mobile Arts & Sports Ass'n v. U.S.*, 148 F.Supp. 311 (D.C. Ala. 1957).

218. Rev. Rul. 61-153, 1961-2 C.B. 114.

219. Rev. Rul. 57-493, 1957-2 C.B. 314.

220. Rev. Rul. 57-297, 1957-2 C.B. 307, *distinguished on another issue by* Rev. Rul. 66-257, 1966-2 C.B. 212.

221. Rev. Rul. 55-439, 1955-2 C.B. 257.

222. Rev. Rul. 66-273, 1966-2 C.B. 222.

223. Rev. Rul. 69-384, 1969-2 C.B. 122.

224. *Lion's Associated Drag Strip v. U.S.*, 13 AFTR2d 973 (D.C. Calif. 1963).

225. Rev. Rul. 64-187, 1964-1 C.B. 187.

226. Rev. Rul. 67-294, 1967-2 C.B. 193.

227. Rev. Rul. 64-313, 1964-2 C.B. 146.

228. Rev. Rul. 65-195, 1965-2 C.B. 164.

229. Rev. Rul. 65-299, 1965-2 C.B. 165.

230. Rev. Rul. 69-148, 1966-1 C.B. 143.

231. Rev. Rul. 66-179, 1966-1 C.B. 139.

232. Rev. Rul. 67-109, 1967-1 C.B. 136.

233. Rev. Rul. 68-118, 1968-1 C.B. 261.

234. Rev. Rul. 68-224, 1968-1 C.B. 262.

235. Rev. Rul. 70-4, 1970-1 C.B. 126, *distinguished by* Rev. Rul. 80-215, 1980-2 C.B. 174.

236. Rev. Rul. 75-286, 1975-2 C.B. 210, *distinguishing* Rev. Rul. 68-14, 1968-1 C.B. 243.

237. Rev. Rul. 75-386, 1975-2 C.B. 211.

238. Rev. Rul. 78-50, 1978-1 C.B. 155.

239. Rev. Rul. 78-68, 1978-1 C.B. 149.

240. Rev. Rul. 78-69, 1978-1 C.B. 156.

241. Rev. Rul. 78-131, 1978-1 C.B. 156.

242. Rev. Rul. 78-429, 1978-2 C.B. 178.

243. Rev. Rul. 79-316, 1979-2 C.B. 228.

244. Rev. Rul. 71-530, 1971-2 C.B. 237.

245. Rev. Rul. 60-193, 1960-1 C.B. 195, *modified on other issues by* Rev. Rul. 66-258, 1966-2 C.B. 213.

246. Rev. Rul. 76-81, 1976-1 C.B. 156.

247. Rev. Rul. 62-167, 1962-2 C.B. 142.

248. Rev. Rul. 80-206, 1980-2, C.B. 185, *distinguishing* Rev. Rul. 73-306, 1973-2 C.B. 179.

249. Rev. Rul. 74-361, 1974-2 C.B. 159, *superseding* Rev. Rul. 66-221, 1966-2 C.B. 220, and *clarifying* Rev. Rul. 71-47, 1971-1 C.B. 92.

250. Treas. Reg. § 1.501(c)(4)-1(b).

251. Treas. Reg. § 1.501(c)(12)-1(b).

252. Rev. Rul. 74-281, 1974-1 C.B. 133.

253. Rev. Rul. 66-59, 1966-1 C.B. 142.

254. Private Letter Ruling 8039002 (1980).

255. Rev. Rul. 66-180, 1966-1 C.B. 144.

256. *Portland Cooperative Labor Temple Ass'n,* 39 B.T.A. 450 (1939).

257. Rev. Rul. 67-7, 1967-1 C.B. 137.

258. Rev. Rul. 68-534, 1968-2 C.B. 217, *superseding* SM 2558 C.B. Dec. 1924, p. 207.

259. Rev. Rul. 75-288, 1975-2 C.B. 212.

260. Rev. Rul. 76-31, 1976-1 C.B. 157.

261. Rev. Rul. 77-154, 1977-1 C.B. 148.

262. Rev. Rul. 59-6, 1959-1 C.B. 121.

263. Rev. Rul. 75-473, 1975 C.B. 213.

264. Rev. Rul. 77-5, 1977-1 C.B. 146.

265. Rev. Rul. 78-42, 1978-1 C.B. 158.

266. Rev. Rul. 77-292, 1977-2 C.B. 191.

267. *Big Spring Cowboy Reunion v. Campbell,* 210 F.2d 143 (5th Cir. 1954).

268. Rev. Rul. 56-245, 1956-1 C.B. 204.

269. Rev. Rul. 55-230, 1955-1 C.B. 71.

270. Rev. Rul. 54-282, 1954-2 C.B. 126.

271. *East Tenn. Artificial Breeders Ass'n v. U.S.,* 12 AFTR2d 5848 (D.C. Tenn. 1963).

272. Rev. Rul. 66-179, 1966-1 C.B. 139.

273. Rev. Rul. 70-372, 1971-2 C.B. 241, *clarified and distinguished by* Rev. Rul. 74-518, 1974-2 C.B. 166.

274. Rev. Rul. 74-518, 1974-2 C.B. 166, *clarifying and distinguishing* Rev. Rul. 70-372, 1971-2 C.B. 241.

275. Rev. Rul. 74-118, 1974-1 C.B. 134.

276. Rev. Rul. 74-488, 1974-2 C.B. 166.

277. Rev. Rul. 76-399, 1976-2 C.B. 152.

278. Rev. Rul. 81-59, 1981-1 C.B. 334.

279. I.R.C. § 501(g).

280. Treas. Reg. § 1.501(c)(6)-1.

281. *Id.*

282. *Id.*

283. *Id.*

284. Rev. Rul. 55-444, 1955-2 C.B. 258.

285. *Retail Credit Ass'n of Minneapolis v. U.S.*, 30 F.Supp. 855 (D.C. Minn. 1938).

286. Rev. Rul. 55-715, 1955-2 C.B. 263.

287. *Amer. Refractories Institute,* ¶ 47,330 P-H Memo TC.

288. *Atlantic Master Printers Club,* ¶ 42,602 P-H Memo TC.

289. *Oregon Casualty Ass'n,* 37 B.T.A. 340 (1938).

290. *Minneapolis Board of Fire Underwriters,* ¶ 38,343 P-H Memo BTA.

291. Rev. Rul. 66-233, 1966-2 C.B. 224.

292. Rev. Rul. 66-260, 1966-2 C.B. 225.

293. *American Woodworking Machinery & Equipment Show, Inc. v. U.S.*, 249 F.Supp. 392 (D.C. N.C. 1966).

294. Rev. Rul. 67-252, 1967-2 C.B. 195.

295. Rev. Rul. 67-264, 1967-2 C.B. 196.

296. *American Plywood Ass'n v. U.S.*, 267 F.Supp. 830 (D.C. Wash. 1967).

297. Rev. Rul. 67-295, 1967-2 C.B. 197.

298. Rev. Rul. 67-393, 1967-2 C.B. 200.

299. Rev. Rul. 67-394, 1967-2 C.B. 201.

300. Rev. Rul. 69-387, 1969-2 C.B. 124.

301. Rev. Rul. 73-567, 1973-2 C.B. 178.

302. Rev. Rul. 74-553, 1974-2 C.B. 168, *distinguished by* Rev. Rul. 76-455, 1976-2 C.B. 150.

303. Rev. Rul. 73-452, 1973-2 C.B. 183.

304. Treas. Reg. § 1.501(c)(7)-1(a).

305. Rev. Rul. 69-68, 1969-1 C.B. 153.

306. *Automobile Club of Michigan v. Comm.*, 353 U.S. 180 (1957); *Smyth v. Calif. State Automobile Ass'n,* 175 F.2d 752 (9th Cir. 1949), *cert. denied,* 338 U.S. 905 (1949).

307. Rev. Rul. 66-179, 1966-1 C.B. 139.

308. Rev. Rul. 67-139, 1967-1 C.B. 129.

309. I.T. 1427, C.B. Dec. 1922, p. 187.

310. Rev. Rul. 68-266, 1968-1 C.B. 270.

311. Rev. Rul. 69-281, 1969-1 C.B. 155.

312. Rev. Rul. 69-573, 1969-2 C.B. 125.

313. Rev. Rul. 73-520, 1973-2 C.B. 180.

314. Treas. Reg. § 1.501(c)(8)-1(a).

315. Rev. Rul. 73-165, 1973-1 C.B. 224, *superseding* I.T. 1516, C.B. Dec. 1922, p. 180, *which overruled* O.D. 690, C.B. Dec. 1920, p. 236.

316. *Family Aid Ass'n v. U.S.*, 36 F.Supp. 1017 (Ct. Cl. 1941).
317. *Id.*
318. Rev. Rul. 55-495, 1955-2 C.B. 259.
319. Rev. Rul. 76-457, 1976-2 C.B. 155.
320. Rev. Rul. 78-87, 1978-1 C.B. 160.
321. Treas. Reg. § 1.501(c)(9)-1(c).
322. Treas. Reg. § 1.501(c)(9)-2(c)(2).
323. Treas. Reg. § 1.501(c)(9)-2(b)(1).
324. Treas. Reg. § 1.501(c)(9)-2(b)(2).
325. Treas. Reg. § 1.501(c)(9)-2(a)(1).
326. Treas. Reg. § 1.501(c)(9)-3(a),(b),(c).
327. Treas. Reg. § 1.501(c)(9)-3(d),(e).
328. Treas. Reg. § 1.501(c)(9)-3(f).
329. Treas. Reg. § 1.501(c)(10)-1(a)(2).
330. Treas. Reg. § 1.501(c)(10)-1(a).
331. Rev. Rul. 76-457, 1976-2 C.B. 155.
332. Rev. Rul. 77-258, 1977-2 C.B. 195.
333. Treas. Reg. § 1.501(c)(12)-1(b).
334. *Id.*
335. Rev. Rul. 72-36, 1972-1 C.B. 151, *modified by* Rev. Rul. 81-109, 1981-1 C.B. 347.
336. Treas. Reg. § 1.501(c)(12)-1(b).
337. Rev. Rul. 57-420, 1957-2 C.B. 308.
338. Rev. Rul. 68-564, 1968-2 C.B. 221, *superseding* I.T. 3286, 1939-1 C.B. 126.
339. Rev. Rul. 67-265, 1967-2 C.B. 205, *superseding* I.T. 167, C.B. June 1923, p. 158.
340. Rev. Rul. 73-453, 1973-2 C.B. 185.
341. Rev. Rul. 83-170, 1983-2 C.B. 97.
342. *N.J. Automobile Club v. U.S.*, 181 F. Supp. 259 (Ct.Cl. 1960).
343. *Consumers Credit Rural Electric Cooperative Corp. v. Comm.*, 319 F.2d 475 (6th Cir. 1963).
344. Rev. Rul. 65-201, 1965-2 C.B. 170.
345. *Lake Petersburg Ass'n*, ¶ 74,055 P-H Memo T.C.
346. *John D. Rockefeller Family Cemetery Corp.*, 65 T.C. 355 (1974); *DuPont de Nemours Cemetery Co.*, 33 T.C.M. 1438 (1974).
347. Treas. Reg. § 1.501(c)(13)-1(a).
348. Rev. Rul. 64-109, 1964-1 C.B. 190.
349. Rev. Rul. 72-17, 1972-1 C.B. 151.
350. Rev. Rul. 71-300, 1971-2 C.B. 238, *withdrawing* Rev. Rul. 69-637, 1969-2 C.B. 127.
351. I.R.C. § 501(c)(14).
352. Rev. Rul. 72-37, 1972-1 C.B. 152, *clarifying* Rev. Rul. 69-282, 1969-1 C.B. 155.
353. Rev. Rul. 69-283, 1969-1 C.B. 156.
354. *U.S. v. Md Savgs-share Ins. Corp.*, 400 U.S. 4 (1970).

355. I.R.C. § 501(c)(15).
356. Treas. Reg. § 1.501(c)(15)-1(a)(1).
357. Rev. Rul. 74-196, 1974-1 C.B. 140, *superseding* GCM 25497, 1948-1 C.B. 60.
358. *Baltimore Equitable Society v. U.S.*, 3 F.Supp. 427 (Ct.Cl. 1933), *cert. denied,*
290 U.S. 662 (1933).
359. I.R.C § 501(c)(16).
360. *Id.*
361. Treas. Reg. § 1.501(c)(16)-1; Treas. Reg. § 1.521-1.
362. I.R.C. § 501(c)(17).
363. Treas. Reg. § 1.501(c)(19)-1(b)(2).
364. Treas. Reg. § 1.501(c)(19)-1(b)(1).
365. I.R.C. § 501(c)(20).
366. I.R.C. § 501(c)(21).
367. I.R.C. § 501(c)(22).
368. I.R.C. § 501(c)(23).
369. I.R.C. § 501(d).
370. Rev. Rul. 80-332, 1980-2 C.B. 34.
371. I.R.C. § 501(e)(1)(A).
372. I.R.C. § 501(f).

4

Organizational Forms

CORPORATE STATUTORY FORMS

Corporations

Most states have adopted nonprofit corporation acts in varying degrees of detail and style. However, some states have merely modified slightly their business corporation acts to include nonprofit corporations (see Table 2).

The typical nonprofit corporation act is a general statute which applies to all nonprofit corporations. Alternatively, some states have adopted a compartmental system in which the various kinds of nonprofit corporations are treated in separate chapters, each devoted to a particular category of organization. There are also hybrid systems of which New York's is the most notable. The New York statute classifies nonprofit corporations into four types.[1] Each of the four types is then treated generally.

The Model Nonprofit Corporation Act has been adopted by a few states but has not been widely accepted since its publication in 1952. The practitioner must look to state statutes for guidance.

The nonprofit corporate form may be used by any organization which qualifies under its state statutes and operates in accordance therewith. The corporate form offers a more rigid framework within which the organization operates than unincorporated associations offer. The relationships within the corporation and between the corporation and third parties are more formal and better suited to associations composed of large or diverse groups.

Of all forms of association the nonprofit corporate form is preferred by more than 20 percent of all nonprofit organizations.[2] Part of this preference may be attributable to the widely held belief that the preferred form of profit-making

Table 2
Types of Nonprofit Corporation Acts

State	Model NonProfit Act	General NonProfit Act	Compartmental Articles	Other
Alabama	X		X	
Alaska		X	X	
Arizona	X			
Arkansas		X	X	
California				
Colorado		X		
Connecticut		X		
Delaware				
District of Columbia	X		X	
Florida		X		
Georgia		X		
Hawaii				
Idaho		X		
Illinois	1	X	X	
Indiana				
Iowa	X			
Kansas			X	
Kentucky		X	X	
Louisiana		X		
Maine		X		
Maryland			X	
Massachusetts		X	X	
Michigan		X		
Minnesota		X		
Mississippi		X		
Missouri	1	X		
Montana		X		
Nebraska				
Nevada			X	
• New Hampshire			X	
New Jersey			X	
New Mexico	X	X		
New York				3
North Carolina	X			
North Dakota	X			
Ohio	1	X	X	
Oklahoma		X		
Oregon	X			
Pennsylvania		X		
Rhode Island		X		
South Carolina		X	X	
South Dakota		X		
Tennessee				2
Texas	X			
Utah				
Vermont				
Virginia	X			
Washington		X	X	
West Virginia				2
Wisconsin	X			
Wyoming		X	X	

1. Similar to Model Act.
2. Contained in for profit corporation act.
3. New York is a hybrid system.

activities is the business corporation because of its characteristics of limited liability, continuity of life, centralized management, and free transferability of interests. Since these attributes are applicable to nonprofit corporations, it follows that there should be a preference for the corporate form for nonprofit associations.

Public Corporations

Public corporations created by state legislatures include municipal, district, and public benefit corporations. The New York Port Authority is an example of a public corporation created by multistate compact.[3] The federal government has created public corporations such as the Commodity Credit Corporation, Federal Deposit Insurance Corporation, Federal Farm Mortgage Corporation, and Farmers Home Corporation.

Public corporations may be created only by express legislative provisions and exercise only those powers expressly granted by the legislature.

Cooperatives

Many states have enacted express legislation governing cooperatives. Cooperatives may be organized for profit or nonprofit purposes. A cooperative is formed to provide mutual assistance or service to or among its membership. The predominant type of cooperative is agricultural.

Mutual Association

Mutual associations are the subject of complex and detailed legislation. Credit unions, credit bureaus, certain banking institutions, and mutual insurance companies are all specifically dealt with in state statutes.

NONCORPORATE FORMS

Trusts

The term "trust" as used in this section is confined to express trusts. Express trusts are classified as either private or charitable trusts. A private express trust is a "fiduciary relationship with respect to property, subjecting the person by whom the title to property is held to equitable duties to deal with the property for the benefit of another person, which arises as a result of a manifestation of an intention to create it."[4] Property which constitutes the trust res or corpus may be land or chattels, tangibles or intangibles, or legal or equitable interests. But, whatever the kind of property involved, no trust exists without the transfer of property to be held in trust.[5]

The trustee and beneficiaries are in a fiduciary relationship which requires the trustee to act for the benefit of the beneficiaries. The standard of duty owed the beneficiaries by the trustee is very high and results from the distinction between law and equity in the English legal system. The equitable duties imposed on the trustee are derived from equity in the Court of Chancery which have survived the merging of law and equity in most jurisdictions in the United States.

A charitable trust is a "fiduciary relationship with respect to property arising as a result of a manifestation of an intention to create it, and subjecting the person by whom the property is held to equitable duties to deal with the property for a charitable purpose."[6]

A charitable trust as opposed to a private trust lacks an ordinary beneficiary and is not required to have a definite beneficiary. A charitable trust is recognized as valid in all the states although there are differences as to how well-defined the charitable purpose must be.

The equitable duties imposed on the trustee of a charitable trust are similar to those imposed on the trustee of a private trust. Because a charitable trust lacks ordinary beneficiaries, the trustee owes no direct duty to a beneficiary, but the equitable duties are enforced by suit of the state attorney general or other public officer.

The charitable trust is the alternative form to the nonprofit corporation for funds and foundations. Charitable trusts may be created for relief of the poor; promotion of education; advancement of religion; and promotion of health, certain governmental or municipal purposes such as erection of public buildings, and others too numerous to list here.[7]

Creation of a charitable trust does not require the strict adherence to form required of nonprofit corporations. The high equitable duties imposed on trustees of charitable trusts by courts of equity to some extent have been lessened by legislatures when the corporate form is used. The statutory form and procedure reduces the discretion of the corporate controlling persons and submits them to the authority of persons other than courts of equity.

Foundations

Foundations may be created as either nonprofit corporations or charitable trusts. If the corporate form is chosen, then the state nonprofit corporation act or special corporation act for foundations is applicable. If the foundation is established as a charitable trust, then the state law regarding charitable trusts applies. Frequently, a charitable trust is created which requires the trustee to incorporate. Occasionally, the trust instrument provides for an option to the trustee to incorporate or not within the trustee's discretion.

Unincorporated Associations

Unincorporated associations for profit and unincorporated associations not for profit must be distinguished. An unincorporated association of two or more persons to carry on as co-owners a business for profit is a partnership.[8] Associations of two or more persons who are not co-owners of a business for profit are not partnerships, and if they are not incorporated, they belong to the vast numbers of nonprofit unincorporated organizations.

Unincorporated nonprofit associations are not legal entities and have no legal existence apart from their memberships. Many states have enacted enabling legislation to permit suits by and against unincorporated associations;[9] however, this legislation generally is considered to be procedural and does not accord legal entity status to such associations.

By and large, state regulation of unincorporated nonprofit associations is sporadic. Moreover, the statutory regulations that exist in some instances do not apply to charitable or fraternal organizations.[10].

Generally, small local organizations are best suited to be unincorporated nonprofit associations. Social clubs, political clubs or committees, and other local musical or literary societies can use the unincorporated nonprofit association form with relative ease. This form of organization is best suited to small, cohesive groups having a single purpose.

Labor Unions

The National Labor Relations Act defines a labor organization as being any organization, or any agency or employee representation committee or plan, in which employees participate and which exists for the purpose, in whole or in part, of dealing with employers concerning grievances, labor disputes, wages, rates of pay, hours of employment, or conditions of work.[11]

Labor unions are unincorporated associations of persons and other unincorporated associations. An unsuccessful attempt was made by the state of Colorado in 1944 to require labor unions to incorporate.[12]

TAX CLASSIFICATIONS

Congress has recognized the corporation, partnership, trust, and unincorporated association as being the major forms of associations for tax purposes.

Corporations

The Internal Revenue Code defines a corporation by merely stating what the term includes. For tax purposes a corporation includes associations, joint-stock companies, and insurance companies.[13] However, the list is not exclusive and includes other organizational forms.[14]

In general, corporation includes business enterprises organized under a state corporation act including professional corporation or association acts, after Treasury Regulations section 301.7701-2(h) was revoked, and also includes unincorporated associations which more closely resemble corporations than not.[15]

The test for whether an unincorporated association more closely resembles a corporation than not was articulated by the U.S. Supreme Court in *Morrissey v. Commissioner*, 296 U.S. 344 (1935).[16] In *Morrissey* the Court listed six basic characteristics of a corporation which are (1) associates, (2) an objective to conduct a business enterprise, (3) centralized management, (4) continuity of life, (5) free transferability of interests, and (6) limited liability of the participants to the property of the organization. If the association has more of these basic characteristics than not, it is treated as a corporation for tax purposes.

Morrissey is applied to partnerships and trusts by discarding those characteristics which the entities have in common. A corporation and partnership have the characteristics of associates and an objective to conduct a business enterprise in common, while a corporation and trust have the remaining four characteristics in common but not associates and an objective to conduct a business enterprise. After discarding the common characteristics, examine the remaining characteristics. If more than half the remaining characteristics are in common with a corporation, the entity is treated as a corporation for tax purposes.

The Treasury Regulations are slanted against finding that a partnership or limited partnership is a corporation for tax purposes if the partnership agreement conforms substantially with the provisions of the Uniform Partnership Act or the Uniform Limited Partnership Act. State partnership acts which deviate from the uniform acts may create tax problems. In *Phillip G. Larson*,[17] the Internal Revenue Service contended that a California limited partnership be treated as a corporation for tax purposes because the California limited partnership act did not provide for dissolution of the partnership on bankruptcy of a general partner and, therefore, had continuity of life which made the partnership more like a corporation than not.

Conversely, there are cases in which a corporation exists under the basic corporation law of a state, but the corporate entity is disregarded for tax purposes. The corporate form will be disregarded for tax purposes if the corporation is purely a passive dummy or is solely used for tax avoidance.[18]

The normal business corporation form is not generally used for tax exempt organizations; however, some states do not have separate nonprofit corporation statutes (see Table 2).

When the term corporation is used in section 501 in conjunction with the distribution constraint, it refers to a nonprofit corporation because the distribution constraint is the primary requirement of a nonprofit corporation.

Partnerships

A partnership is defined in the Internal Revenue Code as a "syndicate, group, pool, joint venture, or other unincorporated organization, through or by means of which any business, financial operation, or venture is carried on, and which is not within the meaning of this title [Code], a trust or estate or a corporation."[19]

A partnership is not one of the forms of organization permitted for a tax exempt organization unless it is considered as a corporation for tax purposes.[20]

Trusts

A trust is not defined in the Internal Revenue Code. Moreover, it is not specifically mentioned as an organizational form in section 501(c)(3), although it is the required organizational form in other subsections of section 501(c) (see Table 3).

While a trust is not specifically mentioned as a permissible organizational form in section 501(c)(3), the enumerated organizational forms of fund and foundation may be trusts. Taxation of private trusts is the subject of subchapter J of the Internal Revenue Code.

Of the two general types of trusts, a business trust is treated as a corporation for tax purposes because it has associates and a business purpose. This section, therefore, deals only with ordinary trusts. Business trusts are considered with corporations, *supra*.

For tax purposes, the existence of a trust is determined on a case-by-case basis considering all the surrounding circumstances, (1) the existence or nonexistence of a trust instrument,[21] (2) grantor's intent,[22] (3) necessity of a trust res or corpus,[23] and (4) requirements of local law.[24] No trust can exist without designation of a trust beneficiary.[25]

An attempted declaration of trust which does not qualify as a trust may be treated as a gift,[26] assignment,[27] or agency relationship.[28]

Other Permissible Tax Exempt Forms

Funds

A fund may describe a charitable trust, a separate organization, or part of another section 501(c)(3) organization. As a separate organization or part of another section 501(c)(3) organization, the fund may be in the form of a corporation. Prior to 1921, corporations and associations could be exempt under section 501(c)(3) but trusts could not. The Revenue Act of 1921 was amended to include "community chest, fund, or foundation." The legislative history indicates that Congress intended to include trusts passing to individuals or unincorporated bodies as well as to corporations.[29]

Table 3
Organizational Forms of Tax Exempt Organizations

Organization	Unincorporated Association	Corporation	Trust	Mutual or Co-operative Company	Community Chest	Foundation	Fund
Instrumentalities of United States Government. Section 501(c)(1).		X					
Organizations Created to Hold Title to Property. Section 501(c)(2).		X					
Charitable Organizations. Section 501(c)(3).		X	X		X	X	X
Civic Leagues. Section 501(c)(4).	X	X					
Labor, Agricultural, or Horticultural Organizations. Section 501(c)(5).	X	X					
Business Leagues, Chambers of Commerce, etc. Section 501(c)(6).	X	X					
Social Clubs, Section 501(c)(7).	X	X					
Fraternal Beneficiary Societies, Orders, or Associations. Section 501(c)(8).	X	X					
Voluntary Employees Beneficiary Association. Section 501(c)(9).	X	X	X				
Domestic Fraternal Societies, Orders, or Associations-No insurance. Section 501(c)(10).	X	X					
Teacher's Retirement Fund Associations. Section 501(c)(11).	X	X	X				X
Benevolent Life Ins. Assoc.,							

64

Type of Organization						
Mutual Ditch or Irrigation Companies, etc. Section 501(c)(12).		X		X		
Cemetery Companies. Section 501(c)(13).	X	X		X		X
Credit Unions—No Capital Stock Section 501(c)(14).		X		X		
Mutual Insurance Companies or Association Other than Life or Marine. Section 501(c)(15).	X	X		X		
Crop Financing Corporations. Section 501(c)(16).		X		X		
Trust for Payment of Supplemental Unemployment Benefits. Section 501(c)(17).			X			
Trusts for Payment of Certain Pension Benefits. Section 501(c)(18).		X	X			
Veteran's Organization. Section 501(c)(19) and (23).		X	X	X	X	
Organization or Trust part of Group Legal Services Plan. Section 501(c)(20).		X	X	X		
Trust—Black Lung Section 501(c)(21).			X			
Multiemployer Retirement Trust. Section 501(c)(22).			X	X		
Religious and Apostolic Organizations. Section 501(d).	X	X				
Cooperative Hospital Service Organizations. Section 501(e).	X	X		X		

Foundations

Foundations generally are created as either corporations or trusts. For tax purposes, foundations are further characterized as private or public. A private foundation is described in section 509 as a domestic or foreign section 501(c)(3) organization except public foundations, organizations described in section 170(b)(1)(A)(i)-(vi), certain related organizations, and organizations formed for testing for public safety.

The section 170(b)(1)(A) exclusions from the definition of private foundation are (1) churches or a convention or association of churches; (2) schools and other educational institutions; (3) organizations that provide medical or hospital care, education, or research; (4) organizations that normally receive a substantial part of their support from governmental units or the general public; (5) a governmental unit; and (6) certain private "operating," "conduit," or "pooled" foundations defined in section 170(b)(1)(D).

A private operating foundation is an organization that makes qualifying distributions directly for the active conduct of the activities which constitute the purpose or function for which the organization is organized and operated.[30] The qualifying distribution must equal substantially all the lesser of the organization's adjusted net income or its minimum investment return.[31] Substantially more than half of the organization's assets must be devoted directly to carrying out its purpose or to functionally related businesses.[32] If the assets of the foundation are stock of a controlled corporation of the foundation, then substantially all the assets of the foundation's controlled corporation must be devoted directly to carrying out its purpose or to functionally related businesses.[33]

A private distributing foundation is a private foundation that, not later than two and one-half months after the close of the taxable year in which it receives contributions, makes qualifying distributions out of the corpus but not out of current or accumulated income in an amount equal to 100 percent of the contributions.[34]

A private community or pooled fund foundation is a private foundation which pools into a common fund all contributions received from its donors, who retain the right to designate the public charities that will benefit from the contribution and the income derived therefrom.[35]

A public foundation is an organization which generally receives substantial support from the public. Substantial support means receiving more than a third of the organization's support from gifts, grants, membership fees, and gross receipts from admissions, sales of merchandise, performance of services, or furnishing facilities in an activity that is not unrelated to trade or business from certain organizations, governmental units, or qualified persons and not more than a third of its support from gross investment income and unrelated business taxable income in excess of the section 511 tax.[36]

For purposes of the support test a "disqualified person" is a substantial contributor as defined in section 507(d)(2); foundation manager as defined in section 4946(b); owner of more than 20 percent of (1) the voting power of a corporation, (2) profits interest in a partnership, or (3) beneficial interest in a trust or unincorporated business if the corporation, partnership, trust, or unincorporated business is a substantial contributor; family members of substantial contributors, foundation manager, or owners of a 20 percent interest; corporation, partnership, trust, or estate in which another disqualified person owns more than a 35 percent interest; a related private foundation which is controlled, directly or indirectly, by the same person or persons or if substantially all contributions to the private foundation in question are made by disqualified persons of the related private foundation in question; and a governmental official as defined in section 4941.[37] These constraints on support are designed to ensure that the foundation is operated for public rather than private uses of a limited number of donors or other persons.[38]

Also excluded from private foundation status are supporting or related organizations.[39] Such an organization must be organized and operated exclusively for the benefit of, to perform the functions of, or to carry out the purposes of one or more section 501(c)(3) organizations which are not private foundations. The organizational test is stated in Treasury Regulations section 1.509(a)-4(c), and the operational test is in Treasury Regulations section 1.509(a)-(4)(b)(1). Further, the related or supporting organization must be operated, supervised, or controlled by or in connection with the organization it is supporting and not be controlled by a disqualified person as defined in section 4946 other than a foundation manager.[40]

Community Chests

A community chest is a permissible form of organization under section 501(c)(3). After World War I, the term community chest came into common use and is probably derived from the practice of raising war chests by organizations to provide relief during World War I. The dictionary meaning is a general fund accumulated from individual subscriptions to defray demands on a community for charity and social welfare.[41]

Government-Owned Organizations

A state or city-owned organization may be exempt if it is a separate entity, does not operate as an integral part of state or city government, and does not exercise enforcement or regulatory powers.[42] A public library which was organized as a separate entity without the power to lay and collect taxes for its operations but which obtained its funds for operation by certifying the tax rate needed to a rate-making authority qualified as a tax exempt organization.[43]

Nonexempt Charitable Trusts and Split-Interest Trusts

Classification as a private foundation is predicated on an organization's obtaining tax exempt status under section 501(c)(3).[44] Unless a section 501(c)(3) organization gives notice to the Internal Revenue Service that it is not a private foundation, it is presumed to be one.[45]

Because trusts are considered to be conduits of income for tax purposes and are taxed only on undistributed income, it was possible for a trust to have the benefits of section 501(c)(3) without applying for the exemption. A trust which contributed all of its income to a qualified charity had an unlimited charitable deduction for the amount distributed[46] and hence no taxable income. Such a nonexempt trust could not be classified as a private foundation and would avoid the restrictions and excise taxes of chapter 42 related to investment income,[47] minimum distribution requirements,[48] self-dealing,[49] excess business holdings,[50] jeopardy investments,[51] and taxable expenditures.[52] To prevent this, Congress enacted section 4947.

Section 4947(a)(1) provides that a trust that is not tax exempt under section 501(a) but in which all of the unexpired interests in the trust are devoted to one or more charitable purposes described in section 170(c)(2)(B) and a charitable deduction was allowed the grantor under section 170, 545(b)(2), 556(b)(2), 642(c), 2055, 2106(a)(2), or 2522 shall be treated as a section 501(c)(3) organization except for purposes of sections 508(a), (b), and (c). Section 170(c)(2)(B) purposes are religious, charitable, scientific, literary, or educational purposes, or to foster national or international amateur sports competition, or for the prevention of cruelty to children or animals. A charitable deduction will be presumed to have been taken if such a deduction would have been allowable.[53] The effect of section 4947(a)(1) is to classify the nonexempt trust as a private foundation and subject it to chapter 42 restrictions and excise taxes.

Although the trust is subject to chapter 42, certain modifications must be considered. If a nonexempt charitable trust is subject to the section 4940 excise tax on investment income, it is subject to the tax imposed by section 4940(b) rather than section 4940(a).[54] Further, if the trust has unrelated business income as defined in section 681(a) on which the tax is imposed under section 641(a), gross investment income does not include the amount on which the section 641(a) tax is imposed.[55]

A section 4947(a)(1) trust is not a substantial contributor for purposes of section 507(d)(2) so that the making of grants and dealing with the trust are not prohibited.[56]

A nonexempt charitable trust may avoid the private foundation classification by requesting a determination of status as a public charity under section 509(a)(3). Section 509(a)(3) classes an organization that is exclusively organized and operated for the benefit of, to perform the functions of, or to carry out the purposes of one or more charitable organizations, not private foundations, and that is operated, supervised, or controlled by or in connection with the charitable organization or organizations as a public charity. Revenue Procedure 72-50[57] provides the guidelines for obtaining such a determination.

A nonexempt charitable trust treated as a private foundation may be required to file IRS forms 990-AR, 1041, 1041-A, 4720, and 5227.

Section 4947(a)(1) may apply to an estate whose administration is considered to be terminated for tax purposes. An estate in which the administrator is required to distribute all the net assets in trust for charitable beneficiaries or free of trust to charitable beneficiaries is not subject to section 4947(a)(1) until the date the estate is considered terminated under Treasury Regulations section 1.641(b)-3(a).[58] The estate thereafter becomes subject to section 4947(a)(1) until the date of final distribution.[59]

Section 4947(a)(2) deals with split-interest trusts. In a split-interest trust, one or more but not all of the unexpired interests are devoted to charitable purposes. The charitable remainder trust and the unitrust are the two most important split-interest trusts for tax purposes. If the charitable interest is for a section 170(c)(2)(B) purpose and a charitable deduction was allowed under sections 170, 545(b)(2), 556(b)(2), 642(c), 2055, 2106(a)(2), or 2522, the split-interest trust is subject to some but not all rules regarding private foundations. The excise taxes on investment income[60] and on failure to distribute income[61] are not applicable.[62] The excise taxes on self-dealing[63] and taxable expenditures[64] are fully applicable.[65] The excise taxes on excessive business holdings[66] and jeopardy investments[67] are applicable except as provided in section 4947(b)(3). Section 4947(b)(3) provides that the taxes on excessive business holdings and jeopardy investments do not apply if all the income interest of the trust is devoted solely to charitable purposes and all amounts in trust for which a charitable contribution was allowed had an aggregate value at the time the deduction was allowed of not more than 60 percent of the fair market value of all amounts in trust or if a charitable deduction was permitted for amounts payable under the trust to every remainderman but not to any income beneficiary (this includes a section 664 unitrust or annuity trust).

Amounts paid to noncharitable income beneficiaries of a split-interest trust are not subject to the private foundation rules.[68] A split-interest trust created by will is considered a split-interest trust under section 4947(a)(2) from the date of death of the grantor.[69] As with nonexempt charitable trusts an estate whose administration is terminated for tax purposes under Treasury Regulations section 1.641(b)-3(a) becomes subject to section 4947(a)(2) from that date until actual distribution if the administrator is required to distribute all the net assets in trust or free of trust to both charitable and noncharitable beneficiaries.[70]

NOTES

1. N.Y. N-PCL § 201.
2. H. Oleck, *The Nature of Nonprofit Organizations in 1979,* 10 U. Tol. L.R. 962, 980-84 (1979).

3. 42 Stat. 174.

4. A. Scott, *Law of Trusts*, § 2.3 (3d ed. 1967).

5. *Id.*

6. *Id.* § 348.

7. *Id.* §§ 368-377.

8. Uniform Partnership Act § 6.

9. *See, e.g.,* N.J. Stat. Ann. tit. 2A §§ 64-1 - 64-6; Ohio Rev. Code Ann. §§ 1745.01, 1745.02.

10. N.J. Rev. Stat. § 64-6.

11. 29 U.S.C. § 152(5).

12. *American Fed'n of Labor v. Reilly,* 113 Colo. 90, 155 P.2d 145 (1944).

13. I.R.C. § 7701(a)(3).

14. I.R.C. § 7701(b).

15. Treas. Reg. § 301.7701-2(a).

16. The *Morrissey* test is incorporated in Treas. Reg. § 301.7701-2.

17. *Phillip G. Larson,* 66 T.C. 159 (1976).

18. *See, William B. Strong,* 66 T.C. 12 (1976); *Moline Properties v. Comm.,* 319 U.S. 436 (1943).

19. I.R.C. § 7701(a)(2).

20. See text accompanying notes 15 and 16.

21. *See, e.g., Myrtle Mercer,* 7 T.C. 834 (1946); *U.S. v. Smither,* 205 F.2d 518 (5th Cir. 1953); *Estate of Robert L. Holt,* 14 B.T.A. 564 (1928); *Van Sciver v. Rothensies,* 36 F.Supp. 577 (D.C. Pa. 1941); *Giovanni Del Drago v. Comm'r,* 214 F.2d 478 (2d Cir. 1954).

22. *The Hanover Bank, Trustee,* 40 T.C. 532 (1963).

23. *Herman Paster,* ¶ 61,240 P-H Memo T.C.

24. Treas. Reg. § 301,7701-4(a).

25. *Morsman v. Comm.,* 90 F.2d 18 (8th Cir.), *cert. denied,* 302 U.S. 701 (1937).

26. Rev. Rul. 55-469, 1955-2 C.B. 519.

27. *Sidney S. Gorham,* 38 B.T.A. 1450 (1938).

28. *Garcia v. U.S.,* 421 F.2d 1231 (5th Cir. 1970).

29. *Fifty-third Union Trust Co. v. Comm.,* 56 F.2d 767 (6th Cir. 1932).

30. I.R.C. § 4942(j)(3).

31. *Id.*

32. *Id.*

33. *Id.*

34. I.R.C. § 170(b)(1)(D)(ii).

35. I.R.C. § 170(b)(1)(D)(iii).

36. I.R.C. § 509(a)(2).

37. I.R.C. § 4946(a).

38. Treas. Reg. § 1.509(a)-3(a)(4).

39. I.R.C. § 509(a)(3).

40. *Id.*

41. *Webster's New Collegiate Dictionary* (1981).

42. Rev. Rul. 60-384, 1960-2 C.B. 172, *amplifying* Rev. Rul. 55-319, 1955-1 C.B. 119.

43. Rev. Rul. 74-15, 1974-1 C.B. 126.
44. I.R.C. § 509(a).
45. I.R.C. § 508(b).
46. I.R.C. § 642(c).
47. I.R.C. § 4940.
48. I.R.C, § 4942.
49. I.R.C. § 4941.
50. I.R.C. § 4943.
51. I.R.C. § 4944.
52. I.R.C. § 4945.
53. Treas. Reg. § 53.4947-1(a).
54. Treas. Reg. § 53.4947-1(b)(1)(ii).
55. Rev. Rul. 74-497, 1974-2 C.B. 383.
56. Rev. Rul. 73-455, 1973-2 C.B. 187.
57. 1972-2 C.B. 830.
58. Treas. Reg. § 53.4947-1(b)(2).
59. *Id.*
60. I.R.C. § 4940.
61. I.R.C. § 4942.
62. I.R.C. § 4947(a)(2).
63. I.R.C. § 4941.
64. I.R.C. § 4945.
65. I.R.C. § 4947(a)(2).
66. I.R.C. § 4943.
67. I.R.C. § 4944.
68. I.R.C. § 4947(a)(2)(A).
69. Treas. Reg. § 53.4947-1(c)(6).
70. Treas. Reg. § 53.4947-1(c)(6)(ii).

5

Organization

Although some nonprofit organizations such as an unincorporated association or oral trust may be organized and operated without formal written organizational documents, tax exempt status may not be obtained without them. Moreover, the Internal Revenue Service generally limits its inquiry to organizational documents in deciding whether to grant a tax exemption.

INCORPORATION

Organization of a nonprofit corporation requires strict adherence to the statutory scheme in the state of incorporation.

Jurisdiction

Selection of jurisdiction for incorporation of a tax exempt organization generally does not rise to the level of importance that is the case with business corporations. If the tax exempt organization is local in its operation, then incorporation should be done in the local jurisdiction.

If choice of jurisdiction is an issue, then consider the following factors:

1. Number of incorporators required
2. Qualifications of incorporators
3. Purposes for which a nonprofit corporation may be incorporated
4. Restrictions on ownership of property
5. Organizational costs such as fees and taxes, if any
6. State securities laws

7. Form of governance allowed

8. Reporting requirements

9. Liabilities of members and trustees or directors

10. Requirements for meetings

11. Compensation restrictions for officers and directors or trustees

12. Merger or consolidation requirements

13. Dissolution procedures and requirements

14. Foreign corporation restrictions

15. Applicability of other statutes such as charitable trust provisions

Corporate Name

After the decision is made as to where to incorporate, the corporate name should be selected and reserved or registered. Certain restrictions are placed on the choice of a corporate name. A corporate name may not be (1) misleading or deceptive; (2) so similar to another corporate name as to cause confusion; (3) merely descriptive indicating geographical location or type of association; (4) vulgar or offensive; or (5) a prohibited name expressly forbidden by the statute.

Unlike business corporations, nonprofit corporations generally do not have to include the words "corporation," "incorporated," or "limited" or an abbreviation thereof in the corporate name. Some states, however, do require that nonprofit corporations that are incorporated for purposes other than religious or charitable include an identifying word such as "corporation," "incorporated," or "limited" in the corporate name.[1] Other states require all nonprofit corporations to be identified as a corporation in the corporate name.[2]

Reserving or registering a corporate name for a nonprofit corporation is essentially the same process as it is for a business corporation. An application to reserve or register a corporate name and the required fee are submitted to the secretary of state or other designated authority setting forth the name and address of the applicant, the name to be reserved or registered, and the basis of the application.

If the name is not otherwise in use or reserved, a certificate of reservation will be issued reserving the name for a short period of time generally from 30 to 180 days depending on the state.

A corporate name which has been registered may be transferred by the registrant to another person or entity. Notice must be given to the secretary of state or designated authority so that the change in registration is officially recorded.

A nonprofit corporation which desires to change its corporate name must comply with the statutory requirements concerning amendment of its articles of incorporation since the corporate name is therein stated. Failure to comply with the statute may result in abandonment of the corporation.[3]

Articles of Incorporation

Each state specifies the contents of articles of incorporation either in a separate nonprofit corporation statute or within the business corporation act. Some states merely state the required content while other states also set forth the required form to be used. Strict adherence to the applicable statutory provision is required.

While no one form is applicable to every jurisdiction, certain essential items are required by almost all states:

1. Heading or title (*e.g.*, Articles of Incorporation or Certificate of Incorporation)
2. Reference to the act or statutory provision under which incorporation is sought
3. Name of the corporation
4. Purpose(s) for which formed
5. Statement of the nonprofit nature of the corporation
6. Location of corporate office or principal place of activity
7. Duration of corporation's life
8. Names and addresses of first directors or trustees
9. Name and address or registered agent for service of process
10. Names and addresses of incorporators and their qualifications
11. Signatures and acknowledgments
12. Consent or approval statement from required governmental body, if any

The drafter must adhere to the statutory requirements of the jurisdiction; nonetheless, the following are fairly representative forms of articles of incorporation. The first form is the model form of articles of incorporation promulgated by ALI-ABA, and the second is the form prescribed by the Texas secretary of state.[4]

ARTICLES OF INCORPORATION
OF
. . . .

The undersigned, acting as incorporator . . of a corporation under the . . . . Non-Profit Corporation Act, adopt . . the following Articles of Incorporation for such corporation:

FIRST: The name of the corporation is . . . .
. . . .

SECOND: The period of its duration is . . . .

THIRD: The purpose or purposes for which the corporation is organized are:
. . . .

FOURTH: Provisions for the regulation of the internal affairs of the corporation, including provisions for the distribution of assets on dissolution or final liquidation, are:
. . . .

(Note 1)

FIFTH: The address of the initial office of the corporation is . . . .
. . . . , and the name of its initial registered agent at such
address is . . . .

SIXTH: The number of directors constituting the initial Board of Directors of
the corporation is . . . . , and the names and addresses of the persons who are to
serve as the initial directors are:

Name   *Address*

. . . .
. . . .
. . . .

SEVENTH: The name and address of each incorporator is:

Name   *Address*

. . . .
. . . .
. . . .

Dated . . . . , 19 . . . .

               . . . .
               . . . .
               . . . .
                         Incorporator

Note 1. If no provisions for the regulation of the internal affairs of the corporation
or for the distribution of assets on dissolution or final liquidation are to be set
forth, insert "None." In an appropriate case provisions relating to members,
their qualifications and rights may be inserted here.

STATE OF . . . .)
COUNTY OF . . . .)

    I, ... , a notary public, hereby certify that on the
. . . . day of . . . . , 19 . . . . , personally appeared before me
. . . . , ... , and
. . . . , declared that . . he . . . .
. . . . the person . . who signed the foregoing document
as incorporator . . , and that the statements therein contained are true.

                        . . . .
                           Notary Public

(NOTARIAL SEAL)

Form Promulgated by Secretary of State
(Non-Profit Corporation)
ARTICLES OF INCORPORATION

ARTICLE ONE

The name of the corporation is . . . .

ARTICLE TWO

The corporation is a non-profit corporation.

ARTICLE THREE

The period of its duration is perpetual.
(May be for a number of years or until a date certain.)

ARTICLE FOUR

The purpose or purposes for which the corporation is organized are:
. . . .
. . . .
(Must be specifically set forth.)

ARTICLE FIVE

The street address of the initial registered office of the corporation is
. . . . , and the name of its initial registered agent at such
address is . . . .
(Use the street, building or rural route address of the registered office; a post office
box number is not sufficient.)

ARTICLE SIX

The number of directors constituting the initial board of directors is
. . . . and the names and the addresses of the persons
who are to serve as the initial directors are: (Must be at least three.)

Name	*Address*
. . . .	
. . . .	
. . . .	

ARTICLE SEVEN

The name and street address of each incorporator is:
(Must be at least three.)

Name	*Address*
. . . .	
. . . .	
. . . .	

(signed)

. . . .
. . . .
. . . .

Incorporators

STATE OF TEXAS   )
COUNTY OF . . . .)
    Before me, a notary public, on this day personally appeared

. . . . , ... , and
. . . . known to me to be the persons whose names are
subscribed to the foregoing document, and, being by me first duly sworn, severally
declared that the statements therein contained are true and correct.
   Given under my hand and seal of the office this . . . . day of
. . . . , A.D., ...

                                    . . . .
                                    (Printed or stamped name)
(Notarial Seal)   Notary Public, State of Texas
                                    My commission expires:
                                    . . . . , 19 . . . .

After the articles of incorporation have been drafted in final form, the articles
must be executed by the incorporators and notarized and acknowledged, if required by the statute. In some states the articles of incorporation must be approved by certain state officials depending on the purpose for which the corporation is being created. For example, a nonprofit corporation created in New York
for the purpose of caring for neglected or dependent children must have the
approval of the commissioner of social services.[5]

Filing and Approval

Once fully executed and approved as required by statute, the completed forms
together with the required fee (check or money order) are sent to the secretary of
state or designated authority for approval and filing.[6] When the secretary of state
or designated authority approves the articles of incorporation or issues the certificate of incorporation, corporate existence begins. Issuance of the certificate of
incorporation is prima facie evidence of incorporation.
   The model nonprofit corporation certificate of incorporation form follows:

STATE OF . . . .
OFFICE OF THE SECRETARY OF STATE
CERTIFICATE OF INCORPORATION
OF
. . . .

   The undersigned, as Secretary of State of the State of
. . . . , hereby certifies that duplicate originals of Articles
of Incorporation for the incorporation of . . . . duly
signed pursuant to the provisions of the . . . . Non-
Profit Corporation Act, have been received in this office and are found to conform
to law.

ACCORDINGLY the undersigned, as such Secretary of State, and by virtue of the authority vested in him by law, hereby issues this Certificate of Incorporation of . . . . and attaches hereto a duplicate original of the Articles of Incorporation.

Dated . . . . , 19 . . . .

. . . .

Secretary of State

Incorporated Charitable Trust or Foundation

In most states a charitable trust may be incorporated under the statutory provisions applicable to nonprofit corporations established for charitable purposes (see incorporation requirements and procedure, *supra*).

As a result of the Tax Reform Act of 1969[7] many states have enacted statutory provisions which impose the limitations and restrictions of I.R.C. §§ 4941–4945 on incorporated foundations in the absence of such express limitations in the articles of incorporation.[8]

Ohio has enacted specific provisions dealing with the incorporation of charitable trusts.[9] The trustee must file with the secretary of state articles of incorporation pursuant to Ohio's nonprofit corporation law[10] together with a certified copy of the deed or will creating the charitable trust.

Defective Incorporation

If the incorporation procedure has been adhered to and the incorporation statute has been substantially complied with, the corporation is a de jure corporation. But, if the incorporation procedure was not followed or there is substantial noncompliance with the incorporation statute, the organization is not technically a corporation as far as the state is concerned. The state attorney general may bring a *quo warranto* proceeding to revoke the charter or articles of incorporation on the grounds of defective incorporation.

Nonetheless, an organization that does not attain de jure status may be a de facto corporation. Traditionally, to be considered a de facto corporation there must be a statute under which the organization could validly have been incorporated, there must be a colorable attempt in good faith to comply with that statute, and there must be some use or exercise of corporate privileges.[11] A determination of de facto status by a court prevents collateral attack by persons other than the state against the corporateness of the organization. The usefulness of the de facto corporation doctrine can be seriously debated. Many courts are hesitant to use it because it is a judicially created concept in opposition to specific statutory requirements. The Model Business Corporation Act has been interpreted as abolishing the de facto corporation doctrine.[12] The Model Business Corporation

Act makes the certificate of authority "conclusive evidence" of incorporation except as against the state.[13] The Model Nonprofit Corporation Act contains language similar to that of the Model Business Corporation Act.[14]

The de facto corporation doctrine cannot be used to cure serious defects in the incorporation process. There is simply no corporation and, hence, no limited liability. The organizers are personally liable for torts and in contract unless the "corporation by estoppel" doctrine is applicable. A person who dealt with a defectively incorporated organization believing it to be a corporation may not later collaterally attack the corporateness of the organization to impose personal liability on the organizers unless it is the only way to prevent injustice.[15]

UNINCORPORATED ORGANIZATIONS

Charitable Trust or Unincorporated Foundation

A charitable trust is the most expeditious way to create a nonprofit tax exempt organization. Creation of a charitable trust requires less formality than incorporation. The trust instrument gives the grantor more control in specifying the uses of the grant or gift and in giving effect to the grantor's wishes. Whereas an incorporated foundation may act within the limits of the nonprofit corporation act, once created it has a will of its own separate and apart from that of its incorporators.

If a charitable trust is chosen as the organizational form, it is important in drafting a charitable trust that the grantor manifest an intention to create a charitable trust.[16]

Although an oral trust in personality may be created in some jurisdictions and recognized for tax purposes,[17] it is foolish to do so. A carefully drafted written instrument is preferred.

The preamble to the trust instrument should identify the grantor and trustee.

WITNESSETH that _____ (hereinafter referred to as "Grantor") and _____ of _____(City)_____, _____(State)_____ (hereinafter referred to as "Trustee") do hereby agree to the following:

The first item of the agreement should be the transfer of the property to the trustee.

Item 1. Grantor does hereby transfer, assign, and convey unto Trustee the property, which is listed on Schedule "A" attached to this instrument and made a part hereof, in trust for the purposes herein stated.

A valid transfer in trust must be made with the same formal requirements that generally apply to transfers of similar property not in trust.

Next, the purpose or purposes for which the transfer in trust is made should be stated with as much specificity as possible. However, to ensure compliance with federal tax law and lapse or failure of charitable purpose, general charitable, religious, and educational purposes should also be stated.

Item 2. The purposes of this trust are to apply to all property of this trust, including income derived therefrom, exclusively for such religious, charitable, scientific, literary, or educational activities as are hereby designated (state purposes) or which may be designated, in writing, by the Trustee and for the payment of incidental expenses and costs of administration of the trust and taxes, if any. Provided, however, that no part of this trust fund shall inure to the benefit of any private entity or individual, and no part of the direct or indirect activities of this trust may consist of carrying on propaganda, attempting to influence legislation, or participating in any political campaign on behalf of any candidate for public office.

The powers granted to the trustee may be specified or granted with reference to and incorporation of the statutory powers of the jurisdiction. Grantor may allow the trustee to act without leave of court.

Item 3. The Trustee shall have all the powers granted by (Statutory provision) and shall include but not be limited to the power to:
(1) Retain all contributions in the original form in which received;
(2) Buy, sell, exchange, or otherwise deal in stocks, bonds, real estate, and other forms of property, at either public or private sale, without advertisement or notice;
(3) Invest and reinvest any funds belonging to the trust at any time in such securities and property, real and personal, as the Trustee in its sole discretion sees fit, irrespective of whether such investment may not be legal investments for trust funds under the laws of the State of _____;
(4) Employ real estate brokers, accountants, attorneys, and other agents, and to compensate them for their services;
(5) Compromise any claims or demand for or against the trust;
(6) Borrow money and secure the same by pledging any of the property of the trust;
(7) Lease any property for any term, notwithstanding the period of the trust;
(8) Vote in person or by proxy any other security, and to take any other action in regard to any reorganization, merger, or bankruptcy, or other proceedings affecting any stock or other property belonging to the trust.
It shall not be required that the Trustee obtain the order or permission of any court or other authority in the exercise of any of the foregoing powers.

If desired the grantor may excuse the trustee from having to make reports or returns to the court of competent jurisdiction.

Item 4. The Trustee is hereby relieved from making any reports or returns to any court.

A provision should be inserted in the instrument governing subsequently acquired property.

Item 5. The Grantor may, from time to time, during the Grantor's life or by Grantor's will add other funds and property to this trust. The same shall be held subject to all the provisions of this instrument and the income used for the aforementioned purposes.

The Trustee may accept contributions from others who may desire to contribute to the trust, provided such contributions are for the same objects and purposes set forth above as to this trust and not inconsistent therewith.

Trustee's compensation, if any, should be set in a separate written instrument incorporated by reference.

Item 6. The Trustee shall receive as compensation for its services rendered hereunder the fees which have been agreed upon between Grantor and Trustee by separate instrument. The fee may be adjusted from time to time as may be required to adequately compensate Trustee for such services by written agreement between Grantor and Trustee or, if Grantor is deceased, between Grantor's Estate and Trustee, or court of competent jurisdiction and Trustee.

In the absence of a provision designating choice of law to be applied, the usual conflicts of laws doctrines apply. To avoid any problems, a choice of law clause should be inserted.

Item 7. This instrument shall be construed and regulated, and all rights hereunder shall be governed by the laws of the State of _____.

To avoid problems arising out of application of the rule against perpetuities, the rule against restraints on alienation, the rule against suspension of the power of alienation, and the rule against unreasonable accumulation, an appropriate savings clause should be used.

Item 8. Unless otherwise terminated the provisions of this trust must terminate one day before the expiration of any time period applicable under any rule of law which would limit the duration of this trust, whether private or charitable.

The grantor must acknowledge and understand that the trust is irrevocable and that grantor retains no right to alter, amend, revoke, or terminate the trust.

Item 9. Grantor understands and declares that this trust is and shall be irrevocable and that upon execution hereof Grantor shall retain no right, title or interest in or power, privilege, or incident of ownership in regard to any of said property or money conveyed and shall have no right to alter, amend, revoke, or terminate this trust in whole or in part.

The trust instrument should be subscribed to by grantor and trustee and witnessed in the form required by the law of the state wherein it is executed.

As an alternative to individually drafted charitable trusts, most bank trust departments have charitable trust forms available which have been adapted for use in the state in which they are located.

Should the donor desire to make testamentary dispositions for a charitable purpose, the donor may direct the executor to establish a foundation to accept donations under the will. Testamentary dispositions must be made in compliance with the formalities of state law governing such dispositions.

Unincorporated Associations

Unincorporated associations often grow out of informal social meetings of two or more persons who are interested in a particular project, idea, or cause. As the purpose of the association formalizes, so should the association by formulating its purpose(s), goal(s), and structure and reducing them to writing in the form of a constitution, charter, or articles of association.

Standard forms may be useful as guidelines but are rarely suitable for adoption without modification. The end product should reflect the desires and wishes of the association's members not those of the drafter of the form. Having disclaimed general applicability of a standard form, an outline containing the essential elements of association follows.

Articles of Association
of
_____

Article 1.

Name. The name of this nonprofit association is _____.

Article 2.

Purpose. The purpose(s) for which this Association is formed is (are) . . .

Article 3.

Duration. The life of this Association shall be _____ years. The death, removal, or resignation of any member of this association shall not terminate the life of this association.

Article 4.

Office. The principal office of the Association shall be located in the City of _____, County of _____, State of _____.

Article 5.

Powers. The Association shall have the power to perform any lawful acts which it deems necessary or desirable in furtherance of its purposes, and for the protection of the lawful rights and interests of its members.

The Association shall have the power to . . . (specify particular powers).

Article 6.

Members. There shall be _____ class(es) of membership. (If more than one class define each class.)

Membership shall be granted by vote of . . . (specify membership, membership committee, etc.) on the application of the applicant. (Specify form of application, if any.)

All newly elected members agree to abide by these Articles of Association, as amended.

(Specify form of enrollment or oath if desired.)

Article 7.

Dues. The annual dues of each member shall be _____ dollars, due and payable on or before _____(date)_____ of each year. (If more than one class of membership, specify dues for each class, if different.)

Article 8.

Governance. The management and government of this Association shall be vested in . . . (specify the membership as a committee of the whole, a Board of Directors, Board of Trustees, or other).

(If a Board specify the following:
1. number of members,
2. qualifications,
3. term of office,
4. quorum,
5. method of election,
6. method of filling vacancies,
7. notice of meetings,
8. meetings (annual and special),
9. salary, if any,
10. reimbursement for expenses incurred in performance of association duties,
11. methods and procedures for removal of board members for cause or without cause, and
12. powers (both general and specific).)

Article 9.

Officers. The Association's officers shall consist of . . . (specify titles such as President, Vice-President, Secretary, and Treasurer).

Officers of the Association shall be elected by _____ during the course of the annual meeting for a term of _____.

The powers and duties of each officer shall be as follows:

(State title and specify powers and duties of each officer.)

(If the officers are to be compensated or reimbursed for expenses, so state and set rate of compensation.)

Article 10.

Committees. Such committees as the (membership or governing body) shall from time to time desire to carry out the purpose(s) of the Association shall be (appointed or elected) by _____ to serve at the pleasure of (membership of governing body).

(Specific committees, if any, method of selection, quorum, control, meetings, and reports should be included here.)

Article 11.

Meetings. The annual meeting of the members of the Association shall be held in the month of _____ at a place in the City of _____, State of _____ to be designated by _____.

Notice of such annual meeting shall be given by . . . (specify method).

(Specify agenda and method of placing items on the agenda.)

(Specify election procedures for directors or officers.)

(Specify methods and procedures for calling special meetings and their agendas.)

Article 12.

Resignations and Removal of Members. (Specify procedure for resignation.) (Specify grounds, notice, and procedure for removal or expulsion.)

Article 13.

Amendments. The Articles of Association may be amended by . . . (specify method and vote requirement).

Article 14.

Termination and Dissolution. The Association shall be terminated by . . . (specify reasons and procedures).

(Specify method or procedure for distributing assets in dissolution.)

Article 15.

Adoption of Articles. These Articles of Association become effective and binding on the persons who duly sign below.

Unions

A labor union may be formed by two or more persons who associate for the purpose of dealing with employers concerning grievances, labor disputes, wages, rates of pay, hours of employment, and conditions of work. A local union may affiliate with a national or international union but need not do so. Affiliation with a national or international union may require that specific language or provisions be included in the local's constitution and by-laws.

No registration or permission to form a labor union is required from the federal government. Labor unions may incorporate under nonprofit corporation acts but rarely, if ever, do so. A state requirement that labor unions incorporate is unconstitutional.[18]

Federal law has preempted the right of states to regulate labor unions in matters dealing with the right to associate and bargain collectively.[19] However, states retain the right to exercise their police power to punish fraud, violence, or other types of misconduct.[20] No specific form of constitution or by-laws is required.

NOTES

1. *See, e.g.,* N-PCL § 301 (McKinney).

2. *See, e.g.,* Ind. Code Ann. § 23-7-1.1-5 (Burns).

3. *Cincinnati Cooperage Co. v. Bate,* 96 Ky. 356, 26 S.W. 538 (1994); *Senn v. Levy,* 111 Ky. 318, 63 S.W. 776 (1901); *Stafford National Bank v. Palmer,* 47 Conn. 443 (1880).

4. Tex. Rev. Civ. Stat. Ann. art. 1396-3.02 (Vernon).

5. N.Y. N-PCL § 404(b) (McKinney).

6. Jurisdictions which require filing with a designated authority other than the secretary of state are Alabama, Alaska, Arizona, District of Columbia, Hawaii, Michigan, New Mexico, Oregon, and Virginia.

7. P.L. No. 91-172, 83 Stat. 487.

8. *E.g.,* Alabama, Maryland, Mississippi, Montana, Nebraska, New Hampshire, New York, Oregon, South Carolina, South Dakota, Washington, Wisconsin, Wyoming.

9. Ohio Rev. Code Ann. §§ 1719.01 to 1719.14 (Page).

10. Ohio Rev. Code Ann. §§ 1702.01 *et seq.* (Page).

11. H. Henn & J. Alexander, *Laws of Corporations,* 329 (3d ed. 1983).

12. *Timberline Equipment Co. v. Davenport,* 267 Ore. 64, 514 P.2d 1109 (1973); *Robertson v. Levy,* 197 A.2d 443 (D.C. Ct. App. 1964); Comments to Model Business Corp. Act §§ 50, 146, 2 Model Business Corp. Act Anno. 205, 908–909 (1971).

13. ABA-ALI Model Business Corp. Act § 56.

14. ABA-ALI Model Nonprofit Corp. Act § 31.

15. H. Henn & J. Alexander, *Laws of Corporations,* 335 (3d ed. 1983).

16. *Giovanni Del Drago v. Comm.,* 214 F.2d 478 (2d Cir. 1954).

17. *John H. Stevens,* 24 B.T.A. 52 (1931).

18. *American Federation of Labor v. Reilly,* 113 Colo. 90, 155 P.2d 145 (1944).

19. *Hill v. Florida,* 325 U.S. 538, *reh. den.,* 326 U.S. 804 (1945).

20. *Id.*

6

Tax Exemptions

FEDERAL INCOME TAX

Merely being organized for one of the exempt purposes enumerated in section 501 does not make an organization tax exempt. The organization must meet all of the requirements of the statute and with certain exceptions must apply for tax exempt status with the Internal Revenue Service.

Pending the issuance of a determination letter or ruling that it is tax exempt, the applicant organization must file the appropriate tax return and pay any tax due. A corporation may be required to file IRS Form 1120; whereas, a trust may be required to file IRS Form 1041. A corporation may avoid the filing of the form 1120 by requesting the automatic three-month extension of time for filing the return.[1] For a trust, a request for an extension of time for filing the return is discretionary, and the trust must establish reasonable cause.[2]

If the organization is a member of a group such as a chapter, local, post, or unit of a large organization such as a church, Boy Scouts or Girl Scouts, veterans' group, or fraternal organization, a group exemption may be obtained, and separate filing is not required.[3] The central organization must show that it maintains adequate control over the subordinate unit and that the subordinate is otherwise qualified for tax exempt status.[4]

Application for section 501(c)(3) organizations is made on IRS Form 1023 while application for exempt status for other organizations is made on IRS Form 1024. Applications for exempt status must be filed in duplicate with the district director for the district in which the principal office or place of business of the organization is located.[5]

Section 501(c)(3) Organizations

For organizations established after October 9, 1969, most section 501(c)(3) organizations will not be treated as such until a form 1023 has been filed with the district director within fifteen months of the end of the month in which the organization was organized.[6] Not only is the organization not treated as a tax exempt organization, but the charitable contribution deductions for income tax and estate and gift tax purposes also are denied for contributions to the nonfiling organization.[7]

Certain organizations are exempt from the filing requirements of section 508(a). These organizations are churches, their integrated auxiliaries, and conventions or associations of churches and any organization which is not a private foundation and the gross receipts of which are normally not more than $5,000 in each taxable year.[8] In addition to the mandatory exceptions, certain educational organizations and other classes of organizations may be excluded if the Internal Revenue Service determines that filing is not necessary for the efficient administration of the provisions dealing with private foundations.[9] Nonetheless, any organization exempt from the notice and filing requirement may file a form 1023 to establish its tax exemption and receive a determination letter or ruling to qualify for tax deductible charitable contributions.[10]

To qualify for tax exempt status under section 501(c)(3), the organization must be both organized and operated exclusively for one or more of the purposes specified in section 501(c)(3). Failure to satisfy the requirements of either the organizational or operational test is disqualifying.[11]

Organizational Test

In 1959, the Internal Revenue Service issued regulations that established the organizational test as an independent test which must be satisfied in order to obtain tax exempt status.[12]

To satisfy the organizational test, the group's organizational documents must limit the purposes for which the organization was created to one or more exempt purposes.[13] In addition, the organizational documents may not expressly empower the organization to engage, other than as an insubstantial part of its activities, in activities that in themselves do not further the exempt purpose or purposes for which the organization was created.[14]

Treasury Regulations section 1.501(c)(3)-1(b)(1)(i) gives examples of statements in the organizational document which will satisfy the organizational test that the organization is being formed or organized for one or more of the exempt purposes stated in section 501(c)(3). The drafter would do well to study them. The following statements will meet the description rule:

1. A statement that the organization is formed for one of the purposes within the meaning of section 501(c)(3)

2. A statement that the organization is created to receive contributions and pay them over to section 501(c)(3) organizations

3. A statement that the organization is formed for charitable purposes

4. A statement that sets forth the purposes of the organization and that describes the manner of operation in detail

The commissioner relies solely on the organizational documents to make the determination of whether the organizational test is met. Qualifying organizational documents are a trust instrument, corporate charter, articles of association, or other written instrument by which the organization is created.[15] The Internal Revenue Service refuses to consider any other evidence of intent to organize as a section 501(c) organization whether manifested in other documents or in actual operation.[16]

This narrow view taken by the Internal Revenue Service is particularly onerous to organizations established before July 28, 1959, which seek recognition of their exempt status subsequent to the adoption of the regulations. Operation exclusively for one or more of the tax exempt purposes in section 501(c)(3) is not sufficient to meet the operational test.[17] Unless the organization amended its organizational document to comply with the 1959 regulations, it will fail the organizational test. Moreover, tax exempt status would only be retroactive to the date of amendment of the requisite document.[18] As a result the Internal Revenue Service could assess taxes against the organization from the date of its conception as a trust or corporation and deny retroactively all charitable deductions based on the mistaken tax exempt status. The statute of limitations would not have been tolled because no return would have been filed.[19] In addition, penalties of up to $5,000 could be assessed for failure to file a return.[20]

The regulation's inquiry solely into the organizational documents is far more restrictive than the congressional mandate in section 501(c)(3). In litigated cases the courts have been more liberal in their inquiries than the Internal Revenue Service by looking beyond the organizational documents to actual operation of the organization.[21] Nonetheless, compliance with the regulations is advised to avoid protracted and expensive litigation over the issue.

To be tax exempt the organization must be organized exclusively for one or more of the purposes enumerated in section 501(c)(3). "Exclusively," however, does not mean "solely" but rather "primarily" or "substantially." Extreme caution must be exercised in drafting organizational documents to avoid going too far. Generally, the purposes stated in the organizational document may be as broad as or more restrictive than section 501(c)(3) without consequence.[22] However, if the organization's stated purposes are broader than those of section

501(c)(3), notwithstanding the actual operation and regardless of extrinsic evidence or the representations of the officers and members, the organization will not meet the organizational test.[23] Likewise, care must be taken that while the stated purposes in the organizational document conform to section 501(c)(3) that the "powers" provision or article not allow the organization to carry on other than an insubstantial amount of its activities which do not further the exempt purposes. For elaboration of this issue see the discussion of action organizations.

The assets must also be dedicated to exempt purposes. An organization's assets will be considered dedicated to an exempt purpose if, upon the organization's dissolution, law or a provision in the organizational documents operates to distribute the assets in any one of the following ways: (1) for one or more exempt purposes, (2) to the federal government, (3) to a state or local government, (4) for a public purpose, or (5) by a court to another organization to be used in such manner as judged by the court that will best accomplish the general purposes for which the dissolved organization was organized.[24] If the assets can be distributed to members, shareholders, or private individuals, under the documents or state law the organization fails the organizational test.[25]

An express provision dedicating the assets and dictating their ultimate disposition should be written into the organizational documents; otherwise, a legal brief detailing state law or the doctrine of *cy pres* in the particular jurisdiction will have to be submitted to the Internal Revenue Service in support of the application.[26] The burden of proof is on the applicant.[27]

A noncharitable organization such as a business corporation may convert to a section 501(c)(3) organization if it meets the organizational test by amending its organizational documents as required at the beginning of the taxable year for which the exemption is sought.[28] Although, pre-1959 case law holds that amendment of the corporate charter was not necessary.[29]

Operational Test

An organization seeking tax exempt status under section 501(c)(3) must independently satisfy the operational test. To qualify, the organization must be operated exclusively for exempt purposes. Operated "exclusively" does not mean "solely" but rather "primarily" or "substantially" so that not more than an insubstantial part of its activities are directed toward nonexempt purposes.[30]

An organization is not operated exclusively for exempt purposes if its net earnings inure in whole or in part to the benefit of private shareholders or individuals.[31] The inclusion of the private inurement prohibition under the operational test subsection of the regulation unnecessarily complicates the matter. It is not clear to what extent the private inurement provision and the insubstantial activities provision are to be read together. The tax court has taken note of the overlap of the private inurement and private purpose prohibitions.[32] Clearly, no private inurement is to be allowed regardless of how substantial or insubstantial it may be.[33] Moreover, courts have shifted the burden of proof regarding private inurement from the organization to the government;[34] whereas, the regulations put the burden of proof on the organization to establish that it is not organized or operated for the benefit of private interest.[35]

Private Foundations

Reacting to a number of well-publicized abuses of tax laws by private foundations, Congress divided section 501(c)(3) organizations into two groups, public charities and private foundations. Any section 501(c)(3) organization in existence on or after October 9, 1969, which does not notify the commission by filing the form 1023 or form 4653 that it is not a private foundation, is presumed to be one.[36]

For taxable years beginning after 1971, no private foundation as defined in section 509 is tax exempt, and no contribution to it is deductible, unless its organizational documents comply with section 508(e). Section 508(e) requires the governing instrument to include provisions to require its income to be distributed in each taxable year to avoid the section 4942 tax and to prohibit the private foundation from engaging in acts of self-dealing under section 4941(d), from retaining any excess business holding under section 4943(c), from making any jeopardy investments under section 4944, and from making any taxable expenditure under section 4945(d). These prohibitions are extended to foundation managers and other disqualified persons who would also be liable for chapter 42 taxes.[37] This requirement of section 508(e) is not met by language sufficient to meet the organizational test under Treasury Regulations section 1.501(c)(3)-1(b) but must make specific reference to the relevant code sections.[38]

The section 508(e) requirement may be satisfied by valid provisions of state law which conform to the section 508(e) requirements by either requiring the private foundation to act in accordance with or incorporate by law such provisions in all governing instruments.[39] Virtually all United States jurisdictions have such provisions.

Private Schools

Private schools must establish that nondiscrimination is a school policy. The school must comply with Revenue Procedure 75-50.[40] Failure to comply results in disqualification for tax exempt status and loss of the charitable deduction by contributors.[41]

To qualify, a school must show by affirmative action that it has adopted a nondiscriminatory policy according to these guidelines:

1. A nondiscrimination provision must be included in the school's charter, by-laws, or other governing instrument.

2. A statement of the school's nondiscriminatory policy must appear in all brochures,

catalogues, and advertising materials concerning the school's admissions, programs, and scholarship.

3. The nondiscriminatory policy must be made known to all segments of the general community it serves.

4. All programs and facilities must be shown to be operated in a racially nondiscriminatory manner.

5. All scholarships must be offered on a racially nondiscriminatory manner.

6. Racial nondiscrimination must be the employment policy regarding the school staff.

Affirmative action that favors racial minority groups does not discriminate if its purpose is to promote, establish, or maintain the school's nondiscriminatory policy.

Other Organizations

The following organizations must file for tax exempt status on IRS Form 1024:

1. Title holding companies (section 501(c)(2))

2. Civic leagues, social welfare organizations (including certain war veterans' organizations), or local associations of employees (section 501(c)(4))

3. Labor, agricultural, or horticultural organizations (section 501(c)(5))

4. Business leagues, chambers of commerce, among others (section 501(c)(6))

5. Social clubs (section 501(c)(7))

6. Fraternal beneficiary societies providing life, sick, accident, or other benefits to members (section 501(c)(8))

7. Voluntary employees' beneficiary associations (section 501(c)(9))

8. Domestic fraternal societies, orders, and others not providing life, sick, accident, or other benefits (section 501(c)(10))

9. Benevolent life insurance associations, mutual ditch or irrigation companies, mutual or cooperative telephone companies, or like organizations (section 501(c)(12))

10. Cemeteries, crematoria, and like corporations (section 501(c)(13))

11. Mutual insurance companies or associations, other than life or marine (section 501(c)(15))

12. Trusts providing for the payment of supplemental unemployment compensation benefits (section 501(c)(17))

13. War veterans' organizations and auxiliary units (section 501(c)(19))

14. Trusts or organizations for prepaid group legal services (section 501(c)(20))

15. Qualified group legal service plans (section 120)

In order to qualify for tax exempt status, an applicant organization must have an organizational instrument or document and otherwise meet the requirements of the particular section of section 501(c) under which it seeks tax exempt status. The purposes and proposed activities of the organization must be described in detail in the organizing documents and in other statements accompanying the application. If the organization issues capital stock, the following information must be provided:

1. The class or classes of such stock
2. The number and par value of the shares
3. The consideration for which the stock was issued
4. A description of the persons holding the stock, if fewer than ten, and the names of the individuals and number of shares held by each
5. Whether the creating instrument authorizes dividend payments on any class of capital stock
6. Whether any such dividends have been paid

A copy of the organization's stock certificate should be attached to the form 1024. Statement of income and expenses and a balance sheet for the current year and for each of the three taxable years immediately preceding must be included, but if the organization has been in existence less than four years, documentation is required only for each year of existence.

To qualify for tax exemption under section 501(c)(2), a corporation must be organized exclusively for the purpose of holding title to property, collecting income therefrom, and turning over the entire amount, less expenses, to another exempt organization. The titleholding corporation must not accumulate its income but must turn over the entire amount, less expenses, to an exempt organization; however, an exempt holding company may retain part of its annual income to apply to indebtedness on property to which it holds title. Retention of such income will be treated as if the parent corporation had received the income and contributed it to the holding corporation.

A civic league or organization that is not organized or operated for profit and that is operated exclusively for the promotion of social welfare may be tax exempt under section 501(c)(4). The primary activity of such an organization must be the promotion of the common good and general welfare of the people of the community by bringing about civic betterments and social improvements. A section 501(c)(4) organization is prohibited from direct or indirect participation or intervention in political campaigns on behalf of or in opposition to any candidate for public office. A social club operated for the benefit, pleasure, or recreation of its members or carrying on of a business with the general public in a manner similar to organizations which are operated for profit is not qualified for exempt status under section 501(c)(4). A social welfare organization may, however, qualify for tax exempt status under section 501(c)(4) even if it is an action organization.

A local association of employees may be tax exempt under section 501(c)(4) if the membership of the association is limited to the employees of a designated person or persons in a particular municipality and if the net earnings of the association are devoted exclusively to charitable, educational, or recreational purposes.

A qualified labor, agricultural, or horticultural organization is prohibited from distributing any of its net earnings to any member and must have as its objective the betterment of the conditions for those actively engaged in labor, agricultural, or horticultural pursuits, the improvement of the grade of their products, and the development of a high degree of efficiency in their respective occupations.

Business leagues, chambers of commerce, real estate boards, boards of trade, and professional football leagues may qualify for tax exemption under section 501(c)(6) if they are not organized for profit and no part of the net earnings inure to the benefit of any shareholder or individual.

Social clubs including college fraternities and sororities which are organized and operated for pleasure, recreation, and other nonprofitable purposes may qualify for tax exemption under section 501(c)(7). Substantially all of the activities of the organization must be for pleasure, recreation, and other nonprofitable purposes inuring to the benefit of the members of the club. However, a club which engages in business such as catering to the general public or making its social and recreational facilities available to the general public or by selling real estate, timber, or other products does not qualify for tax exempt status. Advertising or otherwise soliciting for public patronage of the facilities is prima facie evidence that the club is engaging in business and is not being operated exclusively for pleasure, recreation, or social purposes.

Thirty-five percent or less of the social club's gross receipts may be from investment and from providing facilities and services to nonmembers; however, only 15 percent of the total outside gross receipts may be used to provide outside services. ''Gross receipts'' are those received from normal and usual activities of the club including charges, admissions, investment income, and normal recurring capital gains on investments, but excluding initiation fees and capital contributions. Amounts received from the active conduct of businesses not traditionally carried on by social clubs may not be received within the 35 or 15 percent allowance limitations. The prohibition against private inurement of the net earnings to the benefit of any shareholder applies to social clubs.

Congress has explicitly prohibited discrimination by social clubs for race, color, or religion. No section 501(c)(7) organization may obtain or maintain tax exempt status if its charter, by-laws, or any other governing instrument or any written policy statement of the organization contains a provision which provides for discrimination against any person for race, color, or religion. A club may, however, limit its membership to members of a particular religion in furtherance of the teachings or principles of that religion, provided that it does not exclude individuals of a particular color. Likewise, an auxiliary of a fraternal beneficiary society under section 501(c)(8) may limit its membership to members of a particular religion.

A fraternal beneficiary society operating under the lodge system or for the exclusive benefit of the membership may qualify for tax exemption under section 501(c)(8) if it has established a system for payment of life, sick, accident, or other benefits to its members or their dependents. A domestic fraternal beneficiary society, order, or association which would qualify under section 501(c)(8) except that it does not provide for payment of life, sick, accident or other benefits to its members qualifies for tax exemption under section 501(c)(10) if it devotes its net earnings exclusively to religious, charitable, scientific, literary, educational, and fraternal purposes. Organizations qualified under section 501(c)(7) do not qualify for tax exemption under 501(c)(10).

A voluntary employees' beneficiary association may qualify for tax exemption under section 501(c)(9) if it is an employees' association whose membership is voluntary, if the organization provides for the payment of life, sick, accident, or other benefits to its members or their dependents or designated beneficiaries, and if substantially all of its operations are in furtherance thereof. No part of the net earnings of the organization may inure other than by payment of the benefits to the benefit of any private shareholder or individual. After December 31, 1984, no section 501(c)(9) organization may discriminate in favor of employees who are highly compensated.[42] If the benefits bear a uniform relationship to the total compensation or to the basic or regular rate of compensation of employees covered by the plan, there is no discrimination.[43] Section 505 does not apply to any organization which is part of a plan maintained pursuant to a collective bargaining agreement. After December 31, 1984, no organization shall be treated as tax exempt under section 501(c)(9) for any period before giving notice to the Internal Revenue Service that it is applying for such recognition.[44] Existing section 501(c)(9) organizations must comply with the notice requirement within one year of the date of enactment of the Tax Reform Act of 1984 which was signed by the President on July 18, 1984.[45]

Section 501(c)(12) provides for tax exemption for benevolent life insurance associations of a purely local character, mutual irrigation and ditch companies, mutual or cooperative telephone companies, and like organizations. To qualify for exemption, 85 percent of the income of the organization must be collected from its members for the sole purpose of meeting losses and expenses. Benevolent life insurance associations and organizations like them must be of a purely local character, which means that the business activities are confined to a particular community or district, regardless of political subdivision. Special rules concerning the test for 85 percent of income from members also apply to mutual or cooperative phone companies.

Any nonprofit corporation organized solely for cremation or burial of bodies and which is not permitted under the terms of its organizational document to engage in any business not incident to that purpose may be tax exempt under section 501(c)(13), provided that its earnings do not benefit any private individual or shareholder. The cemetery company or crematorium may perform charitable acts such as burial of paupers and may limit its membership to a particular class of individuals such as family members. No cemetery corporation or crematorium may be tax exempt if it has issued preferred stock after November 27, 1978, unless it was pursuant to a written plan adopted on or before that date. Moreover, a cemetery company or crematorium is not tax exempt if any person has any interest in its net earnings including an equity interest under section 385, a bond or debt instrument which in addition to paying interest at a flat rate also pays an additional interest payment based on income, or a convertible debt obligation issued after July 7, 1975.

To qualify for tax exemption under section 501(c)(15) a mutual insurance company or association and a mutual interinsurer and reciprocal underwriter other than life or marine may not receive during any taxable year from gross investment income from premiums including deposits and assessments more than $150,000. Gross investment income includes interest, dividends, rents, royalties, and trade or business income as defined in the regulations.

A supplemental unemployment benefit trust may be tax exempt under section 501(c)(17) if (1) the trust is a written, valid, existing trust under local law; (2) the trust is part of a written plan established and maintained by an employer, the employees, or both the employees and the employer solely for the purpose of providing supplemental unemployment compensation benefits; (3) the trust is part of a plan which provides that the corpus and income of the trust cannot be used for, or diverted to, any purpose other than the providing of supplemental unemployment compensation benefits, other than necessary or appropriate expenses incurred in connection with the administration of the plan; (4) the trust is part of a plan whose eligibility conditions and benefit do not discriminate in favor of employees who are officers, shareholders, persons whose principal duties consist of supervising the work of other employees, or highly compensated employees; and (5) the trust is part of a plan which requires that the benefits are to be determined according to objective standards and not solely at the discretion of the trustees. After December 31, 1984, no organization shall be treated as tax exempt under section 501(c)(17) for any period before giving notice to the Internal Revenue Service that it is applying for such recognition.[46] Existing section 501(c)(17) organizations must comply with the notice requirement within one year of the date of enactment of the Tax Reform Act of 1984 which was signed by the President on July 18, 1984.[47]

Certain veterans' organizations may be exempt under section 501(c)(19) if they meet the membership requirements and are operated exclusively for one or more of the following purposes:

1. To promote the social welfare of the community

2. To assist disabled and needy war veterans, members of the United States armed forces and their dependents, and widows and orphans of deceased veterans

3. To provide entertainment, care, and assistance to hospitalized veterans and members of the armed forces

4. To carry on programs perpetuating the memory of deceased veterans and members of the armed forces

5. To conduct programs for religious, charitable, scientific, literary, or educational purposes

6. To sponsor programs for activities of a patriotic nature

7. To provide insurance benefits for members and their dependents

8. To provide social and recreational activities for their members

Membership requirements are that at least 75 percent of the members must be war veterans and at least 97.5 percent of the members must be war veterans, present or former members of the armed forces of the United States, cadets, spouses, or widows or widowers of any of them. A unit or society of war veterans may be exempt if it is an auxiliary unit or society of a post or organization of war veterans that is exempt under section 501(c)(19) and meets the following requirements:

1. It is affiliated with and organized in accordance with the by-laws and regulations of the parent organization.

2. At least 75 percent of its members are either war veterans, spouses of war veterans, or are related to a war veteran within two degrees of consanguinity.

3. All of the members are either members of the parent organization or spouses of a member of such organization or related to a member of such organization within two degrees of consanguinity.

4. No part of the net earnings inures to the benefit of any private shareholder or individual.

A trust or a foundation may be exempt under section 501(c)(19) if it is a trust or foundation for a post or organization of tax exempt war veterans and (1) the trust or foundation is in existence under local law, and if organized for charitable purposes, has a dissolution provision otherwise required for a charitable organization under section 501(c)(3); (2) the corpus or income cannot be diverted or used for any purpose other than the funding of a post or organization of tax exempt war veterans or as an insurance set-aside; (3) the trust income is not unreasonably accumulated, and if the trust or foundation is not an insurance set-aside, a substantial portion of the income must in fact be distributed to the post or organization or for section 170(c)(4) charitable purposes; and (4) it is organized exclusively for one or more of the purposes for which a war veterans' organization may be tax exempt.

A trust for qualified group legal services may be tax exempt under section 501(c)(20) if it is a plan satisfying the requirements of section 120(b). Section 120(b) requires a qualified group legal services plan to be a separate written plan of an employer for the exclusive benefit of the employees or their spouses or dependents. The plan is to provide them with specified benefits consisting of personal legal services paid for in whole or in part by the employer through prepayment of or advance provision for legal fees. The plan must not discriminate in favor of employees who are officers, shareholders, self-employed individuals, or highly compensated employees. Section 505 which prohibits discrimination in favor of highly compensated individuals with respect to benefits does not apply to any organization which is part of a plan maintained pursuant to a collective bargaining agreement.

After December 31, 1984, no organization shall be treated as tax exempt under section 501(c)(20) for any period before giving notice to the Internal Revenue Service that it is applying for such recognition.[48] Existing section 501(c)(20) organizations must comply with the notice requirement within one year of the date of enactment of the Tax Reform Act of 1984 which was signed by the President on July 18, 1984.[49]

STATE AND LOCAL TAXES

The three primary state and local taxes that a nonprofit organization encounters are income, property, and sales and use taxes.

Most states which impose an income tax on corporations exempt the generic category of charitable organizations. Many states adopt the federal income tax law concerning exempt organizations within their income tax provisions.

As a matter of constitutional law in most states, the property of nonprofit charitable organizations is exempt from taxation to the extent that it is used predominantly for exempt purposes.

The state statutes exempting nonprofit organizations from the sales and use taxes are diverse. Many times the exemption turns on whether the sale is to an exempt organization or by an exempt organization.

Income Taxes

Exemption from the state corporation income tax statutes is set out below by state, including the District of Columbia.

Alabama (section 40-18-32). The following organizations are exempt from the Alabama corporate income tax:

1. Labor, agricultural, or horticultural organizations
2. Fraternal beneficiary societies
3. Nonprofit business and civic leagues
4. Clubs organized for pleasurable or other nonprofit purposes
5. Farmers' mutual companies or marketing associations
6. Federal land banks and those subject to the state excise tax
7. National farm loan and building and loan associations
8. Certain national banks and financial corporations
9. Building and loan associations
10. Insurance companies subject to the Alabama premium tax
11. Certified or licensed corporations establishing regional mental health programs

Alaska (sections 43.20.010, 43.20.340). Organizations exempt from the federal income tax are exempt from Alaska corporate income tax.

Arizona (sections 20-1566, 43-1201). The Arizona statute essentially enumerates exempt organizations as being those which would be exempt under federal income tax and are as follows:

1. Labor, agricultural, and horticultural organizations, other than cooperatives
2. Fraternal beneficiary societies
3. Cemetery companies
4. Nonprofit religious, charitable, educational, literary, and scientific organizations
5. Organizations operated exclusively for the prevention of cruelty to children or animals
6. Nonprofit business leagues, real estate boards or boards of trade, and chambers of commerce
7. Nonprofit civic leagues
8. Nonprofit social and recreational clubs
9. Holding companies for exempt organizations
10. Voluntary employees' beneficiary organizations
11. Teachers' or public employees' retirement fund organizations of a local character
12. Religious or apostolic organizations
13. United States government voluntary beneficiary organizations
14. Diversified management companies
15. Insurance companies, except title insurance companies
16. Nonprofit mutual, ditch, irrigation, or water companies

Arkansas (section 84-2006). The following are exempted from the Arkansas corporate income tax:

1. Fraternal benefit societies
2. Mutual insurance companies
3. Nonprofit cemetery or charitable corporations
4. Nonprofit business or civic leagues
5. Mutual insurance, ditch or irrigation companies, and mutual or cooperative telephone companies if 85 percent of the income consists solely of members' dues, fees, and assessments
6. Cooperative marketing associations
7. Nonprofit, labor, agricultural, or horticultural organizations

California (Calif. Rev. & T. § 23701). The following organizations are exempt from the California corporate income tax:

1. Labor, agricultural, or horticultural organizations
2. Fraternal beneficiary societies operating under the lodge system and providing payment of life, sickness, accident, or other benefits to its members
3. Nonprofit or membership cemetery companies
4. Nonprofit religious, charitable, scientific, public testing, literary, or educational institutions
5. Nonprofit business leagues, chambers of commerce, real estate boards, or boards of trade
6. Nonprofit civic leagues
7. Nonprofit clubs organized and operated for pleasure and recreational purposes
8. Organizations organized for the exclusive purpose of holding title to property and collecting income for exempt organizations
9. Voluntary employees' beneficiary associations
10. Local teachers' retirement fund organizations
11. Religious corporations with common treasuries
12. Fraternal societies operating under the lodge system
13. Diversified management companies
14. Supplemental unemployment benefit trusts
15. Corporations organized for a political candidate or candidates
16. Employee-funded pension trusts
17. Homeowners' property associations
18. Organizations or trusts forming part of a qualified group legal services plan set up by an employer to provide prepaid legal services for employees

Colorado (section 39-22-302). Colorado exempts from the Colorado income tax all organizations which are exempt from the federal income tax under the provisions of the Internal Revenue Code.

Connecticut (section 12-214). Connecticut exempts nonprofit cooperative housing stock in nonstock organizations and companies exempted under federal income tax law.

Delaware (tit. 30, § 1902). Delaware exempts the following nonprofit organizations:

1. Fraternal beneficiary societies, orders, or associations
2. Cemetery corporations and nonprofit corporations and trusts organized for religious, charitable, scientific, or educational purposes, or for the prevention of cruelty to children or animals
3. Nonprofit business leagues, chambers of commerce, fire companies, merchants' associations or boards of trade
4. Nonprofit civic leagues organized for social welfare
5. Nonprofit clubs organized for pleasure or recreation

District of Columbia (section 47-1554). The following list constitutes exempt organizations in the District of Columbia:

1. Labor organizations
2. Fraternal beneficiary societies
3. Nonprofit membership cemetery companies
4. Nonprofit corporations organized for religious, charitable, scientific, literary, educational, or humane purposes and operating to a substantial extent within the District of Columbia
5. Business leagues, chambers of commerce, and boards of trade
6. Nonprofit civic leagues
7. Holding companies for nonprofit corporations
8. Corporate instrumentalities of the United States
9. Nonprofit voluntary employees' beneficiary corporations
10. Nonprofit voluntary beneficiary corporations of employees of the District of Columbia or the government of the United States
11. Common trust funds

Florida (section 220.03). Florida imposes a franchise tax on corporations which is measured by net income. The term "corporation" does not include proprietorships, state or public fairs or expositions, estates, testamentary trusts, or private trusts.

Georgia (section 92-3105). Organizations which are exempt from federal income tax under sections 401, 501(c), 501(d), 501(e), or 664 are exempt from the Georgia income tax.

Hawaii (section 235-9). The following nonprofit organizations are exempt from the Hawaii tax:

1. Religious, charitable, educational, prepaid legal services, and scientific corporations, trusts, and associations
2. Nonprofit cemetery corporations
3. Nonprofit business leagues, chambers of commerce, real estate boards, and boards of trade
4. Nonprofit civic leagues and organizations, and nonprofit employees' associations devoted to religious, charitable, or recreational purposes
5. Labor organizations
6. Clubs organized for nonprofit purposes
7. Employee trusts exempt under the Internal Revenue Code

Idaho (section 63-3026). Idaho exempts from tax the following organizations:

1. Fraternal beneficiary societies
2. Farmers' or their mutual hail, cyclone, casualty, or fire insurance company
3. Farmers' or fruit growers' associations or like cooperatives
4. Federal land banks and national farm loan associations
5. Corporations exclusively performing contracts with the United States Department of Energy at the Idaho National Laboratory

Illinois (chapter 120, section 2-205). Illinois exempts charitable, religious, civic, and other organizations that are exempt from federal income tax.

Indiana (section 6-3-2-3). Indiana exempts organizations that are exempt from federal income tax under section 501(a).

Iowa (section 422.34). The following organizations are exempt from the Iowa tax:

1. Financial institutions and insurance companies
2. Nonprofit cemeteries and corporations organized for religious, charitable, scientific, or educational purposes
3. Business leagues and labor unions
4. Civic leagues and organizations
5. Nonprofit clubs
6. Marketing associations

Kansas (section 79-32,113). The state of Kansas exempts from Kansas taxes organizations that are exempt from federal income tax under the Internal Revenue Code.

Kentucky (sections 141.040, 290.300, 279.200, 279.350). Kentucky exempts from taxation banks and trust companies, credit unions, savings and loan associations, insurance companies, nonprofit corporations, rural electric cooperatives, and rural telephone cooperatives.

Louisiana (section 47:121). The Louisiana statute exempts the following organizations:

1. Labor organizations
2. Banks and building and loan associations
3. Fraternal beneficiary societies
4. Cemeteries
5. Nonprofit religious, charitable, scientific, or educational organizations and charities which contribute their net earnings to such organizations
6. Business leagues
7. Civic leagues and local associations of employees
8. Clubs
9. Local life insurance associations and mutual ditch, irrigation, and telephone companies
10. Mutual casualty insurance companies
11. Farmers', fruit growers' and like cooperative marketing and purchasing associations, including crop financing corporations organized by them
12. Holding companies for nonprofit religious, charitable, or educational organizations
13. Voluntary employees' associations
14. Local teachers' retirement fund associations
15. Certain agricultural or horticultural organizations

Maine (chapter 61, laws 1971; chapter 801, section 5102). The Maine statute exempts from the Maine corporation tax all organizations that are exempt from the federal income tax as a corporation.

Maryland (section 288, Article 81). Organizations and corporations that are exempt under section 501(c) are exempt from the Maryland income tax.

Massachusetts (chapter 156, section 2). The Massachusetts excise tax does not apply to banks, credit unions, surety companies, safe deposit companies, insurance companies, cemeteries or crematories, railroads, or other public utilities. Agricultural and horticultural associations are also exempt under chapter 157, sections 10 and 18.

Michigan (section 208.35). Michigan exempts from the Michigan business tax organizations that are exempt under the Internal Revenue Code except certain local benevolent life insurance associations and farmers' cooperatives organized to finance operations and limited membership nonprofit civic leagues or organizations exempt under I.R.C. § 501(c)(4).

Minnesota (section 290.05). The following organizations are exempt from the Minnesota corporate income tax:

1. Nonprofit corporations operating cemeteries, public schools, public hospitals, academies, colleges, seminaries, churches, and public charity institutions
2. Nonprofit scientific, literary, religious, charitable, and educational and artistic associations
3. Farmers' mutual insurance companies and credit unions
4. Fraternal beneficiary and public employees' relief associations
5. Cooperative and mutual rural telephone or electric associations
6. Nonprofit labor, agricultural, and horticultural organizations
7. Farmers', fruit growers', and like marketing and purchasing associations, including financing corporations operated by them

Mississippi (section 27-13-64). Exempt from the Mississippi corporation franchise tax are the following:

1. Fraternal beneficial societies, orders, or associations
2. Mutual savings banks, domestic or foreign, and farm loan associations, when organized and operated on a nonprofit basis and for public purposes
3. Nonprofit cemetery corporations, religious, charitable, educational, or scientific associations or institutions, including any community chests, funds, or foundations organized and operated exclusively for religious, charitable, scientific, or educational purposes or for the prevention of cruelty to animals or children in which no part of the net earnings inures to the benefit of any private stockholder or individual
4. Business leagues, labor organizations, agricultural or horticultural associations, chambers of commerce or boards of trade not organized for profit and no part of the net earnings of which inures to the benefit of any private stockholder or individual
5. Civic leagues and social clubs or organizations not organized for profit but operated exclusively for the promotion of social welfare
6. Clubs organized and operated exclusively for pleasure, recreation, and other nonprofit purposes no part of the net earnings of which inures to the benefit of any private shareholder or member
7. Farmers', fishermen's, and fruit growers' cooperatives or other like organizations organized and operated as sales agents for the purpose of marketing the products of the members and turning back to them the proceeds of the sale, less the necessary selling expenses and on the basis of the quantity of produce furnished by them and other nonprofit agricultural organizations organized and operated under the provisions of the cooperative marketing laws of the state of Mississippi
8. Nonprofit cooperative electric power associations or corporations or like associations, when organized and operated for public purposes and when no part of the income inures to the benefit of any private stockholder or individual

9. Insurance companies qualified and regulated by the state of Mississippi

10. State, county, or community fair associations, including any fair association whose fair is held for the benefit of the public where no dividends are declared to the stockholders and where the proceeds are used exclusively for the operation, maintenance, and improvement of the fair

11. Any corporation whose sole function is to own and operate a grammar school, junior high school, high school, or military school within the state of Mississippi, no part of the net earnings of which inures to the benefit of any private stockholder, group, or individual

12. Any organization or corporation whose charter specifically states that it is not organized for profit and where no part of the net earnings of which inures to the benefit of any private stockholder, group, or individual

Missouri (section 147.0101). The Missouri corporation franchise tax does not apply to corporations not organized for profit.

Montana (section 15-31-101). Montana exempts from the corporate income tax a lengthy list of corporations otherwise exempt under section 501(c) as follows:

1. Labor, agricultural, or horticultural organization

2. Fraternal beneficiary society, order, or association operating under the lodge system or for the exclusive benefit of the members of a fraternity itself operating under the lodge system and providing for the payment of life, sick, accident, or other benefits to the members of the society, order, or association or their dependents

3. Cemetery company owned and operated exclusively for the benefit of its members

4. Corporation or association owned and operated exclusively for religious, charitable, scientific, or educational purposes, no part of the net income of which inures to the benefit of any private stockholder or individual

5. Business league, chamber of commerce, or board of trade not organized for profit and no part of the net income of which inures to the benefit of any private stockholder or individual

6. Civic league or organization not organized for profit but operated exclusively for the promotion of social welfare

7. Club organized or operated exclusively for pleasure, recreation, and other nonprofitable purposes, no part of the net earnings of which inures to the benefit of any private stockholder or members

8. Farmers' or other mutual hail, cyclone, or fire insurance company, mutual ditch or irrigation company, mutual or cooperative telephone company, or like organization of a purely local character, the income of which consists solely of assessments, dues, and fees collected from members for the sole purpose of meeting expenses

9. Cooperative association or corporation engaged in the business of operating a rural

electrification system or systems for the transmission or distribution of electrical energy on a cooperative basis

10. Corporation or association organized for the exclusive purpose of holding title to property, collecting income therefrom, turning over the entire amount thereof, less expenses, to an organization which itself is exempt from the tax imposed by the state

Nebraska (section 77-2734). In Nebraska corporate income tax is only imposed on those corporations or other entities that would be taxed as a corporation under the Internal Revenue Code; therefore, any corporation or other entity which is exempt from tax under the Internal Revenue Code is exempt from the Nebraska tax.

Nevada. There is no corporate tax imposed by the state of Nevada.

New Hampshire (section 77-a:1). New Hampshire exempts organizations that are exempt from the federal income tax from the New Hampshire business profits tax.

New Jersey (section 54:10E-3). New Jersey exempts the following from the corporation tax:

1. Cemetery corporations not conducted for pecuniary profit of any private shareholder or individual

2. Nonprofit corporations, associations, or organizations established or chartered without capital stock under the laws of the state of New Jersey or under a special charter or under any similar general or special law of the state and not conducted for pecuniary profit of any private shareholder or individual

New Mexico (section 53-8-28). A corporation incorporated under the not-for-profit act of the state of New Mexico is exempt from the New Mexico franchise act.

New York (N.Y. Tax § 190). The New York corporation tax is imposed only on stock corporations.

North Carolina (sections 57-14 and 105-130.11). Exempt organizations under the federal tax law are exempt from the North Carolina corporate income tax.

North Dakota (section 57-38-09). North Dakota grants tax exempt status to organizations that are tax exempt under the Internal Revenue Code.

Ohio (sections 5733.09, 5733.10). Ohio exempts insurance, fraternal, beneficial, building and loan, bond investment, and other corporations required to file annual reports with the superintendent of insurance.

Oklahoma (section 2359). Organizations that are exempt from the federal income tax are exempt from the Oklahoma income tax.

Oregon (section 317.080). The following organizations are exempt from the Oregon corporation income and excise taxes:

 1. Nonprofit labor, agricultural, and horticultural organizations
 2. Fraternal beneficiary societies
 3. Cemeteries
 4. Nonprofit religious, charitable, or educational corporations
 5. Business leagues
 6. Civic leagues and local employees' associations
 7. Clubs
 8. Mutual irrigation, electric, and telephone companies
 9. Farmers' and fruit growers' associations and finance corporations organized by them
10. Credit unions
11. Corporations engaging in no business or rental activities being organized exclusively to hold title to property used by an exempt organization
12. Student housing corporations
13. Nonprofit corporations furnishing housing and social facilities to older persons
14. People's utility districts

Pennsylvania (title 72, sections 7401 and 7501). Pennsylvania exempts nonprofit corporations from the Pennsylvania tax.

Rhode Island (section 44-11-1). The following organizations are exempted from the definition of corporation under the Rhode Island statute:

1. Public service corporations
2. Corporations not organized for business purposes including nonprofit hospitals and schools
3. Fraternal beneficiary societies
4. Corporations exempt by charter
5. Agricultural cooperatives

South Carolina (section 12-7-330). The South Carolina statute exempts the following organizations:

1. Fraternal beneficiary societies
2. Mutual building and loan associations, cooperative banks and insurance companies
3. Cemeteries and nonprofit religious, charitable, scientific, or educational corporations or trusts
4. Nonprofit business leagues, employees' credit unions, chambers of commerce, textile expositions, or boards of trade
5. Civic leagues
6. Mutual casualty insurance, irrigation, and telephone companies

7. Nonprofit labor, agricultural, and horticultural organizations

8. Pension, profit sharing, stock bonus and annuity trusts established by employers for employees

9. College Greek letter fraternities and sororities

10. Nonprofit corporations providing water and sewage service

11. Homeowners' associations to the extent of their exempt function income

South Dakota. There is no corporate income tax imposed by the state of South Dakota.

Tennessee (section 67-2702). Nonprofit organizations and lodge meeting places are exempt from the Tennessee corporate excise tax.

Texas. Texas does not impose a corporate income tax.

Utah (section 59-13-4). Utah does not impose a tax on the following:

1. Labor, agricultural, and horticultural organizations

2. Fraternal beneficial societies

3. Nonprofit cemeteries

4. Nonprofit religious, charitable, and educational organizations

5. Business leagues

6. Civic leagues

7. Clubs

8. Local life insurance associations and mutual casualty insurance, irrigation, or telephone companies

9. Farmers', fruit growers', and like cooperatives and financing corporations organized by them

10. Corporations holding title to property for exempt organizations

11. Federal agencies

12. Employees' voluntary beneficial associations

13. Local teachers' retirement associations

14. Common trust funds

15. Employees' trusts

Vermont (section 5811). The following organizations are exempt from the definition of corporation:

1. Nonprofit cemeteries, fraternal beneficiary societies, and labor, agricultural, or horticultural organizations

2. Nonprofit sanitary, religious, charitable, educational, or scientific corporations

3. Nonprofit chamber of commerce, business organizations, or boards of trade

4. Civic leagues

5. Clubs

6. Farmers' or other mutual insurance company, mutual water companies and mutual or cooperative telephone companies

7. Farmers', fruit growers', and like cooperatives

8. Credit unions, nonprofit hospital and medical service corporations, and free public library corporations

9. Any political organization exempt from or not owing any federal income tax

Virginia (section 58-151.03). The state of Virginia exempts from taxation religious, charitable, educational, and other organizations not organized for profit and organizations exempt from federal income tax.

Washington. The state of Washington does not impose a corporate income tax.

West Virginia (section 11-24-5). The state of West Virginia exempts from its tax all corporations that are exempt from the federal income tax.

Wisconsin (section 71.01). Wisconsin exempts only mutual insurance companies that are exempt from federal income tax under section 501(c)(15) and governmental and political units of the United States and Wisconsin.

Wyoming. There is no corporate income tax imposed by the state of Wyoming.

Property Taxes

The exemptions from state and local property taxes are set out by state in Table 4.

Sales and Use Taxes

Alabama (section 40-23-4). There are no special exemptions for charitable, religious, and nonprofit organizations from the Alabama sales and use tax, but certain exemptions have been provided by special act of the legislature. Sales to certain veterans' organizations and educational institutions are exempt. Sales by organizations such as the Young Men's Hebrew Association, the YMCA, the YWCA, the Seaman's Home of Mobile, the Knights of Pythias Lodge, and the Cystic Fibrosis Research Foundation, Inc., are excluded from the sales tax.

Alaska. There are no exceptions to the Alaska gross receipts tax.

Arizona (sections 42-1312.15, 42-1409.18, 42-1314, 42-1409). The exemptions from the Arizona sales and use taxes are extended to the purchase of personal property in the state by a nonprofit hospital and sales by a nonprofit organization organized and operated exclusively for charitable purposes.

Arkansas (sections 84-1904, 84-1905, 84-1905.1, 84-3105). Exemptions from the Arkansas sales and use taxes include sales by churches and charitable organizations, sales to charitable hospitals, sales to nonprofit orphans' and children's

Table 4
State and Local Property Tax Exemptions

State	Religious Institutions and Affiliated Property	Charitable Organizations; Community Chest	Educational	Scientific	Literary	Hospitals and Health Care Institutions	Cemeteries	Historical	Social Clubs Including Fraternities and Sororities	War Veterans Organizations	Labor, Agricultural, and Horticultural	Fraternal	Statute
Alabama	X	X	X				X			X		X	§§ 40-8-1 to 40-11-1
Alaska	X	X	X			X	X			X			§29.53.020
Arizona	X	X	X			X	X				X		§ 42-271
Arkansas	X	X	X				X						§ 84-206
California	X	X	X	X		X	X	X		X			Art. XII, Cal. Const.
Colorado	X	X	X				X						§ 39-3-101 to 102
Connecticut	X	X	X	X	X	X		X		X	X		§ 12-81
Delaware	X	X	X				X			X			Tit. 9, § 8103
District of Columbia	X	X	X	X		X	X						§ 47-1208
Florida	X	X	X	X	X	X	X		X		X	X	§ 196
Georgia	X	X	X		X	X	X						§ 92-201
Hawaii	X	X	X			X	X			X			§ 246-32
Idaho	X	X	X			X			X			X	§ 63-105
Illinois	X	X	X			X	X			X			Ch. 120, § 500
Indiana	X	X	X	X	X	X	X		X	X	X	X	§ 6-1.1-10
Iowa	X	X		X	X					X			§ 427.1
Kansas	X	X	X	X	X	X							§ 79-201
Kentucky	Z	Z	Z										Sec. 170, Ky. Const.
Louisiana	X	X	X			X	X		X		X	X	Art. X, § 4 La Const.
Maine	X	X	X	X	X	X				X		X	§ 652
Maryland	X	X	X		X	X	X	X		X		X	§ 9, Art. 81 Code Ann.
Massachusetts	X	X		X	X		X			X	X	X	§ 5, Ch. 59, Gen. Laws
Michigan	X	X	X	X	X		X		X	X	X		§ 211.7
Minnesota	X	X	X			X	X						§ 272.02
Mississippi	X		X		X	X					X		§ 27-31-1 to 27-31-23
Missouri	X	X	X										§ 137.100
Montana	X	X	X			X	X			X	X		§ 15-6-201 to 209
Nebraska	X	X	X				X						§ 77-202

109

Table 4 (continued)
State and Local Property Tax Exemptions

State	Religious Institutions and Affiliated Property	Charitable Organizations; Community Chest	Educational	Scientific	Literary	Hospitals and Health Care Institutions	Cemeteries	Historical	Social Clubs Including Fraternities and Sororities	War Veterans Organizations	Labor, Agricultural, and Horticultural	Fraternal	Statute
Nevada	X	X	X				X						§ 77-202
New Hampshire	X	X	X							X			§ 72:23
New Jersey	X	X	X			X		X		X		X	§ 54:4-3.27
New Mexico	X	X	X				X						§ 3, Art. VIII N.M. Const.
New York	X	X	X	*	*	X	X	*	X	X			§ 421.9
North Carolina	X	X	X	X	X	X	X	X		X			§§ 105-275 to -278
North Dakota	X	X	X						X		X	X	§ 57-02-08
Ohio	X	X	X	X	X	X	X			X			§§ 5709.04-.17
Oklahoma	X	X	X					X				X	§ 2405
Oregon	X ·	X		X	X		X	X	X				§§ 307.130-.150
Pennsylvania	X	X	X				X						Tit. 72, § 5020-201
Rhode Island	X	X	X			X				X		X	§ 44-3-3
South Carolina	X	X	X		X					X		X	§ 12-37-220
South Dakota	X	X	X			X							§ 10-4-9
Tennessee	X	X	X	X			X				X	X	§§ 67-502, 513, 514
Texas	X	X	X				X			X			VACS 11.11, 11.17, 11.18, 11.19, 11.20, 11.21, 11.23
Utah	X	X	X										Art. XIII, § 2 Utah Const.

Table 4 (continued)
State and Local Property Tax Exemptions

State	Religious Institutions and Affiliated Property	Charitable Organizations; Community Chest	Educational	Scientific	Literary	Hospitals and Health Care Institutions	Cemeteries	Historical	Social Clubs Including Fraternities and Sororities	War Veterans Organizations	Labor, Agricultural, and Horticultural	Fraternal	Statute
Vermont	X	X								X			§ 3802
Virginia	X	X				X	X					X	§ 58-12
Washington	X	X	X	X			X	X					§ 84.36 .020, .030, .060
West Virginia	X	X				X							§ 11-3-9
Wisconsin	X	X	X						X	X		X	§ 70.11
Wyoming	X	X	X			X							§ 39-1-201

* Exempt from state property tax but not local property tax.

homes, sales to the Boy Scouts, Girl Scouts, humane societies and 4-H clubs, sales of food stuffs for free distribution to charitable institutions, and sales of religious, professional, trade, and sports publications printed in Arkansas and sold through regular subscriptions.

California (Cal. Rev. & T. §§ 6359 to 6381, 6201). Exempt from the California sales tax are sales to the Red Cross, meals served to students by schools, by any religious organization, to patients in hospitals and mental institutions, to elderly persons in homes for the aged, to children in nurseries, to low-income elderly persons at or below cost by a nonprofit organization or governmental agency, sales by certain charitable organizations, candies sold by youth organizations and nonprofit organizations, commemorative bracelets sold by charitable organizations, flags sold by veterans' organizations, works of art purchased by nonprofit organizations for donation to a museum, medical alert tags furnished by exempt organizations, certain medical equipment such as insulin syringes, or drug infusion devices or medical oxygen delivery systems. California use tax applies to the same exemptions as those for sales except for sales to the Red Cross.

Colorado (section 39-26-102). Excluded from the Colorado retail sales tax are sales to religious, charitable, scientific, literary, humane, amateur sports, or educational organizations and nonprofit schools. Personal tangible property stored, used, or consumed by charitable corporations in the regular conduct of their charitable function is exempt.

Connecticut (sections 12-408, 12-411). The Connecticut sales and use tax does not apply to sales to or the use of personal property by nonprofit charitable hospitals, charitable and religious organizations, sales of food products in school cafeterias, sales of two dollars or under by nonprofit Connecticut eleemosynary organizations to support youth activities or schools or school activities, and personalty owned by nonprofit housing corporations and used in low-income housing.

Delaware. Delaware does not have a sales or use tax.

District of Columbia (section 47-2005). The District of Columbia sales and use tax does not apply to sales to a section 501(c)(3) organization located within the District of Columbia and carrying on its activities to a substantial extent therein.

Florida (sections 212.04, 212.06, 212.08). The exemptions from the Florida sales, use, rental, and admission taxes include articles sold or leased to or by churches or other nonprofit religious, charitable, or educational institutions with the exception that tangible personal property sold by these institutions except for churches is taxable, sales of religious publications, hymnals, bibles, prayer books, and church or ceremonial raiment and equipment, sales of personal tangible property to or by state headquarters of veterans' organizations, property sold to nonprofit scientific institutions, and sales of meals by nonprofit volunteer organizations to invalid and indigent persons.

Georgia (section 92-2150.3). Sales to nonprofit licensed nursing homes, general and mental hospitals, sale or use of bibles, fund-raising sales of a nonprofit religious institution, sales of property or services used exclusively for educational purposes, and property and services sold to the University of Georgia system are exempt from the Georgia sales tax.

Hawaii (sections 237-23, 238-2). There are no exemptions to the Hawaii use tax; however, corporations, associations, or societies operated for religious, charitable, scientific, or educational purposes or operating senior citizen housing facilities, business leagues, hospitals, nonprofit cemetery corporations, and nonprofit shippers' associations are exempt from the general excise tax.

Idaho (section 63-3612). Sales to nonprofit educational institutions, hospitals, and canal companies, sales or use of religious literature sold by a church, sales of meals by schools or churches, and sales to and purchases by forest protective associations are exempt from the Idaho sales and use tax.

Illinois (ch. 120, §§ 439, 441). Sales to charitable, religious, and educational organizations are exempt from the Illinois occupational retail sales tax as well as the Illinois use tax.

Indiana (section 6-2-1-7). Sales of school meals to elementary and nonprofit college and university students and school employees on school premises, sales of meals by a fraternity, sorority, or student cooperative housing organization to its members who are enrolled in the supervising of educational institutions, sales and purchases by nonprofit religious, charitable, educational, or eleemosynary institutions, and all amounts received from a convention, trade show, or exhibition conducted by a nonprofit group, organization, or corporation organized and operated for fraternal or social purposes or as a business league or association are exempt from the Indiana sales and use tax.

Iowa (section 422.45). Iowa exempts the sales of educational, religious, or charitable activities from the gross receipts tax as well as sales or services to private nonprofit educational institutions in Iowa which are exempt from the Iowa sales and use tax.

Kansas (section 79-3606). Sales to the state and its political subdivisions and hospitals, to schools and educational institutions, of food products to contractors for use in preparing meals for homebound elderly or disabled persons, textbook rentals, meals served to employees, sale of prescription drugs and insulin, sales of prosthetics and orthopedic appliances, and leases of tangible personal property are exempt from the Kansas sales tax.

Kentucky (sections 139.480, 139.482). Sales to nonprofit charitable hospitals, educational institutions, charitable institutions, and religious institutions are exempt from the Kentucky sales tax.

Louisiana (section 47:305). Louisiana exempts the following from the sales and use tax: food sold to students at schools, to hospital patients and staff, religious, or medical organizations on an occasional basis if consumed on the premises, sales of admissions by domestic nonprofit corporations presenting musical performances, admissions to entertainment furnished by domestic nonprofit charitable, educational, and religious organizations, sales of personal tangible property at or admission charges for events sponsored by domestic nonprofit civic, educational, historical, charitable, fraternal or religious organizations, membership fees or dues of nonprofit civic organizations, purchases of property or services by war veterans' organizations, and other miscellaneous sales.

Maine (section 1760). Sales to incorporated hospitals, nonprofit nursing homes and home health care agencies, nonprofit medical research corporations, schools, nonprofit organizations operating educational television or radio stations, regularly organized churches or houses of religious worship, incorporated volunteer fire departments, community mental health affiliated nonprofit organizations that operate in residential homes for adults are exempt from the Maine sales and use tax.

Maryland (sections 81-324 to 81-326). Sales to certified nonprofit religious, charitable, or educational organizations situated in Maryland, sales of food by churches and religious organizations and by schools and colleges, including sales by a food concessionaire under contract with the school or college and at hospitals, sales by hospital thrift shops, sales of items manufactured or adapted for the blind, sales by gift shops at mental hospitals operated by the state, and certain sales of electricity to a nonprofit planned retirement community are exempt from the Maryland sales and use tax.

Massachusetts (section 6, chapter 64H, general laws). Sales to charitable, religious, scientific, or educational organizations which are tax exempt under section 501(c)(3) of the Internal Revenue Code are exempt from the Massachusetts sales and use tax.

Michigan (section 205). Sales not for resale to charitable, religious, or educational institutions are exempt from the Michigan sales and use tax unless the activity is mainly a commercial enterprise or vehicle licensed for use on a public highway.

Minnesota (section 297A). Sales to charitable, religious, or educational institutions are exempt if the property purchased is to be used in performance of a charitable, religious, or educational activity.

Mississippi (sections 27-65-29, 27-67-7). Sales of tangible personal property and services to nonprofit hospitals or infirmaries, sales to an orphanage or old people's home supported by a religious, fraternal, or nonprofit organization, sales of taxable tangible personal property or services to a YMCA, YWCA, boys' or girls' club owned and operated by nonprofit associations, and sales to elementary and secondary schools and colleges operated by nonprofit organizations which are exempt from the state income tax are exempt from the Mississippi sales and use tax.

Missouri (section 144). The sales by or to religious or charitable organizations, elementary and secondary schools, and nonprofit civic, social, service, or fraternal organizations are exempt from the Missouri sales and use taxes.

Montana. There is no sales tax imposed by the state of Montana.

Nebraska (section 72-2704). Exempt from the Nebraska sales and use taxes are meals and food served by schools and student or parent-teacher organizations, except sales at public functions, meals and food sold at church functions, and meals and food served to patients of hospitals, sales to religious institutions, schools, colleges, hospitals, or licensed child care agencies, purchases by governmental bodies, sales, lease, rental to or use or consumption by agricultural organizations, purchases by any nonprofit organization that provides services primarily for home health care, and food or food products for human consumption that are eligible for purchase with federal food stamps.

Nevada (section 374.345). Sales to nonprofit religious and charitable organizations and meals for students and teachers are exempt from the Nevada sales and use tax.

New Hampshire. There is no sales tax imposed by the state of New Hampshire.

New Jersey (section 45:32B-9). Sales or amusement charges by or to nonprofit religious, charitable, scientific, or educational organizations are exempt from the New Jersey sales tax.

New Mexico (sections 7-9-12 to 7-9-42). Section 501(c)(3) organizations are exempt from the New Mexico sales and use taxes.

New York (N.Y. Tax §§ 1105, 1116). Sales to nonprofit religious, charitable, educational, or scientific organizations, qualified amateur sports associations, and nonprofit veterans' organizations are exempt from the New York sales and use tax.

North Carolina (section 105.164). Under North Carolina law, nonprofit hospitals and educational institutions, churches, orphanages, and other nonprofit charitable or religious institutions are liable for the sales and use taxes but are entitled to a refund of taxes paid on direct purchases of tangible personal property used in carrying on the work of the institution.

North Dakota (sections 57-39.2-04, 57-40.2-04). Sales of admissions to fairs and gross receipts from educational, religious, or charitable activities unless held in a publicly owned facility, sales of school supplies to private nonprofit schools of higher learning, gross receipts derived by public school districts, sales of meals to nonprofit organizations for delivery to shut-ins, gross receipts from sales of bibles, hymnals, prayer books, or textbooks to nonprofit religious organizations, and sales to hospitals licensed by the state health department are exempt from the North Dakota sales and use tax.

Ohio (sections 5739.02, 5741.02). Sales of tangible personal property to churches and charitable organizations are exempt.

Oklahoma (title 68, sections 1305, 1309, 1404). Oklahoma exempts from the sales and use tax gross proceeds derived from sales of tangible personal property and services to or by churches except where the church may be engaged in business for profit or savings or is competing with other persons engaged in the same or similar business. The sales of tangible personal property or services to state supervisory organizations of the Boy Scouts, Girl Scouts, and Camp Fire Girls are also exempt from the sales tax.

Oregon. There is no sales tax in Oregon.

Pennsylvania (tit. 72, § 7204). Sales to or use by charitable organizations, volunteer firemen's organizations, nonprofit educational institutions, or religious organizations for religious purposes except property or services used in an unrelated trade or business, or materials used in construction or remodeling other than for routine maintenance and repairs are exempt from the Pennsylvania sales and use tax.

Rhode Island (section 44-18-30). Sales to and use by nonprofit hospitals, educational institutions, churches, orphanages, and other institutions or organizations operated exclusively for religious or charitable purposes are exempt from the Rhode Island sales and use tax.

South Carolina (section 12-35). South Carolina does not exempt nonprofit organizations from retail sales and use taxes.

South Dakota (sections 1-45-10, 10-45-13, 10-45-14, 10-46-15). Sales to educational and religious institutions and to hospitals operating as charitable or nonprofit institutions are exempt from the South Dakota sales and use taxes.

Tennessee (sections 67-3010, 67-3012, 67-3014). Sales or donations made directly to nonprofit religious, educational, and charitable institutions are exempt from the sales and use tax.

Texas (Articles 151.309 to 151.313). Texas exempts from the sales and use tax sales to organizations exempt under sections 501(c)(3), (4), (8), (10), and (19).

Utah (section 59-15-6). Sales made to or by charitable or religious institutions in the conduct of their charitable activities are exempt from the Utah sales and use taxes.

Vermont (title 32, section 9743). Organizations that are tax exempt under section 501(c)(3) are exempt from the Vermont sales and use taxes.

Virginia (section 58-441.6). Out of an extensive list of exceptions, the state of Virginia exempts from the retail sales and use tax property used by nonprofit schools, hospitals, and licensed nursing homes, tangible personal property used by a nonprofit institution of learning for use by a construction contractor, tangible personal property bought by a tax exempt church for use in religious worship or education, tangible personal property bought, sold, or used by any chartered not-for-profit organization incorporated under Virginia law and organized for the purpose of preventing cruelty to animals and promoting humane care of animals, federally exempt organizations operated exclusively to provide education, training, and services to Virginia retarded persons, and nonprofit homes for adults.

Washington (sections 82.08, 82.12). Exemptions from the Washington retail sales and use taxes are only tangentially related to nonprofit organizations. Exemptions are for such items as sales of amusement and recreational services by nonprofit youth organizations and sales to, or use by, artistic or cultural organizations of certain art objects acquired for exhibition or presentation.

West Virginia (section 11-15-9). Exempt from tax are sales of property or services to nonprofit religious, charitable, scientific, literary, or educational corporations or organizations which are exempt from the federal income tax under sections 501(c)(3) or (4), provided that the organization only make occasional sales of property or services and that the purchased goods or services are consumed directly by the organization. In addition, sales to national fraternal or social organizations for welfare work, sales of equipment to volunteer fire departments, casual and occasional sales of property or services by nonprofit sections 501(c)(3) and (4) organizations, or sales of property or services to a degree-granting institution whose main campus is in West Virginia and which is also exempt under section 501(c)(3) are exempt.

Wisconsin (section 77.54). The sale of tangible property and services to or use by any certified nonprofit religious, charitable, educational, or scientific organization or organization for the prevention of cruelty to animals is exempt from the Wisconsin sales and use tax.

Wyoming (sections 39-6-401 *et seq.*, 39-6-504). Sales to religious and charitable organizations are exempt from the Wyoming retail sales tax. Occasional sales made by religious or charitable organizations are also exempt.

PRIVATE INUREMENT

The common thread running through state law regulating nonprofit charitable organizations and federal tax law is the requirement that "no part of [the organization's] net earnings . . . inures to the benefit of any private shareholder or individual." This restriction is imposed on charitable organizations under section 501(c)(3), on business leagues and similar organizations under section 501(c)(6), on social clubs under section 501(c)(7), on voluntary employees' beneficiary associations under section 501(c)(9), on teachers' retirement funds under section 501(c)(11), on cemetery companies under section 501(c)(13), and on veterans' organizations under section 501(c)(19). Other provisions, such as sections 501(c)(4), 501(c)(10), 501(c)(21), and 501(c)(22), have restrictions on the use or disposition of the assets or net earnings but not in the same form as the private inurement restriction.

While Congress seems to have placed an absolute prohibition on private inurement in certain of the exemption provisions of section 501(c), it did not provide any further guidelines. The private inurement prohibition is entwined with the organizational and operational tests for section 501(c)(3) organizations, and it is difficult to separate them. One must look to other sources to determine what the prohibition means.

Treasury Regulations section 1.501(a)-1(c) defines a "private shareholder or individual" as any person who has a personal and private interest in the activities of the organization. Treasury Regulations section 1.501(c)(3)-1(d)(1)(ii) provides that an organization, to satisfy the organizational and operational tests, must serve a public rather than a private purpose. This requirement means that the organization may not be organized or operated for the private benefit of designated individuals, the creator or his family, shareholders of the organization, or persons controlled, directly or indirectly, by the organization.[50] The regulation also provides that an organization is not operated exclusively for an exempt purpose if it violates the private inurement prohibition.[51] The entanglement begins.

The relationship between the private inurement prohibitions and the exclusivity requirement of the organizational and operational tests is unclear. "Exclusive" as used in section 501(c)(3) allows for insubstantial activities not in furtherance of the organization's exempt purpose. On the other hand, the private inurement prohibition is absolute. The private inurement prohibition must be liberally construed; otherwise, no organization could qualify since to some extent private individuals, directly or indirectly, benefit from all tax exempt organizations' operations. The key to the liberal application of the private inurement prohibition is the term "net earnings."

While net earnings is not defined in the code or regulations, the courts have lent an all-inclusive construction to the term.[52] Thus, reasonable compensation for goods or services paid by a tax exempt organization to a shareholder or private individual would be permissible since these expenditures are offset against gross income in obtaining net earnings. As long as the compensation is solely for services and is reasonable and necessary, it is not private inurement.[53] Conversely, if it does not meet the test of reasonable and necessary or is a disguised dividend or is not solely as compensation for services, it will be found to be private inurement.[54] Renting the property of shareholders or private individuals or renting the property of the organization to shareholders or private individuals does not constitute private inurement if the rentals are fair. Excessive rentals paid by organizations to shareholders or private individuals or bargain rentals of the organization's property by shareholders or private individuals constitute private inurement.[55]

Loans by the organization on insufficient security or interest free or at reduced rates constitute private inurement.[56]

Likewise, bargain sales of the organization's property or purchases by the organization of shareholders' or private individuals' property at inflated prices constitute private inurement. Transfer of property to a section 501(c)(3) organization subject to a reserved life estate or in exchange for an annuity specifically charged against the asset is not private inurement, particularly if the value of the asset exceeds the value of the annuity contract.[57]

Overlap between the private inurement prohibition and the public purpose requirement occurs in many cases.

Professional associations that have been held not to be exempt because they were not organized for a public purpose have also involved private inurement. For example, a public-interest law firm that charged and accepted attorney's fees did not operate exclusively for charitable purposes;[58] a public-interest law firm that entered into a fee-sharing arrangement with a private attorney lost its exemption;[59] and the owner of a hospital who used control of the hospital to limit the number of staff doctors, to enter into favorable rental agreements with the hospital, and to limit care to essentially his own patients did not operate the hospital exclusively for charitable purposes.[60]

Organizations benefiting a particular group of individuals have been denied or lost their tax exemptions. For example, a trust which provided educational benefits to employees and their families as part of a collective bargaining agreement that required contributions based on amount of work hours accumulated was not exempt;[61] benefits in the form of food, clothing, shelter, medical, educational services, and recreational facilities constitute a private not a public purpose as well as private inurement.[62]

An organization created for personal objectives such as carrying on the founder's feud with a newspaper,[63] advancing the founder's attack on various agencies and institutions,[64] or conducting medical research programs on patients who were charged prevailing fees[65] is not exempt because of private purpose and private inurement.

In the case of private foundations the private inurement prohibition takes the form of the self-dealing proscription.[66] Self-dealing with respect to a private foundation does not initially cause revocation of exempt status but results in the imposition of an excise tax on the foundation and foundation managers. See the discussion concerning self-dealing in Chapter 8 for further details.

NOTES

1. I.R.C. § 6081(b).
2. I.R.C. § 6081(a).
3. Rev. Proc. 80-27, 1980-1 C.B. 677, *superseding* Rev. Proc. 77-38, 1977-2 C.B. 571, *superseding* Rev. Proc. 72-41, 1972-2 C.B. 820.
4. *Id.*
5. Treas. Reg. § 1.501(a)-1(a)(2).
6. Treas. Reg. § 1.508-1(a).
7. I.R.C. § 508(d)(2)(B); Treas. Reg. § 1.508-2(b).
8. I.R.C. § 508(c)(1).
9. I.R.C. § 508(c)(2).
10. Treas. Reg. § 1.508-1(a)(4).
11. *Comm. v. John Danz Charitable Trust,* 284 F.2d 726 (9th Cir. 1960).
12. Treas. Decision 6391 (Proposed 2/26/59, adopted 6/25/59).
13. Treas. Reg. § 1.501(c)(3)-1(b)(1)(i)(a).
14. Treas. Reg. § 1.501(c)(3)-1(b)(1)(i)(b).
15. Treas. Reg. § 1.501(c)(3)-1(b)(2).
16. Treas. Reg. § 1.501(c)(3)-1(b)(1)(iv).
17. *Id.*
18. *Broadway Theatre League v. U.S.,* 293 F.Supp. 346 (W.D. Va. 1968).
19. I.R.C. § 6501(c)(3).
20. I.R.C. §§ 6033(b), 6522(d).
21. *See, e.g., Taxation with Representation v. U.S.,* 585 F.2d 1219 (4th Cir. 1978); *Senior Citizens Stores, Inc. v. U.S.,* 602 F.2d 711 (5th Cir. 1979); *Elisian Guild, Inc. v. U.S.,* 412 F.2d 121 (1st Cir. 1969); *Evergreen Cemetery Ass'n of Seattle v. U.S.,* 444 F.2d 1232 (9th Cir. 1971).
22. Treas. Reg. § 1.501(c)(3)-1(b)(ii).
23. Treas. Reg. § 1.501(c)(3)-1(b)(iv).

24. Treas. Reg. § 1.501(c)(3)-1(b)(4).
25. Id.
26. T.I.R. 54,635 P-H Fed. Taxes 1962.
27. Treas. Reg. § 1.501(c)(3)-1(c)(2).
28. Sebastian Lathe Co. v. Johnson, 110 F.Supp. 245 (S.D.N.Y. 1952).
29. Dillingham Transportation Bldg. Ltd. v. U.S., 146 F.Supp. 953 (Ct. Cl. 1957).
30. Treas. Reg. § 1.501(c)(3)-1(c)(1).
31. Treas. Reg. § 1.501(c)(3)-1(c)(2).
32. See, e.g., Goldsboro Art League v. Comm., 75 T.C., at 345, n.10; People of God
Community v. Comm., 75 T.C. 127, 132, 133 (1980); Western Catholic Church v.
Comm., 73 T.C. 196, 206 n.27 (1979), aff'd in an unpublished opinion, 631 F.2d 736
(7th Cir. 1980).
33. Founding Church of Scientology v. U.S., 412 F.2d 1197, 1199, 1202 (Ct. Cl.
1969), cert. den., 397 U.S. 1009 (1969).
34. Church of the Transfiguring Spirit, Inc. v. Comm., 76 T.C. 1, 5 n.6 (1981).
35. Treas. Reg. § 1.501(c)(3)-1(d)(1)(iii).
36. Treas. Reg. § 1.508-1(b).
37. Treas. Reg. § 1.508-3(b).
38. Id.
39. Treas. Reg. § 1.508-3(d).
40. 1975-2 C.B. 587.
41. Id.
42. I.R.C. § 505.
43. Id.
44. I.R.C. § 505(c).
45. Id.
46. Id.
47. Id.
48. Id.
49. Id.
50. Treas. Reg. § 1.501(c)(3)-1(d)(1)(ii).
51. Treas. Reg. § 1.501(c)(3)-1(c)(2).
52. See, e.g., Passaic United Hebrew Burial Ass'n v. U.S., 216 F.Supp. 500 (D.N.J.
1963).
53. Home Oil Mill v. Willingham, 68 F.Supp. 525 (N.D. Ala. 1946); St. Germain
Foundation, 26 T.C. 648 (1956).
54. Birmingham Business College, Inc. v. Comm., 276 F.2d 476 (5th Cir. 1960); Mabee
Petroleum Corp. v. U.S., 203 F.2d 872 (5th Cir. 1953); Sonora Community Hosp., 46 T.C.
519, aff'd, 397 F.2d 814 (9th Cir. 1968).
55. Birmingham Business College, Inc. v. Comm., 276 F.2d 476 (5th Cir. 1960); F. E.
McGillick Co., 30 T.C. 1130, modified on other gnds, 278 F.2d 643 (3d Cir. 1960); Rev.
Rul. 69-545, 1969-2 C.B. 117; Sonora Community Hosp., 46 T.C. 519, aff'd, 397 F.2d
814 (9th Cir. 1968).
56. Best Lock Corp., 31 T.C. 1217 (1959).
57. Rev. Rul. 69-176, 1969-1 C.B. 150.

58. Rev. Rul. 75-75, 1975-1 C.B. 154.

59. Rev. Rul. 76-5, 1976-1 C.B. 146.

60. Rev. Rul. 69-545, 1969-2 C.B. 117, *modifying* Rev. Rul. 56-185, 1956-1 C.B. 202.

61. *Ohio Teamsters Educational and Safety Training Trust Fund v. Comm.*, 692 F.2d 432 (6th Cir. 1982).

62. *Beth-El Ministries, Inc. v. U.S.*, 44 AFTR2d 79-5190; *Bubbling Well Church of Universal Love, Inc. v. Comm.*, 670 F.2d 104 (9th Cir. 1981).

63. *Puritan Church, et al.*, 209 F.2d 306, *cert. den.*, 347 U.S. 975 (1954).

64. *Save the Free Enterprise System, Inc.*,¶ 81,388 P-H Memo. T.C.

65. Rev. Rul. 69-266, 1969-1 C.B. 151.

66. I.R.C. § 4941.

7

Securities Regulation

In response to perceived abuses in the securities market that contributed to the disastrous crash of 1929, Congress enacted a series of federal statutes dealing with the problems. Six major pieces of legislation were enacted between 1933 and 1940 with one additional major enactment in 1970. Federal securities law consists mainly of the Securities Act of 1933,[1] the Securities Exchange Act of 1934,[2] the Public Utility Holding Company Act of 1935,[3] the Trust Indenture Act of 1939,[4] the Investment Company Act of 1940,[5] the Investment Advisers Act of 1940,[6] and the Securities Investor Protection Act of 1970.[7] Of these seven pieces of federal legislation, tax exempt organizations are likely to encounter the Securities Act of 1933, the Securities Exchange Act of 1934, the Trust Indenture Act of 1939, and the Investment Company Act of 1940.

There is a popular misconception that tax exempt organizations are also exempt from the federal securities law. The basis of the myth seems to be the section 3(a)(4)[8] exemption of charitable organizations from the provisions of the Securities Act of 1933 and the exclusion of certain charitable organizations from the definition of an investment company in the Investment Company Act of 1940.[9] But, these exemptions only apply to certain charitable organizations and only for limited purposes. The rest of the federal securities law still applies to tax exempt organizations. However widespread the myth may be, potential liability may be financially devastating for the unwary who become ensnared in the web of federal securities law.

In addition to federal securities regulation, each of the states regulates issues of securities and their distribution within the boundaries of each state.

THE FEDERAL ACTS

Securities Act of 1933

The Securities Act of 1933 regulates the registration and initial sale of securities by an issuer. The primary purpose of the act is to provide full disclosure of all material facts so that the investor may make an informed decision concerning the investment.

Section 5[10] of the Securities Act makes it unlawful to offer for sale or to sell, in interstate commerce or through the mail, a security that is subject to the act unless a registration statement has been filed with the Securities and Exchange Commission and a prospectus has been provided to potential purchasers of the security.

Section 11[11] of the Securities Act provides for civil liability for misstatements or omissions of material facts in the registration statement. This liability extends to the issuer, underwriters, directors, every person who has signed the registration statement, and specialists or professionals who prepared or certified part of the registration statement.

Section 12[12] of the Securities Act provides a private cause of action for damages by a purchaser against a seller who offers or sells a security in violation of section 5 or who makes an untrue statement of or omits a material fact by means of the prospectus or any oral communication.

Section 17[13] of the Securities Act is a general antifraud provision which applies to the sale of any security whether it is required to be registered or not.

Securities Exchange Act of 1934

Unlike the Securities Act of 1933, which is devoted exclusively to registration and initial distribution of securities issues, the Securities Exchange Act is a hodgepodge. Among other things, the act establishes the Securities and Exchange Commission;[14] requires registration of reporting companies;[15] regulates and requires registration of national exchanges,[16] brokers and dealers, and their associations;[17] regulates secondary distributions;[18] regulates certain intracorporate financial affairs;[19] and contains antifraud provisions.[20]

Section 10[21] of the Securities Exchange Act and its progeny, rule 10b-5[22] have been the workhorses for redressing fraud and misrepresentation in the sale or purchase of a security. Section 10 provides an implied private cause of action for damages to anyone who can prove the necessary elements of a violation of section 10 or rule 10b-5. It is broadly applied to all sales or purchases in interstate commerce or the mails whether the security is registered or not and is in addition to other remedies.

Trust Indenture Act of 1939

Certain debt securities even though registered under the Securities Act of 1933 may not be issued unless they are issued under a trust indenture which qualifies under the Trust Indenture Act of 1939. The act provides for minimum qualifications for corporate trustees with respect to minimum combined capital and surplus.[23] The trust indenture must also contain the powers and duties which the trustee must exercise in the event of default by the issuer.[24]

Investment Company Act of 1940

Publicly owned companies that are primarily engaged in the business of investing, reinvesting, or trading in securities are investment companies regulated by the Investment Company Act of 1940. Excluded from the definition of an investment company are companies organized and operated exclusively for religious, educational, benevolent, fraternal, charitable, or reformatory purposes, in which no part of the net earnings inures to the benefit of any private shareholder or individual.[25] Other tax exempt organizations may be subject to the act.

Investment Advisers Act of 1940

The Investment Advisers Act of 1940 regulates the capital structure of investment companies and the composition of their managements. The Securities and Exchange Commission must approve advisory contacts, changes in investment policy, and transactions between the investment company and its directors, officers, or affiliates. Management compensation and sales charges became subject to supervision following the 1970 amendment.

DEFINITION OF A SECURITY

Although tax exempt organizations, as a rule, do not issue stock or shares in the traditional sense, the definition of a security is far broader than stock or shares and encompasses many instruments issued by tax exempt organizations. The definition of a security is critical since none of the federal securities laws applies if the instrument is not in fact a security. If the instrument is a security, it must be registered unless it is otherwise exempt; however, the antifraud provisions apply whether registration is required or not.

The starting point is section 2(1) of the Securities Act of 1933,[26] which defines a security as

any note, stock, treasury stock, bond, debenture, evidence of indebtedness, certificate of interest or participation in any profit-sharing agreement, collateral-trust certificate, pre-organization certificate or subscription, transferable share, investment contract, voting-trust certificate, certificate of deposit for a security, fractional undivided interest in oil, gas, or other mineral rights, or, in general, any interest or instrument commonly known as a security, or any certificate of interest or participation in, temporary or interim certificate for, receipt for, guarantee of, or warrant or right to subscribe to or purchase, any of the foregoing.

A share of stock by definition is a security; however, the mere designation of a certificate as stock does not necessarily make it a security. In *United Housing Foundation v. Forman*,[27] United Housing required each prospective purchaser of low-cost housing to buy eighteen shares of stock for each room desired. The instruments were identified on their face as stock. The Supreme Court refused to consider the instruments to be securities merely because they were called stock, reasserting disregard of form for substance and placing the emphasis on economic reality.[28] Since the "stock" had none of the attributes of stock such as the right to receive dividends, the right to vote, appreciation in value, free transferability, and right to pledge or hypothecate, it was not a security but rather a security deposit.[29] The economic reality test has been used in one line of cases which holds that notes evidencing ordinary bank loans are not securities because they are commercial transactions rather than investments.[30]

The touchstone for whether or not an instrument is a security is *SEC v. W.J. Howey*.[31] The issue in *Howey* was whether a land sales contract and service contract involving orange groves in Florida constituted an investment contract which is a security as defined in section 2(1) of the Securities Act. The test promulgated by the Supreme Court in *Howey* is whether "the person invests his money in a common enterprise and is led to expect profits solely from the efforts of the promoter or a third party."[32] The last part of the test dealing with the efforts of others has been modified in subsequent decisions to read "the efforts made by those other than the investor are the undeniably significant ones, those essential managerial efforts which affect the failure or success of the enterprise."[33] While the *Howey* case involved an investment contract, the *Howey* test is generally applicable to any security.

Freely transferable memberships in recreational facilities may be securities. In *Riveria Operating Co.*[34] memberships in a tennis club and in *Great Western Campers Association*[35] memberships in a campers' association which were freely transferable but did not convey a right to share in gains or losses of the nonprofit corporation were not exempt because of the free transferability characteristic.

REGISTRATION

The thrust of the Securities Act of 1933 is to provide the ordinary investor with all relevant and material facts necessary to make an informed investment decision. Hence, registration is a disclosure process designed to elicit that information for the benefit of the investor. Unlike many state securities commissions the Securities and Exchange Commission does not pass on the worth or desirability of a particular issue.

The registration statement is really two documents: the prospectus is the selling document provided to all potential purchasers, and Part II contains other information and exhibits not furnished to potential purchasers but kept on file by the commission and made available for public inspection. Section 7[36] of the Securities Act of 1933 prescribes the information which must be included in the registration statement while section 10[37] prescribes the information which must be included in the prospectus.

Registration is accomplished by filing one of the prescribed forms. Form S-1 is the basic form required for registration when no other form is prescribed or authorized. Form S-1 requires the greatest degree of disclosure of all registration forms primarily because the users of Form S-1 have little or no previous contact with the Securities and Exchange Commission.

In 1979, the commission adopted a new form S-18 for use by small issuers. The disclosure requirements are essentially the same as for form S-1 except that the format is simpler and it is not keyed to regulation S-K[38] which regulates disclosure requirements under both the Securities Act of 1933 and the Securities Exchange Act of 1934. Form S-18 may be used only by issuers who are not registered under the Securities Exchange Act of 1934 and only for cash offerings of $5 million or less. Form S-18 may be filed at the nearest commission regional office rather than with the commission in Washington, D.C.

In addition to the forms and instructions contained within it, regulation C, which consists of rules 400 to 485,[39] provides registration procedures and general forms. Registration is a time-consuming, expensive, and complex task not to be undertaken lightly.

Section 8(a)[40] of the Securities Act of 1933 provides that a registration statement becomes effective twenty days after it is filed with the commission. Once the registration statement is effective, the issuer may begin to sell the securities. However, most registration statements do not automatically become effective. The commission expends an enormous amount of its resources on reviewing registration statements. In practice, the commission staff will issue a letter of comment or deficiency letter concerning changes, deletions, or additions or will request other materials prior to making further comment. The twenty-day waiting period begins anew with each change or amendment.

The heart of the Securities Act of 1933 is section 5 which is difficult reading as a result of the amendment process altering the chronological order of the section. There are two dates to keep in mind: the registration filing date and the effective date of the registration.

Section 5(c) prohibits any offer to sell or offer to buy from being made before the filing date except for negotiations between the issuer and underwriters or among the underwriters. No offer may be made to dealers or made by dealers. Between the filing date and the effective date, offers may be made but not sales. While no restrictions are placed on oral offers, an offer in writing is a prospectus and must comply with the requirements of section 10. Rule 431[41] provides for a preliminary prospectus which may be used in the waiting period, and rule 134[42] allows "tombstone ads" so named because of the black borders generally placed around these notices.

After the effective date, offers and sales may be made to anyone, provided that a prospectus is delivered on any sale of securities which is part of an underwriter's unsold public offering and on resales by dealers within a specified time period following the beginning of the public offering.

Exemptions from Registration

Charitable Organizations

Section 3(a)(4)[43] of the Securities Act of 1933 exempts from registration "any security issued by a person organized and operated exclusively for religious, educational, benevolent, fraternal, charitable, or reformatory purposes and not for pecuniary profit, and no part of the net earnings of which inures to the benefit of any person, private stockholder, or individual."

To be exempt from registration under the Securities Act of 1933, an organization must meet the same standards that it does for tax exempt status. They must meet both the exclusive organizational and operational test and the nondistribution prohibition.

The Securities and Exchange Commission brought an action against Children's Hospital of Phoenix, Arizona, to stop the distribution of 8 percent first mortgage bonds that the hospital did not register.[44] The hospital did not claim that the bonds were exempt from registration under section 3(a)(4). Since the burden of proof of the exemption is on the person asserting it, the hospital failed to carry its burden of proof. The court went on to discuss the section 3(a)(4) exemption in terms of the requirement that the organization must be exclusively organized and operated for charitable purposes. Any substantial noncharitable purpose would disqualify the organization from taking advantage of the section 3(a)(4) exemption. The court found a substantial purpose of the promoters to be self-enrichment. An organization must establish that it is not organized or operated for the benefit of private purposes. Failure to do so means loss of the benefits of the exemption.

In another case American Foundation for Advanced Education of Arkansas, a nonprofit corporation, sold debenture bonds which in exchange for $100,000 gave the purchaser the privilege of naming a beneficiary of the foundation, typically a member of the purchaser's family. The debentures were not registered with the Securities and Exchange Commission because the foundation maintained that they were exempt from registration under section 3(a)(4). The court held that the profits were returned to the members by the designation of a family member as a beneficiary of the foundation. Since the private inurement prohibition was violated, the debentures were not exempt from registration.[45]

Section 3(a)(4) is intended to facilitate fund raising by eleemosynary issuers and not to allow promotors or managers to issue securities without registration for their own private benefit.[46]

Small Offerings

Section 3(b)[47] of the Securities Act of 1933 gives the commission the authority to exempt certain securities from registration by rules and regulations provided that registration is not in the public interest or for the protection of the investor and that the aggregate amount of the issue is $5 million or less. Small offerings are included in regulation D along with private offerings.

Private Offerings

Section 4[48] of the Securities Act of 1933 provides for transactional exemptions as opposed to providing an exemption for a class of securities. Section 4(2) exempts transactions by an issuer not involving any public offering.

The bulk of private placements are with institutional investors which is consistent with the policy underlying the section 4(2) exemption. Registration is required to provide the ordinary investor with information he could not otherwise obtain; therefore, investors who have access to the same kind of information that registration would disclose and who are sophisticated investors do not require the protection of the Securities Act of 1933.

To facilitate private offerings, the Securities and Exchange Commission issued rule 146[49] in 1974. Rule 146 was a safe-harbor provision but was not the exclusive means by which a section 4(2) exemption could be obtained. Rule 146 was not workable; therefore, to simplify matters rule 146 was repealed in 1982 and regulation D was adopted.

Regulation D

Regulation D consists of rules 501 to 506.[50] No general solicitation or general offering is permitted under regulation D. Since the purchase of a security under regulation D is not purchased in a public offering, it cannot be resold without registration unless another exemption is available under section 4(1)[51] or rule 144.[52]

Rule 504 allows an issuer to sell an aggregate of $500,000 of securities in any twelve-month period to any number of purchasers without providing any information to the purchasers. The offer must be made in states that require registration of the securities and a disclosure document to be delivered to purchasers prior to sale. Any issuer except an investment company or company registered under the Securities Exchange Act of 1934 may use this exemption.

Rule 505 allows aggregate sales up to $5 million in any twelve-month period to any number of accredited investors and up to thirty-five other purchasers. An accredited investor is defined in rule 501 as follows.

1. Any bank, insurance company, investment company, or employee benefit plan

2. Any business development company

3. Any charitable or educational institution having assets of more than $5 million

4. Any director, executive officer, or general partner of the issuer

5. Any person who purchases at least $150,000 of the offered securities, provided such purchase does not exceed 20 percent of his net worth

6. Any person with a net worth of more than $1 million

7. Any person with an annual income of more than $200,000

If there are any nonaccredited purchasers, then the following information required by rule 502 must be furnished to all purchasers: (1) if the issuer is not registered under the Securities Exchange Act of 1934, (a) the information contained on form S-18 or (b) if the offering exceeds $5 million, the information required on a registration statement on the form that the issuer is entitled to use; (2) if the issuer is registered under the Securities Exchange Act, (a) the most recent annual report to shareholders and proxy statement or (b) updated information contained in the last annual report to the commission. Rule 505 is not available to an investment company or an issuer disqualified from using regulation A by rule 252.[53]

Rule 506 provides that any issuer may sell an unlimited amount of securities to any number of accredited investors and up to thirty-five other purchasers if, prior to the sale, the issuer reasonably believes that each nonaccredited purchaser or his purchaser representative has such knowledge or experience in financial and business matters that he is capable of evaluating the merits and risks of the prospective investment. The information required by rule 502 must be disclosed to nonaccredited purchasers.

Notices of sales pursuant to regulation D must be filed with the commission under rule 503. An issuer who restricts sales solely to accredited investors in an aggregate amount of $5 million or less may take advantage of the section 4(6)[54] exemption as an alternative to regulation D.

Intrastate Exemption

For tax exempt organizations which are local in nature and not proximate to a state line, the intrastate exemption is available. Section 3(a)(11)[55] provides for an exemption for securities offered or sold solely to residents of a single state or territory in which the issuer is a resident and is conducting business or, if the issuer is a corporation, in which the issuer is incorporated and doing business. Intrastate offerings may make use of the mails or other interstate commerce facility. The exemption is not based on the jurisdictional requirements of the Securities Act of 1933.

The rationale for the intrastate exemption is local financing through local investment.[56] The exemption is strictly construed according to its rationale, and an offer or sale to a single nonresident destroys the exemption for all. The offering will remain exempt under the intrastate exemption if no resales are made to nonresidents for at least nine months after the initial distribution is completed.

Regulation A

Regulation A, which consists of rules 251 to 263,[57] was promulgated under the authority of section 3(b) of the Securities Act. Regulation A, however, in practice is not an exemption but rather a simplified registration process for small issues. Regulation A permits an issuer to offer a maximum of $1.5 million and any other person to offer a maximum of $100,000 of the securities during any twelve-month period.

The exemption may not be used by an issuer, underwriter, or other related person convicted of securities offenses, subjected to disciplinary action by the commission, or involved in certain other proceedings within specified periods of the issuance of the securities.

To use regulation A an offering statement must be filed with the regional office of the commission where the issuer has its principal place of business at least ten days before the offering is to begin. The offering statement must contain an offering circular which includes information similar to a prospectus but much less detailed. The "letter of comment" procedure is used for regulation A offerings as well as registration statements.

A copy of the offering circular must be provided to each person to whom a written offer is made or to whom a sale is confirmed. Civil liabilities imposed under section 11[58] do not apply to regulation A offerings because of the exemption from registration under section 3(b); however, section 12[59] liabilities may be imposed.

Antifraud Provisions

The antifraud provisions of the federal securities laws apply to securities whether they are exempt from registration or not or whether they are transactionally exempt or not. Nor is it of any consequence that the issuer is a nonprofit organization.[60] The primary antifraud provisions are section 17[61] of the Securities Act of 1933, section 10(b)[62] of the Securities Exchange Act of 1934, and section 206[63] of the Investment Advisers Act of 1940.

Section 10 and Rule 10b-5

Section 10 is the catchall provision of the Securities Exchange Act of 1934. Its purpose is to provide relief from abuses not otherwise addressed in the act. However, section 10 itself is not a self-executing provision. It is only effective through rules and regulations promulgated by the commission pursuant to the authority of section 10 to make such rules as are necessary or appropriate in the public interest or for the protection of investors. In 1942, rule 10b-5[64] was issued by the commission. Interestingly, rule 10b-5 is merely modified language of section 17(a) of the Securities Act of 1933, the principal modification being that section 17(a) only applies to sales of securities while section 10 applies to purchase or sale.

Rule 10b-5 provides that

It shall be unlawful for any person, directly or indirectly, by the use of any means or instrumentality of interstate commerce, or of the mails, or of any facility of any national securities exchange,

(1) to employ any device, scheme, or artifice to defraud,

(2) to make any untrue statement of a material fact or to omit to state a material fact necessary in order to make the statements made, in the light of the circumstances under which they were made, not misleading, or

(3) to engage in any act, practice, or course of business which operates or would operate as a fraud or deceit upon any person, in connection with the purchase or sale of any security.

Section 10 and rule 10b-5 are stated as prohibitions and give rise to administrative proceedings, suits for injunction by the commission, and criminal actions referred to the Justice Department for prosecution upon conviction for which an individual could be fined up to $10,000 or be imprisoned for a period of not more than five years, or both.[65] However, it was established as early as 1946 that there was an implied civil cause of action for damages in behalf of the defrauded victim.[66]

The elements of a cause of action under rule 10b-5 are (1) use of the mails, an instrumentality of interstate commerce, or any facility of a national securities exchange; (2) a purchase or sale of a security; (3) fraud or deceit or a misstatement or omission of a material fact; (4) scienter; (5) causation; (6) reliance; and (7) damages in a civil action. A private cause of action must be brought by a purchaser or seller.[67] This requirement is strictly applied.

Two of the three clauses of rule 10b-5 deal with fraud or deceit. Fraud does not include overreaching by a controlling shareholder unless accompanied by actual deception. A cause of action for fraud under rule 10b-5 is similar to common law fraud in that there must be a relationship between the parties which gives rise to a duty which is violated. In insider trading cases the insider by virtue of his position gains access to information intended for corporate purposes and not personal benefit. The corresponding duty is to abstain from the marketplace until the information is made public. The insider must not take unfair advantage of information unknown to persons with whom the insider is dealing. In many instances the courts are not clear as to which clause of rule 10b-5 the court is applying, particularly in insider trading cases.

Clause 2 of rule 10b-5 deals with misstatements and omissions of material facts. A fact is material if it is the kind of information that a reasonable investor would consider important in making his investment decision.[68] In the context of an untrue statement of a material fact, the intentional misstatement is akin to common law fraud. In the case of an omission of a material fact where there is a duty to disclose, an element of conjecture is introduced. The test of materiality then becomes whether the reasonable investor would have acted differently had he known of the undisclosed fact.

Since the Supreme Court's decision in *Ernst & Ernst v. Hockfelder*[69] in 1975, scienter is a requirement of a cause of action under section 10b and rule 10b-5. Scienter requires an intent to deceive, manipulate, or defraud.[70] Negligence will not support a cause of action under section 10b and rule 10b-5. The Supreme Court reserved the issue of whether recklessness was equivalent to intentional conduct.[71]

Causation is a necessary element of a cause of action under section 10b and rule 10b-5. The misrepresentation or fraud must be the proximate cause of plaintiff's loss. If the misrepresentation is of a material fact on which plaintiff relied but not the reasonable direct cause of the pecuniary loss, no recovery is allowed.

In fraud cases and cases involving affirmative misstatements of material facts, plaintiff must show actual reliance. The Court of Appeals for the Ninth Circuit, however, has held that if the misleading statement constitutes a fraud on the market, plaintiff does not have to show reliance but only that he bought or sold a security at a price which was affected by the misleading statement.[72] Non-disclosure or complete omission cases present another problem. Plaintiff would have to show that he would have relied on the facts if they were made known to him which in effect means that the omitted facts were material facts. In a nondisclosure case if the plaintiff proves materiality, he has in fact proved reliance.[73]

The measure of damages in most cases is the "out of pocket" rule. The damages award is based on the difference between what plaintiff gave up and the value of what was received in the transaction. The potential for liability is great especially in insider trading cases since liability extends to all persons who traded in the market during the time that the inside information is undisclosed.[74]

Section 17 of the Securities Act of 1933

Whether there exists an implied private cause of action for damages under section 17(a) is a matter of conflict in the different courts of appeals. The Supreme Court has left the issue unresolved.[75]

Since rule 10b-5 is a modified version of section 17(a), one would suspect that the same elements would apply to each. But there are some significant differences. Section 17(a) only applies to the sale of a security and not to a purchase. Fraud by a purchaser is not addressed by section 17(a). The Supreme Court has ruled that only the first clause of section 17(a) requires scienter while negligence will suffice for a cause of action under clauses 2 and 3.[76]

Section 206 of the Investment Advisers Act of 1940

Section 206[77] of the Investment Advisers Act of 1940 is an antifraud provision similar to section 10b and rule 10b-5 of the Securities Exchange Act of 1934 and section 17(a) of the Securities Act of 1933. Section 206 provides that

It shall be unlawful for any investment adviser, by use of the mails or any means or instrumentality of interstate commerce, directly or indirectly—

(1) to employ any device, scheme, or artifice to defraud any client or prospective client;

(2) to engage in any transaction, practice, or course of business which operates as a fraud or deceit upon any client or prospective client;

(3) acting as a principal for his own account, knowingly to sell any security to or purchase any security from a client, or acting as broker for a person other than such client, knowingly to effect any sale or purchase of any security for the account of such client, without disclosing to such client in writing before the completion of such transaction the capacity in which he is acting and obtaining the consent of the client to such transaction. The prohibitions of this paragraph shall not apply to any transaction with a customer of a broker or dealer if such broker or dealer is not acting as an investment adviser in relation to such transaction;

(4) to engage in any act, practice, or course of business which is fraudulent, deceptive, or manipulative. The Commission shall, for the purposes of this paragraph (4) by rules and regulations define, and prescribe means reasonably designed to prevent, such acts, practices, and courses of business as are fraudulent, deceptive, or manipulative.

Unlike section 10b and rule 10b-5 of the Securities Exchange Act of 1934 and possibly section 17(a) of the Securities Act of 1933, section 206 of the Investment Advisers Act of 1940 will not support an implied private cause of action for damages. In a decision in which four justices dissented, the Supreme Court held that Congress provided an express action under section 215 of the Investment Advisers Act of 1940 for recision of the contract and that there was no evidence to indicate Congress intended an implied private cause of action for damages.[78]

Actions under section 206 of the Investment Advisers Act are restricted to Securities and Exchange Commission administrative proceedings and civil or criminal suits brought by the commission.

STATE SECURITIES LAWS

Each of the four major pieces of federal securities regulation carefully preserves the rights of the states to regulate securities within their respective jurisdictions.[79] As a result any issuer contemplating a national issue must comply with the "blue sky" laws[80] of each state and the District of Columbia in addition to federal securities law.

Uniform Securities Act

The commissioners on Uniform State Laws drafted a Uniform Securities Act for adoption by the states in 1956 and amended it in 1958. Since 1956 more than thirty states (see Table 5) have adopted, in whole or in part, the Uniform Securities Act; however, national uniformity even among the adopting states is still lacking. Most states adopting the act did so with substantial changes. Over time, different state courts have interpreted the language of the uniform act differently. The large commercial states such as New York, California, Texas, and Illinois have not adopted any part of the uniform act.

Definition of a Security

The definition of a security in section 401(2) of the Uniform Securities Act is essentially the same as the definition of a security in section 2(1) of the Securities Act of 1933. The drafters of the Uniform Securities Act intended to coordinate the Uniform Securities Act with the federal securities law. There is a slight variation in the wording of the provision regarding oil, gas, and mineral rights or interests, and the last sentence of section 401(2) dealing with insurance, endowment, and annuity contracts does not appear in the federal statute.

In other states the definition of a security has taken an interesting turn. The risk capital test for investment contracts was developed by the California Supreme Court in 1961.[81] Since that decision, other states have turned to the risk capital test to avoid the restrictive nature of the *Howey* test.[82]

In the *Silver Hills Country Club* case, the promoters had purchased land on which to build and operate a country club. In order to finance the operation they sold memberships in the club which entitled the members to use the facilities but did not entitle them to share in the profits of the enterprise. The membership was likened to a beneficial interest in title to property since it was irrevocable except for misconduct or failure to pay dues. The California Supreme Court held that the memberships were securities because the members had supplied the risk capital anticipating a return for their risk—the benefits of club membership.

Table 5
State Securities Laws

State	Uniform Securities Act Adopted	Religious	Educational	Benevolent	Charitable	Fraternal	Social	Athletic	Reformatory	Chamber of Commerce - 1	Other	Filing Required	Permissive Exemption	Comment
Alabama	X	X	X	X	X	X	X	X	X	X				
Alaska	X	X	X	X	X	X	X	X	X	X				
Arizona	X	X	X	X	X	X			X					
Arkansas		X	X	X	X	X	X	X	X	X		X	X	Must be a corporation
California		X	X	X	X	X	X		X	X	X	X		Filing only applies to life income contracts
Colorado	X	X	X	X	X	X	X	X	X	X			X	
Connecticut		X	X	X	X	X	X	X	X	X			X	
Delaware	X	X	X	X	X	X	X	X	X				X	Purpose may be industrial development corporations
District of Columbia	X													
Florida		X	X	X	X	X	X	X	X		X			Must be a corporation
Georgia		X	X	X	X	X	X	X	X	X				
Hawaii	X	X	X	X	X	X	X	X	X		X			
Idaho	X	X	X	X	X	X	X	X	X	X		X	X	Purpose may be local industrial development corporation
Illinois		X	X	X	X	X	X	X	X		X		X	Purpose may be agricultural or trade
Indiana	X	X	X	X	X	X	X	X	X	X		X		
Iowa	X	X	X	X	X	X	X	X	X	X		X	X	
Kansas	X													
Kentucky		X	X	X	X	X	X	X	X	X		X	X	Purpose may be fire protection or fire fighting
Louisiana	X													
Maine		X	X	X	X	X	X	X	X	X			X	

135

Table 5 (continued)
State Securities Laws

State	Uniform Securities Act Adopted	Religious	Educational	Benevolent	Charitable	Fraternal	Social	Athletic	Reformatory	Chamber of Commerce - 1	Other	Filing Required	Permissive Exemption	Comment
Maryland	X	X	X	X	X	X	X	X	X	X			X	
Massachusetts	X	X	X	X	X	X	X	X	X	X			X	
Michigan	X	X	X	X	X	X	X	X	X	X			X	
Minnesota	X													
Mississippi		X	X	X	X	X	X	X	X	X	X	X	X	
Missouri		X	X	X	X	X	X	X	X	X		X	X	
Montana	X	X	X	X	X	X	X		X	X	X			
Nebraska	X	X	X	X	X	X	X	X	X	X				
Nevada	X	X	X	X	X	X	X		X	X	X			
New Hampshire	X	X	X	X	X	X	X		X	X				
New Jersey	X	X	X	X	X	X		X	X				X	
New Mexico	X	X	X	X	X	X	X		X	X				
New York		X	X	X	X	X		X	X	X				
North Carolina	X	X	X	X	X	X	X	X	X				X	Must be a domestic corporation
North Dakota		X	X	X	X	X	X		X		X		X	
Ohio		X				X	X	X	X					All nonprofit purposes including recreational and county

State	Notes
Oklahoma	fairs for cooperative marketing
Oregon	Filing only applies to evidence of indebtedness
Pennsylvania	Must be a domestic corporation
Rhode Island	Filing only applies to evidence of indebtedness
South Carolina	
South Dakota	Must be a domestic corporation
Tennessee	
Texas	Must be a corporation organized in Texas
Utah	
Vermont	Must be a corporation
Virginia	
Washington	
West Virginia	
Wisconsin	Must be a domestic corporation; Filing only applies to evidence of indebtedness

1 – Includes Trade and Professional Associations

Exemption

Nonprofit Organizations

Section 402(a)(9) of the Uniform Securities Act exempts the following securities:

any security issued by any person organized and operated not for private profit but exclusively for religious, educational, benevolent, charitable, fraternal, social, athletic, or reformatory purposes, or as a chamber of commerce or trade or professional operation. . . .

Some states require certain documents to be filed even though the security is exempt. It appears that in many states, as indicated in Table 5, the exemption is not mandatory but merely at the discretion of the state authorities.

Exempt Transactions

State reaction to the federal exemption for issues not involving a public offering under section 4(2) of the Securities Act of 1933 is not uniform and is uncertain after the adoption of regulation D. Some states adopted the language of section 4(2) of the Securities Act of 1933 while other states substantially adopted rule 146 in addition to the statutory language of section 4(2). Other states merely coordinate their exemption with compliance with the federal requirements.

This area of state securities law is in a state of flux following the adoption of regulation D by the Securities and Exchange Commission. The reader should check the latest requirements for particular states.

Registration

Part III of the Uniform Securities Act provides for registration of a security prior to offer or sale of the security. There are three alternative registration procedures: notification, coordination, and qualification.

Notification

Section 302 of the Uniform Securities Act provides for registration by notification. This is the simplest of the three registration procedures. To qualify for registration by notification the issuer must (1) have been in continuous operation for at least five years; (2) not have defaulted in the payment of principal, interest, or dividends of any security within the three fiscal years immediately preceding the registration; and (3) show an average earnings of at least 5 percent on its shares of common stock.

The registration form must contain the following information:

1. Name and address of the issuer
2. Issuer's form of organization
3. State in which organized
4. Date of organization
5. Character of the business
6. Description of the security
7. Offering price
8. Existence of any stock options
9. Certain financial data

A copy of the prospectus or other sales materials must accompany the registration form.

Registration by notification takes place at 3:00 P.M. on the second full business day after filing or sooner if the state authority so determines, provided no stop order is in effect.

Coordination

Coordination is available to an issuer who has filed a registration statement relating to the same offering with the Securities and Exchange Commission under the provisions of the Securities Act of 1933.

Registration by coordination is accomplished by filing the required number of copies of the federal prospectus with the state authorities.

Registration by coordination is automatically effective at the same time that the federal registration is effective, provided there is no stop order in effect, the registration statement has been on file with the state for at least ten days, and a statement regarding proposed offering prices and underwriter discounts and commissions has been on file with the state for at least two full business days unless otherwise waived by the state.

Qualification

Section 304 of the Uniform Securities Act provides for registration by qualification which is to be used by issuers who do not qualify for notification or coordination. The filing requirements for registration by qualification are roughly similar to registration under the Securities Act of 1933. Registration by qualification is not effective until approved by the state authority.

Under the Uniform Securities Act sections 306(a)(2)(E) and (F), registration may be denied if the offering tends to work a fraud upon purchasers or if underwriting compensation, promoter's profits, or options are unreasonable in amount.

Antifraud Provisions

As is the case with the antifraud provisions of the federal securities law, antifraud provisions of the state securities law represent a relaxation of the more stringent requirements of common law fraud. The manifestation of this proposition is contained in section 401(d) of the Uniform Securities Act which provides that " 'Fraud,' 'deceit,' and 'defraud,' are not limited to common law deceit."

The antifraud provision of the Uniform Securities Act bears a striking resemblance to sections 12 and 17(a) of the Securities Act of 1933 and rule 10b-5 under the Securities Exchange Act of 1934. Section 101 of the Uniform Securities Act provides

It is unlawful for any person, in connection with the offer, sale or purchase of any security, directly or indirectly
(1) to employ any device, scheme, or artifice to defraud,
(2) to make any untrue statement of a material fact or to omit to state a material fact necessary in order to make the statements made, in the light of the circumstances under which they are made, not misleading or,
(3) to engage in any act, practice, or course of business which operates or would operate as a fraud or deceit upon any person.

All of the states except New Hampshire authorize the state authority to bring suit for an injunction against fraudulent conduct in the sale of a security, and most states extend that power to the purchase of a security.

The Uniform Securities Act provides only for a cause of action by a defrauded purchaser against his seller and makes no provision for a cause of action by a defrauded seller against his purchaser.[83] This rule is adopted by a majority of the states. New York and Rhode Island make no provision for a private civil cause of action; however, in New York a private civil cause of action may be implied.[84]

The elements of a cause of action for fraud under state securities law are essentially the same as under federal securities law; however, there are some important differences. The scienter requirement which has played an important role in the development of federal rule 10b-5 is treated quite differently under state law. The scienter requirement exists as an element of a civil action, but the burden of proof is shifted from the defrauded purchaser to the seller to prove that the seller was unaware of any misrepresentation or omission of material facts and in the exercise of reasonable care could not have known of any.[85] The reasonable care standard means that negligence is sufficient scienter.

Common law reliance is not required as an element of a civil fraud case under state law; however, the buyer must show that he did not know of the untruths or omission to recover.[86] Purchaser's reliance generally must be reasonable,[87] but some states allow a purchaser to accept the statements made at face value and rely on them.[88]

Generally, materiality is the same under both federal and state securities law utilizing the reasonable man test that the representation be one to which the reasonable man would take into consideration or attach importance in determining his course of action.

The express civil cause of action in most states is granted to the purchaser as against his seller. The remedies granted to a successful plaintiff are recision of the sale or suit for damages if he no longer owns the securities. The Uniform Securities Act and state securities law require privity of contract between the purchaser and seller. The antifraud provisions of state securities law are more in the nature of the express civil liability provision of section 12 rather than section 17(a) of the Securities Act of 1933 or section 10(b) and rule 10b-5 of the Securities Exchange Act of 1934 which support a civil cause of action by any person whether in privity of contract or not. Since section 410(h) of the Uniform Securities Act provides that no cause of action not specified therein may be created, a parallel development of implied civil causes of action for damages to rule 10b-5 is foreclosed.

NOTES

1. 15 U.S.C. §§ 77a *et seq.*
2. 15 U.S.C. §§ 78a *et seq.*
3. 15 U.S.C. §§ 79-79Z-6.
4. 15 U.S.C. §§ 77aaa-77bbbb.
5. 15 U.S.C. §§ 80a-1-80a-52.
6. 15 U.S.C. §§ 80b-1-80b-21.
7. 15 U.S.C. §§ 78aaa *et seq.*
8. 15 U.S.C. § 77c(a)(4).
9. Section 3(c)(10), 15 U.S.C. § 80a-3(c)(10).
10. 15 U.S.C. § 77e.
11. 15 U.S.C. § 77k.
12. 15 U.S.C. § 77l.
13. 15 U.S.C. § 77q.
14. 15 U.S.C. § 78d.
15. 15 U.S.C. § 78l.
16. 15 U.S.C. § 78f.
17. 15 U.S.C. § 78o.
18. 15 U.S.C. § 78e & k.
19. 15 U.S.C. § 78m, n, & p.
20. 15 U.S.C. §§ 78i, j, & s.
21. 15 U.S.C. § 78j.
22. 17 C.F.R. § 240.10b-5.
23. 15 U.S.C. § 77jjj.
24. 15 U.S.C. § 77ppp.
25. 15 U.S.C. § 80a-3(c)(10).

26. 15 U.S.C. § 77b(1).

27. 421 U.S. 837 (1975).

28. 421 U.S. 837, 848 (1975).

29. 421 U.S. 837, 851 (1975).

30. *See, e.g., C.N.S. Enterprises v. G & G Enterprises,* 508 F.2d 1354 (7th Cir. 1975); *McClure v. First Nat'l Bank,* 497 F.2d 490 (5th Cir. 1974).

31. 328 U.S. 293 (1946).

32. 328 U.S. 293, 301 (1946).

33. *SEC v. Glenn W. Turner Enterprises,* 474 F.2d 476, 482 (9th Cir.), *cert. denied,* 414 U.S. 82 (1973).

34. F. Sec. L. Rep. (CCH) ¶ 81, 569 (March 8, 1978).

35. F. Sec. L. Rep. (CCH) [1971–72 Transfer Binder] ¶ 78,386.

36. 15 U.S.C. § 77g.

37. 15 U.S.C. § 77j.

38. 17 C.F.R. part 229.

39. 17 C.F.R. § 230.400 - 230.485.

40. 15 U.S.C. § 77h(a).

41. 17 C.F.R. § 230.431.

42. 17 C.F.R. § 230.134.

43. 15 U.S.C. § 77c(a)(4).

44. 214 F.Supp. 883 (D. Ariz. 1963).

45. 222 F.Supp. 828, 831 (W.D. La. 1963).

46. 214 F.Supp. 883, 891 (D. Ariz. 1963).

47. 15 U.S.C. § 77c(b).

48. 15 U.S.C. § 77d.

49. 17 C.F.R. § 230.146.

50. 17 C.F.R. §§ 230.501 - 230.506.

51. 15 U.S.C. § 77d(1).

52. 17 C.F.R. § 230.144.

53. 17 C.F.R. § 230.252.

54. 15 U.S.C. § 77d(6).

55. 15 U.S.C. § 77c(a)(11).

56. Sec. Act Rel. No. 5450.

57. 17 C.F.R. §§ 230.251 - 230.263.

58. 15 U.S.C. § 77k.

59. 15 U.S.C. § 77l.

60. *SEC v. World Radio Mission, Inc.,* 544 F.2d 535 (1st Cir. 1976).

61. 15 U.S.C. § 77q.

62. 15 U.S.C. § 78j.

63. 15 U.S.C. § 80b-6.

64. 17 C.F.R. § 240.10b-5.

65. Section 32, 15 U.S.C. § 78ff.

66. *Kardon v. National Gypsum Co.,* 69 F.Supp. 512 (E.D. Pa. 1946).

67. *Blue Chip Stamps v. Manor Drug Stores,* 421 U.S. 723 (1975).

68. *TSC Industries, Inc. v. Northway, Inc.,* 426 U.S. 438 (1976).

69. 425 U.S. 185 (1976).

70. *Id.* at 194 n.12.

71. 425 U.S. 185, 193–94 n. 12.

72. *Blackie v. Barrack,* 524 F.2d 891 (9th Cir. 1975).

73. *Affiliated Ute Citizens of Utah v. U.S.,* 406 U.S. 128 (1972), *reh. denied,* 407 U.S. 916.

74. *Shapiro v. Merrill Lynch, Pierce, Fenner & Smith, Inc.,* 495 F.2d 228 (2d Cir. 1974).

75. *Blue Chip Stamps v. Manor Drug Stores,* 421 U.S. 723, 733 n.6 (1975).

76. *Aaron v. SEC,* 446 U.S. 680, 695–700 (1980).

77. 15 U.S.C. § 80b-6.

78.*Transamerica Mortgage Advisors, Inc. v. Lewis,* 444 U.S. 11 (1979).

79. Section 18, Securities Act of 1933, 15 U.S.C. § 77r; Section 28(a) Securities Exchange Act of 1934, 15 U.S.C. § 78bb(a); Section 49, Investment Companies Act of 1940, 15 U.S.C. § 80a-49; Section 222, Investment Advisers Act of 1940, 15 U.S.C. § 80b-18a.

80. So called because of the reference to "blue sky" in *Hall v. Geiger-Jones Co.,* 242 U.S. 539 (1917).

81. *Silver Hills Country Club v. Sobieski,* 55 Cal. 2d 811, 13 Cal. Rptr. 186, 361 P.2d 906 (1961).

82. Alaska, Florida, Georgia, Hawaii, Michigan, Oklahoma, Oregon.

83. Section 410(a)(2), Uniform Securities Act.

84. *Barnes v. Peat, Marwick, Mitchell & Co.,* 69 Misc. 2d 1068, 332 N.Y.S.2d 281 (1972), *modified on other grounds,* 42 A.D.2d 15, 344 N.Y.S.2d 645 (1973).

85. Section 410(a)(2), Uniform Securities Act.

86. *Id.*

87. *S & F Supply Co. v. Hunter,* 527 P.2d 217 (Utah Sup. 1974).

88. *Kaas v. Privette,* 12 Wash. App. 152, 529 P.2d 23 (1974).

8

Operations

ORGANIZATIONAL MEETINGS

The organizational meetings are held following the issuance of the certificate of authority by the secretary of state, corporation commissioner, or other designated state authority. The corporation exists but is not operational until the organizational meetings are held. The initial meetings may include a meeting of the incorporators, a meeting of the initial directors, and a meeting of the members. The statutes vary as to whether or not an organizational meeting is mandatory, which group is required or authorized to meet, and when the group is required to meet. Table 6 outlines these provisions for each state.

The primary purposes of the organizational meeting are to adopt the by-laws and to hold elections. Depending on the constituency of the organizational meeting, the election may be for directors or officers. An organizational meeting should be held whether it is required by the statute or not because there is the risk of a *quo warranto* proceeding being brought by the state for failure of the corporation to organize or to use its power or for inactivity.

To avoid later difficulties, meetings should be held on proper call and proper notice. The organizational meeting may be called by the attorney who incorporated the organization, one of the incorporators, a director, or one or more members. Notice of the meeting should be in writing. A copy of the notice should be retained and included in the minute book with an affidavit by the sender stating to whom and when it was sent. In practice a waiver of notice is often used instead of prior written notice. The waiver may be signed before or after the meeting. Unless the corporation act prohibits its use, the waiver is valid and effective. The signed waiver of notice should be included in the minute book at the organizational meeting.

Table 6
Organizational Meeting

State	Meeting Called by		Place		Days Notice Required by Statute	Authority
	Incorporator	Director	Within State	Outside State		
Alabama	x		x		3	§ 10-3-21
Alaska					3	§ 10.20.166
Arizona	x		x	x	3	§ 10-1032
Arkansas						No provision
California						No provision
Colorado					3	§ 7-21-105
Connecticut					5	§ 33-431
Delaware					2	tit. 8 § 108
District of Columbia			x	x	5	§ 29-1033
Florida						No provision
Georgia					3	§ 22-2705
Hawaii						No provision
Idaho					3	§ 30-324
Illinois	x		x	x	3	ch. 32, § 163a31
Indiana	x				10	§ 23-7-1.1-21
Iowa	x		x	x	3	§ 504A.33
Kansas						No provision
Kentucky	x		x	x	3	§ 273.257
Louisiana						No provision
Maine	x	x			3	§ 406(3)
Maryland						No provision
Massachusetts						No provision
Michigan		x			3	§ 450.2223
Minnesota	x	x				§ 317.14
Mississippi						No provision
Missouri	x		x	x	3	§ 355.060
Montana	x		x	x	3	§ 35-2-205
Nebraska	x		x	x	3	§ 21-1931
Nevada						No provision
New Hampshire						No provision
New Jersey					10	§ 15:1-12
New Mexico	x		x	x	3	§ 53-8-34
New York	x	x	x	x	5	N-PCL § 405
North Carolina		x			3	§ 55A-22
North Dakota	x		x	x	3	§ 10-24-32
Ohio					2	§ 1702.31
Oklahoma	x	x				tit. 18, § 859
Oregon	x		x	x	3	§ 61.325
Pennsylvania	x	x	x	x	5	15 § 7320
Rhode Island	x				5	§ 7-6-6
South Carolina						No provision
South Dakota	x		x	x	3	§ 47-22-31

Table 6 (continued)
Organizational Meeting

State	Meeting Called by		Place		Days Notice Required by Statute	Authority
	Incorporator	Director	Within State	Outside State		
Tennessee						No provision
Texas	x		x	x	3	Art. 1396-3.05
Utah						No provision
Vermont	x		x	x	3	§ 2405
Virginia	x		x	x	3	§ 13.1-234
Washington	x		x	x	3	§ 24.06.180
West Virginia	x		x	x	3	§ 31-1-30
Wisconsin	x		x	x	3	§ 181.34
Wyoming	x		x	x	3	§ 17-6-107

Some corporation acts specify the notice period; however, to avoid disputes a notice period contained in the articles of incorporation or by-laws which otherwise complies with the corporation act must be adhered to. A period of notice of at least ten days is generally safe.

Since the purpose of the organizational meeting is to complete the incorporation process and begin operations, the meeting is generally held in the state of incorporation. Some states allow the organizational meeting to be held outside the state of incorporation. In practice many organizational meetings are held in the office of the attorney who incorporated the organization.

Although no formal procedure is required for the organizational meeting, certain agenda items must be addressed to start operations. Some type of parliamentary procedure should be adopted to facilitate the process. *Robert's Rules of Order* is popular and widely available; *Oleck's Parliamentary Law for Nonprofit Organizations* was designed specifically for the needs of nonprofit organizations.[1]

The following agenda items should be accomplished at the organizational meeting although not necessarily in the following order:

1. Election of temporary chairperson and secretary of the organizational meeting

2. Signing of waiver of notice or filing of copy of formal written notice with the secretary

3. Presentation of minute book and filing of articles and certificate of incorporation therein

4. Adoption of by-laws

5. Election of directors or trustees

6. Election of officers if required by by-laws

7. Meeting is turned over to duly elected directors and officers replacing temporary chairperson and secretary

8. Adoption of corporate seal

9. Authorization to apply for tax exemption

10. Authorization for bank account and bonding of treasurer

11. Designation or confirmation of agent for service of process

12. Membership matters such as dues, acceptance, and qualifications

13. Authorization to pay expenses of organization

14. Authorization and direction to file required reports

15. Adoption of accounting conventions such as fiscal year and accounting methods

16. Set the date and place for subsequent meetings

The organizational meeting of the directors or trustees customarily follows the general organizational meeting. The following agenda is usually followed:

1. Signing waiver of notice or filing of formal written notice

2. Election of chairperson, if not already done

3. Read minutes of general organizational meeting

4. Read by-laws

5. Election of officers, if necessary

6. Set compensation of officers, if necessary

7. Acceptance of contracts or agreements or authorization to enter into contracts in accordance with by-laws

8. Appointment of committees and assignment of tasks

9. New business

10. Set date for next meeting in accordance with by-laws

11. Adjourn

By-Laws

By-laws may be adopted by unincorporated associations as well as by incorporated organizations although they are typically associated more with the latter. Just as the articles of incorporation constitute the relationship between the state and the nonprofit corporation, the by-laws establish the internal relationships of the corporation. By-laws are necessary for frictionless operation but are not always required by the state corporation act although in most instances are assumed under the act. The by-laws regulate the internal management of the organization and define the powers, duties, and relationships among members, directors, and officers or agents. The nature of the relationships is one of contract, and the relationships are binding on the parties accepting them as members. Ordinarily the by-laws have no binding effect on third parties.

Generally, if an organization has members, the power to adopt or amend the by-laws rests with the membership; otherwise, the power rests with the board of directors or trustees. Provisions for each state are outlined in Table 7. The members may delegate their power to alter or amend the by-laws to the board of directors or trustees. By-laws are amended in accordance with the articles of incorporation if addressed there or pursuant to provisions of the by-laws themselves. Amendment usually requires notice and conformance with the established voting requirement at a formal meeting of the authorized group.

The by-laws should contain those items which are appropriate for the particular organizations. The model by-laws prepared by the Committee on Nonprofit Corporations of the American Bar Association which drafted the Model Nonprofit Corporation Act (1964) are set out in an appendix to this chapter.

REGULAR AND SPECIAL MEETINGS

Members' Meetings

Generally, the members of a nonprofit organization meet sometime during the year to elect directors or trustees and consider certain reports. Some state statutes require meetings of the members; other state statutes do not.

Under certain circumstances a meeting of the members is required. Members' approval or vote must be obtained for the following:

1. Election of trustees or directors, if so provided in the by-laws
2. Adoption or amendment of by-laws or articles of incorporation unless otherwise provided
3. Sale or lease of real property or encumbering real property
4. Guaranteeing obligations of others
5. Making substantial grants or donations of the assets
6. Voluntary dissolution
7. Other acts required by articles of incorporation or by-laws

Proper notice of a regular or special members' meeting should be given and in fact is prescribed by statute for certain transactions. Formal written notice must

Table 7
By-Laws

State	Statutory Power to Adopt — Incorporators	Directors	Members	Statutory Power to Amend — Directors	Members	Power to Change Statutory Rule in Articles of Incorporation or by-laws	Quorum to Adopt	Vote Required to Adopt	Authority
Alabama		X		X		X	M	M	§§ 10-3-24, 10-3-65
Alaska		X		X		X		M	§§ 10.20.106, 10.20.056
Arizona		X		X		X	M	M	§§ 10-1012, 10-1020
Arkansas									No provision
California		X	X	X	X	X			Cal. Corp. Code 5150
Colorado									No provision
Connecticut									No provision
Delaware	X	X		X		X			tit. 8, § 109
District of Columbia		X		X		X			§ 29-1013
Florida									No provision
Georgia		X		X		X			§ 22-2706
Hawaii			X	X		X		M	§ 416-79
Idaho		X	X	X	X	X			§ 30-309
Illinois		X		X		X	M	M	Ch. 32, § 163a8, 163a19
Indiana		X		X		X			§§ 23-7-1.1-21, 23-7-1.1-8
Iowa		X		X		X	M	M	§§ 504A.12, 504A.20
Kansas									No provision
Kentucky		X		X		X	M	M	§§ 273.191, 273.217
Louisiana		X	X	X	X	X		M	§ 222
Maine		X		X		X	M		§§ 601, 706
Maryland									No provision
Massachusetts									No provision
Michigan	X	X	X	X	X	X	M		§ 450.2223
Minnesota		X		X	X	X		*	§§ 317.14, 317.15, 317.24
Mississippi									No provision
Missouri		X		X		X	M	M	§§ 355.100, 355.150
Montana		X		X		X	M	M	§§ 35-2-404, 35-2-211
Nebraska		X		X		X	M	M	§§ 21-1911, 21-1919
Nevada			X	X		X		M	§ 81.080
New Hampshire	X							100%	§ 292:6
New Jersey						X			§ 15:1-7
New Mexico		X		X		X	M	M	§§ 53-8-12, 53-8-20

Table 7 (continued)
By-Laws

State	Statutory Power to Adopt — Incorporators	Directors	Members	Statutory Power to Amend — Directors	Members	Power to Change Statutory Rule in Articles of Incorporation or by-laws	Quorum to Adopt	Vote Required to Adopt	Authority
New York	X	X		X		X	M	M	N-PCL §§ 405, 602
North Carolina		X		X		X	M	M	§§ 55A-14, 55A-22
North Dakota		X		X		X	M	M	§§ 10-24-12, 10-24-20
Ohio	X		X			X	M	M	§§ 1702.10, 1702.32
Oklahoma		X			X				tit. 18, § 859
Oregon		X		X		X	M	M	§§ 61.095, 61.135
Pennsylvania	X	X			X	X	M	M	15, §§ 7727, 7320, 7504
Rhode Island									No provision
South Carolina									No provision
South Dakota		X		X		X	M	M	§ 47-22-33
Tennessee									No provision
Texas		X			X	X	M	M	Art. 1396-2.09, 1396-2.17
Utah				X	X		M	M	§§ 16-6-37, 16-6-44
Vermont		X		X	X	X	M	M	§§ 2359, 2367
Virginia		X		X		X	M	M	§§ 13.1-212, 13.1-223
Washington		X		X		X	M	M	§§ 24.06.095, 24.06.140
West Virginia		X		X		X	M	M	§ 31-1-17
Wisconsin		X			X		M	M	§§ 181.13, 181.22
Wyoming		X		X		X			§ 17-6-107

M - Majority
* - A majority of the members but if no voting members 2/3 of the board of directors.

specify the time and place and the purposes of the meeting as provided in the by-laws or statute. The statutory minimum notice requirements control in the event of conflict.

Alternatively, the members may sign a waiver of notice before, during, or after a meeting. This is risky. Disenchanted members may refuse to sign and seek to have the results of the meeting invalidated for lack of proper notice; however, attendance at the meeting without protest constitutes waiver by conduct in some states.[2] Waiver by conduct is not applicable if the lack of notice made it impossible for the member to act as he desired even if the member participated.[3]

The voting requirements are set either by statute or the articles of incorporation or the by-laws and vary from state to state and organization to organization. Generally, the membership list determines who has the right to vote.[4] Any disputes as to who has the right to vote are decided at the meeting where the vote is to take place.[5]

Voting by proxy is allowed in some states and prohibited in others as indicated in Table 8.

A one-member–one-vote rule is in effect in most jurisdictions. Some states permit cumulative voting. For example, if three directors are to be elected, under a cumulative voting system each member has three votes to cast as he chooses. All three may be cast for the same person or allocated among the three candidates. Table 9 gives these specifications for each state.

Minimum quorum requirements for a members' meeting are generally set by statute. Requiring a higher quorum may be provided for in the by-laws.

Directors' Meetings

Most state statutes only provide broad guidelines for meetings of directors or trustees. The statute may provide for a minimum number of directors, their election, and a quorum requirement. Particulars such as notice, place of meeting, and number of meetings are left for the organization to deal with in the by-laws.

Although the statute may not directly provide for meetings, the board collectively is responsible for the management of the corporation and must act collectively. Collective action, however, need not be taken in a boardroom. With the advent of telecommunications a board meeting may take place by conference call. In practice many so-called meetings of the board are not in fact meetings but a series of informal contacts which are subsequently reconstructed to give the impression of a meeting. Assuming that the rights of creditors and other interested third parties are not violated, informal action without a meeting within the scope of the directors' powers is binding if acquiesced by the membership. Moreover, some states validate actions taken without a meeting if the act could have been done at a regular or special meeting and a written record of the action signed by the members of the board otherwise entitled to notice is made and filed in the corporate records.[6]

State statutes generally allow meetings to be held within or outside the state of organization. Convenience is the primary consideration. Time of the meeting is also a matter of convenience. A meeting should not be scheduled on a Sunday if the state has a Sunday blue law invalidating contracts made on Sunday.

Scheduling of meetings is for the most part accomplished in the by-laws. The

Table 8
Proxies

State	Members Proxy Allowed by Statute	Directors Proxy Allowed by Statute	Authority - NFP Corporation Law
Alabama	X		tit. 10 § 3-104
Alaska	X		§ 10.20.071
Arizona	X		§ 10-706A3
Arkansas	X	X	§§ 64-1911, 64-219
California	X		Cal.Corp.Code § 5614
Colorado	X		§ 7-23-106
Connecticut	X		§ 33-471
Delaware	X		tit. 8 § 215
District of Columbia	X		§ 29-603
Florida			No provision
Georgia	X		§§ 22-610, 22-103
Hawaii			No provision
Idaho	X		§§ 30-1002, 30-134
Illinois	X		ch. 32 §163a14
Indiana	X		§ 23.7-1.1-9(c)
Iowa	X		ch. 504 § 496A.32
Kansas	X		§ 17-6505(b)
Kentucky	X		§ 273.201(2)
Louisiana	X	X	§§ 12:232(C), 12:35(F)
Maine	X		c.53 § 28
Maryland	X		Md. Corp. L. § 5-202
Massachusetts			No provision
Michigan			No provision
Minnesota	X		§§ 317.20, 317.22
Mississippi			No provision
Missouri	X		§ 355.120(2)
Montana	X		§ 15-2315
Nebraska	X		§§ 21-1914, 21-1915
Nevada			No provision
New Hampshire			No provision
New Jersey			No provision
New Mexico	X		§ 51-14-57
New York	X		N.Y. NPCL § 609
North Carolina	X		§ 55-A-32(b)
North Dakota	X		§ 10-24-15
Ohio	X		§ 1702.20
Oklahoma	X		tit. 18, §§ 1.60,860
Pennsylvania	X		15 § 7606
Rhode Island	X		§ 7-1.1-31
South Carolina			No provision
South Dakota	X		§ 47-22-26
Tennessee	X		§ 48-1114
Texas	X		Art. 1396-2.13
Utah	X		§ 16-6-30
Virginia	X		§ 13.1-217
Washington	X		§ 24.03.085
West Virginia	X		§ 31-1-20
Wisconsin	X		§ 181.16
Wyoming	X		§ 17-1-130

Table 9
Regular Meetings of Members

State	Minimum Number Days Required	Mail	Waiver	Within State	Outside State	By-Laws	Statutory Quorum	Cumulative Voting for Directors	Minimum Elected	Staggered Terms
Alabama	10			X			10%		3	X
Alaska	10	X	X	X	X	X	10%	X	3	X
Arizona	10	X	X	X	X	X	10%	X	3	X
Arkansas									3	
California	10			X	X	X	M	X	1	
Colorado	10	X	X	X	X	X		X	1	X
Connecticut	7			X	X	X	*	X	3	
Delaware	10	X	X	X	X	X	10%	X	3	X
District of Columbia	10	X	X				10%	X	3	X
Florida	10	X		X	X	X	M	X	3	X
Georgia						X		X	3	X
Hawaii						X		X	3	
Idaho		X				X	10%	X	3	X
Illinois	5	X		X	X	X	10%	X	3	X
Indiana				X		X	M	X	3	
Iowa	10	X	X	X	X	X	10%	X	3	X
Kansas										
Kentucky	10	X	X	X	X	X	10%	X	3	X
Louisiana	10	X				X	M		3	
Maine		X	X			X	10%	X	3	X
Maryland	10					X				
Massachusetts										
Michigan	10	X	X			X	M	X	1	
Minnesota	5			X	X	X	10%	X	3	
Mississippi										
Missouri	5	X	X			X	10%	X	3	X
Montana	10	X		X	X	X	10%	X	3	X
Nebraska	10			X	X	X	10%	X	3	X
Nevada									3	
New Hampshire										
New Jersey	10	X	X	X	X	X	M	X	3	X
New Mexico	10		X			X	10%	X	3	X
New York	10	X	X	X	X	X	M	X	3	X
North Carolina	10	X		X	X	X	10%	X	3	X
North Dakota	10	X	X	X	X	X	10%	X	3	X
Ohio	10	X	X	X	X	X	*		3	
Oklahoma										
Oregon	10	X	X	X	X	X	*	X	3	X
Pennsylvania	5					X	10%	X	1	
Rhode Island										
South Carolina								X	3	
South Dakota	10	X		X	X	X	10%	X	3	X
Tennessee										
Texas		X	X	X	X	X	10%	X	3	

153

Table 9 (continued)
Regular Meetings of Members

State	Minimum Number Days Required	Notice Mail	Notice Waiver	Place Within State	Place Outside State	By-Laws	Statutory Quorum	Election of Directors Cumulative Voting for Directors	Election of Directors Minimum Elected	Election of Directors Staggered Terms
Utah	10	X				X	*		3	
Vermont	10	X	X	X	X	X	10%	X	3	X
Virginia	7	X	X			X	10%	X	1	
Washington	10	X	X	X	X	X	25%		3	X
West Virginia	10	X	X	X	X	X	10%		1	X
Wisconsin	10	X	X	X	X	X	10%		3	X
Wyoming	20								1	X

* Members present constitute a quorum.
M – Majority

by-laws may require annual or regular meetings to be held at a certain time and place. If so, no notice or special call is required. Authorization to call a regular or special meeting should be clearly stated in the by-laws to avoid difficulties.

Unless the time and place of the meeting are fixed in the by-laws, formal written notice is generally required. The written notice should contain precise information as to time, place, and agenda, if any. The notice requirements of the statute or the by-laws should be observed. Lack of notice, however, does not invalidate a meeting if the directors attend and participate without making objection. A waiver of notice may also be executed either before or after the meeting. Continuance of an adjourned meeting at another time and place does not require any notice if the resolution adjourning the meeting specifies time and place of continuation.

The state statute may contain a minimum quorum requirement which must be observed although a greater quorum requirement may be required in the by-laws. If none is stated, a majority constitutes a quorum. If a quorum is not present, no business may be conducted. For purposes of constituting a quorum, a director who was tricked into attending and does not participate, who attended only to protest lack of notice or power to act, or who is an "interested" director should not be counted. If vacancies reduce the board to below a quorum, no business may be conducted until enough vacancies are filled to provide a quorum. If directors leave a meeting and a quorum is then lacking, no further business may be conducted unless the walkout is unreasonable or intended to cripple the board.[7]

Most action taken by a board of directors is by majority vote unless otherwise required by law or articles of incorporation or by-laws. Directors are responsible for the management of the corporation and are required to vote directly and not by proxy. To do otherwise is to delegate their duties and trust, but it is not entirely clear that a proxy is prohibited in some states, and some states have gone so far as to allow directors to vote by proxy (see Table 8).

MISCELLANEOUS

Minutes

The minutes are the official record of the events of a meeting of the members or directors of the organization. The minutes should be kept by the secretary in a minute book. The minute book also contains a copy of the articles of incorporation, certificate of incorporation, by-laws, and chronological records of organizational meetings and subsequent business meetings of the organization. Separate minute books may be maintained for members and directors. Often the minute book is kept in the attorney's office.

The secretary takes the minutes during the meeting and subsequently amplifies and prepares the actual entry in the minute book. At the next meeting the minutes are read, corrected if necessary, and approved as the official record of the meeting.

The minutes are prima facie evidence of the events and actions taken at the meeting.[8] The minutes may be impeached by a person who was present at the meeting, but the presumption of correctness of the minutes is so strong that it is difficult to overcome by oral testimony.[9]

Although not all states require nonprofit corporations to keep minutes, a written record of the meetings is essential to good order and historical accuracy.

Under common law, members had a right to inspect books and records.[10] The right is generally limited to reasonable times at the principal office and for proper purposes. Some states have limited access to books and records of charitable nonprofit organizations to protect donors.[11]

Proxies

The law regarding the use of proxies in meetings of nonprofit corporations is far less developed than the greatly expanded law of proxies used for business corporations. A proxy is merely a special agent of a member or director. The agent is deputized to vote on behalf of the member or director. The proxy may be instructed how to vote or left to his own discretion. No particular form of proxy is required, but it should be in writing and limited according to time and purpose. State statutes (detailed in Table 8) which authorize use of a proxy leave it to the corporation to adopt the use of proxies or limit their use by by-law.

OPERATIONS

The management of a nonprofit corporation is vested in the board of directors as a body. The directors of a nonprofit corporation tend to be more involved in day-to-day operations than their counterparts are in business corporations. A person becomes a director of a nonprofit corporation out of a sense of duty or obligation to serve in the furtherance of a particular cause or for society at large. The level of activity depends on the size of the nonprofit corporation and the time and talents of the director.

Management Structure

Board of Directors

State statutes set minimum qualifications for directors, prescribe a minimum number, provide for classification, and authorize their election and removal. The details are left to the corporation and are set out in the articles of incorporation or by-laws.

Qualifications for a director often include a minimum age and residency requirement. A residency requirement usually only applies to one director and not to all.

Directors may be classified with respect to term of office. While all directors may be elected for the same length of time, their terms are staggered to provide continuity in office.

The minimum number of directors is specified in the state statutes. The minimum number in some states is one but the usual practice is to require three. A few states impose a maximum number of directors (see Table 9).

The initial directors are named in the articles of incorporation. At the organizational meeting these directors may be confirmed in office, or new directors may be elected. If the corporation has voting members, directors are elected by the members. If none of the members has voting rights, the directors are self-perpetuating. Should the elections not be held, the director whose term is expiring remains in office until a successor is chosen.

A director may resign from office at any time. The resignation is effective when it is accepted by the board. A resignation may be withdrawn at any time prior to acceptance. Resignation does not absolve a director from liability incurred prior to resignation.

Most state statutes provide for removal or suspension of directors with or without cause. Removal for cause generally is predicated on misconduct in office, abuse of trust, or waste. Removal for cause is not dependent on the existence of a statute. Removal for cause or without cause may be accomplished by the other directors or members depending on the statutory authority, articles of incorporation, or by-laws. A due process requirement has grown up around removal of directors from office. Notice of the charges, if any, and reasonable opportunity to defend are required.[12] Removal is subject to review by a court of competent jurisdiction.[13]

Whether a vacancy occurs as a result of resignation, removal, or death, the vacancy is filled at a duly called regular or special meeting of the electing body. Unless the vacancy affects the quorum requirement, there is no rush to fill it. Nonetheless, a vacancy should be filled in a reasonable amount of time. Some states require vacancies to be filled within a specific time frame. Failure to fill the vacancy triggers an alternative method to fill the position.

The articles of incorporation or by-laws may authorize the board of directors to divide itself into committees. The committees have and may exercise the authority of the board of directors in all matters except these:

1. Amending, altering, or repealing the by-laws
2. Electing, appointing, or removing a director or officer
3. Amending the articles of incorporation
4. Adopting a plan of merger or consolidation
5. Selling, leasing, exchanging, or mortgaging all or substantially all the property and assets of the corporation
6. Authorizing dissolution or revoking such authority
7. Adopting a plan for distribution of the assets
8. Other acts prohibited by the articles of incorporation or by-laws

The use of committees may allow the board to divide duties along the lines of the directors' expertise.

Directors may receive compensation which is reasonable and solely for services actually rendered unless compensation is otherwise prohibited by statute, the articles of incorporation, or by-laws. Additionally, directors may be reimbursed for out-of-pocket expenses incurred on behalf of the corporation unless those expenses are extravagant. To be safe, compensation and expenses should meet the tests of ordinary and necessary as understood in section 162 and the Treasury Regulations promulgated thereunder.

Officers

Nonprofit corporation acts provide for certain officers such as president, vice-president, secretary, and treasurer by name. Officers are usually elected or appointed by the board of directors unless the articles of incorporation or by-laws provide otherwise. Terms of office may or may not be specified in the statute. The statutes provide little else except that the same person generally cannot be both president and secretary. No description of duties appears in the statutes.

The by-laws should be specific with respect to the powers and limitations of each officer. An officer may be removed from office with or without cause by the body electing or appointing him. Removal proceedings embody some notions of due process regarding notice and hearing. If the officer is under contract, removal may cause a breach of contract and subject the corporation to liability for damages.

An officer is an agent of the corporation and within his express or implied powers can bind the corporation. An officer or agent acting outside the scope of his power may still bind the corporation under the apparent powers doctrine. The corporation is estopped from denying that an officer or agent lacked power if the corporation's conduct gave the officer or agent the appearance of power.

Officers, like directors, may be reasonably compensated for services actually rendered and reimbursed for out-of-pocket expenses incurred on behalf of the corporation.

Powers, Duties, and Liabilities

The powers of a nonprofit corporation are granted by the state legislature. Each corporation shall typically have power to perform the following tasks:

1. To have perpetual succession by its corporate name unless a limited period of duration is stated in its articles of incorporation

2. To sue and be sued, complain and defend, in its corporate name

3. To have a corporate seal which may be altered at pleasure, and to use the same by causing it, or a facsimile thereof, to be impressed or affixed or in any other manner reproduced

4. To purchase, take, receive, lease, take by gift, devise or bequest, or otherwise acquire, own, hold, improve, use and otherwise deal in and with real or personal property, or any interest therein, wherever situated

5. To sell, convey, mortgage, pledge, lease, exchange, transfer and otherwise dispose of all or any part of its property and assets

6. To lend money to its employees other than its officers and directors

7. To purchase, take, receive, subscribe for, or otherwise acquire, own, hold, vote, use, employ, sell, mortgage, lend, pledge, or otherwise dispose of, and otherwise use and deal in and with, shares or other interests in, or obligations of, other domestic or foreign corporations, whether for profit or not for profit, associations, partnerships or individuals, or direct or indirect obligations of the United States, or of any other government, state, territory, governmental district or municipality or of any instrumentality thereof

8. To make contracts and incur liabilities, borrow money at such rates of interest as the corporation may determine, issue its notes, bonds, and other obligations, and secure any of its obligations by mortgage or pledge of all or any of its property, franchises and income

9. To lend money for its corporate purposes, invest and reinvest its funds, and take and hold real and personal property as security for the payment of funds so loaned or invested

10. To conduct its affairs, carry on its operations, and have offices and exercise the powers granted by this Act in any state, territory, district, or possession of the United States, or in any foreign country

11. To elect or appoint officers and agents of the corporation, and define their duties and fix their compensation

12. To make and alter by-laws, not inconsistent with its articles of incorporation or with the laws of this State, for the administration and regulation of the affairs of the corporation

13. Unless otherwise provided in the articles of incorporation, to make donations for the public welfare or for charitable, scientific, or educational purposes; and in time of war to make donations in aid of war activities

14. To indemnify any director or officer or former director or officer of the corporation, or any person who may have served at its request as a director or officer of another corporation, whether for profit or not for profit, against expenses actually and necessarily incurred by him in connection with the defense of any action, suit or proceeding in which he is made a party by reason of being or having been such director or officer, except in relation to matters as to which he shall be adjudged in such action, suit or proceeding to be liable for negligence or misconduct in the performance of duty; but such indemnification shall not be deemed exclusive of any other rights to which such director or officer may be entitled, under any by-law, agreement, vote of board of directors or members, or otherwise

15. To cease its corporate activities and surrender its corporate franchise

16. To have and exercise all powers necessary or convenient to effect any or all of the purposes for which the corporation is organized[14]

With these powers a director has the duty to exercise a high degree of diligence, skill, and care, although there is some controversy as to what degree of diligence, skill, and care is required. The two competing degrees are that of a trustee and that of a business corporate director. Those who argue for the higher standard of a trustee assert that a director of a charitable corporation is more like a trustee of a charitable trust than like a business corporation director.

The prevailing rule uses the lesser standard of the ordinarily prudent man under similar circumstances in one's own affairs. The standard allows reasonable reliance on others such as attorneys and accountants.

Directors and officers owe fiduciary duties to the corporation which require good faith and fair dealing. Such activities as self-dealing, conflict of interest, and appropriation of corporate opportunity are breaches of the fiduciary duty and in some cases amount to fraud. For a discussion of indemnification and liability insurance for officers and directors arising out of breach of fiduciary duty, see Chapter 14.

Although self-dealing and other breaches of fiduciary duty give rise to causes of action under state law either by or on behalf of the corporation, it is the federal income tax law that has the greatest impact in this area particularly regarding private foundations. Self-dealing and other breaches of fiduciary duty violate the prohibition against private inurement found in sections 501(c)(3), (6), (7), (9), (11), (13), and (19) and may result in loss of tax exempt status. With regard to private foundations Congress has imposed penalty taxes on self-dealing.

Tax Consequences of Self-Dealing

It is significant that, although most prohibitions against self-dealing predate the federal income tax, section 4941 regarding private foundations is the broadest sweeping of the proscriptions and the most likely to be adhered to by foundations and foundation managers. It is immaterial that the transaction results in a benefit or a detriment to the private foundation.[15] Knowledge of or an intent to engage in self-dealing is not a prerequisite to liability unlike nontax liability rules. The exception is with respect to a transaction involving a government official.[16]

Self-dealing means engaging directly or indirectly in any one of the enumerated transactions in section 4941(d). Prohibited transactions include the following:

1. Sale or exchange, or leasing, of property between a private foundation and a disqualified person
2. Lending of money, or other extension of credit between a private foundation and a disqualified person
3. Furnishing of goods, services, or facilities between a private foundation and a disqualified person
4. Payment of compensation or reimbursement of expenses to a disqualified person
5. Transfer to, or use by or for the benefit of, a disqualified person of the income or assets of a private foundation
6. Agreement by a private foundation to make any payment of money or other property to a government official except for an agreement to employ the official after termination of his governmental service if the government service will terminate within ninety days of the agreement[17]

For purposes of self-dealing, the disqualified person must have such status prior to the transaction and not acquire it as a result of the transaction.[18] A disqualified person is described in section 4946 as follows:

1. A substantial contributor to the foundation as described in section 507(d)(2)
2. A foundation manager
3. An owner of more than 20 percent of the total combined voting power of a corporation, of a profits interest in a partnership, or of the beneficial interest in a trust or unincorporated enterprise which is a substantial contributor to the foundation
4. A spouse, ancestor, or children, grandchildren, great grandchildren, and their spouses of a substantial contributor, foundation manager, or 20 percent holder
5. A corporation in which the above described persons hold more than 35 percent of the combined voting power, a partnership in which the above described persons hold more than a 35 percent profits interest, or a trust or estate in which the above persons hold more than a 35 percent beneficial interest
6. A government official as defined in section 4946(c)

It is of great import to note that section 4941 prohibits both direct and indirect transactions. The examples of indirect self-dealing in Treasury Regulations section 53.4941(d)-1(b)(8) are evidence of a broad interpretation of "indirect." This is particularly true when considering the definition of "control" used to determine whether or not self-dealing exists. Control of an organization is accomplished by the foundation or one or more of its foundation managers, acting in that capacity, if they can require an organization to engage in an act that would be considered self-dealing if done by the foundation itself or by virtue of aggregating their votes or positions of power.[19] This is clearly broader than the traditional concept of control.

Certain transactions are not considered to be indirect self-dealing. Business transactions between a disqualified person and a controlled organization are excluded if the business relationship was previously established, if the transaction is at least as favorable to the controlled organization as an arm's-length transaction, and if it would cause severe economic hardship on the controlled organization to deal elsewhere or the disqualified person provides a unique product or service.[20] A nonearmarked grant to an intermediary organization which is not controlled by the grantor foundation and which engages in a transaction with a government official is not self-dealing by the grantor foundation.[21] Certain transactions by an administrator or executor of an estate or revocable trust under which the foundation has an interest or expectancy are not indirect self-dealing if the administrator or executor has the power to sell or reallocate the property and the transaction is approved by a probate court.[22] Transactions arising in the normal course of business of a retail business engaged in with the general public, at arm's length, and not exceeding $5,000 per disqualified person per taxable year are excluded from indirect self-dealing.[23]

Specific acts described as self-dealing in section 4941(a)(1) are modified under section 4941(d)(2). Sales or exchanges of property between a private foundation and a disqualified person are acts of self-dealing. This is true without regard to the amount paid. A sale of incidental supplies by a disqualified person to a private foundation is self-dealing, and so is a bargain sale.[24] The transfer of property subject to a mortgage or similar lien is an act of self-dealing unless the mortgage or lien was placed on the property more than ten years before the transfer.[25] This provision is intended to prevent a transferor from taking value out of property before transfer to a private foundation and have the foundation assume the debt or liability.

A lease of property between a private foundation and a disqualified person is self-dealing unless the lease is without charge.[26] A lease is without charge if the foundation pays for such items as janitorial services, utilities, or normal maintenance costs incurred for the use of the property which are not paid directly or indirectly to a disqualified person.[27] However, payment of taxes or mortgage obligations result in indirect benefits and would make the lease an act of self-dealing. A lease of office space by a disqualified person to a private foundation is not self-dealing if the lease was executed prior to October 9, 1969, or renewals thereof, if the lease did not violate section 503(b), and if it was at arm's length.[28]

A loan or other extension of credit between a private foundation and a disqualified person is an act of self-dealing unless the loan is without interest or other charge and the proceeds of the loan are used exclusively for section 501(c)(3) charitable purposes.[29] A promise, pledge or similar arrangement concerning a future gift to a private foundation by a disqualified person which is motivated by a charitable intent and unsupported by consideration is not an extension of credit prior to the maturity date.[30] Neither general banking services nor performance of trust functions by a disqualified person for a private foundation constitute self-dealing.[31]

The furnishing of any goods, services, or facilities such as office space, automobiles, auditoriums, secretarial help, libraries, publications, laboratories, meals, or parking lots constitutes acts of self-dealing.[32] Goods, services, or facilities furnished to foundation managers or employees, including persons who would be considered employees if compensated, in recognition of their services is not self-dealing if the value is reasonable and necessary to the performance of their duties and carrying out the exempt purposes of the foundation.[33] Goods, services, or facilities furnished to a private foundation by a disqualified person without charge are not acts of self-dealing.[34] Costs incurred in obtaining or using the property which are not made directly or indirectly to disqualified persons may be paid without consequence.[35] Furnishing goods, services, or facilities available to the general public to a disqualified person on at least as favorable a basis as with the general public does not constitute an act of self-dealing.[36]

Compensation which is reasonable and necessary to carry out the exempt function may be paid to disqualified persons for services if such amount is not excessive.[37] Excessiveness is determined under Treasury Regulations section 1.162-7 using the same rules as applicable to compensation for personal services rendered in a business context.[38]

The transfer to, use by or for the benefit of, a disqualified person of the income or assets of the private foundation are prohibited.[39] Payment by a foundation of chapter 42 taxes imposed on a foundation manager violates this prohibition.[40] Likewise, the purchase or sale of securities by a private foundation to manipulate the price to the advantage of a disqualified person is prohibited.[41] Liquidations, mergers, redemptions, recapitalizations, or other corporate adjustments by a corporation that is a disqualified person are not self-dealing if all the securities of the same class as held by the foundation are subject to the same terms and conditions.[42]

Prohibited transactions regarding payments to government officials do not include the following:

1. A prize or award excluded from gross income under the terms of section 74(b) for charitable, religious, scientific, educational, artistic, literary, or civic achievement if the government official was selected from the public at large

2. A scholarship or fellowship excluded from gross income under section 117(a) for study at a qualified educational institution

3. An annuity or trust payment which qualifies under section 401 as a stock-bonus, pension, or profit sharing plan

4. An annuity or other payment which qualifies under section 404(a)(2)

5. Contributions, gifts other than money, services, or facilities having an aggregate value of not more than $25 during any calendar year

6. Payments made with respect to government employees' training programs under 5 U.S.C. chapter 41

7. Payment or reimbursement of certain domestic traveling expenses in connection with charitable purposes under section 170(c)(1) or (2)(B)

8. An agreement to employ if within ninety days of the official's termination of government service

9. Certain costs of attending conferences sponsored by private foundations related to their exempt purposes.[43]

Caution is required with respect to transition rules.[44] A foundation may dispose of excess business holdings without engaging in self-dealing if they are within the transition rules of sections 4941 and 4943.[45]

The penalty for self-dealing is a tax on each act of self-dealing imposed on the self-dealer at the rate of 5 percent of the amount involved for each year in the taxable period.[46] The amount involved is the greater of (1) the amount of money and fair market value of other property given or (2) the amount of money and fair market value of other property received.[47] If services are involved, the amount is the excess compensation.[48] Fair market value is determined on the date that the self-dealing occurs.[49] The tax must be paid by the disqualified person unless the disqualified person is a foundation manager and was acting in that capacity when the self-dealing occurred.[50]

In addition to the 5 percent tax imposed on the self-dealer, an additional tax equal to 200 percent of the amount involved is imposed if the act of self-dealing is not corrected within the taxable period.[51] To correct means to undo the transaction to the extent possible.[52] The foundation must be at least in the financial position it would have been in if the disqualified person had acted under the highest fiduciary standards.[53]

The taxable period consists of the period between the act of self-dealing and the earlier of the date the deficiency notice is mailed, the tax is assessed, or the act corrected.[54]

A foundation manager who knowingly participates in an act of self-dealing is subject to a tax of 2.5 percent of the amount involved for each year of the taxable period unless the manager's act or participation was not willful and for reasonable cause.[55] The tax must be paid by the foundation manager; indemnification is not allowed.[56] The maximum tax imposed on a knowing, participating foundation manager is $10,000.[57]

If the foundation manager refuses to agree to all or part of the correction, an additional tax of 50 percent of the amount involved is imposed.[58] The maximum tax imposed on all foundation managers who refuse to agree to the correction is $10,000.[59] All participants are jointly and severally liable for the tax.[60]

Section 4962 does not allow abatement of the initial taxes imposed under section 4941(a).

Foundation managers and disqualified persons should therefore, act with extreme caution and be mindful of their strict fiduciary duties.

Fringe Benefits

Nonprofit corporations are in competition with business enterprises for good managers and other personnel. To be able to compete effectively, nonprofit corporations should offer a complete package of fringe benefits. This is particularly true since salaries or other compensation for employees of nonprofit corporations have traditionally been low and are restricted by the private inurement rule. Reasonable compensation paid to employees for services rendered is permissible without violating the private inurement prohibition.[61]

Beyond payment of reasonable compensation, such fringe benefits as medical, disability, and life insurance are permissible within the guidelines of reasonable compensation. Popular and important fringe benefits are deferred compensation plans. A qualified deferred compensation plan generates three different tax benefits. The employer may deduct contributions to the plan in the year made even though the employee may not actually receive a benefit for many years.[62] Any income earned by the trust on the corpus is tax exempt.[63] Finally, the employee defers tax on the contributions until they are actually received. At that time the employee hopes to be taxed at lower marginal rates.[64] Until recently, deferred compensation plans were restricted to for-profit business enterprises.

Two forms of deferred compensation plans are incentive compensation plans and qualified profit sharing plans. A qualified plan meets the complex requirements of section 401. In a profit sharing plan, the employees participate in the profits they helped generate. An incentive compensation plan is designed to increase efficiency and cost savings by passing all or part of the savings on to the employees. The incentive plan becomes a qualified deferred plan if the savings are paid into a qualified profit sharing trust.

Historically, the Internal Revenue Service has not allowed profit sharing plans to be adopted by tax exempt organizations because they have no "profits" in the traditional business sense of profits.[65] In 1980, the government reversed its position and adopted, for purposes of section 401, a definition of "profit" in the broad accounting sense as being an excess of revenues over expenditures.[66]

However, division of profits by a tax exempt organization is considered a blatant form of private inurement.[67] The government's position appears to be weakening. It has conceded that a profit sharing plan under section 401 may be compatible with section 501(c)(3) provided certain safeguards exist. Amounts contributed to qualified profit sharing plans are deductible as long as they constitute "reasonable compensation."[68] Tax exempt organizations may pay reasonable compensation without violating the private inurement proscription; therefore, it may only be a matter of time before tax exempt organizations can create qualified profit sharing plans to attract and retain quality employees.

Incentive compensation plans have fared slightly better than profit sharing plans. The government has drawn a distinction between profit sharing plans and incentive compensation plans because benefits are not dependent on realization of net profits. Favorable rulings have been issued regarding incentive compensation plans.[69]

The government is currently putting more emphasis on the significant benefit accruing to the employer's exempt purpose from incentive compensation plans than on the benefit derived by the employee. This is a giant step forward.

NOTES

1. Robert, *Robert's Rules of Order,* 1970; H. Oleck *et al., Parliamentary Law,* ABA-ALI Joint Committee, 1979.

2. N.Y. N-PCL § 606 (McKinney); Ohio Rev. Code § 1702.19 (Page); *Beggs v. Myton Canal & Irrig. Co.,* 54 Utah 120, 179 P. 984 (1919).

3. *People ex rel. Carus v. Matthiessen,* 193 Ill. App. 328, *affd,* 269 Ill. 499, 109 N.E. 1056 (1915).

4. *See, e.g., State ex rel. Breger v. Rushe,* 219 Ind. 559, 39 N.E.2d 433 (1942); N.Y. N-PCL § 611(b) (McKinney).

5. *McLain v. Lanova Corp.*, 39 A.2d 209 (Del. 1944).

6. *See, e.g.*, Ohio Rev. Code § 1702.25 (Page).

7. *See, e.g., Duffy v. Loft, Inc.*, 17 Del. Ch. 376, 152 A. 849 (1930); *Comm. v. Vandegrift*, 232 Penna. St. 53, 81 A. 153 (1911).

8. *Stipe v. First National Bank of Portland*, 301 P.2d 175 (Ore. 1956); In re *Mandelbaum*, 80 Misc. 475, 141 N.Y.S. 319 (1913), *affd*, 159 A.D. 909, 144 N.Y.S. 1128 (1913).

9. *Keogh v. St. Paul Milk Co.*, 205 Minn. 96, 285 N.W. 809 (1939).

10. *Ochs v. Washington Hts. Fed. S & L Assn.*, 17 N.Y. 2d 82, 268 N.Y.S.2d 294, 215 N.E.2d 485 (1966).

11. *E.g.*, Ohio Rev. Code § 1702.11(A)(4) (Page).

12. *See, e.g., Kahn v. Colonial Fuel Corp.*, 198 N.Y.S. 596 (1923); *Piedmont Press Assn. v. Record Publ. Co.*, 156 S.C. 43, 152 S.E. 721 (1930).

13. Matter of *Teperman v. Atcos Baths, Inc.*, 4 Misc. 2d 738, 158 N.Y.S. 2d 391 (1951).

14. ABA-ALI Model Nonprofit Corp. Act. § 5.

15. Treas. Reg. § 53.4941(d)-1(a).

16. I.R.C. § 4941(a)(1).

17. I.R.C. § 4941(d)(1).

18. Treas. Reg. § 53.4941(d)-1(a).

19. Treas. Reg. § 53.4941(d)-1(b)(5).

20. Treas. Reg. § 53.4941(d)-1(b)(1).

21. Treas. Reg. § 53.4941(d)-1(b)(2).

22. Treas. Reg. § 53.4941(d)-1(b)(3).

23. Treas. Reg. § 53.4941(d)-1(b)(6).

24. Treas. Reg. § 53.4941(d)-2(a)(1).

25. Treas. Reg. § 53.4941(d)-2(a)(2).

26. Treas. Reg. § 53.4941(d)-2(b).

27. *Id.*

28. I.R.C. § 4941(d)(2)(H).

29. I.R.C. § 4941(d); Treas. Reg. § 53.4941(d)-2(c).

30. Treas. Reg. § 53.4941(d)-2(c)(3).

31. Treas. Reg. § 53.4941(d)-2(c)(4).

32. Treas. Reg. § 53.4941(d)-2(d).

33. Treas. Reg. § 53.4941(d)-2(d)(2).

34. Treas. Reg. § 53.4941(d)-2(d)(3).

35. *Id.*

36. I.R.C. § 4941(d)(2)(D).

37. Treas. Reg. § 53.4941(d)-3(c).

38. *Id.*

39. I.R.C. § 4941(d)(2)(E).

40. Treas. Reg. § 53.4941(d)-2(f).

41. *Id.*

42. I.R.C. § 4941(d)(2)(F).

43. Treas. Reg. § 53.4941(d)-3(e).

44. Treas. Reg. § 53.4941(d)-4.

45. Treas. Reg. § 53.4941(d)-4(b).
46. I.R.C. § 4941(a)(1).
47. I.R.C. § 4941(e)(2).
48. *Id.*
49. I.R.C. § 4941(e)(2)(A).
50. I.R.C. § 4941(a)(1).
51. I.R.C. § 4941(b)(1).
52. I.R.C. § 4941(e)(3).
53. *Id.*
54. I.R.C. § 4941(e)(1).
55. I.R.C. § 4941(a)(2).
56. *Id.*
57. I.R.C. § 4941(c)(2).
58. I.R.C. § 4941(b)(2).
59. I.R.C. § 4941(c)(2).
60. I.R.C. § 4941(c)(1).
61. *Birmingham Business College, Inc. v. Comm.*, 276 F.2d 476 (5th Cir. 1960).
62. I.R.C. §§ 401(a), 404(a).
63. I.R.C. § 501(a).
64. I.R.C. § 402(a)(1).
65. G.C.M. No. 35865 (1974).
66. G.C.M. No. 38283 (1980).
67. Rev. Rul. 56-185, 1956-1 C.B. 202.
68. I.R.C. § 404(a).
69. G.C.M. Nos. 35638 (1974), 36918 (1976), 38283 (1980).

APPENDIX: MODEL BY-LAWS PREPARED BY THE COMMITTEE ON NONPROFIT CORPORATIONS OF THE AMERICAN BAR ASSOCIATION

BY-LAWS[1]

OF

_____

ARTICLE I. OFFICES

The principal office of the corporation in the State of _____,
shall be located in the City of _____, County of _____.
The corporation may have such other offices, either within or without the State of
_____, as the Board of Directors may determine or as the
affairs of the corporation may require from time to time.

The corporation shall have and continuously maintain in the State of
_____ a registered office, and a registered agent whose
office is identical with such registered office, as required by the
_____ Non-Profit Corporation Act. The registered office

may be, but need not be, identical with the principal office in the State of
_____, and the address of the registered office may be
changed from time to time by the Board of Directors.

ARTICLE II. MEMBERS

SECTION 1. Classes of Members.[2] The corporation shall have
_____ class (or classes) of members. The designation of
such class (or classes) and the qualifications and rights of the members of such
class (or classes) shall be as follows:

_____

SECTION 2. Election of Members.[3] Members shall be elected by the Board of
Directors. An affirmative vote of two-thirds of the Directors shall be required for
election.

SECTION 3. Voting Rights.[4] Each member shall be entitled to one vote on each
matter submitted to a vote of the members.

SECTION 4. Termination of Membership. The Board of Directors, by
affirmative vote of two-thirds of all of the members of the Board, may suspend or
expel a member for cause after an appropriate hearing, and may, by a majority
vote of those present at any regularly constituted meeting, terminate the
membership of any member who becomes ineligible for membership, or suspend or
expel any member who shall be in default in the payment of dues for the period
fixed in Article XI of these by-laws.

SECTION 5. Resignation. Any member may resign by filing a written
resignation with the Secretary, but such resignation shall not relieve the member so
resigning of the obligation to pay any dues, assessments or other charges
theretofore accrued and unpaid.

SECTION 6. Reinstatement. Upon written request signed by a former member
and filed with the Secretary, the Board of Directors may, by the affirmative vote of
two-thirds of the members of the Board, reinstate such former member to
membership upon such terms as the Board of Directors may deem appropriate.

SECTION 7. Transfer of Membership.[5] Membership in this corporation is not
transferable or assignable.

ARTICLE III. MEETINGS OF MEMBERS

SECTION 1. Annual Meeting. An annual meeting of the members shall be held
on the _____ in the month of _____ in
each year, beginning with the year 19_____, at the hour of _____ o'clock, _____ M.,
for the purpose of electing Directors and for the transaction of such other
business as may come before the meeting. If the day fixed for the annual meeting
shall be a legal holiday in the State of _____, such
meeting shall be held on the next succeeding business day. If the election of
Directors shall not be held on the day designated herein for any annual meeting, or at
any adjournment thereof, the Board of Directors shall cause the election to be held at
a special meeting of the members as soon thereafter as conveniently may be.

SECTION 2. Special Meetings.[6] Special meetings of the members may be called by the President, the Board of Directors, or not less than one-tenth of the members having voting rights.

SECTION 3. Place of Meeting.[7] The Board of Directors may designate any place, either within or without the State of _____, as the place of meeting for any annual meeting or for any special meeting called by the Board of Directors. If no designation is made or if a special meeting be otherwise called, the place of meeting shall be the registered office of the corporation in the State of _____; but if all of the members shall meet at any time and place, either within or without the State of _____, and consent to the holding of a meeting, such meeting shall be valid without call or notice, and at such meeting any corporate action may be taken.

SECTION 4. Notice of Meetings.[8] Written notice stating the place, day and hour of any meeting of members shall be delivered, either personally or by mail, to each member entitled to vote at such meeting, not less than ten nor more than fifty days before the date of such meeting, by or at the direction of the President, or the Secretary, or the officers or persons calling the meeting. In case of a special meeting or when required by statute or by these by-laws, the purpose or purposes for which the meeting is called shall be stated in the notice. If mailed, the notice of a meeting shall be deemed to be delivered when deposited in the United States mail addressed to the member at his address as it appears on the records of the corporation, with postage thereon prepaid.

SECTION 5. Informal Action by Members.[9] Any action required by law to be taken at a meeting of the members, or any action which may be taken at a meeting of members, may be taken without a meeting if a consent in writing, setting forth the action so taken, shall be signed by all of the members entitled to vote with respect to the subject matter thereof.

SECTION 6. Quorum.[10] The members holding one-_____ of the votes which may be cast at any meeting shall constitute a quorum at such meeting. If a quorum is not present at any meeting of members, a majority of the members present may adjourn the meeting from time to time without further notice.

SECTION 7. Proxies.[11] At any meeting of members, a member entitled to vote may vote by proxy executed in writing by the member or by his duly authorized attorney-in-fact. No proxy shall be valid after eleven months from the date of its execution, unless otherwise provided in the proxy.

SECTION 8. Manner of Acting. A majority of votes entitled to be cast on a matter to be voted upon by the members present or represented by proxy at a meeting at which a quorum is present shall be necessary for the adoption thereof unless a greater proportion is required by law or by these by-laws.

SECTION 9. Voting by Mail. Where Directors or officers are to be elected by members or any class or classes of members, such election may be conducted by mail in such manner as the Board of Directors shall determine.

ARTICLE IV. BOARD OF DIRECTORS

SECTION 1. General Powers. The affairs of the corporation shall be managed by its Board of Directors.[12] Directors need not be residents of the State of _____ or members of the corporation.

SECTION 2. Number, Tenure and Qualifications.[13] The number of Directors shall be _____. Each Director shall hold office until the next annual meeting of members and until his successor shall have been elected and qualified.

SECTION 3. Regular Meetings. A regular annual meeting of the Board of Directors shall be held without other notice than this by-law, immediately after, and at the same place as, the annual meeting of members. The Board of Directors may provide by resolution the time and place, either within or without the State of _____, for the holding of additional regular meetings of the Board without other notice than such resolution.

SECTION 4. Special Meetings. Special meetings of the Board of Directors may be called by or at the request of the President or any two Directors. The person or persons authorized to call special meetings of the Board may fix any place, either within or without the State of _____, as the place for holding any special meeting of the Board called by them.

SECTION 5. Notice. Notice of any special meeting of the Board of Directors shall be given at least two days previously thereto by written notice delivered personally or sent by mail or telegram to each Director at his address as shown by the records of the corporation. If mailed, such notice shall be deemed to be delivered when deposited in the United States mail in a sealed envelope so addressed, with postage thereon prepaid. If notice be given by telegram, such notice shall be deemed to be delivered when the telegram is delivered to the telegraph company. Any Director may waive notice of any meeting. The attendance of a Director at any meeting shall constitute a waiver of notice of such meeting, except where a Director attends a meeting for the express purpose of objecting to the transaction of any business because the meeting is not lawfully called or convened. Neither the business to be transacted at, nor the purpose of, any regular or special meeting of the Board need be specified in the notice or waiver of notice of such meeting, unless specifically required by law or by these by-laws.

SECTION 6. Quorum.[14] A majority of the Board of Directors shall constitute a quorum for the transaction of business at any meeting of the Board; but if less than a majority of the Directors are present at said meeting, a majority of the Directors present may adjourn the meeting from time to time without further notice.

SECTION 7. Manner of Acting. The act of a majority of the Directors present at a meeting at which a quorum is present shall be the act of the Board of Directors, unless the act of a greater number is required by law or by these by-laws.

SECTION 8. Vacancies. Any vacancy occurring in the Board of Directors and any directorship to be filled by reason of an increase in the number of Directors, may be filled by the affirmative vote of a majority of the remaining directors, though less than a quorum of the Board of Directors. A Director elected to fill a vacancy shall be elected for the unexpired term of his predecessor in office.

SECTION 9. Compensation. Directors as such shall not receive any stated salaries for their services, but by resolution of the Board of Directors a fixed sum and expenses of attendance, if any, may be allowed for attendance at each regular or special meeting of the Board; but nothing herein contained shall be construed to preclude any Director from serving the corporation in any other capacity and receiving compensation therefor.

SECTION 10. Informal Action by Directors.[9] Any action required by law to be taken at a meeting of directors, or any action which may be taken at a meeting of directors, may be taken without a meeting if a consent in writing, setting forth the action so taken, shall be signed by all the Directors.

ARTICLE V. OFFICERS

SECTION 1. Officers. The officers of the corporation shall be[15] a President, one or more Vice Presidents (the number thereof to be determined by the Board of Directors), a Secretary, a Treasurer and such other officers as may be elected in accordance with the provisions of this Article. The Board of Directors may elect or appoint such other officers, including one or more Assistant Secretaries and one or more Assistant Treasurers, as it shall deem desirable, such officers to have the authority and perform the duties prescribed, from time to time, by the Board of Directors. Any two or more offices may be held by the same person, except the offices of President and Secretary.

SECTION 2. Election and Term of Office.[16] The officers of the corporation shall be elected annually by the Board of Directors at the regular annual meeting of the Board of Directors. If the election of officers shall not be held at such meeting, such election shall be held as soon thereafter as conveniently may be. New offices may be created and filled at any meeting of the Board of Directors. Each officer shall hold office until his successor shall have been duly elected and shall have qualified.

SECTION 3. Removal.[17] Any officer elected or appointed by the Board of Directors may be removed by the Board of Directors whenever in its judgment the best interests of the corporation would be served thereby, but such removal shall be without prejudice to the contract rights, if any, of the officer so removed.

SECTION 4. Vacancies. A vacancy in any office because of death, resignation, removal, disqualification or otherwise, may be filled by the Board of Directors for the unexpired portion of the term.

SECTION 5. President. The President shall be the principal executive officer of the corporation and shall in general supervise, and control all of the business and affairs of the corporation. He shall preside at all meetings of the members and of the Board of Directors. He may sign, with the Secretary or any other proper officer of the corporation authorized by the Board of Directors, any deeds, mortgages, bonds, contracts, or other instruments which the Board of Directors has authorized to be executed, except in cases where the signing and execution thereof shall be expressly delegated by the Board of Directors or by the by-laws or by statute to some other officer or agent of the corporation; and in general he shall perform all duties incident to the office of President and such other duties as may be prescribed by the Board of Directors from time to time.

SECTION 6. Vice President. In the absence of the President or in event of his inability or refusal to act, the Vice President (or in the event there be more than one Vice President, the Vice Presidents in the order of their election) shall perform the duties of the President, and when so acting, shall have all the powers of and be subject to all the restrictions upon the President. Any Vice President shall perform such other duties as from time to time may be assigned to him by the President or by the Board of Directors.

SECTION 7. Treasurer. If required by the Board of Directors, the Treasurer shall give a bond for the faithful discharge of his duties in such sum and with such surety or sureties as the Board of Directors shall determine. He shall have charge and custody of and be responsible for all funds and securities of the corporation; receive and give receipts for moneys due and payable to the corporation from any source whatsoever, and deposit all such moneys in the name of the corporation in such banks, trust companies or other depositories as shall be selected in accordance with the provisions of Article VII of these by-laws; and in general perform all the duties incident to the office of Treasurer and such other duties as from time to time may be assigned to him by the President or by the Board of Directors.

SECTION 8. Secretary. The Secretary shall keep the minutes of the meetings of the members and of the Board of Directors in one or more books provided for that purpose; see that all notices are duly given in accordance with the provisions of these by-laws or as required by law; be custodian of the corporate records and of the seal of the corporation and see that the seal of the corporation is affixed to all documents, the execution of which on behalf of the corporation under its seal is duly authorized in accordance with the provisions of these by-laws; keep a register of the post-office address of each member which shall be furnished to the Secretary by such member; and in general perform all duties incident to the office of Secretary and such other duties as from time to time may be assigned to him by the President or by the Board of Directors.

SECTION 9. Assistant Treasurers and Assistant Secretaries. If required by the Board of Directors, the Assistant Treasurers shall give bonds for the faithful discharge of their duties in such sums and with such sureties as the Board of Directors shall determine. The Assistant Treasurers and Assistant Secretaries, in general, shall perform such duties as shall be assigned to them by the Treasurer or the Secretary or by the President or the Board of Directors.

ARTICLE VI. COMMITTEES

SECTION 1. Committees of Directors. The Board of Directors, by resolution adopted by a majority of the Directors in office, may designate and appoint one or more committees, each of which shall consist of two or more Directors, which committees, to the extent provided in said resolution, shall have and exercise the authority of the Board of Directors in the management of the corporation, except that no such committee shall have the authority of the Board of Directors in reference to amending, altering or repealing the by-laws; electing, appointing or removing any member of any such committee or any Director or officer of the corporation; amending the articles of incorporation; restating articles of incorporation; adopting a plan of merger or adopting a plan of consolidation with another corporation; authorizing the sale, lease, exchange or mortgage of all or substantially all of the property and assets of the corporation; authorizing the voluntary dissolution of the corporation or revoking proceedings therefor; adopting a plan for the distribution of the assets of the corporation; or amending, altering or repealing any resolution of the Board of Directors which by its terms provides that it shall not be amended, altered or repealed by such committee. The designation and appointment of any such committee and the delegation thereto of authority shall not operate to relieve the Board of Directors, or any individual Director, of any responsibility imposed upon it or him by law.

SECTION 2. Other Committees. Other committees not having and exercising the authority of the Board of Directors in the management of the corporation may be appointed in such manner as may be designated by a resolution adopted by a majority of the Directors present at a meeting at which a quorum is present. Except as otherwise provided in such resolution, members of each such committee shall be members of the corporation, and the President of the corporation shall appoint the members thereof. Any member thereof may be removed by the person or persons authorized to appoint such member whenever in their judgment the best interests of the corporation shall be served by such removal.

SECTION 3. Term of Office. Each member of a committee shall continue as such until the next annual meeting of the members of the corporation and until his successor is appointed, unless the committee shall be sooner terminated, or unless such member be removed from such committee, or unless such member shall cease to qualify as a member thereof.

SECTION 4. Chairman. One member of each committee shall be appointed chairman by the person or persons authorized to appoint the members thereof.

SECTION 5. Vacancies. Vacancies in the membership of any committee may be filled by appointments in the same manner as provided in the case of the original appointments.

SECTION 6. Quorum. Unless otherwise provided in the resolution of the Board of Directors designating a committee, a majority of the whole committee shall constitute a quorum and the act of a majority of the members present at a meeting at which a quorum is present shall be the act of the committee.

SECTION 7. Rules. Each committee may adopt rules for its own government not inconsistent with these by-laws or with rules adopted by the Board of Directors.

ARTICLE VII. CONTRACTS, CHECKS, DEPOSITS AND FUNDS

SECTION 1. Contracts. The Board of Directors may authorize any officer or officers, agent or agents of the corporation, in addition to the officers so authorized by these by-laws, to enter into any contract or execute and deliver any instrument in the name of and on behalf of the corporation, and such authority may be general or confined to specific instances.

SECTION 2. Checks, Drafts, etc. All checks, drafts or orders for the payment of money, notes or other evidences of indebtedness issued in the name of the corporation, shall be signed by such officer or officers, agent or agents of the corporation and in such manner as shall from time to time be determined by resolution of the Board of Directors. In the absence of such determination by the Board of Directors, such instruments shall be signed by the Treasurer or an Assistant Treasurer and countersigned by the President or a Vice President of the corporation.

SECTION 3. Deposit. All funds of the corporation shall be deposited from time to time to the credit of the corporation in such banks, trust companies or other depositories as the Board of Directors may select.

SECTION 4. Gifts. The Board of Directors may accept on behalf of the corporation any contribution, gift, bequest or devise for the general purposes or for any special purpose of the corporation.

ARTICLE VIII. CERTIFICATES OF MEMBERSHIP[18]

SECTION 1. Certificates of Membership. The Board of Directors may provide for the issuance of certificates evidencing membership in the corporation, which shall be in such form as may be determined by the Board. Such certificates shall be signed by the President or a Vice President and by the Secretary or an Assistant Secretary and shall be sealed with the seal of the corporation. All certificates evidencing membership of any class shall be consecutively numbered. The name and address of each member and the date of issuance of the certificate shall be entered on the records of the corporation. If any certificate shall become lost, mutilated or destroyed, a new certificate may be issued therefor upon such terms and conditions as the Board of Directors may determine.

SECTION 2. Issuance of Certificates. When a member has been elected to membership and has paid any initiation fee and dues that may then be required, a certificate of membership shall be issued in his name and delivered to him by the Secretary, if the Board of Directors shall have provided for the issuance of certificates of membership under the provisions of Section 1 of this Article VIII.[19]

ARTICLE IX. BOOKS AND RECORDS

The corporation shall keep correct and complete books and records of accounts and shall also keep minutes of the proceedings of its members, Board of Directors and committees having any of the authority of the Board of Directors, and shall keep at the registered or principal office a record giving the names and addresses of the members entitled to vote. All books and records of the corporation may be inspected by any member, or his agent or attorney for any proper purpose at any reasonable time.

ARTICLE X. FISCAL YEAR

The fiscal year of the corporation shall begin on the first day of January and end on the last day of December in each year.

ARTICLE XI. DUES

SECTION 1. Annual Dues.[20] The Board of Directors may determine from time to time the amount of initiation fee, if any, and annual dues payable to the corporation by members of each class.

SECTION 2. Payment of Dues. Dues shall be payable in advance on the first day of _____ in each fiscal year. Dues of a new member shall be prorated from the first day of the month in which such new member is elected to membership, for the remainder of the fiscal year of the corporation.

SECTION 3. Default and Termination of Membership. When any member of any class shall be in default in the payment of dues for a period of _____ months from the beginning of the fiscal year or period for which such dues became payable, his membership may thereupon be terminated by the Board of Directors in the manner provided in Article III [*sic*] of these by-laws.

ARTICLE XII. SEAL

The Board of Directors shall provide a corporate seal, which shall be in the form of a circle and shall have inscribed thereon the name of the corporation and the words "Corporate Seal. _____(Corporate Name)_____."

ARTICLE XIII. WAIVER OF NOTICE

Whenever any notice is required to be given under the provisions of the _____(State)_____ Non-Profit Corporation Act or under the provisions of the articles of incorporation or the by-laws of the corporation, a waiver thereof in writing signed by the person or persons entitled to such notice, whether before or after the time stated therein, shall be deemed equivalent to the giving of such notice.

ARTICLE XIV. AMENDMENTS TO BY-LAWS

These by-laws may be altered, amended or repealed and new by-laws may be adopted by a majority of the Directors present at any regular meeting or at any special meeting, if at least two days' written notice is given of intention to alter, amend or repeal or to adopt new by-laws at such meeting.

FOOTNOTES

[1]By definition in the Act, the by-laws are the code of rules adopted for the regulation of the corporate affairs, regardless of the name by which the code is designated. The term is here used because of its prevalence in corporate practice.

The initial by-laws are required by the Act to be adopted by the Directors. They may contain any provision for the regulation and management of the affairs of the corporation not inconsistent with law or the articles of incorporation.

[2]The corporation may have one or more classes of members (such as regular, associate, nonresident, honorary, etc.) or it may have no members. If it has no members, that fact shall be set forth in the articles of incorporation or the by-laws. If it has one or more classes, the designation, qualifications and rights of each class may be set forth either in the articles of incorporation or the by-laws. Even though set forth in the articles of incorporation, the statement may be repeated in the by-laws. The qualifications of a class of members may be described in the following manner:

Resident Members. Members of the _____ profession in good standing who reside or have an office within the State of _____ shall be eligible for resident membership.

[3]Members may be chosen in any manner prescribed in the articles of incorporation or in the by-laws. By way of illustration, Section 2 requires election by the Board of Directors. In the case of social clubs and similar organizations a provision that no member shall be elected over the negative vote of a fixed number of Directors may be preferred. In some types of corporations, applications for membership may be deemed desirable, and for such corporations the following paragraphs may be added to Section 2:

Except in the initial election of members, all applicants for membership shall file with the Secretary a written application in such form as the Board of Directors shall from time to time determine.

All applications for membership shall be presented promptly for consideration and investigation to the Board of Directors or to the Admissions Committee, if an Admissions Committee has been appointed by the Board of Directors; and if an Admissions Committee has been appointed, it shall report its recommendations promptly to the Board of Directors. A list of applications for membership shall from time to time be posted at the principal office of the corporation or mailed to each member of the corporation.

Not earlier than _____ days after a list of applications has been posted or mailed to members, the Board of Directors shall pass upon each application included in said list and either accept or reject it. After an applicant has been rejected, he may not make another application for membership within one year thereafter.

[4]The voting rights of members or any class of members may be limited, enlarged or denied under the Act to the extent specified in the articles of incorporation or the by-laws, but unless so specified each member is entitled to one vote.

The right to cumulative voting for Directors (giving each voting member the right to give one candidate a number of votes equal to his vote multiplied by the number of Directors to be elected, or to distribute such votes on the same principle among as many candidates as he shall desire) may be given by the by-laws.

The following alternative provisions may be used where it is desired to give voting rights to some class or classes of members and not to others:

Each member of the resident, sustaining and life classes shall have one vote on each matter submitted to a vote of the members. Members of the nonresident and honorary classes shall have no voting rights.

When all members are to be denied voting rights, the following may be substituted:

No member shall have any voting rights. All voting rights are vested solely in the Directors.

[5]Membership may or may not be transferable as provided by the by-laws. The following is suggested as an alternative in the event that it is desired to have membership be transferable:

Any membership in this corporation may be transferred and assigned by a member whose dues are paid in full, to any person who has the requisite qualifications and whose application is approved by the Board of Directors and elected to membership.

[6]In the absence of a provision fixing the number or percentage of members

entitled to call a meeting, the Act provides that a meeting may be called by members having one-twentieth of the votes entitled to be cast at such meeting.

[7]The Act provides that in the absence of a provision in the by-laws, all meetings shall be held at the registered office of the corporation.

[8]Unless otherwise provided in the by-laws or articles of incorporation, written notice stating the place, day and hour of meetings of members must be sent not less than ten nor more than fifty days prior to the meeting.

[9]The Act expressly confirms the right of members and directors to take action in the manner set forth in this Section.

[10]Unless a different number or percentage is provided by the by-laws, the members holding one-tenth of the votes will constitute a quorum.

[11]Proxy voting by members is authorized unless otherwise provided in the articles of incorporation or the by-laws. Some corporations, such as fraternities, may not wish to have their meetings attended by nonmembers. In view of the statutory permission to limit voting rights, a by-law providing that a proxy may be given only to another member should be valid when the circumstances make this a reasonable restriction.

[12]The Board of Directors may be designated by other titles (such as Board of Governors, Board of Managers, etc.) as provided in the by-laws. The group vested with the management of the affairs of the corporation, by whatever name designated in the by-laws, constitutes the Board of Directors of the corporation as that term is defined in the Act.

The articles of incorporation or the by-laws may prescribe qualifications for Directors.

[13]The number of Directors may be increased or decreased from time to time by amendment to the by-laws, unless otherwise provided in the articles of incorporation. It shall never be less than three. In the absence of a by-law, the number shall be the same as that stated in the articles of incorporation.

Directors need not be elected by members, but may be elected or appointed in the manner and for terms provided in the articles of incorporation or the by-laws.

Directors may be divided into classes and the terms of office of the several classes need not be uniform.

The Directors named in the articles of incorporation hold office until the first annual meeting of the members (unless otherwise specified in the articles or by-laws), and there need be no meeting of the members to elect them.

The by-laws may provide that any one or more officers shall be ex-officio members of the Board of Directors. Provision may be made in the by-laws for conducting elections of Directors by mail.

[14]Unless otherwise provided in the by-laws, a majority of the Directors shall constitute a quorum. In no event shall a quorum consist of less than one-third of the whole Board.

[15]Officers may be designated by other titles (such as Grand Master, Recorder, etc.) as may be provided in the by-laws, but shall always include (but need not be limited to) persons who occupy offices corresponding to those of President, Vice President, Secretary and Treasurer.

[16]Officers may be elected or appointed for such term, not exceeding three years,

as the by-laws provide. In the absence of such provision, officers shall be elected or appointed annually. Where desired, provision may be made in the by-laws for the election of some or all of the officers by the members, and where officers are to be elected by members, the by-laws may provide for conducting the election by mail.

[17]Officers elected or appointed by someone other than the Board of Directors can be removed only by the persons authorized to elect or appoint them.

[18]Certificates evidencing membership may be issued but are not necessary. No shares of stock may be issued and no dividends may be paid. If membership certificates are not desired, this Article of the by-laws may be omitted and the subsequent Articles renumbered; but since its phraseology is permissive it may be retained even though membership certificates are not used.

[19]If Article III [*sic*], Section 7, makes memberships transferable, a section substantially as follows may be added to Article VIII:

Section 3. Transfers of Certificates of Membership. Transfers of certificates of membership shall be made only on the records of the corporation by a registered member or by his attorney thereunto authorized by power of attorney duly executed and filed with the Secretary of the corporation, and on surrender for cancellation of the certificate evidencing the membership to be transferred.

[20]The amount of dues, if any are to be provided for, may be determined by the members if the by-laws so provide, or may be set forth in the by-laws, or determined in some other manner as may be desired by corporations of various types. This Article of the by-laws may be omitted if dues are not to be required from members.

9

Operational Taxation

ACTION ORGANIZATIONS

Organizations strive to attain and retain their tax-exempt status under section 501(c)(3) which requires that the organization be "organized and operated exclusively" for purposes such as religion, charity, and education and confer "no part of the net earnings" upon a private individual. In addition, an organization's legislative activities are limited to only an insubstantial amount, and political campaigning is absolutely prohibited.[1] The benefits flowing from section 501(c)(3) are twofold: (1) the organization itself is exempt from federal taxes, and (2) the organization's donors receive a section 170 deduction for their contributions.

For unfathomable reasons, the limitations on lobbying and campaigning are not imposed on all tax exempt organizations but only on selected ones of which the section 501(c)(3) organizations are the most important. Thus, the section 170 charitable deduction is unavailable under section 501(c)(4),[2] but a section 501(c)(4) organization may engage in substantial lobbying.[3] Obviously, a section 501(c)(3) organization may lose some of its contributions if its donors lose their deduction.[4] An organization loses its preferred status if it is found to be an "action" organization, a term that refers to the statutory limits on legislative activity and the prohibition on political activity.

According to the Treasury Regulation, an action organization (1) as a substantial part of its activities, attempts to influence legislation by either urging the public to contact its legislators (grass-roots lobbying) regarding legislation or advocates the adoption or rejection of legislation (direct lobbying); (2) participates, directly or indirectly, in a political campaign; or (3) has a main objective that may be attained only by legislation or defeat of proposed legislation and advocates the attainment of that objective.[5]

Much uncertainty surrounds the quantity and quality of activity that may be conducted without loss of section 501(c)(3) status. The issue is not purely a matter of interpretation of a federal statute; it invokes constitutional questions as well.

The American roots of the section 501(c)(3) exemption for religious, charitable, and educational organizations date back to 1894.[6] Although that early statute was declared unconstitutional, a similar exemption appeared in 1913.[7] Congress authorized the charitable deduction in 1917.[8] In 1934, Congress added the "no substantial" lobbying limitation to the exemption[9] and corresponding deductions.[10] This limitation was grounded in prior case law and did not represent a change in direction.[11] In *Slee v. Commissioner,* Judge Learned Hand conceded that the American Birth Control League was engaged in a charitable activity, but "agitating" for legislative change violated the exclusively charitable requirement of the section that preceded 501(c)(3). In 1954, Congress added the absolute prohibition on political campaigning to the exemption.[12] In 1969, the same prohibition was added to deductions for income, estate, and gift tax purposes, making similar requirements for the exemption and the corresponding deductions.[13] Congress, in the early 1970s, began to try to standardize the elusive concept of "substantiality" of legislative activity. Ultimately, Congress enacted section 501(h), which is designed to set specific limits for lobbying expenditures for qualified exempt organizations that elect to come within the provision.

Many commentators write that these limitations of tax benefits for charities and their donors are grounded in inequity and are contrary to the public good.[14] They question the constitutionality of restrictions on section 501(c)(3) organizations while other tax-exempt organizations may lobby unencumbered by tests of substantiality.

The U.S. Supreme Court may have permanently silenced their constitutional arguments in *Regan v. Taxation With Representation.*[15] This case addresses the tangential constitutional questions of freedom of speech and equal protection rather than major concerns involving the meaning of substantiality and the types of activities prohibited or limited under section 501(c)(3). *Taxation With Representation* (TWR) was a nonprofit corporation involved in tax reform. The Internal Revenue Service denied its application for section 501(c)(3) tax exempt status because a substantial part of its activities would involve lobbying and other attempts to influence legislation.[16] TWR sued, claiming that the prohibition against substantial lobbying is unconstitutional under the free-speech clause of the first amendment and equal protection implied from the due process clause of the fifth amendment.[17] The Court rejected TWR's argument that the denial of the exemption and the corresponding deductions for lobbying penalized it for its speech.

Congress has not infringed any First Amendment rights or regulated any First Amendment activity. Congress has simply chosen not to pay for TWR's lobbying. We again reject the "notion that First Amendment rights are somehow not fully realized unless they are subsidized by the State" (quoting Justice Douglas's concurrence in *Cammarano v. United States*, 358 U.S. 498, 515 (1950)).[18]

The Court also rejected TWR's argument of denial of equal protection,[19] even though veterans' organizations may lobby unrestricted by limits and still receive a tax exemption under section 501(c)(19), and their donors receive a deduction for contributions under section 170(c)(3).

The Court used a rational relationship analysis rather than a strict scrutiny analysis because no fundamental right was involved.[20] It held that the statutory classifications were valid and rational and within congressional power.

Congress—not TWR or this Court—has the authority to determine whether the advantage the public would receive from additional lobbying by charities is worth the money the public would pay to subsidize that lobbying, and other disadvantages that might accompany that lobbying. It appears that Congress was concerned that exempt organizations might use tax-deductible contributions to lobby to promote the private interests of their members. It is not irrational for Congress to decide that tax exempt charities such as TWR should not further benefit at the expense of taxpayers at large by obtaining a further subsidy for lobbying.[21]

In addition, the beneficial treatment afforded veterans' organizations was also rational. "Our country has a long standing policy of compensating veterans for their past contributions by providing them with numerous advantages. This policy has always been deemed to be legitimate."[22] The recommended approach for TWR would involve a reversion to its dual structure—section 501(c)(3) organization for nonlobbying and section 501(c)(4) for lobbying.[23]

There are four requirements for a section 501(c)(3) tax exemption:

1. That the organization be "organized and operated exclusively" for exempt purposes such as religion, charity, and education

2. That "no part of the net earnings" benefits any private individual

3. That "no substantial part of the activities" is used to carry on "propaganda, or otherwise attempting, to influence legislation (except as otherwise provided in subsection (h))"

4. That the organization "does not participate in, or intervene in (including the publishing or distributing of statements), any political campaign on behalf of any candidate for public office"

These criteria are intertwined. There is room for play because of the structure of this statute itself. The first criterion requires an "exclusive" exempt purpose while the third criterion allows an insubstantial amount of lobbying. The courts and administrative agencies have attempted to ascertain how much legislative and political activity the statute permits before the finding that the exempt organization has become an action organization.[24]

Exclusively

According to the Treasury Regulations, an organization is considered to be organized exclusively for an exempt purpose if it limits its articles of organization to an exempt purpose and limits its involvement in nonexempt purposes to only an insubstantial part of its activities. Because the Internal Revenue Service only examines the organizational documents, they should methodically track the insubstantiality language of section 501(c)(3) rather than venture into new directions and untested language. For example, in *Slee v. Commissioner*,[25] the lower courts intimated that if one of the Birth Control League's stated purposes was to influence legislation, exempt status may be denied for that reason alone. In another example, an organization ceased its legislative activities but failed for two years to change its articles, which authorized such activities.[26] The lower court held that the organization was not entitled to the exemption until its articles were amended. The court of appeals reversed indicating that the courts are willing to consider the issue one of fact. In litigated cases the courts have been more liberal than the Internal Revenue Service and are willing to look beyond the organizational documents to actual operations.

The Treasury Regulations also define "operated exclusively." An organization is operated exclusively for an exempt purpose if it engages primarily in activities that accomplish one or more of such exempt purposes specified in section 501(c)(3). An organization will not be so regarded if more than an insubstantial part of its activities is not in furtherance of an exempt purpose.[27] As a reading of the regulations indicates, exclusively does not mean "solely." Rather, an organization is permitted to engage in an insubstantial amount of nonexempt activities. The issue is how much is insubstantial.

[T]he term "exclusively" is given a connotation differing from the ordinary meaning of that term, as originally used, and activities which are minor, and not substantial, do not disqualify charitable or educational corporations from the benefits of the exemption nor do they disqualify individual contributors to such corporations from deducting them in their income tax returns.[28]

In *Seasongood v. Commissioner*, taxpayers had taken deductions for contributions made to a Good Government League. The League's stated purpose was "to provide an opportunity for discussion of matters of civic importance and to advance good government." The League urged such matters as voter registration and better public health practices.

Seasongood testified that something less than 5% of the time and effort of the League was devoted to the activities that the Tax Court found to be "political." In view of the rule, that this remedial statute must be liberally construed to effect its purpose, and in view of the fact that Seasongood's evidence was not successfully challenged either by adversary witnesses or destructive analysis, we conclude that the so-called "political activities" of the League were not in relation to all of its other activities *substantial,* within the meaning of this section.[29]

Former Secretary of the Treasury Dillon approved of this 5 percent figure;[30] however, recent cases have rejected the utility of the percentage test.

In *Christian Echoes National Ministry v. United States,*[31] the IRS revoked the organization's section 501(c)(3) exempt status. After reviewing its activities, the IRS found: "(1) it was not operated exclusively for charitable, educational or religious purposes; (2) it had engaged in substantial activity aimed at influencing legislation; and (3) it had directly and indirectly intervened in political campaigns on behalf of candidates for public office."[32] The court balanced the political activities within the context of Christian Echoes's objectives to determine whether a substantial amount of its activities were spent influencing or attempting to influence legislation.

A percentage test to determine whether the activities were substantial obscures the complexity of balancing the organization's activities in relation to its objectives and circumstances. An essential part of the program of Christian Echoes was to promote desirable governmental policies consistent with its objectives through legislation. The activities of Christian Echoes in influencing or attempting to influence legislation were not incidental, but were substantial and continuous.[33]

In *Haswell v. United States,*[34] the taxpayer was denied a deduction for contributions made to the National Association of Railroad Passengers, a nonprofit organization designed to improve passenger services of American railroads. The organization used reports and brochures to inform the public of problems affecting rail passengers. The organization also attempted to influence pending interstate commerce legislation by testifying through its representative Haswell before congressional committees. The testimony did not reflect "nonpartisan analysis, study or research" because it "was not the type of full and fair objective expositions that would enable the public to reach an independent conclusion on the subject."[35] In rejecting the *Seasongood* percentage test, the court held

The term "exclusively" is given a connotation that differs from the ordinary meaning of the term, and activities which are minor, and not substantial, do not disqualify charitable and educational organizations from the benefit of the exemption nor do they disqualify individual contributors to such organizations from a deduction. The limitation is remedial and should be liberally construed.

The political efforts of an organization must be balanced in the context of the objectives and circumstances of the organization to determine whether a substantial part of its activities is to influence, or is an attempt to influence, legislation. A percentage test to determine whether the activities are substantial is not appropriate. Such a test obscures the complexity of balancing the organization's activities in relation to its objectives and circumstances in the context of the totality of the organization.[36]

Lobbying

No substantial part of the activities of a section 501(c)(3) organization may be carrying on propaganda or otherwise attempting to influence legislation. To the extent that lobbying is permissible, it must be related to the organization's exempt purpose.

Lobbying is restricted whether it be direct or indirect (grass-roots) lobbying. Direct lobbying consists of communications with a member of a legislative body, the member's staff, or nonlegislative government employee involved in the legislative process for the principal purpose of influencing legislation.[37] The limitation on lobbying applies at all levels of government where legislative action is taken.

Indirect or grass-roots lobbying consists of attempts to influence legislation through public opinion by (1) presenting a one-sided view of an issue in any communications medium,[38] (2) urging the public to contact legislators concerning an issue,[39] (3) publicly advertising a particular point of view concerning legislation,[40] (4) contacting prospective members of an organization concerning a legislative issue,[41] (5) encouraging others to lobby,[42] or (6) making public speeches concerning legislative issues.

Organizations frequently try to characterize their activities toward the public as permissible education and research rather than propaganda. To avoid classification as propaganda, an organization's presentation should be nonpartisan, well balanced, and untainted by selfish or ulterior motives. The Treasury Regulations provide guidance for what constitutes propaganda attempts to affect public opinion within the context of private foundations. The regulation can be analogized to the section 501(c)(3) exemption. The regulations provide that the following activities will not be classified as "propaganda, or otherwise attempting, to influence legislation":

1. Nonpartisan analysis, study, or research
2. Technical advice or assistance (to a governmental body)
3. Decisions affecting the powers and duties of the foundation
4. Examinations and discussions of broad social. economic, and similar problems[43]

For a more detailed discussion of this issue, see the section on taxable expenditures in Chapter 13.

Section 501(h) Lobbying Election

In an effort to add more definition to the judicial and administrative concept of substantiality, Congress in 1976 enacted section 501(h).[44] This section sets optional dollar limits on permissible direct and grass-roots lobbying for qualifying public operating charities. Penalty taxes and a total loss of exemption may result from violation of the limits. These limits are elective, and a charitable organization may well choose to continue under the general section 501(c)(3) rules.[45]

Only certain organizations are eligible to make the section 501(h) election. Not only must the organization be described in section 501(c)(3) and not be a "disqualified group,"[46] but it must be one of the following:

1. Educational institutions[47]
2. Hospitals and medical research organizations[48]
3. Organizations supporting public schools[49]
4. Organizations publicly supported by charitable contributions[50]
5. Organizations publicly supported by admissions, sales, performance of services, or furnishing facilities[51]
6. Organizations supporting public charities provided the charity is not a disqualified organization[52]

The section 501(h) election may not be made by a church, association of churches, integrated auxiliary of a church, or an affiliated group of church-related organizations.[53] Private foundations are regulated under section 4945(d).

The election may be made at any time before the end of the taxable year by filing IRS Form 5768; however, it cannot be revoked for that taxable year after it has begun.[54] This precludes an electing charity from revoking its election should it be approaching the lobbying limits.

If organizations are considered part of an affiliated group, and at least one organization has elected the section 501(h) limits, the lobbying expenditures and exempt purpose expenditures of the group are aggregated.[55] Organizations are affiliated if the governing instruments of one of the organizations requires it to be bound by the decisions of another organization with respect to legislative matters or if the governing board of one organization is controlled by a sufficient number of representatives of another organization such as to cause or prevent action in legislative issues by the controlled organization.[56]

The lobbying election works as follows. A charity must establish its "exempt purpose expenditures"—the total amount devoted to religious, charitable, educational purposes and so forth.[57] The "lobbying nontaxable amounts,"[58] the maximum amounts a charity may spend without incurring a tax, are as follows:

Exempt purposes expenditures of:	*Lobbying nontaxable amount:*
up to $500,000	20% of the exempt purpose expenditure
$500,000 to $1 million	$100,000 + 15% of the excess over $500,000
$1 million to $1.5 million	$175,000 + 10% of the excess over $1 million
More than $1.5 million	$225,000 + 5% of the excess over $1.5 million
	Maximum for any organization is $1 million

A separate limit is placed on grass-roots lobbying.[59] The grass-roots nontaxable amount for any taxable year is 25 percent of the organization's lobbying nontaxable amount for that taxable year.[60] An organization exceeding the general limitation is subject to an excise tax of 25 percent of the amount of the excess lobbying expenditures for that year.[61] An organization exceeding 150 percent of the limits on the average over a four-year period will lose its exempt status under section 501(c)(3).[62]

"Influencing legislation" for purposes of lobbying and grass-roots amounts does not include the following:

1. Making available nonpartisan analysis, study, or research
2. Providing technical advice to a governmental body in response to a written request
3. Appearances before a legislative body regarding matters that might affect the organization's tax status
4. Communications between an organization and its bona fide members
5. A communication with a government official other than: (a) communication with a member of a legislative body (which would constitute the influencing of legislation), or (b) communication for the principal purpose of influencing legislation[63]

This congressional effort to define the elusive substantiality limits does not promise to solve the majority of problems. The provision, being elective, will probably not be used to a great extent because of the extensive disclosure requirements necessary to determine the applicable limits. Section 6033(b)(8) imposes a reporting requirement for lobbying expenditures, lobbying nontaxable amount, grass-roots expenditures, and grass-roots nontaxable amounts. The report is made on IRS Form 990, schedule A, part VII. Any tax due is remitted on IRS Form 4720, schedule F at the same time that the form 990 is filed.

Section 4911(a)(1) imposes a tax on excess lobbying expenditures made by organizations having a section 501(h) election in effect for the taxable year. The excess lobbying expenditures are taxed at a 25 percent rate. Excess lobbying expenditures are the greater of the difference between the lobbying expenditures and the lobbying nontaxable amount for the taxable year or the difference between the grass-roots expenditures and the grass-roots nontaxable amount for the taxable year.[64]

If an organization normally exceeds the lobbying ceiling amount or the grass-roots ceiling amount, it will lose its tax exempt status.[65] The legislative history indicates that Congress intended an aggregate approach. If the expenditures were greater than the ceilings on the average over a consecutive four-year period, the exemption would be lost. This rule does not seem to apply unless the same ceiling is exceeded over the four-year period. Alternating excesses under the two different ceilings would not cause revocation of the tax exempt status.

An otherwise eligible organization cannot become a social welfare organization under section 501(c)(4) if it lost its status as a charity under section 501(c)(3) for excessive lobbying.[66]

Political Campaigning

The "no campaigning" prohibition presents similar considerations to "insubstantial lobbying." Because the prohibition is absolute, the substantiality tests are often irrelevant. "There is no requirement that political campaigning be substantial."[67] Many courts, however, have judicially engrafted the substantiality tests onto political campaigning.[68] The definitional components of impermissible activities, including tests of propaganda, are relevant. In addition, organizations frequently skirt both the lobbying and campaigning clauses because of their interrelated nature.[69]

The no campaigning prohibition arises often within the context of voter education activities. The Treasury Regulations provide guidance as to whether the activity is influencing the outcome of a public election.

[A]n organization shall be considered to be influencing the outcome of any specific public election if it participates or intervenes, directly or indirectly, in any political campaign on behalf of or in opposition to any candidate for public office. The term "candidate for public office" means an individual who offers himself, or is proposed by others, as a contestant for an elective public office, whether such office be national, State or local. Activities which constitute participation or intervention in a political campaign on behalf of or in opposition to a candidate include, but are not limited to:

(i) Publishing or distributing written or printed statements or making oral statements on behalf of or in opposition to such a candidate;

(ii) Paying salaries or expenses of campaign workers; and

(iii) Conducting or paying the expenses of conducting a voter-registration drive limited to the geographic area covered by the campaign.[70]

The IRS has provided the primary source of guidance in this area, however, through its revenue rulings. It formally denied tax exempt status to an organization that sent political candidates a questionnaire and published their responses in a newsletter without editorial comment.[71] The organization sought a section 501(c)(3) exemption for being an organization operated exclusively for educational purposes. The IRS denied the exemption and classified the organization as an action organization because it participated and intervened in a political campaign.[72]

The IRS immediately reversed itself, however.[73] It listed certain voter education activities, which, when conducted in a nonpartisan manner, will be permissible under section 501(c)(3) and will not constitute disqualifying political activity. These situations illustrate permissible and impermissible voter education activity:

Situation 1. An organization annually prepares and makes available to the public the voting records of members of Congress on legislation involving a wide range of subjects. The organization adds no explicit or implicit editorial opinion. This is permissible.

Situation 2. An organization sends a questionnaire to all candidates for a particular office, publishes the answers, and distributes them to the public. The issues are selected based on their importance to the general public as a whole. The organization adds no explicit or implicit editorial opinion. This is permissible.

Situation 3. An organization prepares a publication similar to that in *Situation 2* but evidences a bias on certain issues. That organization will not be tax exempt.

Situation 4. An organization concerned with land conservation publishes a voting guide without any express bias. The guide, however, only concerns conservation issues. Since it is not concerned with broad-ranged voter education but with one narrow issue, it has engaged in an impermissible activity.[74]

Revenue Ruling 80-282 further amplified the Internal Revenue Service's position.[75] The organization published a newsletter that contained the voting records of all incumbents in Congress regarding selected issues of importance to the organization. The organization's position was compared with the incumbents' votes. However, the newsletter was nonpartisan and did not contain any reference to upcoming political campaigns. Even though the format and content of the publication was not neutral, the candidates for reelection could not be identified, and no comment was made on an individual's overall qualifications for office.[76] The IRS ruled that the organization qualified for a tax exemption. It distinguished *Situations 3 and 4* in Revenue Ruling 78-248, primarily because the organization sufficiently divorced itself from political campaigning.

The IRS has made other rulings regarding the political campaigning prohibition.

1. An organization formed to collect campaign speeches, interviews, and other commentary from a candidate for a historically important office for donation to a university or public library qualifies for the section 501(c)(3) exemption.[77]

2. An organization formed to promote and elevate ethics in a political campaign and that distributed information concerning general campaign practices, furnished teaching aides to teachers, and published a proposed code of fair campaign practices qualifies for the section 501(c)(3) exemption.[78]
3. An organization operating a broadcasting station does not lose its section 501(c)(3) exemption by providing air time to candidates in compliance with section 312(a)(7) of the Federal Communications Act of 1934.[79]
4. An organization created to improve public education loses its section 501(c)(3) exemption by announcing its recommended slate of candidates for the school board.[80]

Special Problems of Universities

The Treasury Regulations permit an educational organization to "advocate a particular position or viewpoint so long as it presents a sufficiently full and fair exposition of the pertinent facts as to permit an individual or the public to form an independent opinion or conclusion. . . . [A] mere presentation of unsupported opinion" is impermissible.[81]

Universities encountered section 501(c)(3) problems with the rise of student political activism in the late 1960s and early 1970s. Worried about a loss of their tax exempt status, some university officials began scrutinizing the curriculum and extracurricular activities. Prompted by a concern that student demonstrations over United States foreign policy in Vietnam and Cambodia would jeopardize their exemption, the American Council on Education in 1970 released a set of "Guidelines on Questions Relating to Tax Exemption and Political Activities."

These guidelines stressed that a university should structure its activities to include no campaigning and not more than an insubstantial amount of legislative activities.[82] Problem areas included rearranging the academic calendar—probably permissible as long as no school hours are lost (a shortened year due to a recess before an election to allow faculty and staff to participate in an election might be interpreted as indirect participation in a campaign). Student political groups on campus would probably present no problems. However, if these groups participate in a campaign, beyond the campus, the university should charge and collect appropriate fees for university facilities and services. Also, university officials should separate their personal political views from official university statements regarding a campaign.[83]

Two examples of these concerns of university officials have been treated in revenue rulings. In one, the IRS ruled that a university is not participating in a political campaign by offering a political science course that requires the students to actively participate in a political campaign of their choice.[84] In the other, the IRS ruled that a university's provision of facilities and a professor for the campus newspaper that contains students' editorial opinions on political and legislative matters is not an attempt by the university to influence legislation or participate in a campaign.[85]

Special Problems of Churches

The general problems of educational and charitable organizations apply to religious organizations as well. In *United States v. Dykema*[86] the IRS requested church and individual financial records from the pastor of the Christian Liberty Church to determine whether the church was exempt under section 501(c)(3).[87] The district court denied enforcement of the summons for the information. The court of appeals reversed, holding that the pastor's individual tax liability should be investigated in the same manner as any other taxpayer.[88] The court also granted permission to investigate the church's tax status. "It must be remembered that tax exemption is a privileged status and that the taxpayer claiming it has the burden of demonstrating entitlement thereto."[89]

In another case, it appeared that the church was granted special privileges that *Dykema's* fifteen-member Christian Liberty Church was not afforded. In *Abortion Rights Mobilization, Inc. v. Regan*,[90] the pro-abortion group challenged the Roman Catholic Church's tax-exempt status claiming that the church's involvement in the abortion controversy disqualified it from the exemption. The group is tax exempt under section 501(c)(3) and is contending that the lobbying and campaigning limits are being discriminatorily applied against them. The court treated the case as raising numerous standing questions and did not particularly address the exemption question.

> The complaint also fails to state a violation of § 501(c)(3) by the church defendants. They have received a determination letter from the IRS that confirms their tax-exempt status. Even if, as plaintiffs contend, that letter was erroneously or illegally issued the church is entitled to rely upon it and withhold payment of taxes. The Code imposes no duty upon the church to gain preclearance from the IRS before embarking on activities that might trench upon the § 501(c)(3) prohibitions against political activity. If the church does engage in these proscribed endeavors, then it is liable to revocation of its exemption, but as long as it holds that exemption, it cannot be said to have violated the Code.[91]

An organization must monitor and limit its legislative and political activities to maintain its tax exempt status under section 501(c)(3). It should follow judicial and administrative guidelines for substantiality, since definitive legislative guidelines do not appear to be forthcoming. Particular care must be taken to avoid the appearance of political campaigning, since the prohibition, at least technically, is absolute.

UNRELATED BUSINESS INCOME

The tax on unrelated business income is a congressional attempt to bridge the unfathomable chasm between nonprofit tax exempt activities and business or for-profit activities. The tax on unrelated business income admits that to a limited extent nonprofit tax exempt status is not incompatible with business activities.

An organization that is operated for the primary purpose of carrying on a trade or business is not tax exempt. This is true even if it pays all of its profits to one or more exempt organizations. Such an organization is a "feeder" organization and is taxed on its entire income not just its so-called unrelated business income.[92]

A feeder organization may be utilized by a tax exempt organization to conduct business activities and feed the profits to the tax exempt organization without running the risk of loss of the tax exempt status of the parent organization. This is particularly true of section 501(c)(3) organizations which may carry on, but an insubstantial part of their activities not in furtherance of, their exempt purposes.

The feeder organization may escape taxation itself if its income is derived from rents which would be excluded under section 512(b)(3), if it were applicable, the trade or business is carried on by volunteers without compensation, or the trade or business is the sale of merchandise substantially all of which had been received by the organization as gifts or contributions.[93]

If the tax exempt organization decides to carry on the trade or business rather than use a feeder organization, it will be subject to the tax on unrelated business income.

After 1969, the only tax exempt organizations that are exempt from the provisions on unrelated business income are governmental instrumentalities, which are exempt under the provisions of section 501(c)(1) except for colleges and universities owned or operated by an exempt governmental instrumentality or agency.[94]

Unrelated business taxable income is the organization's gross income from any unrelated trade or business regularly carried on by it less allowable deductions directly connected with the carrying on of the trade or business.[95]

Trade or Business

An unrelated trade or business is not substantially related to the exercise or performance of the organization's exempt purposes.[96] "Related" does not incorporate the need of an organization for income nor the use made by the organization of the profits.[97] In effect, this amounts to a repudiation of the "ultimate destination" test promulgated by the Supreme Court in *Trinidad v. Sagrada Orden de Predicadores*.[98] Under the ultimate destination test the Court looked not to the nature of the activities nor to the source of the income but rather to what was eventually done with the earnings. Under section 513(a) the ultimate use of the earnings is not relevant. The important factor is source.

A trade or business is any activity carried on for the production of income from the sale of goods or performance of services.[99] The activity need not generate a profit to be a trade or business. Under the regulations "trade or business" for purposes of the tax on unrelated business income has the same meaning as under section 162.[100] Therefore, passive investment activities such as the management of an investment portfolio do not constitute a trade or business under section 513 because they do not constitute a trade or business for section 162 purposes.[101] Tying unrelated business income to section 162 gives effect to the congressional purpose to tax only activities that would be in competition with businesses.[102] Hence, income derived from dividends, interest, annuities, royalties, and rents are generally excluded from income.[103]

The tax on unrelated business income is applicable to certain trusts regularly carrying on a trade or business directly or by partnership of which the trust is a member.[104] The tax is imposed on any tax exempt trust, except as relating to a private foundation, which but for the section 501(a) exemption would be subject to subchapter J of the Internal Revenue Code.[105]

Regularly Carried On

The business activity must be regularly carried on to have tax consequence.[106] Keeping in mind the unfair competition concern of Congress, activities which are carried on infrequently or sporadically are not considered to be commercial activities. Given the frequency and continuity with which the activities are conducted and the manner in which they are pursued, if they are generally similar to commercial activities, they are deemed to be regularly carried on.[107] For example, annual fund-raising activity was not regularly carried on although a considerable amount of time was expended in preparation because the actual performances of the fund-raising show were given over one weekend.[108] Conversely, a foundation that built eighty homes over an eighteen-month period to help a church raise funds was regularly carrying on the activity even though it did not intend to continue the activity.[109]

When comparing activities of tax exempt organizations with for-profit business, the normal time span of the activities must be considered. A normal business activity which is generally conducted year-round will not be considered regularly carried on by a tax exempt organization that conducts the same activity for a limited time span as in the first example above.[110] But, carrying on the activity on a regular basis albeit for a relatively short aggregate time span is the regular conduct of a trade or business.[111] Business activity normally conducted on a seasonal basis will be considered to be regularly carried on by an exempt organization if it is conducted for a significant part of the season.[112]

Efforts of exempt organizations must be conducted with the competitive and promotional efforts typical of commercial activities to be considered regular.[113] The rule does not apply to short-term fund-raising activities.[114]

Substantially Related

Treasury Regulations section 1.513-1(d) defines substantially related. Gross income is unrelated business income if the conduct of the trade or business generating it is not substantially related to the tax exempt purpose. There must be a causal relationship between the conduct of the business activity and the exempt purpose other than through the production of income, and the causal relationship must be substantial. This means that the business activity such as the production or distribution of goods or the performance of services which generate the income must contribute importantly to the accomplishment of the exempt purpose to be substantially related.

Not only must the activity contribute importantly to the accomplishment of the exempt purpose, but the magnitude of the activities must be considered. Activities which contribute importantly may generate unrelated business income if conducted on a scale larger than necessary.[115]

Treasury Regulations section 1.513-2(a)(4) also contains a definition of substantially related, and it is not necessarily coextensive with Treasury Regulations section 1.513-1(d). This second definition of substantially related provides that the principal purposes of the trade or business must be to further the exempt purpose of the organization without regard to the production of income. Again, the nature and size of the trade or business must be compared with the nature and extent of the organization's exempt purpose to make a proper determination of substantially related.

Exceptions

Congress specifically excluded certain types of activities from the definition of unrelated trade or business. If substantially all the work performed in carrying on the trade or business is done on a volunteer basis without compensation, the trade or business is not unrelated.[116] This exception does not apply to trusts.[117] Moreover, this exception does not apply if the performance of services is not a material income-producing factor.[118] For example, weekly dances sponsored by a tax exempt organization through volunteer workers did not generate unrelated business income from admission fees charged.[119]

Also excluded from unrelated trade or business is one carried on by a section 501(c)(3) organization or a public college or university primarily for the convenience of its members, patients, officers, or employees.[120] The operation of a university laundry for the convenience of students, staff, and faculty is not an unrelated trade or business.[121] The exclusion extends to any section 501(c)(4) local association of employees organized before May 27, 1969, which sells items of work-related clothes and equipment and vending machine items, snack bars, or other food-dispensing facilities for the convenience of members at their usual place of employment.[122]

Selling merchandise substantially all of which was contributed or donated to the organization is not unrelated.[123] Hence, operation of thrift shops selling donated goods to the public is not unrelated.[124]

Certain activities conducted in connection with trade shows and state fairs are not an unrelated trade or business. Nonprofit charitable (section 501(c)(3)), social welfare (section 501(c)(4)), and agricultural (section 501(c)(5)) organizations which regularly conduct the fair or exposition as one of their substantial exempt purposes may conduct public entertainment activity of the kind traditionally conducted at fairs or expositions promoting agricultural and educational purposes without loss of exemption or tax on the proceeds of the activity.[125] The activity must be conducted in conjunction with an international, national, regional, state, or local fair or exposition.[126] The activity must be conducted under state law permitting such activity to be conducted only by that type of exempt organization or by a governmental entity for a period not exceeding twenty days per year. The state must allow the exempt organization to pay a lesser percentage of the revenues derived than the state would otherwise require from other organizations.[127]

A union (section 501(c)(5)) or a trade association (section 501(c)(6)) that regularly conducts a convention or trade show that stimulates interest in or demand for an industry's product may conduct the kind of activity traditionally associated with conventions, annual meetings, or trade shows without risking tax exempt status or incurring tax on such activities.[128] Rentals of display space to suppliers for sales to members also are excluded from unrelated business income.[129]

A tax exempt hospital may provide certain services to certain other exempt hospitals without tax consequence. The services must be of the kind provided tax free by a cooperative hospital service organization under section 501(e)(1)(A).[130] The recipient hospitals must have facilities limited to 100 or fewer inpatients, and the services must be consistent with the recipient hospital's exempt purpose.[131] The services must be provided at a fee or cost at or below the actual cost of providing the services including allowance for straight-line depreciation and a reasonable return on capital goods used in providing the service.[132]

Congress has excluded income derived by tax exempt organizations and political organizations from bingo games if state or local law permits bingo to be carried on by such organizations and it is not in competition with commercial bingo games.[133] It is irrelevant whether the bingo game is operated by paid workers or volunteers.[134] Moreover, bingo must not be the primary purpose for which the organization was created. The exclusion was limited to bingo and no other game of chance before the Tax Reform Act of 1984.[135] Section 311 of the Tax Reform Act of 1984 extended the bingo exclusion from unrelated business income to any game of chance conducted by a nonprofit organization authorized to conduct such game of chance by a state law in effect as of October 5, 1983, which also prohibited conduct of such game of chance by anyone other than a nonprofit organization. The provision applies to games of chance conducted after June 30, 1981, in taxable years ending after that date. If gambling including bingo is prohibited by state or local law regardless of the degree of enforcement, proceeds from bingo or other games of chance are unrelated business income.[136]

For mutual or cooperative telephone or electric companies, qualified pole rentals under section 501(c)(12)(D) are not unrelated business income.[137]

Taxation of Unrelated Business Income

The tax imposed by section 511(a) is computed on unrelated business taxable income. The tax base of unrelated business income is calculated by determining the organization's ordinary gross income derived from the unrelated trade or business and subtracting therefrom deductions otherwise allowed under chapter 1 of the Internal Revenue Code which are directly connected with the carrying on of the unrelated trade or business.[138] The gross income and deductions are to be computed with certain modifications required by the statute.[139]

Gross Income

Unrelated business taxable income does not include income from the organization's exempt activities but only certain ordinary gross income derived from an unrelated trade or business and a percentage of unrelated debt-financed income.[140]

In general, passive investment income is excluded from the organization's gross income because the generation of passive investment income is not competitive with business organizations. Accordingly, dividends, interest, annuities, royalties (including overriding royalties), and rents predominantly derived from real property are excluded.[141] Also excluded are capital gains and gains on the lapse or termination of options written by the organization in connection with its investment activities to buy or sell securities.[142] All income from research performed for the United States and its agencies or instrumentalities or any state and its political subdivisions is excluded,[143] as well as all income derived by a college, university, or hospital from research.[144] Similarly, all income from research by an organization that is organized and operated to carry out fundamental research and make it freely available to the public is excluded.[145]

Special rules exist with respect to certain types of organizations. Unrelated business taxable income of a foreign organization includes United States source unrelated business taxable income as well as effectively connected unrelated business taxable income.[146]

For social clubs (section 501(c)(7)), employees' associations (section 501(c)(9)), supplemental unemployment compensation benefit trusts (section 501(c)(17)), and group legal services plans (section 501(c)(20)), "exempt function income" is excluded from unrelated business taxable income.[147] Exempt function income means gross income derived from dues, fees, charges, or similar amounts received from members or their dependents as guests for goods, facilities, or services in furtherance of the tax exempt purposes of the organization.[148]

Exempt function income also includes certain amounts set aside exclusively for a charitable purpose or by section 501(c)(9), (17), or (20) organizations to provide payment of life, sick, accident, or other benefits including reasonable costs of administration.[149] A holding company exempt under section 501(c)(2) which pays its income to a social club, employees' association, supplemental unemployment compensation benefit trust, and group legal services plans may exclude exempt function income if it files a consolidated return with the payee organizations. Social clubs, employees' associations, supplemental unemployment compensation benefit trusts, and group legal services plans do not recognize gain on the sale of property used for exempt purposes if other property is purchased within the period beginning one year before and three years after the date of sale for at least the sale price of the old property.[150] Gain is recognized to the extent that the gain is not reinvested in other exempt purpose property.[151]

Unrelated business taxable income does not include amounts attributable to payments for life, sick, accident, or health insurance with respect to the members and their dependents of section 501(c)(19) veterans' organizations which is set aside for paying insurance benefits or used exclusively for charitable purposes.[152]

Payments of rents, royalties, interest, and annuities by a controlled to a control organization may be included in the gross income of the control organization depending on the tax exempt status of the controlled organization.[153] If the controlled organization is tax exempt, the parent or control organization must include in gross income a percentage of the payments received based on the ratio of the controlled organization's unrelated business taxable income to its hypothetical total taxable income if the controlled organization were not an exempt organization.[154] If the controlled organization is not a tax exempt organization, the percentage is based on the ratio of the controlled organization's total taxable income less any amount which would not be unrelated business income if earned by the parent to the controlled organization's taxable income.[155]

If a tax exempt organization is a partner in a partnership which regularly carries on an unrelated trade or business, it must include its distributable share of partnership income in its unrelated business income.[156]

Income derived from advertising is specifically included in unrelated business income whether it is carried on as a principal activity or is merely part of an aggregate of similar activities.[157] The Court of Appeals for the Federal Circuit in *American College of Physicians v. U.S.*, 743 F.2d 1570 (Fed. Cir. 1984) ruled that the sale of advertising in a professional medical journal published by a tax exempt organization is substantially related to the organization's exempt purpose. The decision is based on a finding that the advertising was informational and designed to alert doctors to new developments in pharmaceuticals. Education of internists is one of the organization's exempt purposes. Sale of advertising falls into the category of exploitation of exempt function and will be treated in regard to deductions for expenses incurred.

Deductions

Deductions which are normally allowed business organizations under chapter 1 of the code are allowed to exempt organizations in computing unrelated business taxable income if the expenses are directly connected with the carrying on of the trade or business.[158] Thus, expenses to be deductible must meet the requirements of the particular section in chapter 1 such as section 162 or 168 but also must be directly connected. Congress appears to have overcompensated here by placing an additional requirement on tax exempt organizations not imposed on businesses.

To be directly related, the deduction must have a "proximate and primary relationship" to the carrying on of the trade or business.[159] Directly related expenses fall into one of two categories. Expenses such as salaries paid to full-time employees with respect to the unrelated business activities and depreciation on buildings and equipment solely used in the conduct of the unrelated trade or business are expenses attributable solely to unrelated business activity and are deductible to the extent allowed under chapter 1 of the code. Dual use expenses must be prorated. Dual use implies a combined use, part of which is not unrelated business activity. The allocation must be made on a reasonable basis.[160] Allocation based on hours used is permissible.[161]

Deduction for expenses incurred in unrelated business activity which exploits an exempt activity generally are denied on the grounds that they are not directly connected with the unrelated trade or business activities but are related to the exempt purpose.[162] The regulation gives as an example the sale of advertising in a periodical of an exempt organization which contains editorial material relevant to its exempt purpose.[163] Nonetheless, the deductions may be allowed if the unrelated trade or business activity is the kind that is carried on for profit by business entities and the exempt activity exploited is the kind normally conducted by businesses in pursuit of the business.[164] The deductions are allowed to the extent of the income from the exempt activity and do not create or increase a loss from the unrelated trade or business activity.[165]

Advertising expenses are treated in detail in the regulations. Advertising expenses incurred in the sale of advertising in an exempt organization's periodical include costs directly incurred in selling or publishing the advertising.[166] After expenses of publishing have been allocated between advertising and editorial expenses, the income derived from publication must be allocated to advertising and circulation income.[167] If advertising income does not exceed advertising expenses, the loss may be used against other unrelated business income.[168] If the advertising income exceeds advertising expenses and the circulation income exceeds editorial expenses, the unrelated business income is equal to the difference between the advertising income and advertising expense.[169] However, if the advertising income exceeds advertising expenses and editorial expenses exceed circulation income, the total publication expense is unrelated business income. In this event, losses cannot be carried over or used against other unrelated business income.[170]

Certain deductions are denied as the quid pro quo for excluding the corresponding income item from unrelated business taxable income. Hence, deductions are denied for expenses incurred in generating dividends, interest, payments with respect to securities, loans, annuities, royalties, rents, and research expenses.[171]

A charitable contribution deduction under section 170 is allowed but limited to 10 percent of the unrelated business taxable income computed without regard to the charitable deduction.[172] For trusts under section 511(b) the charitable contribution deduction is allowed under the 50, 30, and 20 percent limitations on percentage of section 170(b).[173]

The net operating loss deduction is allowed but is computed without regard to any item of income or deduction not included in the computation of unrelated business taxable income.[174] Taxable years in which the organization had no unrelated business taxable income are not considered as preceding taxable year(s) for the purposes of section 172.[175] The net operating loss carry-back and carry-over must be computed accordingly.

Each organization having unrelated business income is entitled to a $1,000 deduction which cannot increase or create a section 172 net operating loss.[176] With respect to a diocese, province of a religious order, or a convention or association of churches, each parish, individual church, district, or other local unit is entitled to a deduction equal to the lesser of $1,000 or its gross income derived from an unrelated trade or business regularly carried on by the local unit.[177] If a separate return is filed by the local unit, it must take the deduction, not the parent organization.[178]

Tax

The unrelated business taxable income of an exempt organization is taxed at the rates imposed on corporations in section 11, except for trusts otherwise taxable under subchapter J but for the tax exemption.[179] In this latter case, the trust unrelated business taxable income is taxed at the trust rates provided in section 1(e).[180] No personal exemptions are allowed.[181] Trusts are subject to the minimum tax rate imposed by section 55.[182] Other exempt organizations are subject to the corporate minimum tax of section 56.[183]

Various tax credits are allowed against the tax imposed under section 511. The foreign tax credit is allowed by section 515. Section 48(a)(4) allows an investment tax credit for property used predominantly in an unrelated trade or business, if it is otherwise qualified for the credit. Also available are the credits for possessions taxes, alcohol used as fuel, and increasing research activities.

Filing and Miscellaneous

An exempt organization having unrelated trade or business gross income of at least $1,000 must file IRS Form 990-T, Exempt Organization Business Income Tax Return, on or before the fifteenth day of the fifth month after the close of the taxable year.[184] The tax due must be remitted with the return. The consolidated return provisions are not applicable.[185]

Exempt organizations owing tax on unrelated business taxable income are subject to the same assessment and collection procedures as taxpayers in general.[186] Likewise, the same penalties for negligence, civil fraud, failure to file, and failure to pay apply to exempt organizations having unrelated business taxable income.[187]

Accounting methods and fiscal year selection provisions applicable to other taxpayers apply to exempt organizations having unrelated business taxable income.[188]

State Taxation of Unrelated Business Taxable Income

Some states exempt certain organizations from the state income or franchise tax but impose the tax on unrelated business income. See Table 10 for a list of states that tax unrelated business income.

Table 10
State Taxation of Unrelated Business Income

The following states tax unrelated business income:

Arizona	Sections 20-1566,43-1201
California	Cal. Rev. & Tax § 23731
Colorado	Section 39-22-177
District of Columbia	Section 47-1554
Georgia	Section 1002
Hawaii	Section 235-2.3
Idaho	Section 63-3026
Illinois	Ch. 120, § 2-205
Indiana	Section 6-2-1-7.5
Kansas	Section 79-32,113
Maryland	Art. 81, § 288(d)(5)
Michigan	Section 208.35
Minnesota	Section 290
Montana	Section 15-31-101
New York	N.Y. Tax §§ 290-296
North Carolina	Section 105-130.11
North Dakota	Section 57-38-09
Oklahoma	Section 2359
Oregon	Section 317.930
West Virginia	Section 11-24-5

UNRELATED DEBT-FINANCED INCOME

Some of the forms of passive investment income which are excluded from unrelated business taxable income under section 512 are reincluded as unrelated debt-financed income. The concept of unrelated debt-financed income was designed to curtail abuses of sale-leaseback arrangements such as in the *Clay Brown*[189] and *University Hill Foundation*[190] cases.

The unrelated debt-financed income provisions apply to the same organizations as do the unrelated business income provisions. All of an exempt organization's income derived from debt-financed property held to produce income and not related to the organization's exempt purpose is proportionately subject to the tax on unrelated business income.

Debt-Financed Property

Debt-financed property is subject to acquisition indebtedness at any time during the taxable year or within twelve months of disposition and is held for the production of income.[191] Such property includes realty, tangible personal property, and corporate stock. Debt-financed property does not include the following:

1. Exempt-function or related property (property substantially all of which is used for a substantially related purpose or function constituting the basis of the tax exemption)

2. Property the income from which is taken into account in computing the gross income of any unrelated trade or business, except inventory

3. Property used to generate income from research excluded under section 512(b)(7)-(9)

4. Property used in a business carried on by volunteers without compensation (section 513(a)(1))

5. Property used in a business organized primarily for the convenience of members (section 513(a)(2))

6. Property used in selling contributed or donated property, (section 513(a)(3))[192]

For purposes of the first exception for exempt-function property, "substantially" is defined in the regulations as being at least 85 percent related. If more than 15 percent of the property is not substantially related to the extent that part of the property is used for an exempt purpose, it is not debt-financed property.[193]

To the extent that debt-financed property is used by a related organization, it is treated the same as use by the parent organization.[194] A related organization is one of the following:

1. A section 501(c)(2) holding company and its beneficiary organization

2. An 80 percent owned subsidiary

3. An organization where at least 80 percent of the directors or trustees are, directly or indirectly, representative of the parent organization

4. An organization which has more than 50 percent of its membership in common with another organization

5. A sister organization of another organization both of which are affiliated with a common parent

The exceptions to the definition of debt-financed property enumerated as numbers 1, 4, 5, and 6 also apply to related organizations.[195]

Neighborhood Land

Section 514(b)(3) allows organizations to acquire property for future use without tax consequence. To qualify for this exemption from the classifications of debt-financed property, the property must be acquired for the purpose of using it within ten years of the date of acquisition in the exercise of its exempt purposes, and the property must be located in the neighborhood of other property owned and used by the organization for its exempt purposes.[196] The organization's intent to use for exempt purposes may not be abandoned within the ten-year period.[197] If the exempt organization is a church, the time period is extended to fifteen years, and the property need not be in the neighborhood.[198]

If the property has a structure on it, the ten-year exemption is applicable only if the organization intends to have the structure demolished or removed.[199] If the organization erects a structure on the land after acquisition, the exemption is terminated, and if the property is not used for exempt purposes, it is debt-financed property.[200] Nor does the exemption apply to property on which there is a business lease.[201] Under a business lease, a tenant's use of the property is unrelated to exempt function of the lessor, and the term of which exceeds five years.

Neighborhood land is property contiguous to other property owned by the organization or within a one-mile radius of such land if the acquisition of contiguous property is unreasonable.[202] The application of the neighborhood land rule is automatic for the first five years provided there is no abandonment of the intended exempt use. Thereafter, the organization must satisfy the commissioner that conversion of the property to exempt use will actually occur within the ten-year limit.[203]

Acquisition Indebtedness

Acquisition indebtedness is defined to be indebtedness incurred in acquiring or improving property.[204] The debt may be incurred at a time other than in connection with the acquisition or improvement.[205] Indebtedness incurred before or after acquisition or improvement is considered as acquisition indebtedness under a "but for" test. If the indebtedness would not have been incurred but for the acquisition or improvement, it is acquisition indebtedness.[206] If the indebtedness was incurred afterward and would not have been incurred but for the acquisition or improvement and was reasonably foreseeable at the time of acquisition or improvement, it is acquisition indebtedness.[207] Whether or not debt-financing was reasonably foreseeable depends on the facts and circumstances of each case; however, the regulations indicate that poor planning is not sufficient.[208]

If an exempt organization acquires property subject to a mortgage or similar lien, the amount of the indebtedness is acquisition indebtedness regardless of whether or not the exempt organization assumes or agrees to pay the indebtedness.[209] However, when property that is acquired by an exempt organization by bequest or devise is secured by a mortgage, the amount of the indebtedness is not considered acquisition indebtedness for a ten-year period immediately following acquisition unless the organization makes a payment for the equity of the decedent.[210] If property is acquired by gift and the mortgage was placed on the property more than five years before the date of the gift and was held by the donor for more than five years, the mortgage is not treated as acquisition indebtedness for a ten-year period following the date of the gift unless the organization makes payment for the donor's equity.[211]

A state or local lien for taxes or assessments does not become acquisition indebtedness until after it becomes due and payable and the organization has had an opportunity to pay in accordance with state law.[212]

Other exceptions from the classification of acquisition indebtedness are these:

1. Indebtedness incurred in performing the organization's exempt purpose, such as indebtedness incurred by an exempt credit union in accepting deposits from members[213]

2. An obligation to pay an annuity as sole consideration for debt-secured property provided the value of the annuity is less than 90 percent of the value of the property received, the annuity is payable over a period of not more than two lives in being, and the annuity contract does not guarantee a minimum number of payments or specify a maximum number of payments and is not adjustable with reference to the income received from that property or any other property[214]

3. Obligations insured by the FHA to finance the purchase, rehabilitation, or construction of low- or moderate-income person housing[215]

4. Certain real property acquired by a qualified organization which means an organization described in section 170(b)(1)(A) and its affiliated section 509(a) support organizations and a qualified section 401 trust[216]

Computation of Includable Income

Generally, the income generated from debt-financed property is taxed as unrelated business income in the proportion in which the property is financed by debt. Because the percentage financed by debt changes as the mortgage is reduced, a statutory proportion is provided.

The percentage to be applied to gross income included in unrelated business taxable income as well as to the allowable deductions is the ratio of the average acquisition indebtedness for the tax year to the average adjusted basis of the property for the period of time held during the tax year.[217] The percentage may never exceed 100 percent.[218] The average acquisition indebtedness for the tax year is calculated by finding the average amount due on the mortgage during the year.[219] This may be done by averaging the monthly balances due. The average adjusted basis means the average of the adjusted bases of the property on the first and last days of the tax year that the organization held the property.[220] Proper adjustment must be made to the basis under section 1011 for the entire period following acquisition without regard to the organization's exempt status.[221] If the property was acquired in a complete or partial liquidation of a corporation in exchange for its stock, the organization's basis in the property is the same as it was in the hands of the transferor corporation plus any gain recognized by the transferor upon distribution and any gain included in the organization's unrelated business taxable income by reason of the distribution.[222]

The debt-basis ratio obtained is applied to both gross income and deductions alike. Deductions allowed are those which would be allowed to ordinary businesses under chapter 1 of the code if directly connected with the debt-financed property.[223] Depreciation may only be calculated using the straight-line method.[224] The debt-basis ratio is not applied to a carried back or carried forward capital loss or net operating loss.[225]

Dual use property requires an allocation of income and expenses between the unrelated and exempt uses.[226] This allocation must be done before the application of the debt-basis ratio.

The debt-basis ratio is also applied to gains or losses incurred from the sale or other disposition of debt-financed property.[227] That portion of the gain or loss is included in the organization's unrelated business taxable income.[228] To avoid the tax, the organization must pay off the debt at least one year before the sale.

PRIVATE FOUNDATIONS

Investment Income

All private foundations, except certain operating foundations described in section 4942(j)(3), whether tax exempt or not are subject to an excise tax on net investment income. For tax exempt private foundations the tax rate is 2 percent.[229] The 2 percent tax rate may be reduced to 1 percent in taxable years beginning after December 31, 1984, if the private foundation's qualifying distributions under section 4942(g) for a tax year are equal to or exceed the sum of (1) the amount obtained by multiplying the foundation's assets by the average percentage payout for the base period and (2) 1 percent of the foundation's net investment income for the year.[230] In addition, the average percentage payout for the base period must be at least 5 percent (3.5 percent if it is a private operating foundation).[231]

For purposes of the computation, the base period is the five-year period immediately preceding the taxable year or the period of its existence if less than five years.[232] The percentage payout is the quotient obtained by dividing the amount of the qualifying distributions made during the taxable year by the assets of the foundation for the taxable year.[233] If the tax rate is reduced for any year in a base period as a result of the application of section 4940(e), the amount of the foundation's qualifying distributions for that year is reduced by that amount for purposes of section 4940(e) computation.[234]

If the private foundation is not tax exempt, the tax is equal to the amount by which the sum of 2 percent of the net investment income computed as if the foundation were tax exempt plus the tax which would have been imposed on its unrelated business income had it been a tax exempt foundation exceeds the income tax actually imposed on the foundation.[235]

Since the excise tax is imposed on net investment income, the first step is to determine gross investment income. Gross investment income means the gross amount of income derived from interest, dividends (no exclusion), rents, payments with respect to securities loans, and royalties.[236] To the extent that any of these income items are included in unrelated business income, they are excluded from gross investment income.[237]

Deductions are allowed in the computation of net investment income for all ordinary and necessary expenses paid or incurred for the production or collection of gross investment income or for the management, conservation, or maintenance of property held for the production of income.[238] Depreciation under section 167 is allowed only under the straight-line method.[239] Section 611 depletion deduction is allowed but without regard for percentage depletion in section 613.[240] Expenses attributable to both investment and exempt purposes must be allocated.[241]

Net capital gain or loss is included in net investment income. Gains and losses from the sale or other disposition of property used for the production of interest, dividends, rents, and royalties and property used in the production of income included in the computation of the tax on unrelated business taxable income, except to the extent that such gain or loss is taken into account for the purposes of the section 511 tax, are taken into account.[242] Losses from the sale or other disposition of property are only allowed to the extent of gains from such sales or dispositions.[243] There is no provision for capital loss carry-overs.[244] In computing gain or loss on pre-1970 investments, the basis used is the fair market value of the property on December 31, 1969.[245] No tax is imposed on pre-1970 appreciation.

Sections 103 and 265 are applicable. Net investment income does not include tax exempt interest on certain government obligations nor does it include expenses and interest relating to tax exempt income.[246]

Treasury Regulations sections 53.4940-1(d)(2) and (3) contain two special cases concerning gross investment income. A distribution made by a nonexempt charitable trust (section 4947(a)(1)) does not retain its character in the hands of the distributee. A distribution made after May 26, 1969, by a split-interest trust (section 4947(a)(2)) does retain its character in the hands of the distributee unless taken into account under section 671 (grantor trust provision).[247] For purposes of section 302(b)(1) regarding redemptions of stock, a distribution to a private foundation is not treated as essentially equivalent to a dividend under the following conditions:

1. The stock was donated by a disqualified person.
2. The stock was owned by the foundation on May 26, 1969, or acquired by irrevocable trust or pursuant to a will, or irrevocable testamentary trust in effect or executed before that date.
3. The foundation is required to dispose of the stock to avoid the tax on excess business holdings (section 4943).
4. In exchange for the stock the foundation receives an amount which is equal to or greater than the fair market value at disposition or at the time the contract was executed if the contract constituted a prohibited transaction under section 503(b).[248]

Foreign private foundations are subject to a 4 percent tax on gross investment income from United States sources instead of the tax imposed by section 4940.[249] The source rules of section 861 are applicable.[250] To the extent that a treaty exists between the United States and a foreign sovereign, a private foundation entitled to benefits under the treaty may exercise them rather than be subject to section 4948.[251]

A tax imposed on investment income is reported on IRS Form 990-PF.

Procedures for refund or defenses against asserted deficiencies are similar to those of regular income tax even though the section 4940 tax is an excise tax.[252] Refunds are claimed on IRS Form 843.[253] Claims for refund must be made within three years after the return is filed or two years after the tax was paid, whichever is later.[254] If no return was filed, the two-year period applies.[255] Suits to recover a refund may be instituted after the claim is denied in either United States District Court for the district in which the taxpayer resides or the United States Claims Court.[256] Under the Tax Reform Act of 1969, tax court jurisdiction was extended to all excise taxes under sections 4940 through 4948.[257]

Required Income Distributions

A private foundation must distribute its income within one year after receiving it or be subject to the penalty taxes imposed by section 4942. The calculations require careful attention because miscalculation can be costly.

The amount which must be distributed to avoid the penalty tax is the "distributable amount.'' The distributable amount is equal to the ''minimum investment return'' less the sum of the taxes imposed on the foundation under subtitle A (regular income tax) and section 4940.[258] The ''minimum investment return'' is 5 percent of the excess of the aggregate fair market value of all assets of the foundation not directly used in furtherance of its exempt purpose over its acquisition indebtedness under section 514(c)(1) without regard to the year in which the indebtedness was incurred.[259]

Rules for determining the fair market value of assets are set out in Treasury Regulations section 53.4942(a)-2(c)(4). Securities for which market quotations are available may be evaluated on a monthly basis by any reasonable method commonly accepted for making such appraisals. Cash balances are valued on a monthly basis by averaging the amount of cash on hand as of the first and last days of the month. A foundation's participating interest in a common trust fund (section 584) which is operated pursuant to a plan providing for periodic valuation of participating interest during the taxable year is valued by averaging the reported valuations during the taxable year. Other assets are valued annually, except real property which may be evaluated on a five-year basis. Real property valued every five years must be appraised in writing by a certified, independent appraiser who is neither a disqualified person nor an employee of the foundation.

The tax is imposed on the difference between distributable amount and qualifying distributions if the distributable amount exceeds the qualifying distributions. This difference is the undistributed income.[260]

Qualifying distributions are direct expenditures for charitable purposes described in section 170(c)(2)(B) or an amount paid to acquire an asset used or held for use directly in carrying out the permissible charitable purposes.[261] Distributions may be made to public charities or operating foundations but not to controlled organizations of the distributing foundation or a disqualified person. A payment may be made to a private nonoperating foundation if the payee foundation makes an equal distribution which constitutes a qualifying distribution before the end of the next taxable year. Such distribution must be made out of the payee foundation's corpus, and sufficient eivdence must be submitted to verify that a qualifying distribution was made.[262]

Grant administration expenses paid during a taxable year constitute qualifying distributions up to the excess of (1) 0.65 percent of the sum of the foundation's net assets for the taxable year and the two immediately preceding tax years, over, (2) the aggregate amount of grant administration expenses paid during the two preceding tax years which were taken into account as qualifying distributions.[263] The result is that a private foundation must actually pay amounts equal to 4.35 percent as grants, program-related investments, and other expenditures for the active conduct of its exempt activities including administrative expenses incurred directly in the active conduct of its exempt function. Section 4942(g) is applicable to taxable years beginning after December 31, 1984. During the transition period for taxable years beginning before January 1, 1985, grant administrative expenses may not exceed 0.65 percent of the net assets of the foundation for the taxable year.

Amounts set aside to be paid within sixty months for specific projects may also be qualifying distributions even though they are not actually distributed.[264] The project must have a section 170(c)(2)(B) purpose. The foundation must satisfy the commissioner that the project can better be accomplished by the set-aside than by the immediate payment of funds or that the project will not be completed before the end of the taxable year in which the set-aside is made and minimum cash distribution tests are otherwise satisfied for the start-up and full-payment periods.[265] The start-up period consists of the four taxable years following the taxable year in which the organization was created or became a private foundation. Minimum distribution percentages during the start-up period are set out in section 4942(g)(2)(B)(ii)(III) and range from 20 to 80 percent of distributable amounts.

Private operating foundations are not subject to the minimum distribution requirements of section 4942 since they are subject to other distribution requirements.[266]

For accounting purposes, qualifying distributions made during a taxable year are treated as having been made in the following order:

1. Out of the undistributed income of the immediately preceding taxable year, to the extent thereof, if subject to the section 4942 tax in that year

2. Out of the undistributed income of the taxable year, to the extent thereof

3. Out of the corpus[267]

Excess distributions made when qualifying distributions exceed distributable amounts may be carried over to reduce minimum distributable amounts for the following five years.[268]

If the private foundation does not distribute the distributable amount as qualifying distributions, a penalty tax of 15 percent of the undistributed income not distributed at the beginning of the second tax year after the tax year involved is imposed.[269] The tax is imposed at the beginning of each succeeding tax year that the amount remains undistributed.[270] Failure to distribute as a result of an incorrect valuation not willful and due to reasonable cause is a defense to payment of the tax if actual distribution is made not later than ninety days after the date of mailing of the deficiency notice.[271] The initial tax may also be abated under other circumstances if the violation was due to reasonable cause and not to willful neglect and if corrected within the ninety-day period.[272] The time period may be extended by the commissioner if reasonable and necessary to permit the distribution.[273]

An additional tax equal to 100 percent of the remaining undistributed income is imposed if the foundation has been penalized the initial tax of 15 percent and subsequently fails to make the required distribution by the close of the taxable period.[274] The taxable period ends on the earlier of the date of mailing of the deficiency notice for the initial tax or the date on which the initial tax is assessed.[275]

The task of making the proper evaluations and making the required distributions is one of the most important jobs of a foundation manager.

Excess Business Holdings

In an effort to curtail the involvement of tax exempt organizations in the management and control of business enterprises, section 4943 restricts the combined holdings of foundations and disqualified persons in business enterprises. Excessive holdings are required to be divested or be subject to a penalty tax.

A "business holding" with respect to a stock corporation is voting stock.[276] Nonvoting stock is not considered to be a business holding unless all disqualified persons hold more than 20 percent of the voting power of the corporation.[277] All equity interests that do not have voting power are classed as nonvoting stock.[278] Evidences of indebtedness, including convertible indebtedness, warrants, and other options or rights to acquire stock are not equity interests and do not constitute business holdings.[279]

A business holding in a partnership or joint venture means a "profits interest." A "capital interest" is treated as "nonvoting stock" in the corporate context.[280] A private foundation is not allowed any interest in a sole proprietorship.[281] With respect to trusts and other incorporated interests that are not a partnership or sole proprietorship, a business holding is the "beneficial interest."[282] The beneficial interest of a private foundation or disqualified person in a trust is the beneficial remainder interest as determined under Treasury Regulations section 53.4943-8(b) attribution rules.[283] For other unincorporated businesses beneficial interest means any right to receive a portion of the distributions of profit or portion of the assets on liquidation, except as a creditor or employee, if no distribution of the profits is fixed.[284]

A private foundation may have an interest in certain activities which do not constitute a business enterprise. A business enterprise includes the active conduct of a trade or business and any activity regularly carried on to produce income from the sale of goods or performance of services and which is an unrelated trade or business as defined in section 513.[285] Excluded from the definition of business enterprise are functionally related businesses, program-related investments, and passive investment holding companies.[286] A functionally related business is a trade or business that is not an unrelated trade or business or is an activity carried on within a larger aggregate of similar activities or within a larger complex or other endeavor related to the exempt purposes of the foundation without regard for its need for income or funds or the use made of the profits.[287] Program-related investments include investments in small businesses in central cities or in corporations to assist in neighborhood renovation.[288] A passive holding company is a trade or business in which at least 95 percent of its gross income is derived from passive sources.[289]

Treasury Regulations section 53.4943-8 contains attribution rules for determining ownership of business holdings. The general rule is that any stock or other interest owned, directly or indirectly, by or for a corporation, partnership, estate, or trust is considered to be owned proportionately by or for its shareholders, partners, or beneficiaries.[290] There is an exception under the "myopia rule" for corporations. A business interest owned by a corporation that is actively engaged in a trade or business will not be attributed to the shareholders unless (1) the corporation is not a business enterprise, (2) the assets used in the trade or business are insubstantial compared to the corporation's passive holdings, or (3) the corporation has engaged in a prohibited transaction under Treasury Regulations section 53.4943-7(d)(2).[291]

A passive parent of an affiliated group is treated as an active business for purposes of the rule.[292] Consolidated gross income is used to determine if the parent is a business enterprise.[293] The assets of the entire group are used to determine if the parent is active.[294] In the aggregate a private foundation and disqualified persons are normally permitted to hold a maximum of 20 percent of the business holdings of a business enterprise.[295] A private foundation must reduce its holdings by the holdings of disqualified persons.[296]

If a third party has effective control of the business enterprise, the allowed percentage of ownership by a private foundation and disqualified persons is increased to 35.[297]

Notwithstanding the 20 and 35 percent limitations, a private foundation may own up to 2 percent of the voting stock in a corporation and not more than 2 percent of all outstanding shares of all classes of stock without having an excess business holding.[298]

An initial tax of 5 percent is imposed on the excess business holdings in each business enterprise.[299] The tax is imposed on the last day of the taxable year, but the business holdings are calculated for each business on the day during the taxable year when the excess holdings were largest.[300]

The initial tax does not apply if the foundation disposes of the excess holdings within ninety days if the excess holdings were not acquired by purchase or, if purchased, the foundation did not know or had no reason to know that it exceeded the limitation.[301] The ninety-day period runs from the date the foundation knew or should have known that it had excess business holdings.[302] The initial tax may also be abated under other circumstances if the violation was due to reasonable cause and not to willful neglect and if corrected within the ninety-day period.[303]

An additional tax of 200 percent of the value of the excess business holdings is imposed if the excess business holdings are not disposed of by the earlier of the date of mailing of a deficiency notice with respect to the initial tax or the date the initial tax is assessed.[304]

Section 4943(c)(4) contains elaborate transition rules for private foundations which had excess business holdings on the effective date of the section (May 26, 1969). The transition rules provide for disposition of excess business holdings in a three-phase plan. The first phase which covered a ten-year period should have been completed in 1979. The second and third phases are ongoing. These rules have been further modified by the Tax Reform Act of 1984.[305]

NOTES

1. I.R.C. § 501(c)(3).

2. I.R.C. § 170(c) does not include contributions to section 501(c)(4) organizations.

3. Treas. Reg. § 1.501(c)(3)-1(c)(3)(v).

4. Contributions specifically earmarked for influencing legislation are disallowed as a section 170 charitable deduction. Rev. Rul. 80-275, 1980-2 C.B. 69.

5. Treas. Reg. § 1.501(c)(3)-1(c)(3).

6. 28 Stat. 556 (1894).

7. 38 Stat. 172 (1913).

8. 40 Stat. 330 (1917).

9. 48 Stat. 700 (1934).

10. 48 Stat. 690 (1934).

11. The classic treatment of lobbying limits is by Judge Learned Hand in *Slee v. Comm.*, 42 F.2d 184 (2d Cir. 1930).

12. Pub. L. No. 83-591, 68 Stat. 730.

13. Tax Reform Act of 1969, Pub. L. No. 91-172, amending I.R.C. §§ 170(c)(2), 2055(a)(2), 2522(a)(2).

14. *See, e.g.*, Caplin & Timbie, *Legislative Activities of Public Charities*, 39 Law & Contemp. Probs. 183, 196-201 (1975); Field, *Tax Exempt Status of Universities: Impact of Political Activities by Students*, 24 Tax Law. 157, 440, 452-60 (1970); Geske, *Direct Lobbying Activities of Public Charities*, 26 Tax Law. 305, 305-10 (1973).

15. 461 U.S. 540, 103 S.Ct. 1997 (1983).

16. *Id.* at 1999.

17. *Id.*

18. *Id.* at 2001.

19. *Id.* at 2003.

20. *Id.* at 2002.

21. *Id.* at 2003.

22. *Id.* at 2004.

23. *Id.* at 2004–05 (Blackmun, J., concurring); *accord* Rev. Rul. 60-193, 1960–1 C.B. 195 (organization that encourages greater governmental participation from the business community is not exempt under section 501(c)(3) but may qualify as a social welfare organization under section 501(c)(4)).

24. *See, Comm. v. "Americans United" Inc.*, 416 U.S. 752 (1974) (organization lost its section 501(c)(3) exemption because of substantial lobbying); Rev. Rul. 74-117, 1974-1 C.B. 128 (organization formed to ease the change in administration of the governor's office is an action organization); Rev. Rul. 70-79, 1970-1 C.B. 127 (organization that assists local governments by developing solutions for common regional problems but does not advocate legislative action is not an action organization); Rev. Rul. 67-293, 1967-2 C.B. 185 (organization that promotes legislation to protect animals is an action organization, even though their goals benefit the community); *cf.* Rev. Rul. 71-530, 1971-2 C.B. 237 (organization that represents public interest at governmental hearings on tax matters is an action organization but still qualifies as a section 501(c)(4) social welfare organization).

25. 42 F.2d 184 (2d Cir. 1930), *aff'g* 15 B.T.A. 710 (1929).

26. *Faulkner v. Comm.*, 112 F.2d 987 (1st Cir. 1940), *rev'g* P-H B.T.A. Memo ¶ 39,346 (1939).

27. Treas. Reg. § 1.501(c)(3)-1(c).

28. *Seasongood v. Comm.*, 227 F.2d 907 (6th Cir. 1955).

29. *Id.* at 912.

30. 1 S. Weithorn, *Tax Techniques for Foundations and Other Exempt Organizations* ¶ 34.022, at 34-14.

31. 470 F.2d 849 (10th Cir. 1972), *cert. denied*, 414 U.S. 864 (1973).

32. *Id.* at 853.

33. *Id.* at 855-56.

34. 500 F.2d 1133 (Ct. Cl. 1974).

35. *Id.*

36. *Id.* at 1142.

37. I.R.C. § 4911(d)(1)(B).

38. Treas. Reg. § 53.4945-2(d).

39. Rev. Rul. 78-111, 1978-1 C.B. 41.

40. Rev. Rul. 78-112, 1978-1 C.B. 42.

41. Rev. Rul. 78-114, 1978-1 C.B. 44.

42. I.R.C. § 4911(d)(3)(B).

43. Treas. Reg. § 53.4945-2(b), (d).

44. Tax Reform Act of 1976, Pub. L. No. 94-455, 90 Stat. 1520.

45. I.R.C. § 501(h)(7). The election is made by filing IRS Form 5768.

46. I.R.C. § 501(h)(4).

47. I.R.C. § 170(b)(1)(A)(ii).

48. I.R.C. § 170(b)(1)(A)(iii).

49. I.R.C. § 170(b)(1)(A)(iv).

50. I.R.C. § 170(b)(1)(A)(vi).

51. I.R.C. § 509(a)(2).

52. I.R.C. § 509(a)(3).

53. I.R.C. § 501(h)(5).

54. I.R.C. § 501(h)(6).

55. I.R.C. § 4911(f).

56. I.R.C. § 4911(f)(2).

57. I.R.C. § 4911(e)(1).

58. I.R.C. § 4911(c).

59. I.R.C. § 4911(d)(1)(A).

60. I.R.C. § 4911(c)(4).

61. I.R.C. § 4911(a)(1).

62. I.R.C. § 501(h)(1), (2).

63. I.R.C. § 4911(d)(2).

64. I.R.C. § 4911(b).

65. I.R.C. § 501(h)(1).

66. I.R.C. § 504(a).

67. *I.R.S. Exempt Organizations Handbook* (IRM 7751) § 370(2).

68. *See, St. Louis Union Trust Co. v. U.S.*, 374 F.2d 427, 431-32 (8th Cir. 1967).

69. For example, in *Seasongood v. Comm.*, 227 F.2d 907 (6th Cir. 1955), the League was involved in distributing to the voting public information and notices regarding registration and upcoming elections. *Id.* at 909. Although the activities could be classified as political rather than legislative, the court analyzed the case under the substantiality limits and in doing so promoted its 5 percent test.

70. Treas. Reg. § 53.4945-3(a)(2).

71. Rev. Rul. 78-160, 1978-1 C.B. 153.

72. *Id.*

73. Rev. Rul. 78-248, 1978-1 C.B. 154, *revoking* Rev. Rul. 78-160, 1978-1 C.B. 153.

74. *Id.*

75. Rev. Rul. 80-282, 1980-2 C.B. 178, *amplifying* Rev. Rul. 78-248, 1978-1 C.B. 154.

76. *Id.*

77. Rev. Rul. 70-321, 1970-1 C.B. 129.

78. Rev. Rul. 76-456, 1976-2 C.B. 151.

79. Rev. Rul. 74-574, 1974-2 C.B. 160.

80. Rev. Rul. 67-71, 1967-1 C.B. 125.

81. Treas. Reg. § 1.501(c)((3)-1(d)(3)(i).

82. Statement of the American Council on Education, June 19, 1970, *reprinted in* Exempt Organization Reports (CCH) ¶ 3033.416, at 3644 (1981).

83. *Id.*

84. Rev. Rul. 72-512, 1972-2 C.B. 246.

85. Rev. Rul. 72-513, 1972-2 C.B. 246.

86. 666 F.2d 1096 (7th Cir. 1981).

87. *Id.* at 1098.

88. *Id.*

89. *Id.* at 1099, n.3.

90. 544 F. Supp. 471 (S.D.N.Y. 1982).

91. *Id.* at 487.

92. I.R.C. § 502(a).

93. I.R.C. § 502(b).

94. I.R.C. § 511(a)(2).

95. Treas. Reg. § 1.512(a)-2(a).

96. I.R.C. § 513(a).

97. *Id.*
98. 263 U.S. 578 (1924).
99. I.R.C. § 513(c).
100. Treas. Reg. § 1.513-1(b).
101. *Higgins v. Comm.*, 312 U.S. 212 (1941); Rev. Rul. 56-511, 1956-2 C.B. 170.
102. Treas. Reg. § 1.513-1(b).
103. Treas. Reg. § 1.512(b)-1.
104. I.R.C. § 513(b).
105. I.R.C. § 511(b).
106. I.R.C. § 512(a).
107. Treas. Reg. § 1.513-1(c).
108. *Suffolk Cty Patrolman's Benevolent Ass'n, Inc.*, 77 T.C. 1314 (1981).
109. Rev. Rul. 55-449, 1955-2 C.B. 599.
110. Treas. Reg. § 1.513-1(c)(2)(i).
111. *Id.*
112. *Id.*
113. Treas. Reg. § 1.513-1(c)(2)(ii).
114. Treas. Reg. § 1.513-1(c)(2)(iii).
115. Treas. Reg. § 1.513-1(d)(3).
116. I.R.C. § 513(a)(1).
117. *Cooper Tire & Rubber Co. Employees' Retirement Fund*, 306 F.2d 20 (6th Cir. 1962).
118. Rev. Rul. 78-144, 1978-1 C.B. 168.
119. Rev. Rul. 74-361, 1974-2 C.B. 159, *superseding* Rev. Rul. 66-221, 1966-2 C.B. 220, *clarifying* Rev. Rul. 71-47, 1971-1 C.B. 92.
120. I.R.C. § 513(a)(2).
121. Treas. Reg. § 1.513-1(e).
122. I.R.C. § 513(a)(2).
123. I.R.C. § 513(a)(3).
124. Treas. Reg. § 1.513-1(e).
125. I.R.C. § 513(d)(2).
126. *Id.*
127. I.R.C. § 513(d)(2)(B).
128. I.R.C. § 513(d)(3).
129. Treas. Reg. § 1.513-3(d).
130. I.R.C. § 513(e).
131. *Id.*
132. I.R.C. § 513(e)(3).
133. I.R.C. § 513(f).
134. Treas. Reg. § 1.513-5(c)(3).
135. Treas. Reg. § 1.513-5(d).
136. Treas. Reg. § 1.513-5(c)(3), Ex. (2).
137. I.R.C. § 513(g).
138. I.R.C. § 512(a).
139. *Id.*
140. I.R.C. §§ 512(a)(1); 514(a)(1).

141. I.R.C. §§ 512(b)(1), (2), (3).
142. I.R.C. § 512(b)(5).
143. I.R.C. § 512(b)(7).
144. I.R.C. § 512(b)(8).
145. I.R.C. § 512(b)(9).
146. I.R.C. § 512(a)(2).
147. I.R.C. § 512(a)(3).
148. I.R.C. § 512(a)(3)(B).
149. *Id.*
150. I.R.C. § 512(a)(3)(D).
151. *Id.*
152. I.R.C. § 512(a)(4).
153. I.R.C. § 513(b)(13).
154. *Id.*
155. *Id.*
156. I.R.C. § 512(c).
157. I.R.C. § 513(c).
158. I.R.C. § 512(a)(1).
159. Treas. Reg. § 1.512(a)-1(a).
160. Treas. Reg. § 1.512(a)-1(c).
161. *Rensselaer Polytechic Institute,* 79 T.C. 967 (1982).
162. Treas. Reg. § 1.512(a)-1(d)(1).
163. *Id.*
164. Treas. Reg. § 1.512(a)-1(d)(2).
165. *Id.*
166. Treas. Reg. § 1.512(a)-1(f)(6)(ii).
167. Treas. Reg. § 1.512(a)-1(f)(2).
168. *Id.*
169. *Id.*
170. *Id.*
171. I.R.C. §§ 512(b)(1), (2), (3), (7), (8), (9).
172. I.R.C. § 512(b)(10).
173. I.R.C. § 512(b)(11).
174. I.R.C. § 512(b)(6).
175. *Id.*
176. I.R.C. § 512(b)(12).
177. *Id.*
178. Treas. Reg. § 1.512(b)-1(h)(2)(i).
179. I.R.C. § 511(a).
180. I.R.C. § 511(b).
181. Treas. Reg. § 1.511-1.
182. I.R.C. § 511(d)(2).
183. I.R.C. § 511(d)(1).
184. I.R.C. § 6072(e).
185. I.R.C. § 1504(b)(1).
186. Treas. Reg. § 1.511-3(a).

187. *Id.*
188. Treas. Reg. § 1.511-3(c).
189. *Comm. v. Clay Brown*, 380 U.S. 563 (1965).
190. *University Hill Foundation*, 51 T.C. 548 (1969) which was reversed by the Ninth Circuit after passage of the Tax Reform Act of 1969 amending section 514 (446 F.2d 701 (9th Cir. 1971)).
191. I.R.C. § 514(b).
192. I.R.C. § 514(b)(1).
193. I.R.C. § 514(b)(1)(A)(ii).
194. I.R.C. § 514(b)(2).
195. *Id.*
196. I.R.C. § 514(b)(3)(A).
197. *Id.*
198. I.R.C. § 514(b)(3)(E).
199. I.R.C. § 514(b)(3)(C).
200. *Id.*
201. *Id.*
202. Treas. Reg. § 1.514(b)-1(d).
203. I.R.C. § 514(b)(3)(B).
204. I.R.C. § 514(c).
205. *Id.*
206. I.R.C. § 514(c)(1)(B).
207. I.R.C. § 514(c)(1)(C).
208. Treas. Reg. § 1.514(c)-1(a)(1).
209. I.R.C. § 514(c)(2)(A).
210. I.R.C. § 514(c)(2)(B).
211. *Id.*
212. I.R.C. § 514(c)(2)(C).
213. I.R.C. § 514(c)(4).
214. I.R.C. § 514(c)(5).
215. I.R.C. § 514(c)(6).
216. I.R.C. § 514(c)(9).
217. I.R.C. § 514(a).
218. *Id.*
219. Treas. Reg. § 1.514(a)-1(a)(3).
220. Treas. Reg. § 1.514(a)-1(a)(2).
221. *Id.*
222. I.R.C. § 514(d).
223. I.R.C. § 514(a)(3).
224. *Id.*
225. I.R.C. § 514(a)(2).
226. I.R.C. § 514(e).
227. Treas. Reg. § 1.514(a)-1(a)(1)(v).
228. *Id.*
229. I.R.C. §§ 4940(a), 4940(d).
230. I.R.C. § 4940(e).

231. *Id.*
232. *Id.*
233. *Id.*
234. *Id.*
235. I.R.C. § 4940(b).
236. I.R.C. § 4940(c)(2).
237. *Id.*
238. I.R.C. § 4940(c)(3).
239. I.R.C. § 4940(c)(3)(B)(i).
240. I.R.C. § 4940(c)(3)(B)(ii).
241. Treas. Reg. § 53.4940-1(e)(1)(i).
242. I.R.C. § 4940(c)(4)(A).
243. I.R.C. § 4940(c)(4)(C).
244. *Id.*
245. I.R.C. § 4940(c)(4)(B).
246. I.R.C. § 4940(c)(5).
247. Treas. Reg. § 53.4940-1(d)(2).
248. Treas. Reg. § 53.4940-1(d)(3).
249. I.R.C. § 4948(a).
250. *Id.*
251. Treas. Reg. § 53.4948-1(a)(3).
252. I.R.C. § 7422.
253. I.R.C. § 6402; Treas. Reg. § 301.6402-2(c).
254. I.R.C. § 6511(a).
255. *Id.*
256. I.R.C. § 7422(a).
257. I.R.C. § 6512.
258. I.R.C. § 4942(d).
259. I.R.C. § 4942(e)(1).
260. I.R.C. § 4942(c).
261. I.R.C. § 4942(g).
262. I.R.C. § 4942(g)(3).
263. I.R.C. § 4942(g)(4).
264. I.R.C. § 4942(g)(2).
265. I.R.C. § 4942(g)(2)(B).
266. I.R.C. § 4942(a)(1).
267. I.R.C. § 4942(h).
268. I.R.C. § 4942(i).
269. I.R.C. § 4942(a).
270. *Id.*
271. I.R.C. §§ 4942(a)(2), (j)(2).
272. I.R.C. § 4962.
273. I.R.C. § 4942(j)(2).
274. I.R.C. § 4942(b).
275. I.R.C. § 4942(j)(1).
276. I.R.C. § 4943(c)(2).

277. Treas. Reg. § 53.4943-3(b)(2)(i).
278. *Id.* .
279. *Id.;* Treas. Reg. § 53.4943-10(a)(2).
280. Treas. Reg. § 53.4943-3(c)(2).
281. Treas. Reg. § 53.4943-3(c)(3).
282. Treas. Reg. § 53.4943-3(c)(4)(i).
283. Treas. Reg. § 53.4943-3(c)(4)(ii).
284. Treas. Reg. § 53.4943-3(c)(4)(iii).
285. Treas. Reg. § 53.4943-10(a)(1).
286. Treas. Reg. § 53.4943-10(b), (c).
287. I.R.C. § 4942(j)(4).
288. Treas. Reg. § 53.4943-10(b).
289. Treas. Reg. § 53.4943-10(c).
290. Treas. Reg. § 53.4943-8(a).
291. Treas. Reg. § 53.4943-8(c).
292. *Id.*
293. *Id.*
294. *Id.*
295. I.R.C. § 4943(c)(2)(A).
296. *Id.*
297. I.R.C. § 4943(c)(2)(B).
298. I.R.C. § 4943(c)(2)(C).
299. I.R.C. § 4943(a).
300. I.R.C. § 4943(a)(2).
301. Treas. Reg. § 53.4943-2(a)(1).
302. *Id.*
303. I.R.C. § 4962.
304. I.R.C. § 4943(b).
305. Pub. L. No. 98-369, _____ Stat. _____.

10

Finance

The traditional form of corporate finance—raising capital through the sale of stock or securities—is foreclosed to nonprofit tax exempt organizations.[1] The proscription against issuing stock or securities is grounded in the private inurement prohibition. Stock dividends in the usual sense are distributions of profits which cannot be distributed to private shareholders of nonprofit corporations. Pragmatically, stock issued by a nonprofit corporation may not be saleable because of the lack of a profit motive by the management. Better returns on capital can be had elsewhere. Other avenues of finance must be explored. Capital may be raised by borrowing or issuing bonds, soliciting charitable contributions, and charging fees to users or members.

DEBT FINANCING

Almost all nonprofit corporations have the power to borrow money and issue notes, bonds, or other debt obligations and secure those obligations by mortgage or pledge of all or some of their property, franchises, and income.[2] The interest rate on the obligations is left to the discretion of the management.[3] This is an important consideration because the interest rate determines the attractiveness of the obligation.

Debt securities represent loans to the nonprofit organization, and the purchaser or holder of the debt security is a creditor of the nonprofit organization. The purchaser or holder acquires no right to participate in the management by virtue of being a creditor. The purchaser or holder has the right to repayment of the investment plus the agreed upon interest. The purchaser or holder has priority in dissolution or bankruptcy to be paid out of the assets before certain other groups.

The debt may be secured or unsecured. Unsecured debt is a bare promise to repay with interest. Unsecured creditors must look to the assets as a whole and not to a specific asset or assets. In the event of default, unsecured creditors are subordinate to secured creditors with respect to particular secured assets.

Secured debt provides a creditor with a higher degree of security. In case of default the secured creditor may look to specific assets for payment. The obligation is represented by a bond or note and mortgage agreement which generally requires the debtor corporation to insure the secured asset and keep it free from liens. Personal property security interests are governed by the Uniform Commercial Code except in Louisiana. All security interests in personal or real property should be recorded in the appropriate state or local office.

Large bond issues are generally issued under a trust indenture. The indenture provides for a trustee and procedures to be followed in the event of default. Publicly sold bonds must be issued under a trust indenture which conforms to the requirements of the Trust Indenture Act of 1939.

Bonds, notes, and other debt obligations fall within the definition of a security for purposes of the federal securities law. Extreme caution should be exercised in this area. A more detailed discussion of federal securities law and the Trust Indenture Act of 1939 appears in Chapter 7.

Two states, New York and Pennsylvania, allow variable-return agreements called subventions to be issued. Subventions have several characteristics of preferred stock. Subventions are subordinate to other debt obligations.[4] The interest rate may be variable or fixed as in participating and nonparticipating preferred and may be cumulative or noncumulative.[5]

New York limits the interest rate which may be paid on subventions to two-thirds of the maximum interest rate allowed under the New York usury law.[6] Pennsylvania imposes no limit on interest rates.

Transferability of the subvention certificates is restricted unless the board of directors by resolution provides otherwise.[7] Redemption of the subventions is by resolution of the board of directors at a price not to exceed the original amount or value plus any interest due or accrued.[8] In dissolution the subvention holders are entitled to take after the creditors.[9]

SOLICITATIONS

Large numbers of nonprofit corporations must rely on the generosity of certain segments of society or society at large for support. To garner that support these organizations engage in some sort of solicitation. The solicitation may range from one-on-one meetings with philanthropists to national campaigns.

Fund raising which has received its share of abuse for actual and alleged misdeeds is subject to several layers of regulation. The regulation comes in the form of self-policing and government control at virtually all levels of government.

Self-Regulation

The Code of Professional Practices has been promulgated by the National Society of Fund Raising Executives (NSFRE). Members of the NSFRE must subscribe to the code. Personal honesty, accuracy, and good taste are the keystones of personal conduct in members' fund-raising activities, and fund-raising employment is limited to a fee or salary basis not a percentage of gross take.

While the NSFRE provides standards for fund raisers, the National Information Bureau and the Philanthropic Advisory Service of the Council of Better Business Bureaus developed standards for organizations engaged in fund raising. These standards are directed toward accountability.

Federal Regulation

The most effective federal regulation is that imposed by the federal income tax law. Disclosure is a key element of any regulatory scheme, and the IRS Form 990 is geared toward disclosure. In addition to federal tax law, other areas of federal law regulate fund raising. Mail fraud laws and Title IX, Organized Crime Control Act of 1970[10] also are applicable.

There are constitutional limitations on the regulation of fund raisers. The U.S. Supreme Court in *Village of Schaumburg v. Citizens for a Better Environment*[11] held that a village ordinance that prohibited door-to-door solicitation by charitable organizations that did not use at least 75 percent of receipts for charitable purposes was an infringement on the organization's right to free speech and, therefore, was unconstitutional. The court said that fraudulent misrepresentations can be prohibited and that the penal laws can be used to punish such misconduct without imposing this kind of restriction on solicitation to curtail such activities.

This opinion has far-reaching ramifications considering that a good deal of state regulation goes toward limiting fund-raising costs to a fixed percentage of solicited funds.

The first amendment right of freedom of religion is another constitutional obstacle to regulation of charitable solicitations. As a result, religious organizations are exempt from most state solicitation acts. In *Heritage Village Church and Missionary Fellowship, Inc. (PTL) v. State of North Carolina*[12] the North Carolina Supreme Court found excessive entanglement with religion in the application of the North Carolina solicitation act to churches. Blanket exemption for churches and religious organizations is the rule to avoid such entanglement.

State Regulation

At least thirty-eight states have laws regulating solicitation, and these statutes are listed in Table 11. The laws are not uniform, and the state authority charged

Table 11
State Charitable Solicitation Statutes

Arkansas	Section 64-1601 et seq.
California	Calif. Bus. & Prof. Code § 17510 et seq. and Calif. Government Code § 12580 et seq.
Colorado	Section 18-5-115
Connecticut	Gen. State § 17-21e et seq.
Florida	Chapter 496
Georgia	Section 35-1001 et seq.
Hawaii	Chapter 467B
Idaho	Section 67-1401
Illinois	Ch. 23, §§ 5101-5111
Iowa	Section 122.1 et seq.
Kansas	Section 17-1739
Kentucky	Sections 196.250; 367.510-367.540; 367.650-367.6709.
Maine	Section 5001 et seq.
Maryland	Section 41-103 et seq.
Massachusetts	Section 68-18 et seq.
Michigan	Section 400.271 et seq.
Minnesota	Section 309.50 et seq.
Nebraska	Section 28-1401
Nevada	Section 86.190
New Hampshire	Sections 320.1 et seq.; 31.91
New Jersey	Chapter 45-17A et seq.
New York	N.Y. Exec. L. § 171 et seq.
North Carolina	Section 108-75.1 et seq. (Unconstitutional 1979)
North Dakota	Chapter 50-22
Ohio	Section 1716.01 et seq.
Oklahoma	Section 18-552.1 et seq.
Oregon	Sections 128.610-128.750; 128.805-128.990
Pennsylvania	Section 10-160-1
Rhode Island	Section 5-53-1 et seq.
South Carolina	Section 67-91 et seq.
South Dakota	Section 37-27-1 et seq.
Tennessee	Section 48-2201 et seq.
Texas	Article 1396-1.01 et seq.
Utah	Section 76-10-601
Virginia	Section 57-48 et seq.
Washington	Section 19.09 et seq.
West Virginia	Section 29-19-1 et seq.
Wisconsin	Section 440.41 et seq.

with enforcement varies—for example, secretary of state, attorney general, and consumer protection division.

The state solicitation acts are sporadic in their coverage. For instance, the Illinois Solicitation Act[13] exempts religious corporations; organizations soliciting for religious, charitable, hospital, or educational purposes; certain universities; accredited schools soliciting solely from alumni, faculty, trustees, and their families; certain libraries; fraternal, patriotic, and social organizations soliciting their members; organizations soliciting on behalf of a named person; community chest recipients; volunteer fire fighters; organizations providing nursing services to infants awaiting adoption; federal corporations; and the Boys Club of America. In addition, no registration is required unless the organization solicits and receives more than $4,000 annually. If the organization is covered by the act, it must register with the attorney general's office and file annual reports.

Professional fund raisers must also register under the acts. No person may act as a professional fund raiser unless he has registered with the state and posted a surety bond to guarantee against malfeasance or misfeasance in the conduct of the solicitation.[14]

All contracts between professional fund raisers and commercial co-venturers and charitable or religious corporations must be in writing, and a copy must be filed with the state for a period of time before solicitation begins.[15] A final closing report must be filed disclosing gross receipts and expenditures at the termination of the fund-raising activity.[16]

Civil and criminal sanctions are provided to insure compliance. Violations of registration requirements are misdemeanors.[17] Solicitation by unrecognized charitable organizations, professional fund raisers, or commercial co-venturers constitutes fraud for which the state may bring an action to enjoin the solicitation.[18]

MEMBERSHIPS

Some states allow members to make capital contributions to nonprofit corporations.[19] The contributions may be of money, property, or services but may not be promises of future services of payment. Capital contributions normally are redeemable upon dissolution at not more than the amount contributed. The articles of incorporation may provide for redemption at the option of the corporation.

Many nonprofit organizations glean a large part of their capital from user and membership fees; however, the federal tax law limits the source and amounts obtained from such sources.

Social clubs receive substantial support from charging membership fees and providing facilities and services to members and nonmembers. To retain tax exempt status[20] a social club must not acquire more than 35 percent of its gross receipts from providing facilities and services to nonmembers,[21] nor may more than 15 percent of total outside gross receipts be used to provide outside services.[22]

NOTES

1. *See, e.g.*, ABA-ALI Model Nonprofit Corp. Act § 26.
2. *See, e.g.*, ABA-ALI Model Nonprofit Corp. Act § 5(h).
3. *Id.*
4. N.Y. N-PCL § 504(c) (McKinney); 15 Pa. Cons. Stat. Ann. § 7542 (Purdon).
5. N.Y. N-PCL § 504(d) (McKinney); 15 Pa. Cons. Stat. Ann. § 7542 (Purdon).
6. N.Y. N-PCL § 504(d) (McKinney).
7. N.Y. N-PCL § 504(a) (McKinney); 15 Pa. Cons. Stat. Ann. § 7542(d) (Purdon).
8. N.Y. N-PCL §§ 504(e), (f) (McKinney); 15 Pa. Cons. Stat. Ann. §§ 7542(e), (f) (Purdon).
9. N.Y. N-PCL § 504(g) (McKinney); 15 Pa. Cons. Stat. Ann. § 7542(g) (Purdon).
10. Racketeer Influenced and Corrupt Organizations (RICO), P.L. No. 91-452, 84 Stat. 941 (18 U.S.C. §§ 1961 *et seq.*).
11. 444 U.S. 620, *rehearing den.*, 445 U.S. 972 (1980).
12. 299 N.C. 399 (1980).
13. Ill. Rev. Stat. ch. 23, §§ 5101-5111.
14. *E.g.*, N.Y. EXEC. L. §§ 173, 173-b (McKinney); Ill. Rev. Stat. ch. 23, § 5106.
15. *E.g.*, N.Y. EXEC. L. § 173-a (McKinney), Ill. Rev. Stat. ch. 23, § 5107.
16. *Id.*
17. *E.g.*, N.Y. EXEC. L. §§ 173, 173-a, 173-b (McKinney); Ill. Rev. Stat. ch. 23, §§ 5106, 5107.
18. *E.g.*, N.Y. EXEC. L. § 174 (McKinney); Ill. Rev. Stat. ch. 23, § 5109.
19. *E.g.*, N.Y. N-PCL § 502 (McKinney); 15 Pa. Cons. Stat. Ann. § 7541 (Purdon).
20. I.R.C. § 501(c) (7).
21. S. Rep. No. 1318, 94th Cong., 2d Sess. (1976).
22. *Id.*

11

Charitable Contributions

Charitable giving in 1980 amounted to almost $48 billion of which almost 84 percent was contributed by individuals.[1] Nearly half of all charitable giving goes to religious organizations while educational organizations, hospitals and health organizations, and social welfare organizations combined account for approximately 38 percent of the total.[2]

While the tax law may provide an incentive for charitable giving, it is not clear that the lack of any charitable deduction would significantly affect the generosity of individuals.

THE INCOME TAX CHARITABLE DEDUCTION

Definition

Section 170 of the Internal Revenue Code, within limits, allows a deduction for charitable contributions. A charitable contribution is a contribution or gift to or for the use of:

1. A State, a possession of the United States, or any political subdivision thereof, or the United States or District of Columbia provided the contribution or gift is made exclusively for public purposes

2. A corporation, trust, or community chest, fund, or foundation: (A) created or organized in the United States or in any possession thereof, or under the law of the United States, any State, the District of Columbia, or any possession of the United States; (B) organized and operated exclusively for religious, charitable, scientific, literary, or educational purposes, or to foster national or international amateur sports competition (but only if no part of its activities involve the provision of athletic facilities or

equipment), or for the prevention of cruelty to children or animals; (C) no part of the net earnings of which inures to the benefit of any private shareholder or individual; and (D) which is not disqualified for tax exemption under section 501(c)(3) by reason of attempting to influence legislation, and which does not participate in, or intervene in (including the publishing or distributing of statements), any political campaign on behalf of any candidate for public office

3. A post or organization of war veterans, or an auxiliary unit or society of, or trust or foundation for, any such post or organization: (A) organized in the United States or any of its possessions, and (B) no part of the net earnings of which inures to the benefit of any private shareholder or individual

4. In the case of a contribution or gift by an individual, a domestic fraternal society, order, or association, operating under the lodge system, but only if such contribution or gift is to be used exclusively for religious, charitable, scientific, literary, or educational purposes, or for the prevention of cruelty to children or animals

5. A cemetery company owned and operated exclusively for the benefit of its members, or any corporation chartered solely for burial purposes as a cemetery corporation and not permitted by its charter to engage in any business not necessarily incident to that purpose, if such company or corporation is not operated for profit and no part of the net earnings of such company or corporation inures to the benefit of any private shareholder or individual

Other than for a governmental body or agency, deductible charitable contributions may be made to section 501(c) (3), (8), (10), (13), (19), and (23), 501(e), and 501(f) organizations. Other tax exempt organizations do not qualify to receive deductible charitable contributions. A contribution or gift to an individual regardless of how needy or charitable the purpose is not deductible. A contribution to a foreign charitable organization is not deductible; however, United States-based charitable organizations may use charitable contributions abroad except for contributions by corporations to a trust, chest, fund, or foundation which must be used within the United States or its possessions. However, a domestic charitable organization may not act as a mere conduit for transferring contributions to a foreign organization.[3]

For a transfer of money or property to a charitable organization to be deductible, the transfer must constitute a gift as that term is understood in the field of taxation.

The question of whether or not a transfer constitutes a gift is one of fact not law. As it did with many important terms used in the Internal Revenue Code, Congress declined to provide a statutory definition of "gift." Likewise, the Treasury Regulations tend to be silent with respect to the definition of "gift."

The task of defining the word "gift" has been left to the courts. The U.S. Supreme Court in *Commissioner v. Duberstein*[4] flatly refused to promulgate a test for determining whether a transfer constitutes a gift. Rather, the Court said that the most critical consideration is the transferor's intent. Unwittingly, the Court did promulgate a test which has been used by federal courts since *Duberstein*. "A gift in the statutory sense, . . . proceeds from a 'detached and disinterested generosity' . . . 'out of affection, respect, admiration, charity, or like impulses.' "[5]

A transfer is not a gift if it arises out of the constraining force of a moral or legal duty or from an expected benefit or quid pro quo.[6] Contributions to churches or schools which are in effect disguised tuition payments for the transferor's children's education are not deductible.[7] Transfers to local governments in anticipation of favorable treatment or action for the benefit of the transferor such as a zoning change or approval of a subdivision are not deductible charitable contributions.[8]

Moreover, to be deductible the transfer of the money or property must be complete and irrevocable.[9] The transferor may not reserve the right to reacquire the property or otherwise divest the transference of the property. Contingent transfers of property do not give rise to a charitable deduction until the gift becomes effective or unless the possibility of the contingent event happening is so remote as to be negligible.[10]

No deduction may be allowed for a gift of services to a charitable organization regardless of value to the donee; however, unreimbursed expenses incident to performing such services are deductible as charitable contributions.[11] Reasonable expenses for transportation, meals, and lodging away from home incurred in the course of performing donated services are deductible charitable contributions.[12] The rules regarding "while away from home" under section 162 apply here also.[13]

With the few exceptions discussed later in this chapter, no deduction is allowed for a contribution of less than the transferor's entire interest in the transferred property unless it is transferred in trust or would be allowed as a deduction had it been transferred in trust.[14] Similarly, a gift of a right to use property cannot support a deduction because the right to use constitutes less than the transferor's entire interest.[15]

Timing

Charitable contributions by individuals must actually be paid to be deductible regardless of the transferor's accounting method. A pledge is insufficient to support a charitable deduction even if the transferor is an accrual basis taxpayer. The pledge must actually be paid or otherwise satisfied to be deductible.

Generally, corporations may only deduct charitable contributions which have actually been paid by the close of the taxable year. However, a corporation which uses an accrual method of accounting and whose board of directors has authorized charitable contributions prior to the close of the taxable year may take a charitable deduction in that taxable year, provided it is paid within two and a half months of the close of the corporation's taxable year.[16]

Payment may be made by check, credit card, or transfer by telephone. The gift is complete when a check is mailed or unconditionally delivered to the donee, provided that the check clears the transferor's bank in due course.[17] Payment by credit card is effective when the charge is made regardless of when the credit card issuer actually pays the transferee.[18] If a bank depositer can discharge an obligation by telephoning the bank and directing a transfer of funds, the gift is effective when the bank actually makes payment.[19]

Transfer of donor's own promissory note to the charitable organization is not satisfaction for purposes of the charitable deduction. The deduction is properly taken when the note is satisfied by transfer of money or other property of the donor.[20]

If property is to be transferred to the charitable organization, the contribution is made when the property is irrevocably delivered to the donee. If the transfer of the property is contingent or subject to divestiture, then the charitable deduction must be delayed until the contingency occurs. If the contingency is so remote as to be negligible, then the transfer is effective on delivery.[21]

A transfer of real property is generally effective when possession and the benefits and burdens of ownership are transferred.[22] However, some courts have held that the transfer is made when a properly executed deed to the property is delivered by the transferor to the charitable organization.[23]

A gift of securities is effective when an unconditional delivery of a properly endorsed stock certificate is made to the charitable organization or its agent. The mail box rule of delivery applies. The delivery is complete when the transferor puts the gift in the mail. Delivery of the securities to the transferor's agent or the issuing corporation for transfer of name on the corporate books is effective when the securities are actually transferred on the books; but if the securities are delivered to the donee's agent for transfer on the corporate books, delivery is effective on delivery to donee's agent without regard to the date of actual transfer on the corporation's books.[24]

Limitations on Charitable Deductions by Individuals

Limitations are imposed on the amount deductible by individuals based on the type of property which is contributed, the use to which the contributed property is put by the donee, and the kind of charitable organization receiving the contribution.

Limitations Resulting from Type of Property Contributed

The amount of any charitable contribution of property must be reduced by the amount of gain which would not have been long-term capital gain if, instead, the transferor had sold the property at its fair market value. Charitable deductions for contributions of property whose sale or exchange would give rise to ordinary income are limited to the transferor's tax basis in the contributed property.

A charitable contribution of an inventory item which was included in the cost of goods of a preceding taxable year is limited to transferor's cost; however, a contribution of an inventory item acquired during the current taxable year need not be treated as a charitable contribution but is deductible by the transferor as a cost of goods sold thereby avoiding the limitation.[25] The cost of goods sold is reduced by the lesser of the basis of the property or fair market value on the date of the gift.

Similarly, the amount of a charitable contribution of depreciable personal property, real property, and livestock subject to depreciation recapture provisions of sections 1245 and 1250 must be reduced by the amount of depreciation which would have been recaptured as ordinary income had the property been sold by the transferor at its fair market value.[26]

The charitable deduction allowed as a result of the contribution of any kind of appreciated property to a private foundation, other than an operating, distributing, or community foundation qualifying as a 50 percent-type organization, must be reduced by 40 percent of the amount that would have been recognized as a long-term capital gain had the property been sold by the transferor at its fair market value.[27] The result is that an individual donor may deduct cost plus 60 percent of the unrealized appreciation of the contributed property.

The 40 percent reduction of the amount of the charitable deduction also applies to contributions of tangible personal property if the use of the tangible personal property is unrelated to the charitable purpose or function for which the organization's tax exempt status was granted under section 501 or, if it is a governmental unit, to the strictly public purpose sustaining the deduction.[28] To avoid this restriction, the transferor should be satisfied that the transferee's use of the property will not cause a reduction of the charitable deduction or restrict the use or uses for which the tangible personal property may be used.

If a transferor donates mixed income property which would result in both ordinary income and long-term capital gain if sold by the transferor at its fair market value, then both the ordinary income restriction and the 40 percent reduction on long-term capital gains apply.

Percentage Limitations on Individuals

The general rule is that deductions for charitable contributions cannot exceed 50 percent of the individual donor's contribution base for the taxable year. An individual's contribution base is his adjusted gross income calculated without regard to any section 172 net operating loss carry-back to the taxable year.[29]

The 50 percent limitation applies to contributions to certain charitable organizations specified in section 170(b). Fifty percent organizations include the following:

1. Churches and conventions or associations of churches
2. Schools, universities, and other educational institutions

3. Hospitals and health care institutions providing medical research and education

4. Governmental units

5. Organizations that normally receive a substantial part of their support from governmental units or the general public

6. "Operating" foundations; "conduit," "pass-through," or "distributing" foundations; and "community" or "pooled fund" foundations (see discussion of private foundations in Chapter 4)

Contributions of capital gain property to section 170(b)(1)(A) organizations are not subject to the 50 percent limitation but to a special limitation.[30] Capital gain property is defined as any capital asset which would result in a capital gain if it had been sold at its fair market value including section 1231(b) property used in a trade or business.[31] Section 170(b)(1)(C) limits the deduction on capital gain property to 30 percent of the donor's charitable contribution base, unless the 40 percent reduction of section 170(e)(1)(B) applies. However, contributions of long-term capital gain property, otherwise subject to the special 30 percent limitation, may qualify for the 50 percent limitation at the election of the taxpayer if all long-term capital gain property transferred is subjected to the 40 percent reduction of section 170(e)(1)(B).[32] The election must be made on the individual's tax return for the election year and cannot be revoked for that election year by amended return.[33] This election is generally not advantageous to the transferor unless the total amount of appreciation is insubstantial. Contributions of capital gain property to organizations other than those described in section 170(b)(1)(A) may not exceed the lesser of (1) 20 percent of the taxpayer's contribution base for the taxable year or (2) the excess of 30 percent of the taxpayer's contribution base over the amount of contributions of capital gain property to section 170(b)(1)(A) organizations.[34] Such contributions of capital gain property to other than section 170(b)(1)(A) organizations are taken into consideration after all other charitable contributions.[35]

The 20 percent limitation in section 170(b)(1)(B) was increased to 30 percent by the Tax Reform Act of 1984. The section 170(b)(1)(B) 30 percent of contribution base limitation applies to all contributions to tax exempt organizations which are listed in section 170(c) and which do not qualify for the 50 percent limitation in section 170(b)(1)(A). The 30 percent limitation also applies to contributions made "for the use of" a 50 percent limitation organization as opposed to a direct contribution to the 50 percent limitation organization.[36]

The deduction for section 170(b)(1)(B) 30 percent limitation contributions may not exceed the lesser of (1) 30 percent of the taxpayer's contribution base or (2) the amount of the excess of 50 percent of the contribution base over the allowable amount of deductions to 50 percent limitation organizations.[37] For purposes of the second computation above, special 30 percent limitation contributions are considered with the 50 percent limitation contributions to reduce the amount available for section 170(b)(1)(B) 30 percent limitation contributions.[38]

These rules are summarized in Table 12 in an easy-to-read ready reference format.

Carry-overs by Individuals

Charitable contributions in excess of the overall 50 percent limitation may be carried over. Excess contributions to 50 percent limitation organizations may be carried over in the five succeeding taxable years.[39] If charitable contributions of capital gain property are subject to the special 30 percent limitation, the excess over 30 percent of the contribution base is carried over in the five succeeding taxable years in which it remains subject to the special 30 percent limitation.[40] A taxpayer should not exceed 30 percent of the contribution base to prevent loss of the deduction. Moreover, section 170(b)(1)(B) 30 percent limitation deductions depend on the amount of 50 percent limitation deductions allowed in the current taxable year and in succeeding carry-over taxable years.

In any taxable year, current 50 percent limitation deductions (including the special 30 percent limitation deductions) are taken first, then carry-overs of 50 percent and section 170(b)(1)(B) 30 percent limitation deductions are taken. Thirty percent limitation deductions to nonsection 170(b)(1)(A) organizations are always taken last.[41]

If a taxpayer in any taxable year makes the election to have special 30 percent limitation property treated as 50 percent limitation property, then for all prior years the carry-over must be redetermined as if the property had been 50 percent limitation property in each of those taxable years.[42] The redetermination is only for purposes of recomputing carry-overs and does not affect any charitable deduction allowed in a prior year.

Excess capital gain property contributions to organizations other than section 170(b)(1)(A) organizations may be carried over for five succeeding taxable years as capital gain property to organizations other than section 170(b)(1)(A) organizations.[43] This carry-over provision applies to taxable years ending after July 18, 1984.

Limitations on Charitable Deductions by Corporations

Charitable contributions made by corporations are not limited by the type of organization receiving them as in the case of individuals. Corporate charitable deductions may not exceed 10 percent of corporate taxable income before contributions are deducted.[44] Excess actual contributions over 10 percent of taxable income are carried over in the next five succeeding taxable years, subject to the 10 percent limitation in each of those taxable years.[45]

Corporations are subject to the same limitations on charitable deductions arising out of transfers of ordinary income property as are individuals with some minor exceptions. For contributions of inventory and certain other property used

Table 12
Limitations on Charitable Deductions by Individuals

Type of Contribution	Classification of Charitable Organization				
	50% Limitation Organization		30% Limitation Organization		
	Amount Deductible	Percentage Limitation	Amount Deductible		Percentage Limitations
			Private Foundations	Other 30% Organizations	
			Amount Contributed	Amount Contributed	
1. Cash	Amount Contributed	50%	Amount Contributed	Amount Contributed	30%
2. Ordinary income property (inventory, certain depreciable property, agricultural products, oil and gas property, art work donated by creator, section 306 stock, short term capital gain assets.)	Cost	50%	Cost	Cost	30%
3. Long term capital gain property					
a. General rule	Fair market value	30%	Cost + 60% unrealized appreciation	Fair market value	20%
b. Election to reduce	Cost + 60% unrealized appreciation	50%	---	---	---
c. Tangible personal property, use by donee unrelated to exempt purpose or function	Cost + 60% unrealized appreciation	50%	Cost + 60% unrealized appreciation	Cost + 60% unrealized appreciation	20%

231

in a trade or business, a corporation (other than a subchapter S corporation) may deduct an amount equal to its tax basis plus one-half of the unrealized appreciation but not more than twice the tax basis, provided that no deduction is allowed for any amount which would represent recapture of ordinary income had the property been sold.[46] A corporation may deduct the lesser of its tax basis plus one-half the unrealized appreciation or twice the tax basis for transfers to colleges and universities of certain scientific equipment manufactured by the transferor.[47]

The 40 percent reduction for individuals on long-term capital gain property and tangible personal property not used in relation to the exempt purpose or function of the exempt organization is changed to a 28/46 reduction for corporations.[48]

TRANSFERS

Outright Gifts

The simplest method of making a charitable contribution is to make an outright gift of cash or property. A gift of cash dispenses with evaluation problems, and substantiation is easily obtained by receipt from the donor or canceled check. The amount deductible is limited to either 50 percent or 30 percent of the contribution base depending only on the type of organization receiving the contribution.

Treasury Regulations section 1.170A-1(a)(2) requires that taxpayers furnish with their tax returns the name of the donee organization, the amount of the contribution, and the date of actual payment of each contribution. If more than one cash contribution is made to the same organization, the taxpayer only needs to list total cash payments rather than itemize. In practice, the tax return instructions require only a reporting of total cash contributions made for which the taxpayer has receipts, canceled checks, or other written evidence for donations which exceed $3,000 to any one organization when the name of the donee organization must be reported.

An outright gift of property is more complex than a gift of cash because the gift may be subject to reduction as discussed above and valuation. A charitable gift of property does not cause a taxpayer to recognize gain on the transfer,[49] and, correspondingly, a taxpayer cannot recognize a loss on such a transfer.[50] A taxpayer holding appreciated property should transfer the property directly to a charitable organization, and a taxpayer who would sustain a deductible loss should sell the property and contribute the proceeds. The donor should take care that a sale of the donated property immediately upon receipt by the donee not be attributed to the donor. The donor should never engage in negotiations with the prospective buyer of the property prior to contribution.

It should be noted that the effect of the 40 percent long-term capital gain reduction and ordinary income property treatment is similar to the result obtained if the donor sold the property and contributed the proceeds of the sale to the charitable organization.

Valuation of property contributed is critical to the amount of the charitable deduction. Ideally, the donor would get a charitable deduction to the full extent of the fair market value. However, overstating value can result in assessment of a penalty.[51] The penalty is a graduated addition to the income tax, hence it is not deductible. The penalty is assessed on valuations which exceed 150 percent of correct valuation and ranges from 10 percent to 30 percent of the amount by which the donor's income tax is understated as a result of the inflated evaluation.[52] No penalty is assessed if the underpayment of the tax is less than $1,000[53] or if the overvaluated property has been held by the taxpayer for more than five years.[54] Appraiser's fees for valuations of donated property are deductible as an expense incurred in the determination of a tax under section 212(3).

The donor is required to furnish detailed information with respect to gifts of property for which a charitable deduction in excess of $200 is claimed.[55] In addition, as donee, the charitable organization may be required to furnish information with respect to the gift.[56]

Bargain Sales

A bargain sale (sometimes referred to as a donative sale) is a sale of appreciated property to a charitable organization in an amount less than its fair market value. This practice allows the donor to recoup his investment in appreciated property and use the appreciated value as a charitable contribution.[57] The transferor's intent must be clear that he intended to make a donation of the appreciated value of the property.

The property donated must be long-term capital gain property. If the donated property is short-term capital gain property, no charitable contribution is allowed for short-term appreciation.

Unlike the usual rule wherein the tax basis is first allocated against the sale, the tax basis must be prorated between the sale and gift if the bargain sale results in a charitable contribution deduction.[58] The allocation of tax basis is made by multiplying the tax basis times the ratio of the sale price to the fair market value. A bargain sale of appreciated property to a charitable organization at its tax basis will result in recognition of some gain but less than a sale at fair market value.

To determine whether a charitable contribution deduction is allowable for application of the basis allocation rule, the gift part of the transaction must be reduced by the amount required under the reduction rules applicable to outright contributions of property. If the gift part of the bargain sale does not exceed the overall reduction amount, no basis allocation is required.

No basis allocation is required if no charitable deduction is allowed because of the 20 percent limitation. However, basis allocation is required when the charitable deduction is deferred to a subsequent year under the 30 or 50 percent limitations. Gain is recognized in the year of the bargain sale even if the charitable deduction must be carried over to a subsequent year.[59]

A transfer of encumbered property to a charitable organization will trigger the bargain sale provision even if the transferor receives no cash but the charitable organization assumes the liability or takes the property subject to the encumbrance.[60] The amount received by the transferor is the amount of the liability assumed or taken subject to.

Deferred Giving

The concept of deferred giving is like having your cake and eating it too. The transferor gets a charitable contribution deduction in the taxable year in which the transfer is made but still retains the right to receive or dispose of the income from the transferred property. The donee organization's full ownership rights are delayed until a future time depending on the terms of the trust instrument.

The charitable deduction is allowed for the contribution of the remainder interest in property but only if the transfer is made in trust.[61] A transfer of a partial interest in property not in trust is deductible only to the extent that it would be deductible if made in trust[62] with a few exceptions being transfers of a remainder interest in a personal residence or farm,[63] of an undivided interest in property,[64] and exclusively for conservation purposes.[65] The three acceptable trust forms are a charitable remainder annuity trust, a charitable remainder unitrust, and a pooled income fund.

Charitable Remainder Annuity Trust

A charitable remainder annuity trust is a trust whereby the grantor, through a single transfer of property, confers an economic benefit on a charitable organization and either retains the income interest or conveys it to a third party.

To qualify for the charitable contribution deduction, the charitable remainder annuity trust instrument must provide that

1. A sum certain must be paid to at least one noncharitable beneficiary living at the time that the trust is created,
2. The sum certain must be paid at least annually for either the life or lives of the noncharitable beneficiary or beneficiaries or a term of years not to exceed twenty years,
3. The minimum payment to the income beneficiary or beneficiaries be equal to at least 5 percent of the initial net fair market value of the trust corpus,
4. No other noncharitable person may receive a distribution from the trust, and

5. The remainder interest be transferred to or for the use of a qualified charitable organization or retained by the trust for such use.[66]

Revenue Ruling 72-395[67] sets out mandatory and optional provisions for inclusion in charitable remainder annuity trusts. Sections 4 and 5 of the revenue ruling provide:

SEC. 4. CHARITABLE REMAINDER ANNUITY TRUST; MANDATORY PROVISIONS

.01 Creation of annuity amount for a period of years or life
The trustee shall pay to A during his life an annuity amount of $Y in each taxable year of the trust. The annuity amount shall be paid in equal quarterly installments from income and, to the extent that income is not sufficient, from principal. Any income of the trust for a taxable year in excess of the annuity amount shall be added to principal.
.02 Creation of remainder interest in charity
Upon the death of A, the trustee shall distribute all of the then principal and income of the trust, other than any amount due A, to M charity.
.03 Selection of alternate charitable beneficiary if remaindermen do not qualify under section 170(c) of the Code at time of distribution
If M charity is not an organization described in section 170(c) of the Internal Revenue Code of 1954 at the time when any principal or income of the trust is to be distributed to it, the trustee shall distribute such principal or income to one or more organizations then described in section 170(c) as the trustee shall select in his sole discretion.
.04 Computation of annuity amount in short and final taxable years
In determining the annuity amount, the trustee shall prorate the same, on a daily basis, for a short taxable year and for the taxable year of A's death.
.05 Prohibition of additional contributions
No additional contributions shall be made to the trust after the initial contribution.
.06 Prohibitions governing private foundations
Except for the payment of the annuity amount to A, the trustee is prohibited from engaging in any act of self-dealing as defined in section 4941(d) of the Internal Revenue Code of 1954, from retaining any excess business holdings as defined in section 4943(c) of the Code which would subject the trust to tax under section 4943 of the Code, from making any investments which would subject the trust to tax under section 4944 of the Code, and from making any taxable expenditures as defined in section 4945(d) of the Code. The trustee shall make distributions at such time and in such manner as not to subject the trust to tax under section 4942 of the Code.

SEC. 5. CHARITABLE REMAINDER ANNUITY TRUST; OPTIONAL PROVISIONS

.01 Dollar amount annuity may be stated as a fraction of a percentage
The trustee shall pay to A in each taxable year of the trust during his life an annuity amount equal to Y percent of the initial net fair market value of the assets constituting the trust. In determining such value, assets shall be valued at their values as finally determined for Federal tax purposes. If the initial net fair market value of the assets constituting the trust is incorrectly determined by the fiduciary, then within a reasonable period after

such final determination, the trustee shall pay to A in the case of an undervaluation or shall receive from A in the case of an overvaluation an amount equal to the difference between the annuity amount properly payable and the annuity amount actually paid. The annuity amount shall be paid in equal quarterly installments from income and, to the extent that income is not sufficient, from principal. Any income of the trust for a taxable year in excess of the annuity amount shall be added to principal.

.02 Deferral of annuity amount during a period of administration or settlement

All the rest, residue and remainder of my property and estate, real and personal, of whatever nature and wherever situated, I give, devise, and bequeath to my trustee in trust, to invest and reinvest the same during the life of A and in each taxable year of the trust to pay to A an annuity amount equal to Y percent of the initial net fair market value of the assets constituting the trust. In determining such value, assets shall be valued at their values as finally determined for Federal tax purposes. If the initial net fair market value of the assets constituting the trust is incorrectly determined by the fiduciary, then within a reasonable period after such final determination, the trustee shall pay to A (in the case of an undervaluation) or shall receive from A (in the case of an overvaluation) an amount equal to the difference between the annuity amount properly payable and the annuity amount actually paid. The annuity amount shall be paid in equal quarterly installments from income and, to the extent that income is not sufficient, from principal. Any income of the trust for a taxable year in excess of the annuity amount shall be added to principal. The obligation to pay the annuity amount shall commence with the date of my death, but payment of the annuity amount may be deferred from the date of my death until the end of the taxable year of the trust in which occurs the complete funding of the trust. Within a reasonable time after the end of the taxable year in which the complete funding of the trust occurs, the trustee must pay to A, in the case of an underpayment, or must receive from A, in the case of an overpayment, the difference between:

(a) Any annuity amounts actually paid, plus interest on such amounts computed at 6 percent a year, compounded annually; and

(b) The annuity amounts payable, plus interest on such amounts computed at 6 percent a year, compounded annually.

.03 Annuity amount may be allocated to class of noncharitable beneficiaries in discretion of trustee

The trustee shall pay an annuity amount of $Y in each taxable year of the trust to such member or members of a class of persons consisting of A, B, and C in such amounts and proportions as the trustee in its absolute discretion shall from time to time determine until the last to die of A, B, and C. The trustee may pay the annuity amount to any one member of said class or may apportion it among the various members in such manner as the trustee shall from time to time deem advisable. The annuity amount shall be paid first from income and, to the extent that income is not sufficient, from principal. Any income of the trust for a taxable year in excess of the annuity amount shall be added to principal.

.04 Reduction of annuity amount if part of corpus is paid to charity on death of first recipient

During the joint lives of A and B, the trustee shall, in each taxable year of the trust, pay to A an annuity amount of $X and pay to B an annuity amount of $Y. The annuity amounts shall be paid in equal quarterly installments from income and, to the extent that income is not sufficient, from principal. Any income of the trust for a taxable year in excess of the annuity amounts shall be added to principal. Upon the death of the first to die of A and B, the trustee shall distribute $Z (or P percent of the trust assets) to M charity, and thereafter the trustee shall pay, in equal quarterly installments, to the survivor of A and B, for his life, an annuity amount, in each taxable year of the trust, which bears the same ratio to 5 percent of the initial net fair market value of the trust assets as the net fair market value of the trust assets, valued as of the date of distribution, less $Z (or P percent of the trust assets bears), to such fair market value as of the date of distribution.

.05 Distributions to charity in kind

During the life of A, the trustee may pay to M charity any income of the trust in excess of the annuity amount payable to A for the taxable year of the trust in which the income is earned. The adjusted basis for Federal income tax purposes of any trust property which the trustee distributes in kind to charity during the life of A must be fairly representative of the adjusted basis for such purposes of all trust property available for distribution on the date of distribution.

.06 Termination of annuity amount on payment date next preceding death of recipient

The trustee shall pay to A during his life an annuity amount of $Y in each taxable year of the trust. However, the obligation of the trustee to pay such annuity amount shall terminate with the payment next preceding the death of A. The annuity amount shall be paid in equal quarterly installments from income and, to the extent that income is not sufficient, from principal. Any income of the trust for a taxable year in excess of the annuity amount shall be added to principal.

.07 Retention of testamentary power to revoke noncharitable interest

The trustee shall pay to the settlor during his life an annuity amount of $Y and upon the death of the settlor, if B survives him, the trustee shall pay to B during her life an annuity amount of $Y. The settlor hereby expressly reserves the power, exercisable only by his will, to revoke and terminate the interest of B under this trust. Upon the first to occur of (i) the death of the survivor of the settlor and B or (ii) the death of the settlor if he effectively exercises his testamentary power to revoke and terminate the interest of B, the trustee shall distribute all of the then principal and income of the trust other than any amount due A or B, to M charity. The annuity amount shall be paid in equal quarterly installments from income and, to the extent that income is not sufficient, from principal. Any income of the trust for a taxable year in excess of the annuity amount shall be added to principal.

.08 Investment restrictions on trustee

Nothing in this trust instrument shall be construed to restrict the trustee from investing the trust assets in a manner which could result in the annual realization of a reasonable amount of income or gain from the sale or disposition of trust assets.

.09 Distribution from trust used to administer an estate to a charitable remainder trust

The trustee shall pay to A all of the income from the trust assets for A's life, during which the trust shall be fully revocable by A. Upon A's death the trust shall become irrevocable and the trustee shall pay the debts, taxes and other expenses of the administration of A's estate. After the payment or satisfaction of all such debts, taxes and expenses, the trustee shall transfer all of the then principal and income of the trust to the trustee of the charitable remainder annuity trust hereinafter established to be held, administered and distributed in the manner and according to the terms and conditions hereinafter provided.

A charitable remainder annuity trust should be used by a donor who is concerned primarily with receiving or guaranteeing to the income beneficiary a predictable amount of income during the term of the trust. The amount of the annual distribution may be predetermined by the donor as long as it is at least 5 percent of the fair market value of the trust corpus on date of transfer to the trust. The fixed amount of the annual annuity payment must be made even if the trust corpus must be invaded thereby giving a degree of protection to the income beneficiary from loss of value of the trust corpus or economic fluctuations in general.

A word of caution in this respect is that the Internal Revenue Service has taken the position that no charitable deduction is allowed if there is more than a 5 percent probability that a noncharitable beneficiary will survive the exhaustion of the fund in which the charity has the remainder interest.[68] This 5 percent probability test is troublesome because there is no authority on which to base its existence.

Certain kinds of property such as bonds are particularly suited to the annuity trust. The required annual distribution percentage can be determined by reference to the current effective interest rate on the bonds. Municipal bonds are attractive because the required annual annuity payment is tax free to the income beneficiary.

A charitable remainder annuity trust has several disadvantages. First, the trust affords the income beneficiary no protection against inflation since the annual annuity payment is fixed at the time of creation of the trust. Second, the income producing assets may decline in value. Third, no additional assets may be contributed to the annuity trust to replace or increase the deteriorating corpus. Any subsequent contribution to the charitable organization would require creation of a new annuity trust.

The amount of the charitable deduction allowed to the grantor on transfer of property to a charitable remainder annuity trust is the excess of the fair market value of the property transferred over the present value of the fixed annuity to be paid to the noncharitable income beneficiaries. The present value of the annuity is determined with reference to the estate tax regulations mortality tables discounted at a rate of 10 percent.[69] A pay-out rate of between 5 and 10 percent results in a larger charitable deduction than a unitrust at the same pay-out rate.

Charitable remainder annuity trusts are exempt from taxation unless the trust has "unrelated business income."[70] Generally, charitable remainder trusts have no unrelated business income.

The income beneficiaries of charitable remainder annuity trusts are not exempt from taxation. Income received by a noncharitable income beneficiary must be treated in the following order:

1. Ordinary income to the extent that the trust has ordinary income in the current taxable year or undistributed ordinary income from prior taxable years

2. Capital gains to the extent that the trust has capital gains for the current taxable year or undistributed capital gains from prior taxable years

3. Other income such as tax exempt income to the extent that the trust has other income in the current taxable year or undistributed other income from prior taxable years

4. Distributions of the trust corpus[71]

Note that this required treatment is contrary to the normal rule characterizing trust distributions proportionately in relation to the different kinds of income which constitute the trust's distributable net income.[72]

Charitable Remainder Unitrusts

A unitrust like an annuity trust is a charitable remainder trust. The primary differences are that a unitrust may be used to make additional charitable gifts to the same trust and that the income distribution scheme may be in the form of a variable annuity.

To qualify for the charitable deduction the charitable remainder unitrust instrument must provide the following:

1. A fixed percentage, not less than 5 percent, of the net fair market value of the trust assets must be paid to at least one noncharitable beneficiary living at the time that the trust is created.

2. The trust assets must be valued annually to determine the amount of the payment to the income beneficiary or beneficiaries.

3. Payments to noncharitable income beneficiaries must be made for the life or lives of those beneficiaries or a term of years not to exceed twenty years.

4. No other noncharitable person may receive a distribution from the trust.

5. The remainder interest must be transferred to or for the use of a qualified charitable organization or retained by the trust for such use.[73]

Revenue Ruling 72-395 sets out mandatory and optional provisions for inclusion in charitable remainder unitrusts. Sections 6 and 7 provide:

SEC. 6. CHARITABLE REMAINDER UNITRUST:
MANDATORY PROVISIONS

.01 Creation of unitrust amount for a period of years or life
The trustee shall pay to A in each taxable year of the trust during his life a unitrust amount equal to Y percent of the net fair market value of the trust assets valued as of the first day of each taxable year of the trust. The unitrust amount shall be paid in equal quarterly installments from income and, to the extent that income is not sufficient, from principal. Any income of the trust for a taxable year in excess of the unitrust amount shall be added to principal.
.02 Creation of remainder interest in charity
Upon the death of A, the trustee shall distribute all of the principal and income of the trust, other than any amount due A, to M charity.

.03 Selection of alternate charitable beneficiary if remaindermen do not qualify under section 170(c) of the Code at the time of distribution

If M charity is not an organization described in section 170(c) of the Internal Revenue Code of 1954 at the time when any principal or income of the trust is to be distributed to it, the trustee shall distribute such principal or income to one or more organizations then described in section 170(c) as the trustee shall select in his sole discretion.

.04 Adjustment for incorrect valuations

If the net fair market value of the trust assets is incorrectly determined by the fiduciary for any taxable year, then within a reasonable period after the final determination of the correct value, the trustee shall pay to A in the case of an undervaluation or shall receive from A in the case of an overvaluation an amount equal to the difference between the unitrust amount properly payable and the unitrust amount actually paid.

.05 Computation of unitrust amount in short and final taxable years

In determining the unitrust amount, the trustee shall prorate the same, on a daily basis, for a short taxable year and for the taxable year of A's death.

If the valuation date selected does not occur in a taxable year of the trust, other than the year in which the noncharitable interests terminate, the trust assets shall be valued as of the last day of such taxable year. In the case of the taxable year in which the noncharitable interests terminate, if the selected valuation date does not occur before the day the noncharitable interests terminate, the trust assets shall be valued as of the day the noncharitable interests terminate.

.06 Additional contributions

If any additional contributions are made to the trust after the initial contribution in trust, the unitrust amount for the taxable year in which the assets are added to the trust shall be Y percent of the sum of (a) the net fair market value of trust assets (excluding the assets so added and any income from, or appreciation on, such assets) and (b) that proportion of the value of the assets so added that was excluded under (a) which the number of days in the period which begins with the date of contribution and ends with the earlier of the last day of the taxable year or A's death bears to the number of days in the period which begins on the first day of such taxable year and ends with the earlier of the last day in such taxable year of A's death. In the case where there is no valuation date after the time of contribution, the assets so added shall be valued at the time of contribution.

.07 Prohibitions governing private foundations

Except for the payment of the unitrust amount to A, the trustee is prohibited from engaging in any act of self-dealing as defined in section 4941(d) of the Internal Revenue Code of 1954, from retaining any excess business holdings as defined in section 4943(c) of the Code which would subject the trust to tax under section 4943 of the Code, from making any investments which would subject the trust to tax under section 4944 of the Code, and from making any taxable expenditures as defined in section 4945(d) of the Code. The trustee shall make distributions at such time and in such manner as not to subject the trust to tax under section 4942 of the Code.

SEC. 7. CHARITABLE REMAINDER UNITRUST; OPTIONAL PROVISIONS

.01 Unitrust amount expressed as the lesser of income or a fixed percentage

The trustee shall pay to A in each taxable year of the trust during his life an amount equal to the lesser of (a) the trust income for such taxable year (as defined in section 643(b) of the Internal Revenue Code of 1954 and the regulations thereunder) and (b) Y percent of the net fair market value of the trust assets valued as of the first day of such taxable year decreased as elsewhere provided in the case where the taxable year is a short taxable year or is the taxable year in which A dies and increased as elsewhere provided in the case where there are additional contributions in the taxable year. If the trust income for any taxable year exceeds the amount determined under (b), the payment to A shall also include such excess income to the extent that the aggregate of the amounts paid to A in prior years is less than Y percent of the aggregate net fair market value of the trust assets for such years. Payments to A shall be made in quarterly installments. Any income of the trust in excess of such payments shall be added to principal.

.02 Deferral of unitrust amount during a period of administration or settlement

All the rest, residue and remainder of my property and estate, real and personal, of whatever nature and wherever situated, I give, devise, and bequeath to my trustee in trust, to invest and reinvest the same during the life of A and in each taxable year of the trust to pay, in equal quarterly installments, to A, a unitrust amount equal to Y percent of the net fair market value of the trust assets valued as of the first day of each taxable year of the trust. The unitrust amount shall be paid from income and, to the extent income is not sufficient, from principal. Any income of the trust for a taxable year in excess of the unitrust amount shall be added to principal. The obligation to pay the unitrust amount shall commence with the date of my death, but payment of the unitrust amount may be deferred from the date of my death until the end of the taxable year of the trust in which occurs the complete funding of the trust. Within a reasonable time after the end of the taxable year in which the complete funding of the trust occurs, the trustee must pay to A, in the case of an underpayment, or must receive from A, in the case of an overpayment, the difference between:

(a) Any unitrust amounts actually paid, plus interest on such amounts computed at 6 percent a year, compounded annually and

(b) The unitrust amounts payable, determined under the method described in section 1.664-1(a)(5)(ii) of the federal income tax regulations, plus interest on such amounts computed at 6 percent a year, compounded annually.

.03 Unitrust amount may be allocated to a class of noncharitable beneficiaries in discretion of trustee

The trustee shall pay, in each taxable year of the trust, a unitrust amount equal to Y percent of the net fair market value of the trust assets valued as of the first day of such taxable year to such member or members of a class of persons consisting of A, B, and C in such amounts and proportions as the trustee in its absolute discretion shall from time to time determine until the last to die of A, B, and C. The trustee may pay the unitrust amount to any one member of said class or may apportion it among the various members in such manner as the trustee shall from time to time deem advisable. The unitrust amount shall be paid first from income and, to the extent that income is not sufficient, from principal. Any income of the trust for a taxable year in excess of the unitrust amount shall be added to principal.

.04 Reduction of unitrust amount if part of corpus is paid to charity on death of first recipient

During the joint lives of A and B, the trustee shall, in each taxable year of the trust, pay to A a unitrust amount equal to X percent of the net fair market value of the trust assets valued as of the first day of such taxable year and pay to B a unitrust amount equal to Y percent of the net fair market value of the trust assets valued as of the first day of such taxable year. The unitrust amounts shall be paid in equal quarterly installments from income and, to the extent that income is not sufficient, from principal. Any income of the trust for a taxable year in excess of the unitrust amounts shall be added to principal. Upon the death of the first to die of A and B, the trustee shall distribute $Z (or P percent of the trust assets) to M charity, and thereafter the trustee shall pay to the survivor of A and B for his life a unitrust amount in each taxable year of the trust equal to 5 percent of the net fair market value of the trust assets valued as of the first day of such taxable year.

.05 Distribution to charity in kind

During the life of A, the trustee may pay to M charity any income of the trust in excess of the unitrust amount payable to A for the taxable year of the trust in which the income is earned. The adjusted basis for Federal income tax purposes of any trust property which the trustee distributes in kind to charity during the life of A must be fairly representative of the adjusted basis for such purposes of all trust property available for distribution on the date of distribution.

.06 Termination of unitrust amount on payment date next preceding death of recipient

The trustee shall pay to A in each taxable year of the trust during his life a unitrust amount equal to Y percent of the net fair market value of the trust assets valued as of the first day of such taxable year. However, the obligation of the trustee to pay such unitrust amount shall terminate with the payment next preceding the death of A. The unitrust amount shall be paid in equal quarterly installments from income and, to the extent that income is not sufficient, from principal. Any income of the trust for a taxable year in excess of the unitrust amount shall be added to principal.

.07 Retention of testamentary power to revoke noncharitable interest

The trustee shall pay to the settlor during his life a unitrust amount equal to Y percent of the net fair market value of the trust assets valued as of the first day of each taxable year of the trust and upon the death of the settlor, if B survives him, the trustee shall pay to B during her life a unitrust amount equal to Y percent of the net fair market value of the trust assets valued as of the first day of each taxable year. The settlor hereby expressly reserves the power, exercisable only by his will, to revoke and terminate the interest of B under this trust. Upon the first to occur of (i) the death of the survivor of the settlor and B or (ii) the death of the settlor if he effectively exercises his testamentary power to revoke and terminate the interest of B, the trustee shall distribute all of the then principal and income of the trust, other than any amount due A or B, to M charity. The unitrust amount shall be paid in equal quarterly installments from income and, to the extent that income is not sufficient, from principal. Any income of the trust for a taxable year in excess of the unitrust amount of income shall be added to principal.

.08 Investment restrictions on trustee

Nothing in this trust instrument shall be construed to restrict the trustee from investing the trust assets in a manner which could result in the annual realization of a reasonable amount or gain from the sale or disposition of trust assets.

.09 Distribution from trust used to administer an estate to a charitable remainder trust

The trustee shall pay to A all of the income from the trust assets for A's life, during which the trust shall be fully revocable by A. Upon A's death the trust shall become irrevocable and the trustee shall pay all debts, taxes and other expenses of the administration of A's estate. After the payment or satisfaction of all such debts, taxes and expenses, the trustee shall transfer all of the then principal and income of the trust to the trustee of the charitable remainder unitrust hereinafter established to be held, administered and distributed in the manner and according to the terms and conditions hereinafter provided.

A charitable remainder unitrust is the best hedge against inflation because the annual distribution is determined annually based on fair market value of the trust assets.

The unitrust is more flexible than an annuity trust since it can receive subsequent contributions of assets eliminating the cost of setting up a separate new trust. The annual income distribution can be limited to the trust's actual income thereby preventing an invasion of the trust corpus and possible trouble with the 5 percent rule of Revenue Ruling 77-374. The income deficiency may be made up in a subsequent year when trust income exceeds the projected annual distribution.

Disadvantages of a unitrust are the nonpredictability or uncertainty of annual income by the noncharitable income beneficiaries and continued annual valuation problems particularly if the trust corpus is difficult to evaluate.

The amount of the charitable deduction allowed to the grantor on transfer of property to a charitable remainder unitrust is the excess of the fair market value of the property transferred over the present value of the variable annuity to be paid to the noncharitable income beneficiaries. The present value of the annuity is determined with reference to the estate tax regulations mortality tables discounted at a rate of 10 percent.[74] A pay-out rate in excess of 10 percent will yield a greater charitable deduction than an annuity trust on the same corpus at the same pay-out rate.

Charitable remainder unitrusts are exempt from taxation unless the trust has "unrelated business income."[75] Generally, charitable remainder trusts have no unrelated business income.

The income beneficiaries of charitable remainder unitrusts are not exempt from taxation. Income received by a noncharitable income beneficiary must be treated in the following order:

1. Ordinary income to the extent that the trust has ordinary income in the current taxable year or undistributed ordinary income from prior taxable years

2. Capital gains to the extent that the trust has capital gains for the current taxable year or undistributed capital gains from prior taxable years

3. Other income such as tax exempt income to the extent that the trust has other income in the current taxable year or undistributed other income from prior taxable years

4. Distributions of the trust corpus[76]

Note that this required treatment is contrary to the normal rule characterizing trust distributions proportionately in relation to the different kinds of income which constitute the trust's distributable net income.[77]

Pooled Income Fund

A pooled income fund is a form of charitable remainder trust which receives gifts of money or property from several different donors and commingles the property. The pooled income fund pays the donor or designated beneficiary a pro rata share of the income earned attributable to the value of the contribution. A pooled income fund is an investment fund commonly operated by charitable organizations. The remainders are donated to the charitable organization.

To be deductible, a transfer to a pooled income fund must meet the following requirements:

1. An irrevocable remainder interest in property must be transferred to or for the use of a 50 percent limitation charitable organization.
2. An income interest must be retained for the life of at least one beneficiary.
3. The property must be commingled with property received from other donors.
4. The trust may not invest in tax exempt securities.
5. The trust may not accept transfers which do not qualify under the pooled income fund requirements.
6. The trust must be maintained by the organization to which the remainder interest is donated.
7. No donor or income beneficiary of the pooled income fund can be a trustee of such pooled income fund.
8. The income distributed to the income beneficiary each year must be determined by the rate of return earned by the trust during the year.[78]

These are the advantages of a pooled income fund:

1. The donor is able to diversify investments without incurring tax liability imposed on conversion of the property to other types of property (The donor's assets are exchanged for a share of the pooled income fund.).
2. The pooled income fund is generally professionally managed at relatively low cost to each donor.
3. The pooled income fund is the best vehicle for smaller contributors.
4. The fund only distributes its income and does not invade the corpus of the trust.

Disadvantages of the pooled income fund are that (1) the fund cannot invest in tax exempt securities; (2) the income interest is for life not a term of years; and (3) only certain types of 50 percent limitation charitable organizations may receive a remainder interest in property under a pooled income fund.

The amount of the charitable contribution deduction is the excess of the fair market value of the property transferred over the present value of the income interest retained. The present value of the income interest is determined under Treasury Regulations section 1.642(c)-5(b) and depends on the age of the donor and rate of return earned by the fund. These tables are also based on mortality and a 10 percent interest factor.

Unlike the charitable remainder annuity trusts and unitrusts, pooled income funds are not exempt from taxation but are subject to the ordinary rules treating taxation of ordinary trusts in subchapter J.[79] A pooled income fund is allowed a deduction for amounts of long-term capital gains permanently set aside for charitable purposes.[80]

Taxation of income beneficiaries is the same as under the normal trust rules rather than under the special rules that apply to income beneficiaries of annuity trusts or unitrusts.[81]

Caution Areas

Annuity trusts, unitrusts, and pooled income funds should not be used without consulting competent legal counsel. Moreover, a donor should not fund a charitable remainder trust until after a favorable letter ruling has been obtained from the Internal Revenue Service. Some of the more significant problem areas encountered in creating such a trust are briefly discussed.

The amount of the charitable deduction is a function of the life expectancy of the income beneficiary. The rules allow the donor to reserve income for the life of another person or for a life in addition to the donor's life. Such designations can substantially alter the amount of the charitable deduction by either designating a person with a shorter life expectancy than the donor or a person or persons whose life expectancy or expectancies are longer than the donor's.

Another problem in connection with designating other lives or multiple lives is that the tables promulgated in the Treasury Regulations only involve one life and may not be used to value the remainder interest in a trust involving joint lives. In such a case, the Internal Revenue Service has promulgated additional tables which may be used for certain two-life plans. If these tables are not appropriate, then the information should be submitted to the Internal Revenue Service for determination of the proper factors to be used in calculating the remainder interest.

The transfer of property subject to a liability where the transferee either assumes the liability or takes the property subject to the liability may result in income tax liability. The transaction will be treated as part sale and part gift.[82] The amount realized on the sales part of the transaction is the amount of the liability assumed or taken subject to.[83] This is true even if the amount of the liability exceeds the fair market value of the property at the time of transfer.[84] The bargain sales rules may apply to the transaction, and the tax basis would be allocated between the sale and the gift. The Treasury Regulations governing bargain sales may be fairly interpreted to cover transfers to annuity trusts and unitrusts.

It is permissible for the donor to be the trustee of a charitable remainder annuity trust or unitrust but not a pooled income fund. The powers retained by the trustee must be carefully written to avoid creating a grantor trust whereby the trust income is attributable to the grantor and no charitable deduction is allowed.[85] Retention of the power to affect or alter the beneficial enjoyment of the annual income distributions of the trust is fatal to the deductibility of the contribution. The drafter of the trust instrument must make sure that state law governing the trust does not disqualify the trust through its grant of powers to the trustee. To avoid the problem, the trust instrument should expressly limit the trustee's powers to those permissible to qualify the trust for the charitable deduction.

Likewise, the trust cannot be created and funded conditionally. Conditioning the transfer of property on the deductibility of the charitable contribution is impermissible; however, conditioning the transfer on receipt of a favorable revenue ruling is permissible.[86] This result is brought about by the proscription against paying an amount to any noncharitable person other than the required annual income distribution to the designated income beneficiaries.

The donor may, however, alter or substitute the remainderman in the event that the named remainderman is not a qualified charitable organization.[87] Care must be taken not to designate a remainderman which would not qualify for the 50 percent limitation.[88]

The limitations imposed on charitable deductions arising out of outright contributions of appreciated property likewise apply to deferred giving. A charitable deduction is reduced to the extent of inherent ordinary income or short-term capital gain. Long-term capital gain property may be subject to the 40 percent reduction. (See the limitations discussed under outright gifts, *supra*.)

A deduction for a contribution of tangible personal property to a charitable remainder trust is postponed until all intervening life interests have expired.[89] If contemplating an immediate deduction, the donor should not give tangible personal property to a charitable remainder trust.

An income beneficiary would prefer to have the income from the trust tax free. One way to accomplish this would be for the trust to sell the contributed property and invest the proceeds in tax exempt securities. The sale of the contributed property generally results in no gain or loss recognized by the donor. Congress prohibited pooled income funds from investing in tax exempt securities.[90] The Internal Revenue Service in its *Pomona College* ruling has accomplished the same result with respect to annuity trusts and unitrusts.[91] The ruling states that if a donor transfers property to a charitable organization under an express or implied obligation to sell the property and reinvest in tax exempt securities—the income from which is to be paid to an income beneficiary designated by the donor and the charitable remainder to the organization—the donor must recognize any gain on the sale of the property. Unless or until the *Pomona College* ruling is overturned, such a plan should not be used. Moreover, the Internal Revenue Service has indicated that it will extend the ruling to any express or implied sale requirement whether the reinvestment is to be in tax exempt securities or other property.

Estate and Gift Tax Consequences

No transfer of property to a charitable remainder trust should be undertaken without giving due consideration to estate and gift tax consequences of the transaction.

If the grantor of a charitable remainder trust merely retains an income interest for himself for a term of years, no gift of an income interest has been made, and no gift tax liability arises. The gift-over to the charitable remainderman qualifies for the gift tax charitable deduction which results in no gift tax liability.[92] However, if the grantor dies before the expiration of the term of years, the full value of the trust assets must be included in the grantor's gross estate.[93] The estate is entitled to the estate tax charitable deduction so that only the remaining value of the income interest is included in the estate for tax purposes.[94]

If the grantor retains an income interest for life, there are no detrimental estate or gift tax consequences. The gift of the charitable remainder is offset by the gift tax charitable deduction,[95] and on the death of the grantor the value of the trust assets is offset by the estate tax charitable deduction.[96]

Problems arise when another life is used to set the term of the trust or another person is designated as the income beneficiary. A gift to a charitable remainder trust with an income interest for another person for a term of years constitutes two gifts. The gift of the income interest to another person constitutes a taxable gift. The gift of the remainder interest to the charitable organization is subject to the gift tax charitable deduction so that no tax liability arises out of it.[97] Since the donor has retained no interest, the value of the assets of the trust is not included in the gross estate whether the donor dies during or after the term of years. Under the unified estate and gift tax, the amount of the taxable gift resulting from transfer of the income interest must be considered when calculating the estate tax due because the amount of any gift tax paid will reduce the estate tax liability.[98] However, if the donor dies within three years of the income interest gift, the amount of the gift tax paid must be included in the donor's gross estate.[99]

If the donor retains an income interest for his life plus for a survivor beneficiary, a gift may be made if the income interest for the survivor is made without reservation.[100] The gift tax consequences may be avoided if the donor retains the power to revoke the survivor's income interest by will on donor's death.[101] The full value of the trust assets is included in donor's gross estate on his death.[102] Should the survivor beneficiary predecease the donor or should the donor revoke by will the survivor's income interest, no estate tax liability arises because the estate receives the estate tax charitable deduction for the full amount of the trust assets received by the charitable remainderman.[103] However, if the survivor beneficiary should survive the donor without revocation of the survivor's income interest, the value of the survivor's life estate in the income must be included in the net estate for tax purposes.[104] The gift to the charitable remainderman presents no detrimental tax consequence because the value of the gift is offset by the gift tax charitable deduction.[105]

The antidistribution rule for amounts paid other than the required annual income payment prohibits the trust from paying any estate or gift tax liability incurred. Other arrangements must be made for payment of the estate or gift tax liability.

Charitable Gift Annuities

A charitable gift annuity is a popular form of charitable contribution. The donor gives cash or other property to the charitable organization in exchange for the right to receive a specified amount each year for the remainder of the donor's or other's life. The value of the annuity is less than the charitable gift so that the excess value supports a charitable contribution deduction while providing lifetime income.[106]

The present value of the annuity is to be determined by reference to the cost of a comparable contract purchased from an insurance company.[107] Nonetheless, the Internal Revenue Service has published a revenue ruling which provides the rates to be used in determining present value of the annuity.[108]

If appreciated property is used to purchase the gift annuity, the transfer is treated as a bargain sale which may result in recognition of a gain on the transfer (see bargain sales, *supra*).

If the annuity is not assignable or only assignable to the issuing charitable organization and the donor or the donor and designated survivor annuitants are the only annuitants, the gain recognized on the transfer, if any, is recognized ratably over the expected number of years that the annuity will be paid.[109] Otherwise, any recognizable gain is recognized in the year in which the transfer occurs.

Because annuity payments represent both a return of the initial payment and a return on the investment, the part of the payment that represents the return of capital is excluded from gross income while the balance of the payment is included in gross income. Section 72 provides an exclusion ratio which is the ratio of the amount of the investment in the annuity contract to the expected return on the annuity contract. Expected return is calculated by multiplying the annual annuity payment by the life expectancy of the annuitant or joint life expectancy, if more than one annuitant. The amount which represents gross income is ordinary income.

An annuity contract which involves the life of someone other than the donor or an additional life will have the same adjustments as a charitable remainder trust. The variation in life expectancy will alter the present value of the annuity contract and either increase or decrease the amount of the charitable deduction.

Likewise, designating another person as an annuitant will result in a taxable gift to that person in the amount of value of the annuity. Donor's spouse may be an annuitant without gift tax consequence because of the marital deduction.[110] Any gift tax paid on a gift within three years of donor's death will result in inclusion of the amount of the gift tax in donor's gross estate.[111]

Gifts of Partial Interests

As noted above, only certain gifts of partial interests in property will support a deduction for income, estate, or gift tax purposes unless the transfer is in trust or would meet the requirements of a transfer in trust.[112] The exceptions to this strict rule are (1) a remainder interest in a personal residence or farm,[113] (2) an undivided interest in the donor's entire interest in the property,[114] (3) transfers exclusively for conservation purposes,[115] and (4) certain transfers of copyrighted works of art, but only for estate and gift tax purposes.[116]

Remainder Interest in Personal Residence or Farm

A personal residence is any property used by its owner as a personal residence but not restricted to principal residence.[117] Therefore, a vacation home used as a personal residence part of the year,[118] stock in a cooperative housing corporation if the unit was used as a personal residence,[119] and a yacht if the owner lived on board part of the year[120] constitute a personal residence.

A farm is any land and improvements on such land used by the donor or donor's tenant to produce crops, fruit, or other agricultural products or to sustain livestock.[121] For this purpose the acreage may be subdivided; it need not be the whole farm.[122]

The property itself must be contributed and not the proceeds from the sale of the property.[123] While the amount of the charitable deduction depends on the fair market value of the personal residence or farm, the calculation is complicated by the requirements that depreciation and depletion must be taken into account as well as discounting the resulting value at 10 percent per annum to obtain the fair market value of the remainder interest.[124]

Undivided Interest in Property

To be deductible a gift of an undivided interest in property must be a fraction or percentage of the donor's entire ownership rights and extend over the entire period of donor's ownership.[125] A deductible undivided interest includes a transfer of an interest as a tenant in common with the donor where possession and control of the property is divided along percentage of ownership lines.[126] This method will result in an immediate deduction for a gift of an undivided interest in tangible personal property which would not otherwise be deductible until all intervening interests or rights to actual possession or enjoyment have expired or are held by a person other than the donor or a person standing in close relationship to the donor.

The amount of the charitable contribution of an undivided interest is calculated by taking the donated percentage and multiplying it by the fair market value of the property.

Gift Exclusively for Conservation Purposes

A gift exclusively for conservation purposes must be a qualified conservation contribution to be deductible. A qualified conservation contribution is a contribution of a qualified real property interest to a qualified organization exclusively for conservation purposes in perpetuity.[127] A qualified real property interest is the donor's entire interest, a remainder interest, or a perpetual restriction on use.[128] A qualified organization is a governmental unit or a publicly supported charity.[129] The conservative purpose must be preservation of land areas, protection of natural wildlife habitat, preservation of open space for scenic enjoyment or government conservation policy, or preservation of historically important land or historic structures.[130]

The donor may retain subsurface mineral rights and the right to access thereto except for surface mining which must be prohibited.[131] The amount of the charitable contribution is the fair market value of the real property interest transferred.

Copyrighted Works of Art

Partial interests in certain copyrighted works of art may give rise to a gift and estate tax charitable deduction but not a charitable contribution deduction under section 170.[132]

Nondeductible Partial Interests

A series of revenue rulings has established that the following gifts of partial interests to charitable organizations are not deductible:

1. A bequest of a remainder interest in the household furnishings of a personal residence[133]
2. A bequest of a remainder interest in a personal residence where the residence was placed in trust[134]
3. A bequest of part of the proceeds of the sale of a personal residence on the death of the life tenant[135]
4. A bequest of the remainder interest in a personal residence to a charitable organization and an individual as tenants in common[136]

5. A bequest of the entire proceeds of the sale of a personal residence on the death of the life tenant[137]

6. A gift of an annuity contract acquired by the donor under a split insurance plan that provided for term insurance at favorable rates in addition to the annuity contract.[138]

7. A gift of corporate stock where the donor retained the right to vote the stock[139]

Income Contributions

The converse of the charitable remainder trust is the charitable income or lead trust. In a charitable lead trust, the trust income is contributed to a charitable organization while the remainder interest is either retained by the donor or given to another noncharitable beneficiary. There are two types of charitable lead trusts each having a different purpose.

Qualified Lead Trust

A qualified lead trust will support a deduction for income, gift, and estate tax purposes. To qualify for a gift or estate tax deduction, the charitable lead trust must set up the income interest in the form of a guaranteed annuity or as a fixed percentage of the fair market value of the trust assets valued annually and distributed at least annually as in a unitrust income interest.[140] In addition to the requirements for an estate or gift tax deduction, the trust must be a grantor trust to qualify for an income tax deduction.[141] In a grantor trust, the grantor is treated as the owner of the trust, and the trust income, therefore, is attributable to the grantor.[142]

A charitable lead trust is not subject to the minimum pay-out requirements imposed on charitable remainder trusts. Any guaranteed annuity or fixed pay-out percentage may be used.[143] Nor are charitable lead trusts subject to the twenty-year term restriction imposed on charitable remainder trusts, so any term of years may be used.[144]

The charitable deduction is an amount equal to the present value of the income interest in the year of transfer. The same tables as those used to calculate the value of the income interest in a charitable remainder trust are used for qualified charitable lead trusts. Since the charitable deduction is taken in the year of transfer and the trust income is attributable to the grantor in the years in which it is earned, the effect of the qualified charitable lead trust is to exchange the tax value of the current charitable deduction for income tax liabilities in subsequent years.

Since a gift to a charitable lead trust is "for the use of" rather than "to" a charitable organization, the charitable contribution is subject to the 30 percent limitation.[145] Extreme caution is urged because of the possible double penalty of loss of the charitable contribution because of the 30 percent limitation plus no carry-over of the deduction and future tax liability on the income. A qualified charitable lead trust is best suited to a situation in which the grantor has an unusually large amount of income in a particular year subject to tax. The income recognized in subsequent years would be taxed at lower rates. Another good use of a qualified lead trust is to fund the trust with tax exempt securities so that future income is not taxed to the grantor who gets the charitable deduction in the year of transfer.

A qualified charitable lead trust may be effectively used as an estate planning tool because the estate is allowed an estate tax charitable deduction to the extent of the value of the income interest.

The funding of a qualified charitable lead trust results in a gift to a charitable organization. The gift is offset by the gift tax charitable deduction if the qualified charitable lead trust meets the requirements of a qualified charitable lead trust for estate and gift tax deductions, and no gift tax liability is imposed.[146] Note that a qualified charitable lead trust is a private foundation for purposes of certain restrictions.[147] (For discussions of private foundations see other chapters of this book.)

Nonqualified Charitable Lead Trusts

A nonqualified charitable lead trust is primarily an income splitting device. The trust is not a grantor trust so that the trust income is not attributable to the grantor. The benefits that the grantor receives are a reduction in tax liability by shifting income to the trust to be taxed at a lower rate which lessens the estate tax burden on intrafamily transfers.

Contributions of income from a nonqualified charitable lead trust are not deductible by the donor for any purpose. To the extent that the income is contributed to a charitable organization, the trust has an unlimited deduction for its required payments.[148] A nonqualified charitable lead trust may be used by an individual or corporation which because of the limitations cannot make use of a charitable deduction but wishes to make contributions in any event.

To avoid having the gift of all future income completed in the year that the nonqualified charitable lead trust is created, the donor may reserve the power to designate annually the charitable income beneficiaries or the right to change such beneficiaries before the income is actually distributed.[149] Reservation of such power will not make the trust a grantor trust.[150] For gift tax purposes, the gift is complete each year when paid and should escape gift tax liability since the gift tax charitable deduction will offset it.[151] However, this arrangement can cause severe estate tax consequences if the donor dies before termination of the trust because retention of the power to designate income beneficiaries means that the fair market value of the remainder interest on date of death must be included in donor's gross estate.[152] The estate tax consequences may cause a potential grantor to reject a nonqualified charitable lead trust alternative.

Miscellaneous Forms of Contributions

Life Insurance

A donor may take a charitable contribution deduction for gifts of life insurance policies to a charitable organization. The donor must transfer all ownership interests in the policy; otherwise, it is a transfer of a partial interest in property, and no deduction is allowed. Merely designating a charitable organization as beneficiary will not support a charitable deduction.

The amount of the charitable contribution varies depending on the continued payment of premiums and intent to surrender the policy for cash value. If the policy is paid up (no further premiums due), the amount of the deduction is the policy's replacement cost but not to exceed the donor's tax basis in the policy.[153] If premiums remain to be paid, the amount of the deduction is the interpolated terminal reserve value of the policy which is generally slightly in excess of the cash surrender value.[154] If there are substantial loans against the policy, if the donor is not the insured, or if the donee intends to cash the policy in, the amount of the deduction is the cash surrender value of the policy.[155]

Group term life insurance paid by donor's employer represents an opportunity to provide a substantial charitable contribution at no cost. An employer may provide up to $50,000 of group term life insurance to an employee without inclusion of the premium amount in the employee's gross income.[156] Amounts of group term life insurance in excess of $50,000 provided by an employer result in gross income to the employee unless the employer names a charitable organization as the beneficiary of the life insurance in excess of $50,000.[157]

Unreimbursed Expenses

An individual who incurs expenses on behalf of a charitable organization and is not reimbursed may take a charitable deduction in the amount of the expenses.[158] Examples of deductible unreimbursed expenses are (1) cost of operation, repair, and maintenance of a motor vehicle used to provide gratuitous services (the standard mileage rate is twelve cents per mile),[159] (2) expenses of delegates or representatives of charitable organizations at conventions,[160] (3) expenses of local officials who serve without pay in the performance of official duties,[161] (4) expenses of dinner parties to promote a charity ball except benefits received by donor and family.[162]

Membership Fees

Membership fees and subscriptions paid to charitable organizations are deductible to the extent that the payments exceed the monetary value of benefits and privileges available to members.[163]

Legal Fees

Legal fees incurred in preserving the original purpose for which property was contributed to a charitable organization are deductible.[164]

Raffle Tickets and Admissions

The cost of a raffle ticket or admission is deductible only to the extent that the amount paid exceeds the fair market value of the benefits or privileges received.[165] To receive a charitable deduction in the full amount, an outright gift should be made by refusing or returning the admission ticket before the event.[166] Generally, the cost of a raffle ticket is not deductible because of the difficulty of establishing that the value of the chance purchased is less than the cost.

THE ESTATE TAX CHARITABLE DEDUCTION

A charitable bequest, legacy, devise, or transfer to certain charitable organizations will give rise to a charitable estate tax deduction. To be deductible the charitable bequest, legacy, devise, or transfer must be made:

(1) to or for the use of the United States, any State, any political subdivision thereof, or the District of Columbia, for exclusively public purposes;

(2) to or for the use of any corporation organized and operated exclusively for religious, charitable, scientific, literary, or educational purposes, including the encouragement of art, or to foster national or international amateur sports competition (but only if no part of its activities involve the provision of athletic facilities or equipment), and the prevention of cruelty to children or animals, no part of the net earnings of which inures to the benefit of any private stockholder or individual, which is not disqualified for tax exemption under section 501(c)(3) by reason of attempting to influence legislation, and which does not participate in, or intervene in (including the publishing or distributing of statements), any political campaign on behalf of any candidate for public office;

(3) to a trustee or trustees, or a fraternal society, order, or association operating under the lodge system, but only if such contributions or gifts are to be used by such trustee or trustees, or by such fraternal society, order, or association, exclusively for religious, charitable, scientific, literary, or educational purposes, or for the prevention of cruelty to children or animals, such trust, fraternal society, order, or association would not be disqualified for tax exemption under section 501(c)(3) by reason of attempting to influence legislation, and such trustee or trustees, or such fraternal society, order, or association, does not participate in, or intervene in (including the publishing or distributing of statements), any political campaign on behalf of any candidate for public office; or

(4) to or for the use of any veterans' organization incorporated by Act of Congress, or of its departments or local chapters or posts, no part of the net earnings of which inures to the benefit of any private shareholder or individual.[167]

The amount of the charitable estate tax deduction is the fair market value of the bequest.[168] There are no percentage limitations nor distinctions made among types of qualified donees or property contributed as in the case of an income tax charitable deduction.[169] The amount of the deduction must be reduced by the amount of any death taxes paid out of the bequest, legacy, or devise. Further, the amount of the deduction cannot exceed the value of the transferred property included in the gross estate.[170]

Bequest of a Remainder Interest

A testator may make a charitable bequest of a remainder interest. The charitable estate tax deduction is only allowed if the remainder interest is in the form of an annuity trust, unitrust, or pooled income fund.[171] The amount of the charitable estate tax deduction is computed in the same manner as for the income tax charitable deduction. (See the discussion of these charitable remainder trusts, *supra.*)

Bequest of Income

A testator may establish a charitable lead trust in the testator's will. The gift of income will support a charitable estate tax deduction only if the income interest is in the form of a guaranteed annuity or a fixed percentage of the fair market value of the trust assets valued annually and distributed annually.[172] (See the discussion of charitable lead trusts, *supra.*)

NOTES

1. American Association of Fund-Raising Counsel, *Report on 1980 Charitable Giving.*
2. *Id.*
3. Rev. Rul. 63-252, 1963-2 C. B. 101.
4. 363 U.S. 278 (1960).
5. 363 U.S. 278, 285 (1960).
6. *Bogardus v. Comm.,* 302 U.S. 34, 41 (1937).
7. *See, e.g., Winters v. Comm.,* 468 F.2d 778 (2d Cir. 1972); Rev. Rul. 79–99, 1979-1 C. B. 108.
8. *Karl D. Petit,* 61 T. C. 634 (1974).
9. *Threlfall v. U.S.,* 302 F. Supp. 1114 (D. C. Wis. 1969).
10. Treas. Reg. § 1.170A-1(e).
11. Treas. Reg. § 1.170A-1(g).
12. *Id.*
13. *Id.*

14. I.R.C. § 170(f)(3).

15. I.R.C. § 170(f)(3)(A).

16. I.R.C. § 170(a)(2); Treas. Reg. § 1.170A-11(b).

17. Treas. Reg. § 1.170A-1(b).

18. Rev. Rul. 78-38, 1978-1 C.B. 67, *revoking* Rev. Rul. 71-216, 1971-1 C. B. 96.

19. Rev. Rul. 80-335, 1980-2 C.B. 170.

20. Rev. Rul. 68-174, 1968-1 C.B. 81; *Norman Petty,* 40 T.C. 521 (1963); *Sheldon B. Guren,* 66 T.C. 118 (1976).

21. Treas. Reg. § 1.170A-1(e).

22. Rev. Rul. 69-93, 1969-1 C.B. 139.

23. *See, e.g., Johnson v. U.S.,* 280 F. Supp. 412 (D.C.N.Y. 1967).

24. Treas. Reg. § 1.170A-1(b).

25. Treas. Reg. § 1.170A-1(c)(4).

26. I.R.C. § 170(e)(1)(A).

27. I.R.C. § 170(e)(1)(B)(ii).

28. I.R.C. § 170(e)(1)(B)(i).

29. I.R.C. § 170(b)(1).

30. I.R.C. § 170(b)(1)(C)(i).

31. I.R.C. § 170(b)(1)(C)(iv).

32. I.R.C. § 170(b)(1)(C)(iii).

33. Treas. Reg. § 1.170A-8(d)(2)(iii); Rev. Rul. 77-217, 1977-1 C.B. 64.

34. I.R.C. § 170(b)(1)(D).

35. *Id.*

36. I.R.C. § 170(b)(1)(B); Treas. Reg. § 1.170A-8(c)(1)(ii).

37. I.R.C. § 170(b)(1)(B); Treas. Reg. § 1.170A-8(c)(2).

38. I.R.C. § 170(b)(1)(B)(ii).

39. I.R.C. § 170(d)(1)(A).

40. I.R.C. § 170(b)(1)(C)(ii).

41. I.R.C. § 170(b)(1)(B); Treas. Reg. § 1.170A-8(c)(2)(ii); Treas. Reg. § 1.170A-8(f), Example (8).

42. I.R.C. § 170(b)(1)(C)(iii); Treas. Reg. § 1.170A-8(d)(2)(i)(b).

43. I.R.C. § 170(b)(1)(D).

44. I.R.C. § 170(b)(2).

45. I.R.C. § 170(d)(2).

46. I.R.C. § 170(e)(3).

47. I.R.C. § 170(e)(4).

48. I.R.C. § 170(e)(1)(B).

49. Rev. Rul. 55-138, 1955-1 C.B. 223, *modified by* Rev. Rul. 68-69, 1968-1 C.B. 80; Rev. Rul. 55-275, 1955-1 C.B. 295; Rev. Rul. 55-531, 1955-2 C.B. 520.

50. Rev. Rul. 55-410, 1955-1 C.B. 297.

51. I.R.C. § 6659.

52. I.R.C. § 6659(b).

53. I.R.C. § 6659(d).

54. I.R.C. § 6659(c).

55. Treas. Reg. § 1.170A-1(a)(2).

56. Treas. Reg. § 1.170A-1(a)(2)(iii).

57. *Elizabeth H. Potter,* 38 T.C. 951 (1962), *acq.* 1964-2 C.B. 7; Treas. Reg. § 1.1001-1(e)(1).

58. I.R.C. § 170(e)(2).

59. Treas. Reg. § 1.1011-2(a)(2); Treas. Reg. § 1.1011-2(c), Example (3).

60. Treas. Reg. § 1.1011-2(a)(3); Rev. Rul. 81-163, 1981-1 C.B. 433.

61. I.R.C. §§ 170(f)(2)(A), 2055(e)(2)(A), 2522(c)(2)(A).

62. I.R.C. § 170(f)(3)(A).

63. I.R.C. § 170(f)(3)(B)(i).

64. I.R.C. § 170(f)(3)(B)(ii).

65. I.R.C. §§ 170(f)(3)(B)(iii) & (iv).

66. I.R.C. §§ 508(e), 664(d)(1); Treas. Reg. § 1.664-2(a).

67. 1972-2 C.B. 340, *modified by* Rev. Rul. 80-123, 1980-1 C.B. 205, *clarified by* Rev. Rul. 82-165, 1982-2 C.B. 117. Sections 5.02 and 7.02 are mandatory provisions for charitable remainder trusts with respect to decedents who die after May 5, 1980.

68. Rev. Rul. 77-374, 1977-2 C.B. 329.

69. Treas. Reg. § 1.664-2(c); Treas. Reg. § 20.2031-10.

70. I.R.C. § 664(c).

71. I.R.C. § 664(b).

72. I.R.C. §§ 652(b), 661(b).

73. I.R.C. §§ 664(d)(2), 508(e); Treas. Reg. § 1.664-3(a).

74. Treas. Reg. § 1.664-4(b)(5).

75. I.R.C. § 664(c).

76. I.R.C. § 664(b); Treas. Reg. § 1.664-1(a)(5)(iii).

77. I.R.C. §§ 652(b), 661(b).

78. I.R.C. § 642(c)(5); Treas. Reg. § 1.642(c)-5(b).

79. I.R.C. § 664 does not apply to pooled income funds.

80. I.R.C. § 642(c)(3).

81. I.R.C. § 661(b).

82. Treas. Reg. § 1.1011-2(a)(1).

83. *Crane v. Comm.,* 331 U.S. 1 (1947).

84. *Comm. v. Tufts,* 461 U.S. 300, 103 S. Ct. 1826 (1983).

85. I.R.C. §§ 671-679.

86. Rev. Proc. 80-20, 1980-1 C.B. 633, *modified by* Rev. Proc. 81-33, 1981-2 C.B. 564.

87. Rev. Rul. 76-7, 1976-1 C.B. 179; Rev. Rul. 76-8, 1976-1 C.B. 179; Rev. Rul. 76-371, 1976-2 C.B. 305.

88. Rev. Rul. 79-368, 1979-2 C.B. 109.

89. I.R.C. § 170(a)(3).

90. I.R.C. § 642(c)(5)(C).

91. Rev. Rul. 60-370, 1960-2 C.B. 203.

92. I.R.C. §§ 2522(a),(c).

93. I.R.C. § 2036(a). *But see,* Rev. Rul. 76-273, 1976-2 C.B. 268.

94. I.R.C. §§ 2055(a),(e).

95. I.R.C. §§ 2522(a),(c).

96. I.R.C. § 2036(a).

97. I.R.C. §§ 2522(a),(c).

98. I.R.C. § 2001(b).

99. I.R.C. § 2035(c).

100. *Burnet v. Guggenheim*, 288 U.S. 280 (1933); Treas. Reg. § 25.2511-2(b).

101. Treas. Reg. § 25.2511-2(c).

102. I.R.C. § 2036(a).

103. I.R.C. §§ 2055(a),(e).

104. I.R.C. § 2036(a).

105. I.R.C. §§ 2055(a),(e).

106. Treas. Reg. § 1.170A-1(d)(1); Rev. Rul. 55-388, 1955-1 C.B. 233; Rev. Rul. 80-281, 1980-2 C.B. 282.

107. Treas. Reg. § 1.170A-1(d)(2); Treas. Reg. § 1.101-2(e)(1)(iii)(b)(2).

108. Rev. Rul. 62-137, 1962-2 C.B. 28, *supplemented by* Rev. Rul. 62-216, 1962-2 C.B. 30, *as clarified by* Rev. Rul. 67-39, 1967-1 C.B. 19, and *amplified by* Rev. Rul. 72-438, 1972-2 C.B. 38.

109. Treas. Reg. § 1.1011-2(a)(4)(ii).

110. I.R.C. § 2523(b)(1).

111. I.R.C. § 2035(d).

112. I.R.C. §§ 170(f)(3)(A), 2522(c)(2), 2055(e)(2).

113. I.R.C. §§ 170(f)(3)(B), 2522(c)(2), 2055(e)(2).

114. *Id.*

115. *Id.*

116. I.R.C. §§ 2522(c)(3), 2055(e)(4).

117. Treas. Reg. § 1.170A-7(b)(3).

118. *Id.*

119. *Id.*

120. Private Ltr. Rul. 8015017.

121. Treas. Reg. § 1.170A-7(b)(4).

122. Rev. Rul. 78-303, 1978-2 C.B. 122.

123. Rev. Rul. 77-169, 1977-1 C.B. 286.

124. Treas. Reg. §§ 1.170A-7(b)(3), -12.

125. Treas. Reg. § 1.170A-7(b)(1).

126. *Id.;* Private Ltr. Ruls. 7728046 and 7733075.

127. I.R.C. § 170(h)(1).

128. I.R.C. § 170(h)(2).

129. I.R.C. § 170(h)(3).

130. I.R.C. § 170(h)(4).

131. I.R.C. §§ 170(h)(5),(6).

132. I.R.C. §§ 2055(e)(4), 2522(c)(3).

133. Rev. Rul. 76-165, 1976-1 C.B. 279.

134. Rev. Rul. 76-357, 1976-2 C.B. 285.

135. Rev. Rul. 76-543, 1976-2 C.B. 287, *amplified by* Rev. Rul. 77-169, 1977-1 C.B. 286.

136. Rev. Rul. 76-544, 1976-2 C.B. 288.

137. Rev. Rul. 77-169, 1977-1 C.B. 286.

138. Rev. Rul. 76-1, 1976-1 C.B. 57.

139. Rev. Rul. 81-282, 1981-2 C.B. 78.

140. I.R.C. §§ 170(f)(2)(B), 2055(e)(2)(B), 2522(c)(2)(B).

141. I.R.C. § 170(f)(2)(B).

142. I.R.C. §§ 671-679.

143. I.R.C. § 170(f)(2)(B).

144. Treas. Reg. § 1.170A-6(c)(2)(i)(A).

145. Treas. Reg. §§ 1.170A-8(a)(2), (c)(1)(ii).

146. I.R.C. §§ 2522(a), (c)(2)(B).

147. I.R.C. § 4947.

148. I.R.C. § 642(c)(1).

149. Treas. Reg. § 25.2511-2(c); Rev. Rul. 77-275, 1977-2 C.B. 346.

150. I.R.C. § 674(b)(4).

151. I.R.C. § 2522(a).

152. I.R.C. §§ 2036, 2038.

153. *U.S. v. Ryerson,* 312 U.S. 260 (1941); Treas. Reg. § 25.2512-6(a), Example (3); I.R.C. § 170(e)(1)(A).

154. Rev. Rul. 59-195, 1959-1 C.B. 18.

155. *Tuttle v. U.S.,* 436 F.2d 69 (2d Cir. 1970).

156. I.R.C. § 79(a); Treas. Reg. § 1.79-1(a)(2).

157. I.R.C. § 79(b)(2)(B); Treas. Reg. 1.79-2(c)(3).

158. Treas. Reg. § 1.170A-1(g); Rev. Rul. 58-240; 1958-1 C.B. 141, *clarified by* Rev. Rul. 71-135, 1971-1 C.B. 94; Rev. Rul. 84-61, 1984-1 C.B. 40.

159. Rev. Rul. 58-279, 1958-1 C.B. 145; Rev. Proc. 80-32, 1980-2 C.B. 767, *modifying* Rev. Proc. 80-7, 1980-1 C.B. 590; I.R.C. § 170(j).

160. Rev. Rul. 61-46, 1961-1 C.B. 51.

161. Rev. Rul. 59-160, 1959-1 C.B. 59.

162. Private Ltr. Ruls. 7726018, 7922060.

163. Rev. Rul. 68-432, 1968-2 C.B. 104.

164. *Archbold v. U.S.,* 444 F.2d 1120 (Ct.Cl. 1971).

165. Rev. Rul. 67-246, 1967-2 C.B. 104.

166. *Id.*

167. I.R.C. § 2055(a).

168. I.R.C. §§ 2055(a),(d).

169. I.R.C. § 2055(c).

170. I.R.C. § 2055(d).

171. I.R.C. § 2055(e)(2)(A).

172. I.R.C. § 2055(e)(2)(B).

12

Financial Management

Historically, the law governing the management of institutional funds has been uncertain and confusing. Part of this problem is attributable to the form of organization the institution uses. The law governing charitable trusts grew out of the English Statute of Charitable Uses and the English Court of Chancery. Nonprofit corporation law is derived from acts of legislative bodies. Nonprofit corporation acts are less restrictive than the law of charitable trusts probably because they used business corporation acts as models. In addition, within the trust law area there is confusion as to whether the law of private trusts regarding financial management should also apply to charitable trusts. Moreover, the demarcation line is not strictly between unincorporated charitable trusts and nonprofit corporations. An unincorporated charitable trust may have a corporate trustee. Conversely, some states apply trust law to nonprofit corporations if the assets are transferred to a charitable corporation on condition that the corpus be preserved and only the income be used for the charitable purpose. Out of an abundance of caution, managers and trustees of institutional funds were reluctant to exceed the bounds of private trust law in their institutional dealings. Cary and Bright in their work *The Law and the Lore of Endowment Funds* concluded that these self-imposed restrictions had little basis in law but instead were based on myth.

UNIFORM MANAGEMENT OF INSTITUTIONAL FUNDS ACT

In an effort to bring order to this area of the law, the commissioners on Uniform State Laws promulgated the Uniform Management of Institutional Funds Act in 1972. Twenty-eight states have adopted the act in whole or part, as detailed in Table 13.

260

Table 13
Uniform Management of Institutional Funds Act

Table of Jurisdictions Wherein Act Has Been Adopted

For text of Uniform Act, and variation notes and annotation materials for adopting jurisdictions, see Uniform Laws Annotated, Master Edition, Volume 7A.

Jurisdiction	Statutory Citation
California	West's Ann. Civ. Code, §§ 2290.1 to 2290.12.
Colorado	C.R.S. 1973, 15-1-1101 to 15-1-1109.
Connecticut	C.G.S.A. §§ 45-100h to 45-100p.
Delaware	12 Del.C. §§ 4701 to 4708.
District of Columbia	D.C. Code §§ 32-401 to 32-409.
Illinois	S.H.A. ch. 32, ¶¶ 1101 to 1110.
Kansas	K.S.A. 58-3601 to 58-3610.
Kentucky	KRS 273.501 to 273.590,
Louisiana	LSA-R.S. 9:2337.1 to 9:2337.8.
Maryland	Code, Estates and Trusts, §§ 15-401 to 15-409.
Massachusetts	M.G.L.A. c. 180A, §§ 1 to 11.
Michigan	M.C.L.A. §§ 451.1201 to 451.1210.
Minnesota	M.S.A. §§ 309.62 to 309.71.
Montana	MCA 72-30-101 to 72-30-207.
New Hampshire	RSA 292-B:1 to 292-B:9.
New Jersey	N.J.S.A. 15:18-15 to 15:18-24.
New York	McKinney's N-PCL §§ 102, 512, 514, 522.
North Dakota	NDCC 15-67-01 to 15-67-09.
Ohio	R.C. §§ 1715.51 to 1715.59.
Oregon	ORS 128.310 to 128.355.
Rhode Island	Gen. Laws 1956, §§ 18-12-1 to 18-12-9.
Tennessee	T.C.A. §§ 35-1101 to 35-1109.
Vermont	14 V.S.A. §§ 3401 to 3407.
Virginia	Code 1950, §§ 55-268.1. to 55-268.10.
Washington	West's RCWA 24.44.010 to 24.44.900.
West Virginia	Code, 44-6A-1 to 44-6A-8.
Wisconsin	W.S.A. 112.10.

The Uniform Act applies to institutional funds held by incorporated or unincorporated organizations organized and operated exclusively for educational, religious, charitable, or other eleemosynary purposes or to a governmental organization to the extent that it holds funds exclusively for one of the above purposes.[1] The act applies primarily to section 501(c)(3) organizations. The fund must be held by and for the exclusive use, benefit, or charitable purpose of a charitable institution.[2] The act does not apply to funds not held by charitable institutions even if the fund is held for the use or benefit of a charitable organization.[3] Thus, the act does not apply to charitable remainder trusts held by institutions until the noncharitable interest is terminated at which point the trust becomes an institutional fund.

Section 4 of the Uniform Act is a broad grant of investment authority to the governing board which is the body responsible for the management of the institution or the institutional fund. The act is clear that the governing board is not limited to traditional investments authorized to trustees under charitable or private trust law.

The governing board may do any of the following:

1. Invest and reinvest an institutional fund in any real or personal property deemed advisable by the governing board, whether or not it produces a current return, including mortgages, stocks, bonds, debentures, and other securities of profit or nonprofit corporations, shares in or obligations of associations, partnerships, or individuals, and obligations of any government or subdivision or instrumentality thereof

2. Retain property contributed by a donor to an institutional fund for as long as the governing board deems advisable

3. Include all or any part of an institutional fund in any pooled or common fund maintained by the institution

4. Invest all or any part of an institutional fund in any other pooled or common fund available for investment, including shares or interests in regulated investment companies, mutual funds, common trust funds, investment partnerships, real estate investment trusts, or similar organizations in which funds are commingled and investment determinations are made by persons other than the governing board

The governing board is held to a standard of care similar to that imposed on the board of directors of a business corporation. The standard of care imposed on the governing board by section 6 of the Uniform Act is to exercise ordinary business care and prudence under the facts and circumstances prevailing at the time of the action or decision. In making that decision or taking the action, the governing board shall consider (1) the long- and short-term needs of the institution in carrying out its charitable purposes, (2) the institution's present and anticipated financial requirements, (3) expected total return on its investments, (4) price level trends, and (5) general economic conditions.

The Uniform Act makes it clear that a governing board of a private institution or institutional fund may delegate its investment management powers unless a particular gift instrument prohibits such delegation. The governing board of a governmental organization must operate within the governmental framework. The governing board may delegate to one of its committees, officers, employees, or agents, including investment counsel, the authority to act in place of the governing board in the investment and reinvestment of institutional funds.[4] Further, the governing board may contract with independent investment advisers, investment counsel or managers, banks, or trust companies to act on behalf of the governing board and authorize payment of compensation for investment advice or services.[5]

The Uniform Act addresses the oft-encountered problem of gift restrictions to uses which could no longer be feasibly administered or to investments no longer available or productive. Prior law or uncertainty concerning prior law left a governing board virtually paralyzed. The doctrine of *cy pres* was not a satisfactory solution to the problem; however, the Uniform Act is careful not to limit the *cy pres* doctrine. The Uniform Act allows the governing board to obtain the written consent of the donor to release, in whole or in part, a restriction imposed on the use or investment of an institutional fund by the gift instrument.[6] If the donor's written consent cannot be obtained because of death, disability, unavailability, or impossibility of identification, the governing board may petition a court of competent jurisdiction for a release of the restriction.[7] Proper notice must be given to the state attorney general or other designated state authority, and an opportunity to be heard must be provided to the attorney general or other official designated.[8] The release procedure is not available to allow use of the fund for a purpose other than the charitable purposes of the petitioning institution.

Another practical problem encountered by a governing board is whether realized capital gains on institutional endowment funds may be used as income or must be allocated to principal. Cary and Bright in their work came to the conclusion that there was no substantial authority under prior law to require the treatment of realized capital gains as principal.[9] Conversely, Thomas E. Blackwell and John W. Wheeler concluded that Cary and Bright were wrong and that realized capital gains constituted principal.[10] A more considerable issue is presented with respect to unrealized appreciation on capital assets held by an institution. The more conservative managers took the Blackwell-Wheeler approach.

The Uniform Act allows appropriation of net appreciation for expenditure for the uses and purposes for which the endowment fund was created.[11] The appreciation may be realized or unrealized appreciation over the historic dollar value of the fund which essentially is the aggregate fair market values of the endowed assets determined as of the date of acquisition.[12] In appropriating the realized or unrealized net appreciation, the governing board must use the same standard of care that it uses for investments.[13] The act does not allow appropriation if it would be contrary to the donor's expressed intent in the gift instrument.[14]

The appropriation provision is retroactive in effect.[15] The commissioners' comments indicate that there is no substantial authority that prohibits retroactive application of the act. There is no constitutional obstruction to retroactive treatment because the act deals with trust administration and not with vested property rights.

TRADITIONAL RULES REGARDING INVESTMENTS

Under the traditional view, rules governing investments made by trustees of private trusts apply to investments made on behalf of charitable trusts.[16]

Kinds of Investments

The type of investment allowed depends on the trust instrument and state law, or both. Within the limits of state law the trust instrument is controlling.

Statutory regulation may be mandatory or permissive. If the regulation is mandatory, the trustee is limited to the types of investments specified in the statute unless otherwise provided in the trust instrument. If permissive, the statute lists types of investments which are permissible but leaves it up to the trustee to choose from other types of investments. Most state statutes do not draw a distinction between individual and corporate trustees with respect to the kinds of investments that may be made.

Standard of Conduct

A trustee must conduct himself as a reasonably prudent and skillful man would in the conduct of his own affairs.[17] Speculation is prohibited, and the safety of the fund should be the trustee's primary concern. In the absence of specific authorization, a trustee may not invest in either speculative or nonincome producing properties.[18] A prudent man would diversify investments for safety; therefore, a trustee has the obligation to diversify.[19]

If gift restrictions are no longer feasible or possible to carry out, the doctrine of *cy pres* is used to reform the trust. No trust fails altogether if the grantor has a general intention to give the property for charitable purposes. *Cy pres* is also available where it is impracticable but not impossible to carry out specific instructions.[20]

TAX RESTRICTIONS ON INVESTMENTS

A private foundation and its managers are subject to tax penalties if the private foundation invests its assets in a manner that jeopardizes the carrying out of any of its exempt purposes.[21] A jeopardy investment is an investment made by foundation managers who, in making the investment, failed to exercise ordinary business care and prudence, under the facts and circumstances at the time they made the investment, in providing for the long- and short-term financial needs of the foundation to carry out its exempt purpose.[22] This is not the prudent trustee test although there is some evidence that Congress intended for the prudent trustee test to apply.[23] In fact, the test set out in the regulation is more liberal. The object of the treasury test is preservation of the exempt purpose.

In the exercise of ordinary business care and prudence, foundation managers may take into account (1) the expected return (both income and appreciation of capital), (2) the risks of rising and falling price levels, and (3) the need for diversification within the investment portfolio.[24]

The determination of whether the investment jeopardizes the exempt purpose for which the private foundation was created is made on an investment-by-investment basis, taking into account the entire portfolio.[25] There are no per se jeopardy investments, but the regulation lists some that will be closely scrutinized.

These investments probably should be avoided: (1) trading in securities on margin, (2) trading in commodity futures, (3) investments in working interests in oil and gas wells, (4) purchase of "puts" and "calls" and "straddles," (5) purchase of warrants, and (6) selling short.[26] Also in the suspect category are (1) "spreads," "strips," and "straps,"[27] (2) special options,[28] (3) low-interest loans,[29] (4) loans unattractive to normal commercial sources,[30] and (5) stock classified as high-risk by investment services.[31] The common thread in the Treasury Department's position is the efforts of speculators or traders whether successful or not. These efforts are inconsistent with the proper management of the affairs of a private foundation.[32]

Once it is determined that a particular investment does not jeopardize the carrying out of the foundation's exempt purpose, that determination is final and may not be opened even if the investment subsequently results in a loss to the foundation.[33] Hindsight may not be used to make a subsequent determination.

Note that section 4944 does not relieve foundation managers from other obligations or fiduciary duties imposed by other federal or state law concerning the operation or administration of a trust or other organization subject to section 4944.[34] Moreover, no state may exempt or relieve a person from any obligation, duty, responsibility, or standard of conduct imposed by section 4944 and the regulations promulgated thereto.[35]

Section 4944(a) does not apply to these investments:

1. Program-related investments[36]
2. An investment made by any person which is later gratuitously transferred to a private foundation[37]
3. An investment acquired by a private foundation solely as a result of a corporate reorganization under section 368(a)[38]

A program-related investment is defined as follows:

1. The primary purpose of the investment is to accomplish one or more of the charitable purposes described in section 170(c)(2)(B).
2. No significant purpose of the investment is the production of income or the appreciation of property.
3. No purpose of the investment is to influence legislation or participate in or intervene in any political campaign on behalf of any candidate for public office.[39]

An investment has as its primary purpose a charitable purpose if it significantly furthers the accomplishment of the private foundation's exempt purposes and if it would not have been made "but for" the relationship between the investment and the accomplishment of the foundation's exempt purposes.[40] Three types of investments that were intended to qualify for program-related investments by the Senate Finance Committee are (1) low-interest loans to needy students, (2) high-risk investments in low-income housing, and (3) loans to small businesses where commercial sources of funds are unavailable.[41] Treasury Regulations section 53.4944-3(b) contains examples of program-related investment.

A program-related investment may cease to be program-related because of a critical change in circumstances.[42] The foundation has thirty days after the foundation managers have actual knowledge of such critical change to withdraw the investment; otherwise, it will become a jeopardy investment. However, changes in the form or terms of the investment made primarily for exempt purposes and not for any significant purpose involving the production of income or appreciation of property will not disqualify a program-related investment.[43]

If a private foundation makes a jeopardy investment, a tax equal to 5 percent of the amount of the jeopardy investment is imposed on the private foundation for each year or part of a year that the investment continues during the taxable period. The taxable period begins with the date of the investment and ends on the earlier of the date of mailing of a deficiency notice with respect to the tax, the date on which the tax is imposed, or the date the amount is removed from jeopardy. No maximum penalty can be assessed; nor is a defense available to the foundation itself.

In addition to the penalty tax on the foundation, any foundation manager who participated in the making of the jeopardy investment may be subject to the 5 percent penalty tax. However, foundation managers' maximum tax liability at this stage is $5,000. Regardless of how many foundation managers participate, the total tax is 5 percent of the amount. All participants are jointly and severally liable. But, a foundation manager who lacked knowledge of the jeopardy and whose action was not willful and was due to reasonable cause is not liable for the tax. If a penalty tax is imposed on a foundation manager, the foundation manager must pay the penalty tax; otherwise, it is self-dealing if the foundation pays it, and the amount paid is subject to tax under section 4941.

Under section 4962 the initial tax may be abated under certain circumstances if the violation was due to reasonable cause and not to willful neglect and if corrected within the taxable period.

If the initial penalty tax is imposed on the private foundation and the jeopardy investment is not removed within the taxable period, an additional tax of 25 percent of the amount of the investment is imposed on the private foundation. There is no limit to the amount of the penalty tax imposed. Again, the foundation has no defense.

A foundation manager who refuses to agree to part or all of the removal from jeopardy is assessed an additional 5 percent penalty tax. All foundation managers who refuse to agree have a maximum of $10,000 tax liability in the aggregate.

If a foundation is guilty of repeated violations concerning jeopardy investments or if any particular act (or failure to act) concerning an investment is done without reasonable cause and is both willful and flagrant, the foundation may lose its tax exempt status and be subject to a tax equal to the lesser of the aggregate tax benefits received from tax exempt status or the value of the net assets of the foundation.[44]

In such a case the foundation managers are subject to penalty taxes equal to 100 percent of the penalty taxes previously imposed on the investments unless the manager can show reasonable cause and that his actions were not willful or flagrant.[45]

A private foundation must annually report jeopardy investments on form 990 or 1041-A or both depending on its exempt status and type of organization and file a form 4720. Failure to file a form 4720 results in a $10-per-day penalty up to $5,000,[46] 6 percent per annum interest resulting from underpayment of the tax,[47] and a possible fraud penalty of up to 50 percent of the underpayment imposed on the foundation.[48] A foundation manager may be subject to the $10-per-day penalty if he fails to file the form 4720 within a reasonable period after having received written demand to file.[49]

A new foundation manager coming on board should carefully scrutinize the foundation's portfolio of investments before accepting the position.

NOTES

1. Uniform Management of Institutional Funds Act (UMIFA) § 1(1).
2. UMIFA § 1(2).
3. *Id.*
4. UMIFA § 5.
5. *Id.*
6. UMIFA § 7.
7. *Id.*
8. *Id.*
9. Cary, William L., & Bright, Craig B., *The Law and The Lore of Endowment Funds* 5–6, Ford Foundation, 1969.
10. 2 J. Coll. & U.L. 210.
11. UMIFA § 2.
12. UMIFA § 1(5).
13. UMIFA § 2.
14. UMIFA § 3.
15. *Id.*
16. A. Scott, *Law of Trusts,* § 389 (3d ed. 1967).
17. *Harvard College v. Amory,* 9 Pick. 446 (1930).

18. *Estate of Carlton v. Comm.*, 298 F.2d 415 (2nd Cir. 1962).

19. *See, e.g., Steiner v. Hawaiian Trust Co.*, 393 P.2d 96, 105 (Hawaii 1964); *Mandel v. Cemetery Bd.*, 185 Cal. App.2d 657, 8 Cal. Rptr. 342 (1960); 7 Ind. Stat. Ann. § 31-507 (Burns 1968 Supp); 6 Tenn. Code Ann. §§ 35-309 to 35-311 (1955); Wis. Stat. § 320.01(1) & (2).

20. A. Scott, *Law of Trusts*, §§ 399.3, 399.4 (3d ed. 1967).

21. I.R.C. § 4944(a).

22. Treas. Reg. § 53.4944-1(a)(2).

23. S. Rep. No. 552, 91st Cong., 1st Sess. *reprinted in* 1969-3 C.B. 423.

24. Treas. Reg. § 53-4944-1(a)(2).

25. *Id.*

26. *Id.*

27. Treas. Dept. Report on Private Foundations 53 (Comm. Print 1965).

28. *Id.*

29. Treas. Reg. § 53.4944-3(b)(1).

30. Treas. Reg. § 53.4944-3(b)(3).

31. Treas. Reg. § 53.4944-1(c), Ex. 1.

32. Treas. Dept. Report on Private Foundations 53 (Comm. Print 1965).

33. Treas. Reg. § 53.4944-1(a)(2).

34. *Id.*

35. *Id.*

36. I.R.C. § 4944(c).

37. Treas. Reg. § 53.4944-1(a)(2)(ii)(a).

38. Treas. Reg. § 53.4944-1(a)(2)(ii)(b).

39. Treas. Reg. § 53.4944-3(a)(1).

40. Treas. Reg. § 53.4944-3(a)(2)(i).

41. S. Rep. No. 552, 91st Cong., 1st Sess., *reprinted in,* 1969-3 C.B. 423.

42. Treas. Reg. § 53.4944-3(a)(3).

43. *Id.*

44. I.R.C. § 507.

45. I.R.C. § 6684.

46. I.R.C. § 6652(d)(1).

47. I.R.C. § 6601(a).

48. I.R.C. § 6653(b).

49. I.R.C. § 6653(d)(3).

13

Accountability

ANNUAL REPORTS

Annual reports serve several purposes. The annual report provides governmental authorities with information concerning the activities of an organization and uses to which the organization is putting its assets. The information disclosed in the annual report is used by potential patrons and current donors to determine whether to support or to continue to support the organization. If the organization provides for membership, the annual report allows the members to evaluate the performance of the organization's activities. Because the annual report is virtually the only source of information available to the different consumers of the reports, it is essential that the reports be comprehensive and informative. Unfortunately this is not often the case.

Nonprofit Corporation Law

Most states require both domestic and foreign corporations to submit annual reports to the secretary of the state's office. The annual report requirements tend to be brief and relatively uninformative. A typical example is the recommended form promulgated by the drafters of the Model Nonprofit Corporation Act, which follows:

ANNUAL REPORT

OF

_____

To the Secretary of State
of the State of _____ :
    Pursuant to the provisions of Section _____ of the _____

Non-Profit Corporation Act, the undersigned corporation submits the following annual report:

FIRST: The name of the corporation is _____
_____ .

SECOND: It is incorporated under the laws of _____ .
THIRD: The address of its registered office in your State is _____
_____

and the name of its registered agent in your State of such address is _____
_____ .

FOURTH: If a foreign corporation, the address of its principal office in the state or country under the laws of which it is incorporated is
_____ .

FIFTH: The character of the affairs which it is actually conducting in your State, briefly stated, is _____
_____ .

SIXTH: The names and respective addresses of its directors and officers are:

Name	Office	Address
_____	Director	_____
_____	Director	_____
_____	Director	_____
_____	President	_____
_____	Vice President	_____
_____	Secretary	_____
_____	Treasurer	_____

Dated _____, 19____

_____ (Note 1)

By _____ (Note 2)

Its _____

Notes: 1. Exact corporate name of corporation making the report.
         2. Signature and title of officer signing for the corporation.
(Add verification, if required.)
STATE OF _____
COUNTY OF _____
I, _____, a notary public hereby certify that on this
_____ day of _____, 19_____, personally appeared before me
_____, who, being by me first duly sworn, declared that
he is the _____ of _____
_____; that he signed the foregoing document as
_____ of the corporation; and that the statements therein contained are
true.

_____

Notary public

(NOTARIAL SEAL)

Failure or refusal to file the report on time may result in a *de minimis* fine but, more importantly, may cause the state to bring an action for involuntary dissolution of the corporation.

The majority of states only require that the annual report be filed with the office of the secretary of state, and no provision is made for dissemination of the report to the members, although the filed annual report should be available for inspection by the members at the corporate offices. Some states, such as California and New York, do require that annual reports be made by the directors to the members.

The New York statute requires a report verified by the president and treasurer or a majority of the directors or a report certified by outside accountants.[1] The report must contain in appropriate detail the assets and liabilities of the corporation, including trust funds, and the principal changes in the assets and liabilities, including trust funds, over the fiscal reporting period.[2] An income statement or its equivalent showing revenue or receipts and expenses or disbursements for general and restricted purposes must be included.[3]

Under New York law the report must be presented at the annual meeting of the members, and a copy of the report must be included in the minutes of the annual meeting of the members.[4] If the corporation has no members, the annual report shall be presented at the annual meeting of the board of directors and included in the minutes of that meeting.[5]

California law requires that the annual report actually be sent to members of certain corporations, not just presented at the annual meeting of the members.[6] A nonprofit corporation which received less than $25,000 in gross revenues or receipts during the fiscal year or which solicits, in writing, at least 500 persons and mails a copy of the report promptly to anyone solicited who requests it and publishes the annual report in a newspaper of general circulation in the county where the corporation's general office is located need not send copies of the report to the members.[7] An annual report need only be sent with the frequency with which members' meetings are held.[8]

The content of the report is similar to that required by New York with respect to reporting of assets and liabilities, including trust funds, and principal changes in each during the fiscal year.[9] An income statement is also required showing revenue or receipts and expenses or disbursements for both general and restricted purposes.[10] The report must be certified that it was prepared without audit or be accompanied by a report from independent accountants.[11] Falsification of any report required to be filed with the state will subject the perpetrator to criminal liability.[12]

Solicitation Statutes

A majority of states have enacted charitable solicitation statutes which require certain organizations soliciting funds for charitable purposes to register with the state and provide financial reports. Table 14 gives details of the statute requirements for each state.

The acts are more notable for the number of exemptions from the reporting requirements than anything else. For example, the New York statute[13] exempts the following groups:

1. Religious corporations and other religious agencies and organizations
2. State-approved educational institutions and educational institutions confining solicitation to students, alumni, faculty, trustees and their families
3. Fraternal, patriotic, social, and alumni organizations and historical societies chartered by the state of New York which confine solicitations to their respective memberships
4. Solicitations for the relief of any particular named individual, provided all contributions are given to the named individual without deduction
5. Organizations soliciting $10,000 or less during a fiscal year, if fund raisers are unpaid for their services
6. Certain veterans' organizations, volunteer fire departments, volunteer ambulance services, and their auxiliaries

If an organization is not exempt, the annual report requirements under the solicitation act are not burdensome. Generally, a balance sheet and statement of income and expense are to be attached or submitted with the form required by the state reporting officer, which is usually the attorney general.

Charitable Trust Statutes

Most states have charitable trust statutes; however, prior to 1951 only New Hampshire had enacted legislation requiring trustees to report the existence and administration of property held for charitable purposes to the state. The Uniform Supervision of Trustees for Charitable Purposes Act[14] has served as a model for many of the existing statutes requiring such reporting.[15]

The Uniform Supervision of Trustees for Charitable Purposes Act and the statutes patterned after it apply not only to trusts but also to unincorporated and incorporated charitable organizations.[16] The acts do not apply to noncharitable nonprofit organizations. Moreover, certain entities such as governmental units and their political subdivisions, religious organizations holding property for religious purposes, and charitable corporations organized and operated primarily for educational, religious, or hospital purposes are exempted.[17] Other entities such as cemeteries and homes for the aged also have been exempted.[18]

Under the act the attorney general establishes and maintains a register of trustees who are required to report. The initial filing required of a trustee who has received property for charitable purposes is for a copy of the instrument provid-

Table 14
Reports Required by States

State	Nonprofit Corp. Act Frequency	Nonprofit Corp. Act Statute	Solicitation Act	Charitable Trust Provisions
Alabama	--	none	none	none
Alaska	Biennial	§ 10.20.260	none	none
Arizona	Annual	§ 10-1081	none	none
Arkansas	--	none	§ 64-1602	none
California	--	none	Cal. Gov.§ 17510	Cal. Gov. §§ 12585-12586
Colorado	Annual	§ 31-24-89	none	none
Connecticut	Biennial	§ 33-435	§ 19-323	none
Delaware	--	none	none	none
District of Columbia	Annual	§ 29-1083	§ 2-2101	none
Florida	--	none	§ 496.01 et seq.	none
Georgia	Annual	§ 14-3-270	§ 43-17-1 et seq.	none
Hawaii	Annual	§ 416-96	§ 467B-1 et seq.	none
Idaho	Annual	§ 30-601	none	none
Illinois	Annual	ch. 32, § 62	ch. 23, § 5101	ch. 14, § 51
Indiana	Annual	§ 23-7-1.1	none	none
Iowa	Annual	§ 504A.83	§ 122.1	none
Kansas	--	none	§ 17-1	none
Kentucky	Annual	§ 273.367	none	none
Louisiana	--	none	none	none
Maine	--	none	§§ 5001-5014	none
Maryland	--	none	§ 103A-103L	none
Massachusetts	--	none	ch. 68, §§ 18-33	ch. 12, § 8F
Michigan	Annual	§ 450.81	§ 400.271 et seq.	§ 14.251 et seq.
Minnesota	--	none	§ 309.50 et seq.	none
Mississippi	--	none	none	none
Missouri	Annual	§ 355.325	none	none
Montana	Annual	§ 35-9-901	none	none
Nebraska	Biennial	§ 21-1981	§ 28-1401 et seq.	none
Nevada	Annual	ch. 81, § 18	none	none
New Hampshire	--	none	§ 320:20	§ 7:28
New Jersey	--	none	§ 45:17A	none
New Mexico	Annual	§ 53-8-82	§ 57-22-1 et seq.	none
New York	--	none	N.Y. Exec. L. § 171-176	N.Y. EPTL § 8-1.14
North Carolina	--	none	§ 131C-1 et seq.	§ 36-19
North Dakota	--	none	§ 50-22-01 et seq.	none
Ohio	--	none	§ 1716.01 et seq.	§ 109.23
Oklahoma	--	none	§ 552.1 et seq.	none
Oregon	Annual	§ 61.805	§ 128.805 et seq.	§ 128.610 et seq.; § 128.070
Pennsylvania	--	none	§ 160-1 et seq.	none
Rhode Island	Biennial	§ 7-6-14	§ 5-53-1	none
South Carolina	--	none	§ 33-55-10 et seq.	§ 21-31-10 et seq.
South Dakota	Annual	§ 47-27-18	§ 37-27-1 et seq.	none
Tennessee	--	none	§ 48-2201 et seq.; § 8-312	none

Table 14 (continued)
Reports Required by States

State	Nonprofit Frequency	Corp. Act Statute	Solicitation Act	Charitable Trust Provisions
Texas	4 years	Art. 9.01	none	none
Utah	Annual	§ 16-6-97	none	none
Vermont	Annual	§ 2701	none	none
Virginia	Annual	§ 13.1-282	§ 57-48 et seq.	none
Washington	Annual	§ 24.03.395	§ 19.09.010 et seq.	§ 19.10.010 et seq.
West Virginia	--	none	§ 29-19-1 et seq.	none
Wisconsin	--	none	§ 440.41 et seq.	none
Wyoming	--	none	none	none

ing for the trustee's title, powers, or duties.[19] Thereafter, periodic written financial reports must be made to the attorney general.[20]

The uniform act provides that the reports shall be made available for public inspection;[21] however, there is no provision for disclosure to members or patrons.

Federal Securities Regulation

Reporting companies must file certain reports with the Securities and Exchange Commission pursuant to section 12 of the Securities Exchange Act of 1934. The purpose of such filings is to make public information concerning certain publicly traded securities.

A reporting company is any issuer whose stock is traded on a national securities exchange or who has assets in excess of $1 million in value and at least 500 shareholders.[22] An issuer organized and operated exclusively for religious, educational, benevolent, fraternal, charitable, or reformatory purposes and not for pecuniary profit, in which no part of the net earnings inures to the benefit of any private shareholder or individual is exempt from the reporting requirement.[23] Other nonprofit organizations may have to file if they meet the requirements of section 12(g)(1) and are not otherwise exempt under section 12(g)(2) of the Securities Exchange Act of 1934. In 1982, the Securities and Exchange Commission exempted small issuers with assets of less than $3 million in value from the filing requirements.[24]

Section 12 of the Securities Exchange Act of 1934 requires that a detailed statement about the issuer be filed when the issuer first registers under that act.

Section 13 of the act requires annual reports to be filed on form 10-K, quarterly reports to be filed on form 10-Q, and certain monthly reports to be filed on form 8-K. The annual report on the form 10-K must be signed by the principal executive, financial, and accounting officers and at least a majority of the board of directors.[25]

Any person who makes or causes to be made a false or misleading statement of a material fact in a required report is liable in damages to any person who bought or sold a security in reliance on the statement at a price which was affected by that statement.[26] Under section 18 of the Securities Exchange Act of 1934 the plaintiff must show that he had no knowledge that the statement was misleading or false. Good faith and no knowledge that the statement was false or misleading constitutes a defense to such an action.

Tax Returns

Exempt Organizations other than Private Foundations

Section 6033 requires annual returns to be filed on IRS Form 990 by certain organizations that are tax exempt under section 501(a). The following organizations are exempt from filing form 990:

1. A church, an interchurch organization of local units of a church, a convention or association of churches or an integrated auxiliary of a church such as a men's or women's organization, religious school, mission society, or youth group

2. A school below college level affiliated with a church or operated by a religious order

3. A mission society sponsored by or affiliated with one or more churches or church denominations, if more than half of the society's activities are conducted in, or directed at persons in, foreign countries

4. An exclusively religious activity of any religious order

5. A state institution whose income is excluded from gross income under the provisions of section 115

6. Corporations organized under an act of Congress that are instrumentalities of the United States and are tax exempt under said act pursuant to section 501(c)(1)

7. A private foundation described in section 509(a) and tax exempt under section 501(c)(3)

8. A black lung benefit trust exempt under section 501(c)(21)

9. A section 401 qualified stock bonus, pension, or profit-sharing trust

10. A religious or apostolic organization exempt under section 501(d)

11. Certain organizations whose gross receipts are normally $25,000 or less[27]

Section 6033(b) requires annual reporting of the following information:

1. Gross income for the year

2. Expenses attributable to gross income incurred within the year

3. Disbursements within the year for its tax exempt purposes
4. A balance sheet showing the organization's assets, liabilities, and net worth as of the beginning of the year
5. The names and addresses of all substantial contributors and the total contributions and gifts received during the year
6. Names and addresses of its foundation managers and highly compensated employees and the amounts of compensation and other payments made to each
7. Organizations which have a section 501(h) election in effect for the reporting year must provide the following information: (a) lobbying expenditures, (b) lobbying nontaxable amount, (c) grass-roots expenditures, and (d) grass-roots nontaxable amounts.

The IRS Form 990 is available for public inspection in the national office of the Internal Revenue Service and in the office of the district director in the district where the tax exempt organization operates.[28]

A copy of the form 990 and schedule A (form 990) may be used to satisfy the annual reporting requirements of some states in place of all or part of their financial report forms.[29] You should check the state requirements and substitution allowable by state officials before submitting a form 990 to them. Table 15 lists states that will and will not accept form 990.

Table 15
States Accepting and Not Accepting IRS Form 990 for Charitable Registration Purposes

States that will accept the Form 990 for charitable registration purposes:

Arkansas	New Hampshire
California	New Jersey
Connecticut	New York
District of Columbia	North Carolina
Florida	Ohio
Georgia	Oregon
Illinois	Pennsylvania
Maine	Rhode Island
Maryland	South Carolina
Massachusetts	South Dakota
Michigan	Tennessee
Minnesota	Virginia
Nebraska	West Virginia
Nevada	Wisconsin

States which will not accept the Form 990 for charitable registration purposes:

Hawaii	Kansas
North Dakota	Oklahoma

Source: National Association of State Charity Officials

Private Foundations

Private foundations are required to provide information in addition to that required by section 6033(b) and file an IRS Form 990-PF.[30]

The additional information required is the information that would have been required under the provisions of section 6056 (repealed 1980) in addition to that required by section 6033(b). The additional information is (1) an itemized statement of the private foundation's securities and all other assets at the close of the year, showing both book and market value; (2) an itemized list of all grants and contributions made or approved for future payment during the year, showing the amount of each grant or contribution, the name and address of the recipient, any relationship between any individual recipient and the foundation managers or substantial contributors, and a concise statement of the purpose of each grant or contribution; (3) the address of the principal office of the foundation and the place where its books and records are maintained, if different.

Foundation managers must make the annual return available for inspection during regular business hours at the principal office of the foundation and provide a free copy to any person requesting inspection in accordance with section 6104(d). Notice that the private foundation's annual return is available for inspection, and notice of its availability must be published in a newspaper of general circulation in the county where the foundation's principal place of activity is located. The published notice must appear by the due date for filing the annual report. A copy of the notice must be attached to the annual return filed with the Internal Revenue Service. Substantial penalties of up to $5,000 may be imposed for failure to publish and file the notice with the annual return.

Foundation managers must provide a copy of the annual report to the attorney general of the state of organization or incorporation, the state in which the principal office is located, the states in which the private foundation is carrying on activities, and any other state attorney general who requests it. Only one copy of the annual report needs to be filed with a state attorney general even if it satisfies other reporting requirements to that state attorney general. Required filings with other state agencies or officers is not satisfied by filing the required copy with the state attorney general. A Return of Certain Excise Taxes on Charities and Other Persons Under Chapters 41 and 42 of the Internal Revenue Code (form 4720) must be attached to the form 990-PF provided to each state attorney general.

ACCOUNTING

Accountability required by state and federal law to the respective governmental bodies, members, contributors and others creates the need for a system of financial management. Systems of financial management for nonprofit organizations are relatively new. The American Institute of Certified Public Accountants (AICPA) issued industry guides for hospitals in 1972, colleges and universities in 1973, voluntary health and welfare organizations in 1974, and state and local governmental units in 1974. In 1978, the industry guide for certain other nonprofit organizations was approved.

The 1978 industry guide is intended to cover the following types of organizations:

1. Cemetery organizations
2. Civic organizations
3. Fraternal organizations
4. Labor unions
5. Libraries
6. Museums
7. Other cultural institutions
8. Performing arts organizations
9. Political parties
10. Private and community foundations
11. Private elementary and secondary schools
12. Professional associations
13. Public broadcasting stations
14. Religious organizations
15. Research and scientific organizations
16. Social and country clubs
17. Trade associations
18. Zoological and botanical societies[31]

Organizations not intended to be covered by these accounting principles are those organizations that operate essentially as a commercial business for the direct economic benefit of members or stockholders.[32] This group includes pension plans, mutual insurance companies, mutual banks, trusts, and farm cooperatives.[33]

The guide is intended to provide necessary information to users of the financial statements including (1) contributors, (2) beneficiaries of the organization, (3) trustees or directors of the organization, (4) employees of the organization, (5) governmental bodies, (6) the organization's current and future creditors, and (7) constituent organizations.[34]

The principal purpose of the financial statement is to communicate the ways resources have been allocated and used in carrying out the organization's mission.[35] Second, the financial statement should identify the organization's principal programs and their costs.[36] Third, the degree of control exercised by donors over the use of resources should be illuminated.[37] Finally, the financial statement should assist the user in evaluation of the organization's ability to carry out its fiscal objectives.[38]

The guide recommends that financial statements be prepared using the accrual basis of accounting; however, books may be kept using a cash basis of accounting.[39]

Three basic financial statements are recommended: a balance sheet, statement of activity, and statement of changes in financial position.[40] The balance sheet is intended to reflect financial position and should summarize the assets, liabilities, and fund balances of the organization.[41] The statement of activity, including changes in fund balances, is intended to present results of operations. It should report the support, revenue, capital or nonexpensable additions, and functional expense categories.[42] The statement of changes in financial position provides a summary of available resources and their use during the accounting period. It should contain information about the methods of financing programs and activities and about the use and investment of resources during the accounting period.[43]

Combined or combining financial statements of interrelated organizations are more informative and present a fairer picture of activities than separate statements. Interrelated organizations are organizations where one exercises control, directly or indirectly, over the direction of management and policies through ownership, by contract, or otherwise.[44] Combined financial statements are necessary if one organization controls another and (1) separate entities solicit funds in the name of and with the expressed or implicit approval of the reporting organization, and substantially all the solicited funds are intended by the donor or are otherwise required to be transferred to the reporting organization or to be used at its discretion or direction, (2) a reporting organization transfers some of its resources to another separate entity whose resources are held for the benefit of the reporting organization, or (3) a reporting organization assigns functions to a controlled organization whose funding is primarily derived from sources other than public contributions.[45]

For the treatment of particular items such as capital additions, current restricted or unrestricted gifts, grants, bequests, or other income, donated services, membership fees, investment income, depreciation, and other expenses, the industry guide should be consulted. In addition, the industry guide contains illustrative financial statements in Appendix C which may prove helpful.

EXPENDITURES

State Law

Trusts

If a trustee of a charitable trust commits a breach of trust, the trustee is treated the same as a trustee of a private trust who commits a breach of trust. The general rule is that a trustee only commits a breach of trust if he is in some way personally at fault either through negligence or intentional conduct. With respect to his duty to administer the trust, a trustee is held to a reasonable man standard. A good faith intention to do the best he can is not sufficient.

A trustee is personally liable for any loss which results from an improper investment. A trustee is under an obligation to invest trust funds in such a way as to generate income without incurring risk of loss of the principal.[46] The trustee must exercise reasonable care in selecting the investment keeping in mind the preservation of the corpus.[47]

Should a trustee make an improper investment, he has a duty to dispose of that investment within a reasonable period of time and reinvest in a proper investment.[48] This same duty applies even if the investment was proper when made but subsequently becomes improper.[49] Misappropriation of trust funds constitutes a breach of trust and may give rise to criminal prosecution. A trustee is under an obligation to restore the money or property to the trust.[50]

Corporations

Corporate officers and directors owe their corporations the fiduciary duties of care and loyalty. The same is true of officers and directors of nonprofit corporations.

The standard of care is that of the reasonably prudent person under similar circumstances.[51] Officers and directors are only liable for damages actually caused by their negligence.[52] Officers and directors owe a duty of undivided allegiance to the corporation.[53] The duty owed by officers and directors of nonprofit corporations is to the membership, patrons or contributors, and general public.

Nonprofit corporations have the power to contract and incur liabilities. The business judgment rule generally applies. As long as the officers and directors act within the scope of their authority and such action is reasonable and in good faith and not adverse to the best interests of the corporation, a court will not substitute its judgment for that of the officers and directors. Nonprofit corporation law in this area has lessened the standards of charitable trust law.

Unauthorized expenditures which constitute waste or misappropriation of corporate assets breach both the duties of care and loyalty; in which event, the guilty officer or director must restore the amount misappropriated or pay damages resulting from his action. The officer or director also may be prosecuted for embezzlement or fraud.

In many states, either the secretary of state or attorney general has the power to inquire into the activities of a nonprofit corporation to ascertain whether or not the nonprofit corporation is complying with the state nonprofit corporation act.[54] Officers and directors are required under threat of criminal penalty to respond truthfully and fully to such inquiries.[55]

The power of a state attorney general to oversee expenditures of contributions by a nonprofit corporation was brought into question in the case of the *Worldwide Church of God.* Section 9505 of the California Corporations Code empowered the attorney general to ascertain the condition of the affairs of a nonprofit corporation, to take corrective action, and, if necessary, to put the church into receivership. The uproar from religious groups was immediate. In the aftermath, section 9505 was repealed, and section 9230 of the California Corporations Code was enacted.

Section 9230 of the California code severely restricted the power of the attorney general with respect to religious organizations. Enforcement of the charitable purpose for which money is solicited may be instituted only after notice of such intent has been given to the religious organization. No civil action may be taken by the attorney general if the directors or members in good faith conclude that the stated purpose for which the money or property was solicited is no longer in accord with the policies of the corporation and ratify the use of the property for other purposes.

Taxable Expenditures

The Tax Reform Act of 1969[56] restricted the purposes for which a private foundation could make expenditures. Prohibited expenditures result in the imposition of a tax under section 4945(a) on the private foundation or foundation managers, or both. These prohibited expenditures are termed "taxable expenditures" and mean any amount paid or incurred by a private foundation for the following reasons:

1. To carry on propaganda or otherwise attempt to influence legislation
2. To influence the outcome of any specific public election or to carry on, directly or indirectly, any voter registration drive (with some exceptions discussed below)
3. As a grant to an individual for travel, study, or other similar purposes unless the grant satisfies certain requirements
4. As a grant to an organization testing for public safety or a private foundation unless the private foundation-grantor exercises expenditure responsibility over the grant
5. For any purpose other than religious, charitable, scientific, literary, or educational, to foster national or international amateur sports competition, or for the prevention of cruelty to children or animals[57]

Propagandizing or Attempting to Influence Legislation

Section 501(c)(3) has long contained the requirement for tax exempt status: "no substantial part of the activities of which is carrying on propaganda, or otherwise attempting, to influence legislation." After the Tax Reform Act of 1969 the "substantial" element is removed with respect to private foundations.

Activity which is permissible under section 501(c)(3) may be a taxable expenditure under section 4945(e). Extreme caution should be observed by foundation managers in this area.

Section 4945(e) prohibits attempts to influence legislation by affecting public opinion or a segment of public opinion and by communicating with any member or employee of a legislative body, or with any other government official or employee who may participate in the formulation of the legislation. However, technical advice or assistance may be provided to a governmental body or to a committee or other subdivision thereof in response to a written request from such body or committee. The results of nonpartisan analysis, study, or research may be made available to the public and to legislators and other persons connected with the legislative process.

The first of the two prohibitions regarding public opinion is directed at grassroots campaigns or other attempts to encourage the public to contact legislators or other officials to propose, oppose, or support legislation. This provision is parallel to the limitation on ordinary and necessary business expense deductions in section 162(e)(2) with respect to for-profit businesses. No deduction is allowed in connection with any attempt to influence the general public or a segment of it with respect to legislative matters. Section 4945(e) also parallels the loss of section 501(c)(3) tax exempt status for action organizations.[58]

The second prohibition of section 4945(e) is against lobbying activities. Communications with any member or employee of a legislature or with any other government official or employee who may participate in the formulation of the legislation with the intent to influence the legislation is prohibited. Communications lacking the intent to influence are permissible.

Neither the code nor the regulations indicate whether the prohibited communications include not only direct but also indirect communications through related persons or other third parties. Caution is recommended.

The type of legislation within the prohibited category includes action by Congress, including treaties pending ratification, by any state, by any local council or similar governing body, or by the public in a referendum, initiative, constitutional amendment, or similar procedure.[59] Legislation does not include executive, judicial, or administrative actions by such bodies as school boards, housing authorities, sewer and water districts, zoning boards, and other similar federal, state, or local special purpose bodies whether appointed or elected.[60] Communication is prohibited through the whole legislative process from introduction of the legislation through enactment, defeat, or repeal of the legislation.[61]

Jointly funded projects with another organization or a governmental body are not taxable expenditures if they meet the criteria specified in the regulations. A grant to another organization is not a taxable expenditure merely because the grant is made on the condition that the grantee obtain a matching support appropriation from a governmental body.[62]

Taxable expenditures do not include amounts paid or incurred in discussing a jointly funded program or the possibility of a new jointly funded program by the foundation and a governmental body. The purpose of the discussions must be the exchange of data and information concerning the jointly funded program, and the discussions are limited to the jointly funded program and may not include other legislative issues.[63]

A private foundation may not make a grant to a section 509(a)(1), (2), or (3) organization (public charity) for the purpose of influencing legislation and avoid the restrictions of section 4945(d).[64] Grants that are not earmarked to be used for prohibited activities are not taxable expenditures.[65] A grant is earmarked for a prohibited activity if an oral or written agreement exists between the grantor and grantee that the grant will be used for prohibited activities or that the grantor retains the right to select the recipient of the grant.[66]

An amount paid or incurred by a recipient of a program-related investment in connection with an appearance before or communication with a legislative body, with respect to legislation or proposed legislation of direct interest to the recipient, is not attributable to the private foundation-grantor if the funds are not earmarked for prohibited activities and if a section 162 deduction is allowable to the recipient for the amount expended.[67]

The three statutory exceptions to taxable expenditures relating to influencing legislation are (1) making available the results of nonpartisan analysis, study, or research; (2) giving technical advice or assistance provided to a governmental body or to a committee or other subdivision in response to a written request by that body or subdivision; and (3) appearing before, or communicating with a legislative body concerning a possible decision of that body which will affect the existence of the private foundation, its powers and duties, its tax exempt status, or the deduction of contributions to the foundation.

Nonpartisan analysis, study, or research means independent and objective exposition of a particular subject matter including educational activities.[68] Nonpartisan analysis, study, or research may advocate a particular position or viewpoint provided there is a sufficiently full and fair exposition of the pertinent facts to enable the public or an individual to form an independent opinion or conclusion.[69] But the mere presentation of unsupported opinion does not qualify.[70] The nonpartisan analysis, study, or research must not reach the level of substantial, thereby violating the proscription of section 501(c)(3) and inviting the loss of tax exempt status.

The results of the nonpartisan analysis, research, or study may be made available by any suitable means such as oral or written presentations; distribution of reprints of speeches, articles, or reports; conferences, meetings, and discussions; and dissemination to the news media including radio, television, and newspapers.[71] If the results are broadcast by a noncommercial educational broadcasting station or network, the station or network must adhere to the

Federal Communications Commission regulations and its fairness doctrine which requires balanced, fair, and objective presentation of issues.[72] If the presentation is part of a series, the determination of nonpartisan analysis, study, or research will be based on the series as a whole rather than on each presentation.[73] All broadcasts within a six-month period may be considered as part of a series.[74] Presentations may not be limited to or directed entirely toward persons who are interested solely in one side of a particular issue.[75]

The second statutory exception is giving technical assistance. The technical assistance must be made in response to a written request in the name of the governmental body, committee, or subdivision making the request and not in the name of an individual member of the body, committee, or subdivision.[76] The technical assistance does not have to be nonpartisan analysis, research, or study.[77] Opinions and recommendations are permissible if given in response to specific requests.[78]

Apparently, if a foundation contacts the governmental body, committee, or subdivision first and is then requested to provide technical assistance, a taxable expenditure would be incurred. Likewise, presenting an unsolicited opinion or recommendation regardless of its significance renders all expenditures in connection with rendering the technical assistance as taxable expenditures.

The final statutory exception under section 4945(d) relates to possible decisions by a legislative body which might affect the existence, powers and duties, tax exempt status, or deduction of contributions to a private foundation. There are no limitations on communications with the entire legislative body, individual congressmen or legislators, members of their staffs, or representatives of the executive branch involved in the legislative process which relate to the prescribed subject matter.[79] No grass-roots campaign is permitted, however.[80]

Elections and Voter Registration Drives

Amounts expended to influence the outcome of any specific public election or to carry on, directly or indirectly, a voter registration drive are taxable expenditures.[81] An organization is deemed to be influencing the outcome of any specific public election if it participates or intervenes, directly or indirectly, in any political campaign on behalf of or in opposition to any candidate for public office.[82] A candidate for public office is an individual who offers himself, or is proposed by others, as a contestant for an elective public office at the national, state, or local level.[83]

The following activities are prohibited: (1) publishing or distributing written or printed statements or making oral statements on behalf of or in opposition to a candidate, (2) paying salaries or expenses of campaign workers, and (3) conducting or paying the expenses of conducting a voter-registration drive limited to the geographical area covered by the campaign.[84]

Certain organizations are not subject to the prohibition contained in section

4945(d)(2). To qualify for the exemption under section 4945(f), the organization must be tax exempt under section 501(c)(3). The activities must be nonpartisan and not confined to one specific election period and carried on in at least five states. Substantially all (85 percent) of the organization's income must be expended directly for the active conduct of the activities constituting the purpose or function for which it is organized and operated. The organization must receive at least 85 percent of its support (other than gross investment income) from exempt organizations, governmental units, or the general public. No more than 25 percent of its support may be received from any one exempt organization. Not more than half of its support may be derived from gross investment income. The support tests are computed on a five-year "moving average" rather than yearly, which enables the organization to occasionally exceed the 25 percent support test.[85] Contributions may not be conditioned on use in specified geographical areas or limited to specific elections.

An advance ruling may be requested that the organization qualifies under section 4945(f) for its first year of operation.[86] The organization must establish that it can reasonably be expected to satisfy the requirements of section 4945(f).[87] Contributors to the organization, including private foundations, may rely on the ruling until public notice is given that the organization is not qualified, even if it is ultimately determined not to qualify under section 4945(f) unless the grantor was aware of, or in part responsible for, the organization's failure to meet the statutory standards.[88]

The expenditure responsibility requirement of section 4945(d)(4) does not apply to grants made by a private foundation to a donee voter registration organization qualified under section 4945(f).

Grants to Individuals

A grant to an individual for travel, study, or other similar purpose is a taxable expenditure unless the grant is awarded on an objective and nondiscriminatory basis pursuant to an approved procedure and (1) the grant constitutes a scholarship or fellowship grant under the terms of section 117(a) and is used for study at an educational institution described in section 170(b)(1)(A)(ii), (2) the grant is a prize or award excluded from gross income under the terms of section 74(b), provided the recipient is selected from the general public, or (3) the grant's purpose is to achieve a specific objective, produce a report or other similar product, or improve or enhance a literary, artistic, musical, scientific, teaching, or other similar capacity, skill, or talent of the grantee.[89]

Grants include not only scholarships, fellowships, internships, prizes, and awards but also student loans and program-related investments.[90] Program-related investments consist of investments in such things as small businesses in central cities or businesses that assist in neighborhood renovation. But grants do not include salaries or other compensation paid to employees including educational payments to employees which are required to be included in the employees' gross income.[91] Contracts for personal services in assisting a foundation in planning, evaluating, or developing projects or areas of program activity by consulting, advising, or participating in conferences organized by the grantor-foundation are not grants.[92] A grant for a purpose other than those described in section 4945(d)(3) is not a taxable expenditure.[93]

A grant by a private foundation to another organization which in turn makes a grant for purposes included under section 4945(d)(3) is not considered to be a grant by the original grantor to an individual under section 4945(d)(3) if the requirements of the regulation are met. The original grantor-foundation may not earmark the use of the grant for any named individual but may have expectations that certain individuals may derive benefits from the grant.[94] The selection process must be completely independent of the original grantor-private foundation.[95] There may not be any oral or written agreement whereby the original grantor-private foundation may effect the selection of the individual grantee.[96]

A grant to a section 509(a)(1), (2), or (3) public charity which in turn makes payments to an individual for purposes described in section 4945(d)(3) is not a grant to an individual under section 4945(d)(3) if the grant is made for a project under the control of the public charity which controls the selection of the individual grantee.[97] The original grantor-private foundation may first suggest a recipient, provided there is an objective manifestation that the selection process is under the control of the grantee-public charity.[98]

If the grantee organization is a state, a possession of the United States, or any political subdivision thereof, or the United States or District of Columbia, the grantor-private foundation does not made a section 4945(d)(3) grant to an individual even if it is earmarked for a particular individual.[99] To qualify, the governmental body must satisfy the commissioner of Internal Revenue in advance that the program (1) is in furtherance of a charitable purpose, (2) requires the individual to make reports, and (3) requires the governmental body to investigate jeopardized grants.[100]

The foundation's selection process must be objective and nondiscriminatory. An objective and nondiscriminatory process is one in which the foundation's activities are consistent with its section 501(c)(3) purposes and the allowance of a charitable deduction pursuant to section 170.[101] The group from which the grantees are selected must be sufficiently broad so that the giving of grants would be considered to fulfill a section 170(c)(2)(B) charitable purpose, be sufficiently large to constitute a charitable class, and be reasonably related to the purpose of the grant.[102] Considerations such as exceptional qualifications to carry out the purpose of the grant and criteria calculated to effect the charitable purposes of the grant rather than benefit a particular individual may be used to restrict the size and nature of the selection group.[103] The criteria used in selecting the recipient should be related to the purpose of the grant. Those who select the grantees should not be in a position to derive any direct or indirect private benefit from the selection of any particular grantee over others.[104]

The selection procedure must be approved by the commissioner in advance with respect to the system of standards, procedures, and follow-up designed to result in grants.[105] The request for approval must fully describe the procedures and contain the following:

1. A statement detailing the selection process
2. A description of the terms and conditions under which the foundation ordinarily makes grants
3. A detailed description of the procedure for exercising supervision over the grants
4. A description of the procedure for review of grantee reports, for investigation of diversion of grant funds from their proper purpose, and for recovery of diverted grant funds[106]

The Internal Revenue Service has forty-five days to deny approval of the grant procedures; otherwise, they are considered approved until receipt of actual notice that the procedures do not meet the standards. The request for approval is submitted to the director of the district in which the private foundation's principal place of operation is located.

The regulation does not provide guidelines for supervision of grants other than scholarships and fellowships. The private foundation must make arrangements with the educational institution to obtain reports of the grantee's grades and courses taken in each academic period.[107] The report must be submitted at least annually.[108] Should the grantee be preparing research papers or projects instead of courses, a progress report must be submitted which has been approved by the supervising faculty member.[109] A final report must also be submitted.[110] No supervision is necessary if the fellowship or scholarship is paid by the private foundation to an educational institution described in section 151(e)(4) (i.e., one that maintains a regular faculty and curriculum) and if the institution agrees to use the grant to defray the recipient's expenses or to pay the recipient only if enrolled and whose standing is consistent with the purposes and conditions of the grant.[111]

Annual reports must be submitted on the progress made by grantees of section 4945(g)(3) grants.[112] A final report which includes an accounting of all funds received under the grant and a report of the grantee's accomplishments must be submitted.[113]

A private foundation has a mandatory obligation to investigate jeopardized grants. If it appears from any of the required reports submitted or other information that the grant is not being used in furtherance of the purposes for which it was made, the grantor must investigate.[114] Pending the investigation, further payments, if any, must be withheld until it is determined that no part of the grant was improperly used or, if so, until the misapplied funds have been recovered and the grantee has made assurances that future misapplications will not occur.[115] If the diversion is discovered and the grantor takes no action or fails to take all reasonable and appropriate action to recover or restore the funds, the foundation will be deemed to have made a taxable expenditure to the extent of the diverted funds and possibly of the amount of any future funds to the same grantee.[116]

The grantor-private foundation must keep records of the following information concerning all individual grants:

1. All information obtained by the foundation which evaluates potential grantees
2. The identity of all grantees
3. The amount and purpose of each grant
4. Progress reports concerning fellowships, scholarships, and grants to enhance a skill
5. Any information obtained pursuant to a mandatory investigation[117]

Grants to Organizations

A grant by a private foundation to another organization which is not a public charity under the terms of section 509(a)(1), (2), or (3) is a taxable expenditure unless the grantor exercises expenditure responsibility over the grant.[118] Expenditure responsibility means that the grantor-private foundation must exert all reasonable efforts and establish adequate procedures to see that the grant is spent solely for the purposes for which it was made, to obtain full and complete reports as to how the funds were spent, and to make full and detailed reports regarding such expenditures to the Internal Revenue Service.[119]

Expenditure responsibility does not extend to grants to section 509(a)(1), (2), or (3) organizations or to exempt operating foundations nor to grants under section 4945(f). With respect to a foreign organization which does not have a determination or ruling that it is a section 509(a)(1), (2), or (3) organization, it will be treated as one if the grantor has made a good faith determination that it is such an organization.[120] The good faith determination should ordinarily be based on an affidavit by the grantee foreign organization or opinion of grantor's or grantee's counsel that it qualifies as a section 509(a)(1), (2), or (3) organization.[121] The affidavit or opinion must contain sufficient information for the Internal Revenue Service to make such a determination.[122]

A private foundation does not have to exercise expenditure responsibility for secondary grants provided it does not earmark the grant for use by the secondary grantee.[123] A grant is not earmarked if the original grantor does not cause the selection of the secondary grantee even though it may expect that a particular organization may derive benefits from the grant.[124] An independent selection process is the key.

A grant made to a governmental body described in section 170(c)(1) which is earmarked for use by another organization need not be supervised if the governmental body satisfies the Internal Revenue Service in advance that the grant-making program is in furtherance of one of its section 170(c)(2)(B) purposes and that the governmental body will exercise expenditure responsibility.[125]

Expenditure responsibility is a burdensome obligation. Before making the grant, the grantor must conduct a limited inquiry concerning the potential grantee.[126] The limited inquiry should be complete enough to give a reasonable man assurance that the grantee will use the grant for proper purposes.[127] The inquiry should be concerned with (1) the identity, prior history and experience, if any, of the grantee organization and its managers; and (2) any knowledge which the private foundation has or which is readily available concerning the management, activities, and practices of the grantee organization.[128] The scope of the inquiry will vary from case to case depending on the size and purpose of the grant, the period over which it is to be paid, and prior experience with the grantee.[129]

Each grant that is subject to the expenditure responsibility requirements must be made under a written commitment signed by an appropriate officer or trustee or director of the grantee.[130] The written agreement must include an agreement by the grantee (1) to repay any portion of the grant which is not used for grant purposes, (2) to submit full and complete annual reports concerning how the funds were spent, (3) to maintain records of receipts and expenditures and to make its books and records available to the grantor at reasonable times, and (4) not to use the funds for propaganda or otherwise attempt to influence legislation under section 4945(d)(1), not to influence the outcome of any specific election or carry on a voter registration drive under section 4945(d)(2), not to make any grants outside of the terms of sections 4945(d)(3) and (4) or undertake any activity outside of the purposes specified in section 170(c)(2)(B).[131] Failure to comply subjects the grant to the tax on taxable expenditures.[132]

Included with its annual report under section 6033 must be a report with respect to every grant made during the taxable year that is subject to the expenditure requirement.[133] The report must contain these items:

1. The name and address of the grantee
2. The date and the amount of the grant
3. The purpose of the grant
4. The amounts expended by the grantee
5. Any diversion of funds from the purpose of the grant
6. Dates of reports from the grantee and dates and results of their verification[134]

The grantor-private foundation must make available to the Internal Revenue Service at the grantor's principal office copies of all agreements covering grants subject to the expenditure responsibility requirements, of each grantee report, and of reports of audits or investigations made with respect to the exercise of expenditure responsibility.[135]

Diversions of grant funds by the grantee for other purposes may result in the amounts diverted being classed as taxable expenditures.[136] However, the grantor will not be treated as having made a taxable expenditure if it takes all reasonable and appropriate steps to recover the diverted funds or insure their restoration, if future payments, if any, to the grantee are withheld until the grantee assures that no future diversions will occur, and if extraordinary precautions are taken to prevent reoccurrence.[137]

Expenditures for Noncharitable Purposes

An amount paid or incurred for any noncharitable purpose outside of the meaning of section 170(c)(2)(B) is a taxable expenditure.[138] Charitable purpose includes religious, charitable, scientific, literary, or educational uses, or for the prevention of cruelty to children or animals. Treasury Regulations section 53.4945-6(b) contains seven exceptions to the rule. The following are not taxable expenditures:

1. Expenditures to acquire investments entered into for the purpose of obtaining income or funds for the furtherance of its charitable purposes

2. Reasonable expenses incurred in acquiring such investments

3. Payment of taxes

4. A deductible expense incurred in connection with unrelated business income

5. A payment which constitutes a qualifying distribution under section 4942(g) or an allowable deduction under section 4940

6. Reasonable expenses incurred in evaluating, acquiring, modifying, and disposing of program-related investments

7. Business expenditures by the recipient of a program-related investment

Any expenditures for unreasonable administrative expenses, including compensation, consulting fees, and other fees for services rendered are ordinarily taxable expenditures unless the grantor can show that the expenses were paid or incurred in the good faith belief that they were reasonable and consistent with ordinary business care and prudence.[139]

A private foundation may not make a grant to a noncharitable organization unless the making of the grant itself constitutes a direct charitable act or a program-related investment or the grantor is reasonably assured that the grant will be used exclusively for charitable purposes described in section 170(c)(2)(B).[140]

Taxes on Taxable Expenditures

Section 4945(a) imposes on the private foundation a tax equal to 10 percent of the amount of each taxable expenditure. Any foundation manager who knowingly agrees to make a taxable expenditure is subject to a 2.5 percent tax on the amount of the taxable expenditure unless the manager can show that the agreement was not willful and was due to reasonable cause.[141] The maximum tax which may be imposed on a foundation manager under the subsection is $5,000.[142] The initial taxes may also be abated under other circumstances if the violation was due to reasonable cause and not to willful neglect and if it was corrected within the taxable period.[143]

Additional taxes are imposed on the foundation and its managers if the taxable expenditure is not corrected within the taxable period.[144] Correction requires recovery of the diverted amount or performing such corrective action as may be required by the Internal Revenue Service.[145] The foundation is not required to bring legal action unless it is probable that it will result in satisfaction of execution on a judgment.[146] The additional tax imposed on the foundation is 100 percent of the amount of the taxable expenditure.[147] The tax imposed on the foundation manager is 50 percent of the amount of the taxable expenditure if the manager refuses to agree to part or all of the correction.[148] The maximum additional tax which may be imposed on a foundation manager is $10,000.[149]

NOTES

1. N.Y. N-PCL § 519(a) (McKinney).
2. *Id.*
3. *Id.*
4. N.Y. N-PCL § 519(b) (McKinney).
5. N.Y. N-PCL § 519(c) (McKinney).
6. Cal. Corp. Code § 6321(a) (West).
7. Cal. Corp. Code §§ 6321(c), (f) (West).
8. Cal. Corp. Code § 6321(d) (West).
9. Cal. Corp. Code § 6321(a) (West).
10. *Id.*
11. Cal. Corp. Code § 6321(b) (West).
12. *See, e.g.,* ABA-ALI Model Nonprofit Corp. Act, § 86.
13. N.Y. EXEC. L. § 172-a (McKinney).
14. 9C Uniform L. Ann. 210-15 (1957).
15. Uniform Act adopted by California, Illinois, Michigan, and Oregon. Similar statutes exist in New Hampshire, Rhode Island, Ohio, and Massachusetts.
16. Uniform Supervision of Trustees for Charitable Purposes Act (USTCPA), § 2.
17. USTCPA § 3.
18. *See, e.g.,* Cal. Gov. Code § 12583 (West); Ill. Stat. ch. 14 § 54; O.R.S. §§ 61.755 to 61.775.

19. USTCPA § 5.

20. USTCPA § 6.

21. USTCPA § 10.

22. 15 U.S.C. § 781(g)(1) (1976).

23. 15 U.S.C. § 781(g)(2) (1976).

24. 17 C.F.R. § 240.12(g)-1 (1983).

25. Securities Exchange Act Rels. 17114 (1980); 17524 (1981).

26. 15 U.S.C. § 78r (1976).

27. I.R.S. Instructions for Form 990.

28. I.R.C. § 6104(b); Treas. Reg. § 301.6104-2(c).

29. I.R.S. Instructions for Form 990.

30. I.R.C. § 6033(c).

31. *Accounting Principles and Reporting Practices for Certain Nonprofit Organizations,* Dec. 31, 1978, American Institute of Certified Public Accountants, pp. 3–4.

32. *Id.* at 3.

33. *Id.*

34. *Id.* at 5.

35. *Id.*

36. *Id.*

37. *Id.*

38. *Id.*

39. *Id.* at 6.

40. *Id.* at 7.

41. *Id.*

42. *Id.* at 8.

43. *Id.* at 9.

44. *Id.* at 11.

45. *Id.*

46. A. Scott, *Law of Trusts,* § 227 (3d ed. 1967).

47. *Id.*

48. *Id.* § 230.

49. *Id.* § 231.

50. *Id.* § 386.

51. H. Henn & J. Alexander, *Laws of Corporations;* 621–625 (3d ed. 1983).

52. *Id.*

53. *Id.* at 625–628.

54. *See, e.g.,* ABA-ALI Model Nonprofit Corp. Act § 87.

55. *See, e.g.,* ABA-ALI Model Nonprofit Corp. Act § 86.

56. Pub. L. No. 91-172, 83 Stat. 487 (1969).

57. I.R.C. § 4945(d).

58. Treas. Reg. § 1.501(c)(3)-1(c)(3).

59. Treas. Reg. § 53.4945-2(a)(2).

60. *Id.*

61. *Id.*

62. Treas. Reg. § 53.4945-2(a)(3).

63. *Id.*

64. Treas. Reg. § 53.4945-2(a)(5).
65. *Id.*
66. *Id.*
67. Treas. Reg. § 53.4945-2(a)(4).
68. Treas. Reg. § 53.4945-2(d)(1)(ii).
69. *Id.*
70. *Id.*
71. Treas. Reg. § 53.4945-2(d)(1)(iv).
72. Treas. Reg. § 53.4945-2(d)(1)(ii).
73. Treas. Reg. § 53.4545-2(d)(1)(iii).
74. *Id.*
75. Treas. Reg. § 53.4545-2(d)(1)(iv).
76. Treas. Reg. § 53.4945-2(d)(1)(i).
77. Treas. Reg. § 53.4945-2(d)(1)(ii).
78. *Id.*
79. Treas. Reg. § 53.4945-2(d)(3).
80. S. Rep. No. 91-552, 91st Cong. 1st Sess. p. 49, 1969-3 C.B. 455.
81. I.R.C. § 4945(d)(2).
82. Treas. Reg. § 53.4945-3(a)(2).
83. *Id.*
84. *Id.*
85. Treas. Reg. § 53.4945-3(b)(3).
86. Treas. Reg. § 53.4945-3(b)(4).
87. *Id.*
88. *Id.*
89. I.R.C. § 4945(g).
90. Treas. Reg. § 53.4945-4(a)(2).
91. *Id.*
92. *Id.*
93. Treas. Reg. § 53.4945-4(a)(3)(i).
94. Treas. Reg. § 53.4945-4(a)(4)(i).
95. *Id.*
96. *Id.*
97. Treas. Reg. § 53.4945-4(a)(4)(ii).
98. *Id.*
99. *Id.*
100. *Id.*
101. Treas. Reg. § 53.4945-4(b).
102. *Id.*
103. *Id.*
104. *Id.*
105. Treas. Reg. § 53.4945-4(d).
106. *Id.*
107. Treas. Reg. § 53.4545-4(c)(2).
108. *Id.*
109. *Id.*

110. *Id.*
111. Treas. Reg. § 53.4545-4(c)(5).
112. Treas. Reg. § 53.4945-4(c)(3).
113. *Id.*
114. Treas. Reg. § 53.4545-4(c)(4).
115. *Id.*
116. *Id.*
117. Treas. Reg. § 53.4945-4(c)(6).
118. I.R.C. § 4945(d)(4).
119. I.R.C. § 4945(h).
120. Treas. Reg. § 53.4945-5(a)(5).
121. *Id.*
122. *Id.*
123. Treas. Reg. § 53.4945-5(a)(6)(i).
124. *Id.*
125. Treas. Reg. § 53.4945-5(a)(6)(ii).
126. Treas. Reg. § 53.4945-5(b)(2).
127. *Id.*
128. *Id.*
129. *Id.*
130. Treas. Reg. § 53.4945-5(b)(3).
131. *Id.*
132. Treas. Reg. § 53.4945-5(e)(3)(ii).
133. Treas. Reg. § 53.4945-5(d)(1).
134. Treas. Reg. § 53.4945-5(d)(2).
135. Treas. Reg. § 53.4945-5(d)(3).
136. Treas. Reg. § 53.4945-5(e).
137. *Id.*
138. I.R.C. § 4945(d)(5).
139. Treas. Reg. § 53.4945-6(b)(2).
140. Treas. Reg. § 53.4945-6(c).
141. I.R.C. § 4945(a)(2).
142. I.R.C. § 4945(c)(2).
143. I.R.C. § 4962.
144. I.R.C. § 4945(b).
145. I.R.C. § 4945(i)(1).
146. Treas. Reg. § 53.4945-1(d)(1).
147. I.R.C. § 4945(b)(1).
148. I.R.C. § 4945(b)(2).
149. I.R.C. § 4945(c)(2).

14

Liability Insurance and Indemnification

STATE LAW

Corporations

Business Corporations

Every business corporation statute in the United States has an indemnification provision for reimbursement of expenses incurred by directors, officers, and other corporate personnel. There are two general forms of statutes; some speak to the power of a corporation to indemnify, and others are drafted in terms of a right of indemnification.

Most indemnification statutes are traceable to the original Model Business Corporation Act,[1] the 1967 Model Act—Delaware version,[2] the 1980 Model Act revision,[3] the 1963 New York statute,[4] and the 1977 California statute.[5]

The statutes distinguish between actions by or in the right of the corporation to procure a judgment in its favor and other proceedings. Most statutes are not limited to derivative actions. Legislatures have been more liberal with indemnification for liability arising out of third-party actions than for derivative suits.

To be eligible for indemnification, the person must meet the prescribed standard of conduct which generally requires good faith and reasonable belief that the conduct was in or at least was not opposed to the best interests of the corporation.[6] In an action by or in the right of the corporation, negligence or misconduct in the performance of the duty owed to the corporation is a bar to indemnification.[7] In a criminal proceeding the person must have reasonable belief that the conduct was lawful.[8] Self-dealing is also a bar to indemnification.[9]

Unless court ordered, indemnification must be authorized; therefore, a finding must be made that the person to be indemnified met the required standard of conduct. That determination is typically made by the board of directors by majority vote of a quorum present, who were not parties to the conduct or action or legal counsel, in a written opinion submitted to the board of directors.[10] Sometimes the decision is made by the shareholders if they were not parties to the conduct or action,[11] or infrequently the determination is made by a court.[12] Success on the merits or otherwise in defense affords the person seeking indemnification the right to indemnification.[13]

If the state corporation act is unclear or general in content, the corporation should provide detailed indemnification procedures and guidelines in its by-laws.

Most modern corporate statutes expressly provide that a corporation may purchase and maintain liability insurance on behalf of corporate personnel even if the corporation would not have the power to indemnify such persons against such liability.

Insurance coverage has two aspects whether in a single policy or several. First, the policy provides for reimbursement of amounts paid by the corporation for indemnification of corporate personnel. Second, the policy provides for payment of liabilities of directors and officers who are not indemnifiable by the corporation. The latter aspect generally covers judgments and settlements in derivative actions for negligence but not claims arising out of self-dealing, bad faith, and knowing violations of federal securities law and other willful misconduct. The policies generally have high deductibles and some have co-insurance provisions.

Nonprofit Corporations

Indemnification and liability insurance provisions in state nonprofit corporation acts are for the most part modeled after the provisions in the business corporation statutes.

The Model Nonprofit Corporation Act of 1957 adopted the pre-1967 version of the Model Business Corporation Act indemnification clause.[14] The Model Nonprofit Corporation Act was drafted in terms of the power of the nonprofit corporation to indemnify. No mention is made of liability insurance.

The persons who may be indemnified are directors, officers, former officers or directors, and other persons who have served at the request of the nonprofit corporation as a director or officer of another corporation whether for profit or not for profit. Further, the defense of the action, suit, or proceeding must be by reason of being a party who was or is an officer or director. No indemnification is permitted if the officer or director is liable for negligence or misconduct in the performance of his duty.

The indemnification power described is not exclusive. Indemnification may be provided by the nonprofit corporation's by-laws, a separate agreement, vote of either the board of directors or members, or some other method or agreement.

Many states have adopted the model act provision, and they are listed in Table 16. The 1967 Model Business Corporation Act—Delaware version has also been incorporated in many state nonprofit corporation acts.[15]

Table 16
Basic Types of Indemnification Statutes

State	Model NFP Corporation Act (1957)	1967 MBCA- Delaware Version	Business Corporation Act	Comment
Alabama	X			§ 10-3-120
Alaska				Other. § 10.20.015 (14)
Arizona		X		§ 10-1005(17)
Arkansas		X	X	No NFP statutory provision
California				CAL. CORP. CODE §§ 5238,9246
Colorado				Similar to Alaska. § 7-22-101(n)
Connecticut		X		§ 33-454(a)
Delaware			X	No separate NFP Act
District of Columbia	X			§ 29-505(14)
Florida		X	X	§ 617.028 refers to 607.014
Georgia				Mere grant of power. § 22-2202
Hawaii	X			§ 416-26(16)
Idaho		X	X	§ 30-3-3 refers to Business Corporation Law
Illinois		X		§ 24a, 163a23.1
Indiana	X			§ 23-7-4(9)
Iowa	X			§ 504A.4(14)
Kansas		X	X	No NFP provision
Kentucky	X			§ 273.171(14)
Louisiana		X		§ 12:227
Maine		X		13-B § 714
Massachusetts				other C.180 § 6
Michigan		X		§ 450.2561
Minnesota				Mere grant of power. § 317.16
Mississippi			X	No NFP provisions. § 79-3-7(o) 1959 MBCA
Missouri		X	X	No NFP provision
Montana	X			§ 35-2-107(14)
Nebraska		X		§ 21-1904(14)
Nevada		X	X	No NFP provision
New Hampshire		X	X	No NFP provision
New Jersey				Precedent for California. § 14:3-5
New Mexico				Other § 53-8-26
New York				N.Y. N-PCL §§ 721-727
North Carolina				Other § 55A-17.1
North Dakota				Other § 10-24-5
Ohio		X		§ 1702.12(E)
Oklahoma		X	X	§ 856 refers to Business Corporation Law

Table 16 (continued)
Basic Types of Indemnification Statutes

State	Model NFP Corporation Act (1957)	1967 MBCA-Delaware Version	Business Corporation Act	Comment
Oregon		X		§ 61.205
Pennsylvania				Mere grant of power § 7502(17)
Rhode Island		X	X	No NFP provision
South Carolina			X	1980 MBCA. No NFP provision
South Dakota	X			§ 47-22-65
Tennessee			X	N.Y. BUS. CORP. Model
Texas				Other Art. 1396-2.22
Utah	X			§ 16-6-22(14)
Vermont	X			§ 2352(14)
Virginia		X		§ 13.1-205.1
Washington	X			§ 24.06.030(15)
West Virginia		X		§ 31-1-9
Wisconsin	X			§ 181.04(13)
Wyoming	X			§ 17-6-103(ix)

The 1967 version is more detailed than the earlier versions and typically contains seven subsections. The first subsection applies to actions, suits, or proceedings (civil, criminal, or investigative) other than those by or in the right of the corporation. Any person who is a party by reason of being a director, officer, employee, or agent may be eligible to be reimbursed for amounts paid in settlements, judgments, fines, and other expenses including attorney's fees incurred in connection with the action, suit, or proceeding. The person must have acted in good faith and in a manner reasonably believed to be in or not opposed to the best interests of the corporation. If a criminal action or proceeding is involved, the person must have reasonably believed that the conduct was lawful.

The second subsection applies to actions, suits, or proceedings by or in the right of the corporation to procure a judgment in its favor. Under this subsection the person is not entitled to indemnification if adjudged liable for negligence or misconduct in the performance of his duty to the corporation. However, the court in which the action or suit was brought may determine that, despite the adjudication of liability and in view of all the circumstances of the case, the person is fairly and reasonably entitled to indemnification for such expenses as the court deems proper.

Subsection (c) or (3) provides for indemnification for actual and reasonable expenses to any person who is successful on the merits of or otherwise in defending the action, suit, or proceeding specified in the first two subsections.

The fourth subsection provides for authorization of indemnification for actions, suits, or proceedings specified in the first two subsections on a finding of the applicable standard of conduct by (1) the board of directors by majority vote of a quorum of directors who were not parties to the action, suit, or proceeding, (2) independent legal counsel, in a written opinion, if a quorum of disinterested directors is not available or at the direction of such a quorum, or (3) by the members of the nonprofit corporation. This subsection does not apply if a court orders indemnification.

The fifth subsection allows prepayment of expenses as authorized by the board of directors on receipt of an undertaking to repay such amount to the corporation unless it is ultimately determined that the person was entitled to be indemnified by the corporation.

Subsection (f) or (6) provides that the indemnification section is not exclusive and that indemnification may be had by by-law, agreement, vote of members, or disinterested directors.

The last subsection authorizes the nonprofit corporation to purchase and maintain liability insurance on behalf of its officers and directors whether the corporation would have the power to indemnify the officer or director or not under this indemnity section.

Some nonprofit corporation acts merely give the corporation the power to indemnify or provide liability insurance.

The California Nonprofit Public Benefit Corporations Law and Nonprofit Religious Corporation Law have virtually identical indemnification provisions.[16] The provisions broadly apply to any person who is or was a director, officer, employee, or other agent in a threatened, completed, or pending civil, criminal, administrative, or investigative action or proceeding.

In a proceeding other than an action by or in the right of the corporation, an action against an interested director for self-dealing under section 5233 or section 9243 of the California Corporation Code, or an action brought by the attorney general or a person granted relator status for breach of duty relating to assets held in charitable trust, a party may be indemnified for expenses, judgments, fines, settlements, and other amounts, provided the person acted in good faith and in a manner reasonably believed to be in the best interests of the corporation. If the action is a criminal proceeding, the person must reasonably have believed that the action was lawful.

In a proceeding by or in the right of the corporation, a section 5233 or 9243 action, or action by the attorney general or a person granted relator status for breach of duty relating to assets held in charitable trust, the person made party may be indemnified against actual and reasonable expenses, including attorney's fees, provided the person acted in good faith and in a manner reasonably believed to be in the best interest of the corporation and with such care as an ordinary prudent man in a like position would under similar circumstances. No indemnification is permitted unless (1) the court finds that a person, who has been adjudged liable to the corporation in the performance of that person's duty, is fairly and reasonably entitled to indemnification; (2) the court approves payment to settle or to otherwise dispose of a threatened or pending claim; or (3) if settled without court approval, with approval of the attorney general.

If a party is successful on the merits regardless of the type of claim, that person is entitled to indemnification for expenses. Otherwise, a determination must be made as to whether or not the person met the applicable standard of conduct. The standard of conduct shall be determined by (1) a majority vote of a quorum of directors who are not parties to the proceeding, (2) approval of the members who are not party to the proceeding, or (3) the court having jurisdiction over the controversy.

Expenses may be advanced by the corporation prior to final disposition upon receipt of an undertaking to repay such amount unless it is ultimately determined that the person is entitled to indemnification.

Indemnification of officers and directors is exclusively determined under the statute. Other agents and employees may be indemnified beyond this limitation. The corporation may purchase and maintain liability insurance to cover liabilities whether or not the corporation could indemnify the person except for self-dealing.

The New York Not For Profit Law contains extensive indemnification provisions.[17] The New York statute is the exclusive means of indemnification for officers and directors. Other corporate personnel are not so limited.

In proceedings by or in the right of the corporation, the party may be indemnified for expenses, including attorney's fees, except in actions arising out of breach of such party's duty to the corporation. No indemnification is allowed for amounts paid in settling or otherwise disposing of threatened or pending actions, and expenses may only be paid with respect to settlements or other dispositions with court approval.

In other proceedings (civil or criminal) the party to the action may be indemnified for amounts paid in settlement, judgments, fines, and reasonable expenses, including attorney's fees, if the party acted in good faith and in a manner reasonably believed to be in the best interest of the corporation and if a criminal action had no reasonable cause to believe the conduct was unlawful.

A party who is successful on the merits in any proceeding is entitled to indemnification. Otherwise indemnification must be authorized by court order or (1) vote of a quorum of directors who are not parties to the proceeding that the person met the prescribed standard of conduct, or (2) if a quorum is not obtainable, by (a) the board of directors on written opinion of independent legal counsel that indemnification is proper under the circumstances, or (b) the members by a finding that the applicable standard of conduct was met.

If the corporation fails to indemnify the person, he may apply to the court having jurisdiction of the proceeding or to the Supreme Court in a separate proceeding to procure indemnification. Such costs may also be indemnified. Unless indemnification is ordered by a court, the corporation must give notice to its members of any such indemnification.

A New York nonprofit corporation may purchase and maintain liability insurance to indemnify the corporation for payments made to indemnify officers and directors whether they could be indemnified by the corporation or not. However, no insurance may pay if the judgment or other final disposition adverse to the insured director or officer established that his acts of active and deliberate dishonesty were material to the cause of action or that he gained in fact a financial profit to which he was not legally entitled.

Private foundations and foundation managers should take note of federal law before authorizing indemnification under a state statute or before purchasing and maintaining liability insurance for foundation managers. The tax aspects of indemnification of foundation managers are discussed later in this chapter.

Trusts

Liability for litigation costs, including attorney's fees, generally lies with the estate or trust and not the trustee or fiduciary acting in good faith and in the exercise of reasonable judgment in his representative capacity.[18] Several states have statutes which provide that litigation expenses are expenses of the estate or trust provided the trustee or fiduciary was acting in good faith in a representative capacity.[19] The same result has been reached in the absence of such a statute.[20]

Litigation costs incurred in disputes among co-trustees have been assessed against the trust where the purpose of the suit was to obtain instructions or to construe the trust.[21]

Costs of suits by beneficiaries against a trustee whose acts seemingly required investigation and of unsuccessful suits charging misconduct by the trustee have been assessed against the trust.[22]

A trustee who is not negligent and acts on advice of legal counsel may be allowed to recover costs even if the advice and subsequent action taken pursuant to the advice turn out to be wrong.[23] Conversely, a trustee who misconceives his duty albeit in good faith is personally liable for litigation costs concerning the misconception.[24]

A trustee is personally liable for litigation expenses, including attorney's fees, occasioned by his own negligence or fault.[25] Moreover, a trustee is not entitled to reimbursement for expenses incurred by the trustee in asserting unfounded claims against the trust.[26]

SECURITIES

Potential liabilities which may arise under sections 11, 12, and 17 (a) of the Securities Act of 1933 and section 10b and rule 10b-5 of the Securities Exchange Act of 1934 may be draconian. Officers, directors, controlling persons, and underwriters may be exposed to substantial financial liability. The right to indemnification for litigation expenses or for liabilities and fines incurred in direct or derivative actions brought on behalf of the corporation or in third-party actions arising out of actions taken in a representative capacity is first determined under state law. However, an indemnification agreement permissible under state law may not be enforceable with respect to violation of the federal securities law.

Indemnification of officers, directors, controlling persons, and underwriters for violation of federal securities law is contrary to public policy.[27] The goal of the civil liability provisions of federal securities law is deterrence and not compensation of victims.[28] Indemnification would thwart that goal by passing on the cost of the liability ultimately to the corporation and its shareholders, many of whom might be victims of the fraud.[29]

The Securities and Exchange Commission refuses to accelerate the effective date of a registration statement if an indemnification agreement is in existence unless the issuer agrees to submit the question of indemnification to a court before making any indemnification payment.[30]

Conversely, contribution among joint wrongdoers is allowed and expressly provided for in section 11 of the Securities Act of 1933 and sections 9 and 18 of the Securities Exchange Act of 1934. Contribution is also allowed when liability is predicated on section 10b and rule 10b-5 of the Securities Exchange Act of 1934 so that one or more of the joint wrongdoers may not escape liability by leaving the prompt or diligent wrongdoer with the burden of payment.[31]

Ironically, the Securities and Exchange Commission does not view liability insurance in the same way as indemnification regardless of who pays the premium. In either event the deterrent power is thwarted. Nonetheless, liability insurance seems to be permissible.

TAX ASPECTS OF INDEMNIFICATION AND INSURANCE
OF DIRECTORS AND OFFICERS
OF PRIVATE FOUNDATIONS

Assuming that a private foundation may indemnify or insure its directors and officers under state law, and assuming that its governing instruments (articles of incorporation, by-laws, and so forth) comply with section 508(e) by prohibiting certain acts and requiring the distribution of income to avoid penalty taxes, the extent of indemnification and its tax effect should be examined.

Indemnification or Insurance for Liabilities Incurred
for Violation of Chapter 42

A foundation manager who knowingly commits an act that is a violation of certain provisions of chapter 42[32] is subject to penalty taxes unless his action is not willful or is due to reasonable cause. Section 4941 addresses self-dealing; section 4944 defines jeopardy investments; and section 4945 deals with incurring taxable expenditures.

The definition of foundation manager in section 4946(b) is broader than for director or officer. A foundation manager is (1) an officer, director, or trustee of a foundation or similar person having such powers or responsibilities as an officer, director, or trustee and (2) any employee of the foundation having authority or responsibility to act (or for failure to act).

A private foundation may indemnify a foundation manager for expenses (other than taxes, penalties, or expenses of correction), including attorney's fees, incurred in defense in a judicial or administrative proceeding involving chapter 42 or state laws relating to mismanagement of a charitable organization's funds if (1) the expenses were reasonably incurred in connection with the proceeding, (2) the foundation manager is successful in such defense, or the proceeding is settled, and (3) the foundation manager did not act willfully and without reasonable cause with respect to the act or failure to act which gave rise to chapter 42 liability.[33] Similarly, a private foundation may pay premiums for insurance to reimburse the foundation for a permissible indemnification payment.[34]

The indemnification for expenses is treated as payment of compensation for personal services.[35] To avoid having the payment for expenses classed as self-dealing, the payment must be treated as compensation for performance of personal services which are reasonable and necessary to carry out the exempt purpose of the private foundation.[36] Reasonable and necessary have the same meaning as in section 162(a). Excessive compensation as determined under Treasury Regulations section 1.162-7 is self-dealing under section 4941(d)(1)(E). Moreover, such excessive compensation may be a taxable expenditure if it is not paid for one of the charitable purposes specified in section 170(c)(2)(B),[37] and it may be subject to a penalty tax.[38]

In Revenue Ruling 82-223[39] the Internal Revenue Service held that indemnification of attorney's fees and court costs of a foundation manager who had not acted willfully or without reasonable cause constituted expenses which were treated as part of the compensation paid to the foundation manager.

Indemnification for the principal liability or penalty taxes is self-dealing and constitutes a taxable expenditure. The payment of any tax imposed on a disqualified person (here the foundation manager) by chapter 42 is treated as a transfer of income or assets of a private foundation for the benefit of a disqualified person.[40] Similarly, the payment of insurance premiums by a private foundation to insure against liability to a foundation manager for chapter 42 taxes is an act of self-dealing unless the amount of the premiums is treated as part of the foundation manager's compensation.[41] Direct indemnification by the foundation for the chapter 42 taxes subjects the payments to the penalty taxes on both the foundation and its manager. The taxes are the personal liability of the foundation manager and are not an expense of the foundation. However, a foundation may pay premiums on liability insurance to reimburse the manager for the penalty tax if the premium is included in the foundation manager's compensation and such compensation is not excessive.

Indemnification or Insurance for Liabilities Arising under State Law

Part of Revenue Ruling 82-223 deals with indemnification by a private foundation for liabilities and expenses arising out of a suit by state officials against a foundation manager for mismanagement of the funds of a charitable organization. The dispute was settled during trial, and the foundation manager agreed to reimburse the foundation for the value of the assets lost. Under an existing indemnification agreement, the foundation would indemnify its manager for attorney's fees, court costs, and the settlement amount paid.

The ruling holds that reimbursement of court costs and attorney's fees are expenses of the foundation within the meaning of Treasury Regulations section 53.4941(d)-2(f)(3). Such reasonable expenses are incurred for charitable purposes within the meaning of section 170(c)(2)(B). The amount of the reimbursement is included in the foundation manager's compensation, and if such compensation is not excessive, the reimbursement is not considered self-dealing under section 4941(d)(1)(E) or a taxable expenditure under section 4945(d)(5).

Reimbursement of the settlement amount constitutes both self-dealing and a taxable expenditure. The settlement amount is not an expense of the foundation but rather a personal expense of the foundation manager that is assumed by the foundation. The amount of the settlement is subject to the penalty taxes imposed under chapter 42.

Situation 2 in Revenue Ruling 82-223 involves payment of premiums by a private foundation for liability insurance for a foundation manager's liabilities, including settlement amounts arising out of a state judicial or administrative proceeding involving mismanagement of a charitable organization's funds. Payment of the premiums is not self-dealing under section 4941(d)(1)(E) if the amount of the premiums paid by the foundation is included in the foundation manager's compensation and such compensation is not excessive. Likewise, the payment of the premium is not a taxable expenditure under section 4945(d)(5) since the expenditure is a reasonable administrative expense incurred for charitable purposes within the meaning of section 170(c)(2)(B).

To be able to attract competent managers, private foundations must offer incentives comparable to those of the private business sector. The best protection for foundation managers is through liability insurance rather than an indemnification agreement.

NOTES

1. 1959 ABA-ALI Model Business Corp. Act, § 4(o).
2. 1967 ABA-ALI Model Business Corp. Act, § 4A.
3. ABA-ALI Model Business Corp. Act, § 5.
4. N.Y. Bus. Corp. Law §§ 721-726. (McKinney).
5. Cal. Corp. Code § 317 (West).
6. *See, e.g.*, 1967 and 1980 Model Business Corp. Act versions.
7. *See, e.g.*, pre-1967 and 1967 Model Business Corp. Act versions.
8. *See, e.g.*, 1967 and 1980 Model Business Corp. Act versions.
9. 1980 ABA-ALI Model Business Corp. Act §§ 5(c), (d)(2)(B).
10. *See*, 1967 and 1980 Model Business Corp. Act versions.
11. *Id.*
12. *See*, Comment, *Court-Ordered Indemnification of Corporate Officers and Directors*, 1979 Ariz. St. L.J. 639.
13. *See*, 1967 and 1980 Model Business Corp. Act versions.
14. 1957 ABA-ALI Model Business Corp. Act, § 4(o).
15. 1967 ABA-ALI Model Business Corp. Act, § 4A.
16. Cal. Corp. Code §§ 5238, 9246 (West).
17. N.Y. N-PCL §§ 721-727 (McKinney).
18. *Sterling v. Gregory*, 149 Cal. 117, 85 P. 305 (1906); *Bank of Am. Nat'l Trust & Savings Ass'n v. Long Beach Fed. Saving and Loan Ass'n*, 141 Cal. App.2d 618, 297 P.2d 443 (1956); *Burns v. Turnbull*, 268 App. Div. 822, 49 N.Y.S.2d 538 (1944); *Hartman v. City of Pendleton*, 96 Ore. 503, 186 P. 572, 190 P. 339 (1920); *Account of First Nat'l Bank & Trust Co. (Landis Trust)*, 382 Pa. 486, 115 A.2d 167 (1955); *First Nat'l Bank v. Stricklin*, 347 P.2d 652 (Okla. 1959).
19. Cal. Code Civ. Pro. § 1026; Cal. Civ. Code § 2273; N.Y. Civ. Prac. Law § 8110.
20. *Hartman v. Pendleton*, 96 Ore. 503, 186 P. 572, 190 P. 339 (1920); *Nelson v. Mercantile Trust Co.*, 335 S.W.2d 167 (Mo. 1960).
21. *Detroit Trust Co. v. Blakely*, 359 Mich. 621, 103 N.W.2d 413 (1960); *Thurlow v. Berry*, 249 Ala. 597, 32 So.2d 526 (1947).
22. *Atwood v. Kleberg*, 163 F.2d 108 (5th Cir. 1947); *Freeman's Trust*, 247 Minn. 50, 75 N.W.2d 906 (1956); *In re Bishop's Will*, 277 App. Div. 108, 98 N.Y.S.2d 69 (1950); *Estate of Coulter*, 379 Pa. 209, 108 A.2d 681 (1954); *Weidlich v. Comley*, 267 F.2d 133 (2d Cir. 1959).
23. *American Nat'l Bank v. Biggs*, 274 S.W.2d 209 (Tex. Civ. App. 1954).
24. *Dickerson v. Camden Trust Co.*, 1 N.J. 459, 64 A.2d 214 (1949).
25. *In re Lewis' Estate*, 349 Pa. 455, 37 A.2d 559 (1944).
26. *Estate of Vokal*, 121 Cal. App.2d 252, 263 P.2d 64 (1953).
27. 17 C.F.R. § 230.460; *Globus v. Law Research Service, Inc.*, 418 F.2d 1276 (2d Cir. 1969), *cert. denied*, 397 U.S. 913 (1970).
28. *Globus v. Law Research Service, Inc.*, 418 F.2d 1276 (2d Cir. 1969), *cert. denied*, 397 U.S. 913 (1970).
29. *Id.*
30. Item 512(i), Regulation S-K, 17 C.F.R. part 229.

31. *Globus v. Law Research Service, Inc.*, 318 F.Supp. 955, *aff'd per curiam*, 442 F.2d 1346 (2d Cir. 1971), *cert. denied sub nom.*, *Law Research Service, Inc. v. Blair & Co.*, 404 U.S. 941.

32. I.R.C. §§ 4941, 4944, 4945.

33. Treas. Reg. § 53.4941(d)-2(f)(3).

34. *Id.*

35. Treas. Reg. § 53.4941(d)-3(c).

36. *Id.*

37. I.R.C. § 4945(d)(5).

38. I.R.C. § 4945(a)(1).

39. 1982-2 C.B. 301.

40. Treas. Reg. § 53.4941(d)-2(f).

41. *Id.*

15

Insolvency, Bankruptcy, and Reorganization

INSOLVENCY

This section deals with equity insolvency as opposed to bankruptcy insolvency. Equity insolvency is defined as the inability to pay debts as they become due in the ordinary course of affairs;[1] whereas, bankruptcy insolvency means that liabilities exceed assets in the book accounting sense.

Equity insolvency generally is temporary and results from an inadequate cash flow. If it is more serious, certain nonbankruptcy remedies under state law are available. Although state law insolvency provisions are sporadic and do not specifically apply to nonprofit organizations, the debtor-creditor relationship is generally unaffected by the nonprofit nature of the debtor.

Composition

If the number of creditors is relatively few and the creditors and debtor can agree, they may compromise. The compromise is called a "composition" or "creditor's agreement." The composition may provide for a pro rata reduction of the creditors' claims against the debtor or may even provide for a fresh infusion of capital to tide the ailing debtor over to better times. The composition is only binding on the parties thereto and not on dissenters. The advantages of a composition are that the debtor continues to operate and avoids legal proceedings and piecemeal grabbing of the debtor's assets.

Assignment for Benefit of Creditors

A statutory alternative to a composition is a general assignment for the benefit of creditors, which is regulated by state law. It is an assignment of all or substantially all the assets of the debtor to an assignee (trustee) for the purpose of marshalling the debtor's assets, selling them, and distributing the proceeds among the creditors. A general assignment for the benefit of creditors cannot work a discharge of the debtor's obligation. To do otherwise would violate the constitutional grant of power in bankruptcy matters to Congress.[2] The debtor remains liable for the unpaid balance. Judgment creditors are prohibited from levying against the assigned property. Proper notice must be given to creditors, and compliance with the state statute is required.

Receiverships—Nonbankruptcy

Appointment of a receiver has traditionally been a function of a court of equity. The power of a court of equity is not derived from statutes,[3] although the procedure for appointing a receiver today is largely statutory.

On application of an insolvent debtor or creditor, a disinterested receiver may be appointed to receive and hold the debtor's assets pending the court's decision as to the ultimate disposition among the creditors. The receiver is charged with marshalling the assets but makes no decision as to disposition. In this respect a receiver is an officer of the court. Ancillary receivers may be appointed in other states to marshall out-of-state assets and hold them until ordered to dispose of the assets by the court.

Under certain circumstances a court may appoint a receiver even if the organization is solvent. A court may appoint a receiver without notice to the organization to seize the assets of the organization if the officers of the organization are misapplying the assets;[4] however, evidence of fraud or improper conduct must be clear and convincing.[5]

Appointment of a receiver is to be done only as a last resort when all other remedies are exhausted.[6] No receiver may be appointed to seize the assets and dissolve a solvent corporation if dissolution would not be in the best interest of the members.[7]

BANKRUPTCY

For purposes of federal bankruptcy law[8] insolvency means that the debtor's aggregate debts exceed the aggregate value of the debtor's property at a fair evaluation.[9]

Generically there are two kinds of bankruptcy cases—voluntary and involuntary. A voluntary bankruptcy case may be filed under one of the chapters of the federal act by an entity that may be a debtor under that chapter.[10] An involuntary bankruptcy case may be filed under chapter 7 or 11 of the federal bankruptcy act.[11] However, an involuntary bankruptcy action may not be brought against a corporation that is not a moneyed business or commercial corporation. This provision is unchanged from the prior law.[12] The exception is primarily for charitable organization that would be tax exempt under I.R.C. § 501(c)(3). Other tax exempt organizations may be adjudicated to be bankrupt. Under the prior law, nonprofit cooperative associations or corporations[13] were adjudicated to be bankrupt and so was an unincorporated masonic lodge.[14] But, a nonstock, nonprofit, cooperative corporation may not be the subject of an involuntary bankruptcy proceeding.[15]

Nonprofit organizations may file for voluntary bankruptcy. The debtor may apply for liquidation under chapter 7 or reorganization under chapter 11. However, the bankruptcy court may not transfer a petition for reorganization by a nonprofit organization to chapter 7 liquidation unless it is made at the request of the nonprofit debtor.[16] In a decision under the prior bankruptcy law, a labor union is entitled to file a voluntary petition in bankruptcy.[17]

REORGANIZATION

Nonprofit corporations as well as business corporations have the statutory power to reorganize themselves by altering their infrastructure, merging or consolidating, or selling their assets. Dissolution is discussed in chapter 16. Special consideration must be given to special application of trust fiduciary principles when dealing with a charitable corporation and to federal tax law when dealing with a tax exempt organization.

Statutory Framework

Changes in Infrastructure

An internal reorganization of a nonprofit organization may be accomplished by amending the articles of incorporation and by-laws of the corporation. The initial step is taken by the board of directors or trustees who adopt a resolution setting forth the proposed amendments. If the corporation has members who are entitled to vote, then the proposed amendments are adopted or rejected at a regular or special meeting of the members. The meetings must conform to the requirements of the statute. (See discussions of regular and special meetings of the board of directors or trustees and members and procedures to amend the articles of incorporation and by-laws in chapter 8.)

Merger or Consolidation

In general, any two nonprofit corporations may merge or consolidate pursuant to the state statute by adopting a plan of merger or consolidation. The plan typically sets forth the following:

1. The names of the nonprofit corporations proposing to merge or consolidate, the name of the surviving corporation, if a merger takes place, or the name of the new corporation, if a consolidation takes place
2. The terms and conditions of the proposed merger or consolidation
3. The changes or required statements to be included in articles of incorporation of either the surviving corporation or the new corporation being organized
4. Other provisions desired or deemed necessary

The plan is approved by the board of directors or trustees at a regular or special meeting which complies with the statutory requirements for meetings. If no members are entitled to vote, the plan is approved or disapproved. If members are entitled to vote on the merger or consolidation, then the proposed plan is submitted to the membership for approval at a regular or special meeting which complies with the statutory requirements.

After approval, the articles of merger or consolidation are executed by the corporate officers and filed with the state authority, usually the secretary of state. The merger or consolidation generally is effective upon issuance of a certificate of merger or consolidation by the state authority.

The effect of the merger or consolidation is that the separate existence of the corporations, except for the surviving corporation or new corporation, ceases. The surviving or new corporation succeeds to all the rights, privileges, immunities, and franchises of each of the merging or consolidating corporations as well as all property and debts due on whatever account, all other choses in action, and all other interests belonging to each of the merged or consolidated corporations. All title to real estate, or any interest therein, vested in any of the corporations shall not revert or be in any way impaired because of the merger or consolidation.

If one of the corporations involved is a foreign corporation, additional requirements may be imposed such as providing authenticated articles of merger or consolidation from the foreign state authority.

Letters of intent and the proposed plan should retain the right to withdraw from the plan of merger or consolidation at any time prior to filing the certificate of merger or consolidation with the state authority. This is particularly important when dealing with charitable corporations to avoid breach of fiduciary duty or adverse federal and state tax consequences.

Sale of Assets

A sale, lease, exchange, mortgage pledge, or other disposition of all, or substantially all, the property and assets of a nonprofit corporation may be made on such terms and conditions and for such consideration as may be authorized by the board of directors or trustees and members, if they are entitled to vote. Meetings must conform to statutory requirements. This method of reorganization may be used to accomplish certain objectives such as nonassumption of liabilities of the selling corporation.

Charitable Trust Restrictions

Transfers of unrestricted assets in a reorganization generally fall within a trustee's discretion and generally do not require court approval.

Charitable gifts which are dedicated to a particular or restricted purpose require careful attention in a contemplated reorganization. Transfer of the assets to another corporation by sale, merger, or consolidation is permissible provided that the acquiring corporation continues the charitable purpose.

Transfers of restricted assets or transfer of assets to a corporation having a substantially different charitable purpose may require court approval. Ordinarily, a court will invalidate or enjoin a transfer of assets which violates the conditions set forth by the donor in the governing documents. To avoid difficulties, the nonprofit corporation should apply to the appropriate court for guidance if the reorganization makes it impossible to use restricted assets in accordance with the donor's wishes.

The doctrine of *cy pres* may be used when the donor's charitable purpose has become impossible or impracticable to fulfill or has become illegal.[18] If the donor had manifested a general charitable intent as well as the specific purpose, the court may approve transfer of the assets for use in a charitable purpose within the donor's general intent. In an application for *cy pres* the state attorney general and donor or his successor must be joined and approve. *Cy pres* is not available when the original purpose can possibly be accomplished, nor can *cy pres* prevent a gift-over to another charity or third party if the original purpose fails.

Tax Restrictions

Preservation of tax exempt status is paramount in reorganizations of tax exempt organizations. Tax exempt status may be lost because of a violation of the private inurement requirement, or preferential tax status may be lost by transforming a public charity into a private foundation. Tax liability may be incurred if one of the tax exempt organizations generates unrelated business income. No reorganization should be undertaken without obtaining a private letter ruling from the Internal Revenue Service in advance.

For tax exempt organizations subject to the private inurement disqualification, none of the assets may ever inure to the benefit of a shareholder or individual. Extreme care must be taken in a reorganization to prevent any private inurement. All parties to the reorganization must be subject to the private inurement restriction, and no shareholder or individual should be enriched by the reorganization.

Entities that generate unrelated business income should be avoided or isolated in reorganizations. Otherwise, the unrelated business income of one of the parties becomes the tax liability of the reorganized entity.

Merger or consolidation of a public charity and a private foundation must be structured to avoid designation of the merged or consolidated corporation as a private foundation subject to the various restrictions and limitations of the Internal Revenue Code.

Transfer of Assets from Private Foundation to Public Charity

A private foundation may transfer all of its assets to a public charity or charities as defined in section 170(b)(1)(A) (except for clauses (vii) and (viii)) provided the transferee public charities have been in continuous operation for a period of at least sixty consecutive months preceding the transfer.[19] The private foundation must not be guilty of willful repeated acts (or failures to act) or a willful and flagrant act (or failure to act) giving rise to liability for taxes imposed under chapter 42 of the code.[20]

To terminate private foundation status, notice must be provided to the Treasury Department (district director), and the tax imposed by section 507(c) must be paid or abated.[21] In the case of a transfer to a public charity, the tax imposed by section 507(c) does not apply.[22]

To qualify under section 507(b)(1) the private foundation must transfer all its rights, title, and interest in or to all its net assets to one or more public charities.[23] To effect such a transfer, the transferor private foundation may not impose any material restriction or condition that restricts the transferee public charities from freely and effectively employing the transferred assets or the income derived therefrom in furtherance of their charitable purposes.[24] The materiality of a restriction or condition is determined from all the facts and circumstances of the transfer including this information:

1. Whether the public charity (including a participating trustee, custodian, or agent in the case of a community trust) is the owner in fee of the assets it receives from the private foundation

2. Whether such assets are to be held and administered by the public charity in a manner consistent with one or more of its exempt purposes

3. Whether the governing body of the public charity has the ultimate authority and control over such assets and the income derived therefrom

4. Whether and to what extent the governing body of the public charity is organized and operated to be independent from the transferor[25]

The presence of any one of the following factors is considered as preventing the transferee public charity from freely and effectively employing the transferred assets or the income derived therefrom in furtherance of its exempt purpose:

(1) Distributions. (a) With respect to distributions made after April 19, 1977, the transferor private foundation, a disqualified person with respect thereto, or any person or committee designated by, or pursuant to the terms of an agreement with such a person (hereinafter referred to as "donor"), reserves the right, directly or indirectly, to name (other than by designation in the instrument of transfer of particular section 509(a)(1), (2), or (3) organizations) the person to which the transferee public charity must distribute, or to direct the timing of such distributions (other than by direction in the instrument of transfer that some or all of the principal, as opposed to specific assets, not be distributed for a specified period) as, for example, by a power of appointment. The Internal Revenue Service will examine carefully whether the seeking of advice by the transferee from, or the giving of advice by, any donor after the assets have been transferred to the transferee constitutes an indirect reservation of a right to direct such distributions. In any such case, the reservation of such a right will be considered to exist where the only criterion considered by the public charity in making a distribution of income or principal from a donor's fund is advice offered by the donor. Whether there is a reservation of such a right will be determined from all of the facts and circumstances.

(b) The presence of some or all of the following factors will indicate that the reservation of such a right does not exist:

(i) There has been an independent investigation by the staff of the public charity evaluating whether the donor's advice is consistent with specific charitable needs most deserving of support by the public charity (as determined by the public charity);

(ii) The public charity has promulgated guidelines enumerating specific charitable needs consistent with the charitable purposes of the public charity and the donor's advice is consistent with such guidelines;

(iii) The public charity has instituted an educational program publicizing to donors and other persons the guidelines enumerating specific charitable needs consistent with the charitable purposes of the public charity;

(iv) The public charity distributes funds in excess of amounts distributed from the donor's fund to the same or similar types of organizations or charitable needs as those recommended by the donor; and

(v) The public charity's solicitations (written or oral) for funds specifically state that such public charity will not be bound by advice offered by the donor.

(c) The presence of some or all of the following factors will indicate the reservation of such a right does exist:

(i) The solicitations (written or oral) of funds by the public charity state or imply, or a pattern of conduct on the part of the public charity creates an expectation, that the donor's advice will be followed;

(ii) The advice of a donor (whether or not restricted to a distribution of income or principal from the donor's trust or fund) is limited to distributions of amounts from the donor's fund, and the factors described in (b)(i) or (ii) or this section are not present;

(iii) Only the advice of the donor as to distributions of such donor's fund is solicited by the public charity and no procedure is provided for considering advice from persons other than the donor with respect to such fund; and

(iv) For the taxable year and all prior taxable years the public charity follows the advice of all donors with respect to their funds substantially all of the time.

(2) Other action or withholding of action. The terms of the transfer agreement, or any expressed or implied understanding, require the public charity to take or withhold action

with respect to the transferred assets which is not designed to further one or more of the exempt purposes of the public charity, and such action or withholding of action would, if performed by the transferor private foundation with respect to such assets, have subjected the transferor to tax under chapter 42 (other than with respect to the minimum investment return requirement of section 4942(e)).

(3) Assumption of leases, contractual obligations, and liabilities. The public charity assumes leases, contractual obligations, or liabilities of the transferor private foundation, or takes the assets thereof subject to such liabilities (including obligations under commitments or pledges to donees of the transferor private foundation), for purposes inconsistent with the purposes or best interests of the public charity, other than the payment of the transferor's chapter 42 taxes incurred prior to the transfer to the public charity to the extent of the value of the assets transferred.

(4) Retention of investment assets. The transferee public charity is required by any restriction or agreement (other than a restriction or agreement imposed or required by law or regulatory authority), express or implied, to retain any securities or other investment assets transferred to it by the private foundation. In a case where such transferred assets consistently produce a low annual return of income, the Internal Revenue Service will examine carefully whether the transferee is required by such restriction to retain such assets.

(5) Right of first refusal. An agreement is entered into in connection with the transfer of securities or other property which grants directly or indirectly to the transferor private foundation or any disqualified person with respect thereto a right of first refusal with respect to the transferred securities or other property when and if disposed of by the public charity, unless such securities or other property was acquired by the transferor private foundation subject to such right of first refusal prior to October 9, 1969.

(6) Relationships. An agreement is entered into between the transferor private foundation and the transferee public charity which establishes irrevocable relationships with respect to the maintenance or management of assets transferred to the public charity, such as continuing relationships with banks, brokerage firms, investment counselors, or other advisers with regard to the investments or other property transferred to the public charity (other than a relationship with a trustee, custodian, or agent for a community trust acting as such). The transfer of property to a public charity subject to contractual obligations which were established prior to November 11, 1976, between the transferor private foundation and persons other than disqualified persons with respect to such foundation will not be treated as prohibited under the preceding sentence, but only if such contractual obligations were not entered into pursuant to a plan to terminate the private foundation status of the transferor under section 507(b)(1)(A) and if the continuation of such contractual obligations is in the best interests of the public charity.

(7) Other conditions. Any other condition is imposed on action by the public charity which prevents it from exercising ultimate control over the assets received from the transferor private foundation for purposes consistent with its exempt purposes.[26]

Restructuring a Private Foundation as a Public Charity

Section 507(b)(1)(B) provides for two ways to transform a private foundation into a public charity. The twelve-month rule described in section 507(b)(1)(B)(i) was intended to be a transition rule for the first taxable year beginning after December 31, 1969, and no longer has viability.

Section 507(b)(1)(B)(ii) provides that if the private foundation gives notice to the secretary of the treasury (district director) of its intent to terminate private foundation status and become a public charity as defined in section 509(a)(1), (2), or (3) and complies with the sixty-month requirement, it will be reclassified as a public charity. The private foundation must meet the requirements of section 509(a)(1), (2), or (3) for sixty continuous calendar months beginning with the first day of the taxable year following notice to the treasury. Although section 507(b)(1)(B) prohibits a change to a public charity during a taxable year, a change of accounting period may accelerate the process by terminating the current taxable year and beginning a new taxable year immediately after giving notice.[27] No form of notice is prescribed, so a letter will suffice if it includes the requisite information prescribed in Treasury Regulations section 1.507-2.

Immediately after the expiration of the sixty-month period, the organization must establish that it complied with section 509(a)(1), (2), or (3) during the entire period.[28] Failure to meet the sixty-month requirement means that the organization will be treated as a private foundation for taxable years that it did not qualify as a public charity. For those taxable years in which the organization did meet the section 509(a)(1), (2), or (3) requirement, it shall be treated as a public charity, and grants or contributions made to it shall be treated as if they were made to a section 509(a)(1), (2), or (3) organization.[29] Moreover, for the taxable years in which the organization qualified as a public charity, sections 507 through 509 and chapter 42 do not apply.[30] If the private foundation does establish that it met the sixty-month requirement, it is treated as if it had been a public charity for the entire period.[31]

To qualify as a section 509(a)(1) organization, the organization must be one of those listed in sections 170(b)(1)(A)(i)-(vi) for the entire 60-month period. Any support received prior to commencement of the sixty-month period is not taken into consideration in determining public support.[32] Either the 33.3 percent or the 10 percent support test set forth in Treasury Regulations section 1.170A-9(e)(2) must be satisfied during the sixty-month period not during the usual four-year period specified in Treasury Regulations section 1.170A-9(e). All other organizational and operational tests for a public charity under sections 170(b)(1)(A)(i)-(vi) must be met for the entire sixty-month period.

A private foundation seeking to qualify as a section 509(a)(2) organization must meet the tests for the entire sixty-month period not for any shorter period in the Treasury Regulations promulgated pursuant to section 509(a)(2).[33]

A section 509(a)(3) organization does not have to meet any public support test. A private foundation must meet the section 509(a)(3) requirements during the entire sixty-month period. Compliance should be carefully observed because of the lack of a public support test.

A private foundation seeking to terminate its status under section 507(b)(1)(B) may apply for an advance ruling that it can be expected to satisfy the sixty-month requirement.[34] Factors to be considered in issuing the advance ruling are (1) organizational structure, (2) proposed programs or activities, (3) intended method of operation, and (4) projected sources of support.[35] The organization may not rely on an advance ruling, and the tax which would be due remains collectible if the organization fails the sixty-month requirement.[36] Grantors and contributors may rely on the advance ruling until notice is given of revocation or unless the grantor or contributor is responsible for the organization's failure to meet the sixty-month requirement.[37]

A conversion from private foundation to public charity is not a termination of private foundation status under section 507(a); therefore, the tax imposed by section 507(c) is not applicable and need not be abated.

Merger and Other Reorganizations of Private Foundations

A section 507(b)(2) transfer is any liquidation, merger, redemption, recapitalization, or other adjustment, organization, or reorganization involving a transfer of assets from one private foundation to another private foundation.[38] The transferee organization is not treated as a newly created organization but as possessing certain attributes and characteristics of the transferor organization.[39]

The transferee organization succeeds to the aggregate tax benefit of the transferor prorated by multiplying the aggregate tax benefit by the ratio of the fair market value of the transferred assets (less encumbrances) to the fair market value of the transferred assets (less encumbrances) immediately before the transfer.[40] Fair market value is determined as of the date of transfer.[41] The aggregate tax benefit is limited to the fair market value of the transferred assets unless the transferor and transferee organizations are controlled, directly or indirectly, by the same person or persons.[42] The aggregate tax benefit resulting from section 501(c)(3) status of a private foundation is the sum of the following:

1. The aggregate increases in tax under chapters 1, 11, and 12 of the Internal Revenue Code which would have been imposed with respect to all substantial contributors to the foundation if deductions for all contributions made by the substantial contributors had been disallowed

2. The aggregate increases in tax under chapter 1 of the Internal Revenue Code if: (a) the organization had not been tax exempt under section 501(a), and (b) in the case of a trust, deductions under section 642(c) had been limited to 20 percent of the taxable income of the trust (computed without the benefit of section 642(c) but with the benefit of section 170(b)(1)(A))

3. Interest on the increases in tax determined under subparagraphs 1 and 2 above from the first date on which each increase would have been due and payable to the termination date of the private foundation[43]

A person who is a substantial contributor of the transferor foundation is treated as a substantial contributor of the transferee foundation(s) whether or not that person meets the $5,000 two percent test with respect to the transferee foundation(s) at any time.[44] A substantial contributor means any person who contributes or bequeaths an aggregate amount of more than $5,000 to a private foundation provided that amount is more than 2 percent of the total contributions and bequests received by the foundation before the end of the foundation's year in which the contribution or bequest is received.[45]

In a case where transferee liability applies, the transferee foundation takes the assets subject to any liability incurred by the transferor foundation for taxes and penalties imposed under chapter 42 prior to the transfer.[46] A transfer of assets under section 507(b)(2) is not a section 507(a) termination, and the tax imposed by section 507(c) is not applicable.

A private foundation is required to meet the distribution requirements of section 4942 for the taxable year in which the section 507(b)(2) transfer takes place. The transfer itself satisfies part of the requirement to the extent that the amount transferred meets the requirements of section 4942(g).[47]

Hospital Reorganizations

A relatively large number of hospitals have reorganized into multiorganizational groups and sought private letter rulings concerning the tax consequences of the reorganization. The hospitals and new organizations generally are tax exempt under section 501(c)(3), are section 170(b)(1)(A)(i)-(iv) organizations, and are not private foundations under section 509, although some of the organizations involved are taxable entities.

The reorganized group often shares assets and services and is controlled by the same persons. The Internal Revenue Service has ruled that these reorganizations do not change the organization's status under sections 170, 501(c), or 509. Moreover, the reorganizations do not cause the tax exempt organizations to realize any unrelated business income on the transfers.[48]

NOTES

1. ABA-ALI Model Nonprofit Corp. Act, § 2(h).
2. U.S. Const., Art. I, Sec. 8, cl. 4.
3. *Popper v. Supreme Council,* 61 A.D. 405, 407, 70 N.Y.S. 637 (1901).
4. *Southern Maryland Agric. Ass'n v. Magruder,* 81 A.2d 592 (Md. 1951).
5. *Rabinowitz v. Steinberg,* 112 N.Y.S.2d 758 (1952).
6. *See, e.g., Northern Pac. Ry. v. Boyd,* 228 U.S. 482 (1913); *Case v. Los Angeles L. Co.,* 308 U.S. 106 (1939).
7. *In re Sentinel Pub. Co.,* 113 Ohio St. 608, 149 N.E. 882 (1925); *Martin Oil Co. v. Clokey,* 277 So.2d 343 (Ala. 1973).
8. 11 U.S.C. §§ 1 *et. seq.* (1982).
9. 11 U.S.C. § 101(26) (1982).
10. 11 U.S.C. § 301 (1982).
11. 11 U.S.C. § 303(a) (1982).

12. Section 4(b) of the prior bankruptcy law.

13. *Schuster v. Ohio Farmers' Co-op Milk Ass'n*, 61 F.2d 337 (6th Cir. 1932); *In re Wisconsin Co-operative Milk Pool, First Wisconsin National Bank of Milwaukee v. Wisconsin Co-operative Milk Pool*, 119 F.2d 999 (7th Cir. 1941).

14. *In re William McKinley Lodge No. 840*, F. & A.M., 4 F.Supp. 280 (D.C.N.Y. 1933).

15. *In re Dairy Marketing Ass'n of Ft. Wayne, Inc.*, 8 F.2d 626 (D.C. Ind. 1925).

16. 11 U.S.C. § 112(c) (1982).

17. *Highway & City Freight Drivers, Dockmen and Helpers, Local Union No. 600 v. Gordon Transports, Inc.*, 576 F.2d 1285 (8th Cir. 1978).

18. A. Scott, *Law of Trusts*, § 399 (3d ed. 1967).

19. I.R.C. § 507(b)(1)(A).

20. I.R.C. § 507(b).

21. I.R.C. § 507(a).

22. Treas. Reg. § 1.507-2(a)(1).

23. Treas. Reg. § 1.507-2(a)(7).

24. Treas. Reg. § 1.507-2(a)(8).

25. *Id.*

26. Treas. Reg. § 1.507-2(a)(8)(iv).

27. Rev. Rul. 77-113, 1977-1 C.B. 152.

28. I.R.C. § 507(b)(1)(B)(iii).

29. Treas. Reg. § 1.507-2(f)(2).

30. *Id.*

31. Treas. Reg. § 1.507-2(f)(1).

32. Treas. Reg. § 1.507-2(d)(1).

33. Treas. Reg. § 1.507-2(d)(1)(iii).

34. Treas. Reg. § 1.507-2(e).

35. *Id.*

36. Treas. Reg. § 1.507-2(e)(4).

37. Treas. Reg. § 1.507-2(e)(3).

38. Treas. Reg. § 1.507-3(a).

39. *Id.*

40. Treas. Reg. § 1.507-3(a)(2).

41. *Id.*

42. *Id.*

43. I.R.C. § 507(d)(1).

44. Treas. Reg. § 1.507-3(a)(3).

45. I.R.C. § 507(d)(2).

46. Treas. Reg. § 1.507-3(a)(4).

47. Treas. Reg. § 1.507-3(a)(5).

48. Private Ltr. Ruls. 8405088, 8405089, and 8405090; 8403035; 8403042; 8403109; 8402089 and 8402097; 8352091, 8352092, and 8352093; 8350110, 8350111, 8350117, and 8350118; 8347068, 8347069, 8347070, 8347071, and 8347072; 8347073, 8347074, 8347075, and 8347076.

16

Dissolution

Dissolution of nonprofit organizations is formally governed by state law. However, many nonprofit organizations just seem to disappear without going through the formal process of dissolution. Although this informal disbanding of the members of the organization may be expedient, there may be unexpected or adverse consequences later concerning such things as creditors' rights, ownership or title to property, liability for certain taxes, and breach of fiduciary duty. The informed person will comply with the formalities of dissolution to avoid future difficulties.

VOLUNTARY DISSOLUTION

Unincorporated Associations

Unincorporated associations may be voluntarily dissolved by (1) vote of the members, (2) expiration of the period of duration of life expressed in the articles of association, or (3) lapse of membership by death or withdrawal.

Nonprofit Corporations

A nonprofit corporation may be voluntarily dissolved by expiration of the period of duration as provided in the articles of incorporation or action taken by the board of directors or trustees and members pursuant to the articles of incorporation or the by-laws.

At common law, unanimous consent of the members was necessary to voluntarily dissolve a corporation. State statutes have reduced the required vote which ranges from a simple majority to two-thirds of the members. See Table 17 for

Table 17
Dissolution—Nonprofit Corporation Statutes

Jurisdiction	Voluntary Dissolution		Involuntary Dissolution		
	Required vote of		Certification by	Court of Equity by	
	Board of Directors	Eligible Membership	Secretary of State	Member	Creditor
Alabama	M	2/3		X	X
Alaska	M	2/3	*	X	X
Arizona	M	M	*	X	X
Arkansas[1]					
California	M	M		X	
Colorado	M	2/3	X	X	X
Connecticut	M	2/3	X	X	X
Delaware[1]					
District of Columbia	M	2/3		X	X
Florida[1]					
Georgia	M	2/3	X	X	X
Hawaii[1]					
Idaho[1]					
Illinois	M	2/3	X	X	X
Indiana	M	M			
Iowa	M	2/3	X	X	X
Kansas[1]					
Kentucky	M	2/3	X	X	X
Louisiana		2/3	X		
Maine	M	M		X	X
Maryland[1]					
Massachusetts	M				
Michigan	M	M		X	
Minnesota	M	M			
Mississippi		2/3			
Missouri	M	2/3	X	X	X
Montana	M	2/3		X	X
Nebraska	M	2/3	X	X	X
Nevada[1]					
New Hampshire[1]					
New Jersey	M	2/3		X	
New Mexico	M	2/3	*	X	X
New York	M	2/3			
North Carolina	M	2/3		X	X
North Dakota	M	2/3	X	X	X
Ohio	M	M		X	
Oklahoma	M				
Oregon	M	2/3		X	X
Pennsylvania	M	M		X	X
Rhode Island	M	M	X	X	X
South Carolina		2/3			
South Dakota	M	2/3	X	X	X
Tennessee	M	2/3		X	
Texas	M	2/3	X	X	X
Utah	2/3	2/3		X	X

Table 17 (continued)
Dissolution—Nonprofit Corporation Statutes

Jurisdiction	Voluntary Dissolution		Involuntary Dissolution		
	Required vote of		Certification by	Court of	Equity by
	Board of Directors	Eligible Membership	Secretary of State	Member	Creditor
Vermont	M	2/3	X	X	X
Virginia	M	2/3	*	X	X
Washington	M	2/3	X		
West Virginia	M	M		X	X
Wisconsin	M	2/3	X	X	X
Wyoming	M	2/3	X		

　　1 - No nonprofit corporation act provision. Refer to Business
　　　　Corporation act.
　　M - Majority
　　* - Corporation Commission

dissolution statute requirements for each state. The articles of incorporation may require a higher percentage of the members voting to adopt a resolution of dissolution than does the statute.

Procedurally, the board of directors or trustees adopts by majority vote a resolution recommending that the corporation be dissolved. If there are no members or no members entitled to vote, the dissolution is authorized by the vote of the board of directors or trustees. If members are entitled to vote, the board of directors or trustees gives notice of a meeting of the members to decide whether the corporation should be dissolved. The resolution to dissolve is effective on passage by the requisite vote of the members.

After the resolution to dissolve is authorized, a plan of distribution of the assets must be adopted. The plan is adopted by majority vote of the board of directors or trustees if there are no members or no members entitled to vote. Otherwise the board resolution is submitted to the membership at a regular or special meeting of the members for their approval by the requisite vote. The meeting must conform to the statutory requirements for calling and holding a meeting of the members.

On adoption of the resolution to dissolve, the corporation must cease to conduct its affairs except for winding up its affairs, marshalling the assets, and distributing them.

Following the discharge of all debts, liabilities, and obligations of the corporation and the distribution of the remaining property and assets, articles of dissolution are executed by the corporate officers and filed with the appropriate state authority. The information required for inclusion in the articles of dissolution is substantially the same as set out below in the Model Nonprofit Corporation Act (1957).

ARTICLES OF DISSOLUTION
OF

_____

Pursuant to the provisions of Section _____ of the
_____ Non-Profit Corporation Act, the undersigned
corporation adopts the following Articles of Dissolution for the purpose of
dissolving the corporation:

FIRST: The name of the corporation is _____

_____

SECOND: A resolution to dissolve the corporation was adopted in the following
manner:

(Note 1)

THIRD: All debts, obligations and liabilities of the corporation have been paid
and discharged, or adequate provision has been made therefor.

FOURTH: All remaining property and assets of the corporation have been
transferred, conveyed or distributed in accordance with the provisions of the
_____ Non-Profit Corporation Act.

FIFTH: There are no suits pending against the corporation in any court in respect
of which adequate provision has not been made for the satisfaction of any
judgment, order or decree which may be entered against it.

Dated _____ 19_____

_____ (Note 2)

By _____

Its _____ President

(Note 3)

and _____

Its _____ Secretary

(Add Verification)

Notes:

1. Insert whichever of the following statements is applicable:
   (a) "The resolution to dissolve the corporation was adopted at a meeting of
       members held on _____ at which a quorum
       was present, and the resolution received at least two-thirds of the votes
       which members present or represented by proxy at such meeting were
       entitled to cast."
   (b) "The resolution to dissolve the corporation was adopted by a consent in
       writing signed by all members entitled to vote in respect thereof."
   (c) "The resolution to dissolve the corporation was adopted at a meeting of
       the Board of Directors held on _____ and
       received the vote of a majority of the Directors in office, there being no
       members having voting rights in respect thereof."
2. Exact corporate name of corporation making the statement.
3. Signatures and titles of officers signing for the corporation.

At any time prior to the issuance of the certificate of dissolution by the appropriate state authority, the resolution to dissolve may be revoked by the same procedure by which the resolution authorizing dissolution was adopted. On receipt of the articles of dissolution the appropriate state authority endorses and files the articles and issues a certificate of dissolution to the dissolved corporation. The corporation ceases to exist on issuance of the certificate of dissolution except for suits or other proceedings and appropriate corporate action by directors, officers, and members to wind up the corporation's affairs and distribute the assets.

INVOLUNTARY DISSOLUTION

Unincorporated Associations

Unincorporated associations may be involuntarily dissolved by court order on application of a creditor or member or by action of state authorities for improper action or conduct by the organization.

Nonprofit Corporations

Actions by State

A nonprofit corporation may be involuntarily dissolved by a court decree in an action brought by the state attorney general or other designated authority if

1. The corporation fails to file its annual report within the statutory time limits,
2. The articles of incorporation were procured by fraud,
3. The corporation continuously exceeds or abuses its authority under state law,
4. The corporation failed for ninety days to appoint and maintain a registered agent in the state,
5. The corporation fails to notify the secretary of state or other designated state authority of a change in its registered agent, or
6. The corporation fails to pay its state tax liability.

To institute an involuntary dissolution proceeding, the secretary of state or other designated authority annually certifies to the attorney general the names of all corporations which have failed to file their annual reports or otherwise have given cause for dissolution under the state statute. Notice of such action is concurrently mailed to the corporation.

The attorney general files suit in a court of competent jurisdiction unless the corporation cures the defect before suit is filed. After suit is filed, the action is abated if the corporation cures the defect and pays the costs of the action.

The corporation is dissolved on issuance of the court decree dissolving the corporation, and the corporation ceases to exist.

Courts of Equity

In the absence of statutory authority for involuntary dissolution, it is generally conceded that a court of equity, without statutory authority, may dissolve a corporation by appointment of a receiver to protect creditors and members.[1]

Many state nonprofit corporation acts contain statutory authorization for courts of equity to entertain suits brought by creditors or members. A suit by a member may be brought when (1) the directors are deadlocked in the management of the corporate affairs and the corporation is suffering irreparable injury or is threatened by reason of the deadlock, and the members are unable or powerless to break the deadlock; (2) the acts of the directors or controlling persons are illegal, oppressive, or fraudulent; (3) the corporate assets are being misapplied or wasted; or (4) the corporate purpose cannot be carried out.

A creditor generally may seek dissolution when (1) the claim of the creditor is reduced to judgment and returned unsatisfied because the corporation is insolvent, or (2) an insolvent corporation admits in writing that the claim of the creditor is due and owing.

Some states allow a corporation to have its dissolution conducted under the supervision of a court. The state attorney general or other designated authority may apply for court supervision if it is determined that liquidation precede dissolution.

In court proceedings to liquidate the assets and affairs of a corporation, the court may issue injunctions and appoint a receiver *pendente lite* with such powers as the court directs to preserve the corporate assets and carry on the affairs of the corporation until the full hearing is held.

Creditors must file their claims in accordance with the state statute or be barred from participating in the assets. After the full hearing the court may appoint a liquidating receiver to collect the assets and to sell, convey, or dispose of the assets, subject to court supervision, at public or private sale.

After all the debts, obligations, and liabilities of the corporation have been paid and discharged and the remaining property and assets, if any, are distributed, the court will enter a decree of dissolution at which time the corporation ceases to exist.

DISTRIBUTION OF ASSETS

The distribution of assets of a nonprofit organization, particularly a charitable nonprofit corporation, must conform to strict rules of nonprofit corporations and charitable trusts. In general, the distribution of assets is as follows:

1. Court costs and related expenses, if court supervised
2. Liabilities and obligations of the corporation or association
3. Assets held under condition or limitation that they be returned, transferred, or conveyed on dissolution
4. Assets held by a charitable nonprofit organization limiting their use to a charitable purpose but not required to be returned, transferred, or conveyed because of dissolution must be transferred or conveyed to another charitable organization having a similar purpose
5. Other assets, if any, are distributed in accordance with the articles of incorporation or association or by-laws, to the extent that the articles of incorporation or association or by-laws govern
6. The remaining assets, if any, are distributed in accordance with the plan of distribution or court order, if court supervised

TERMINATION OF A PRIVATE FOUNDATION

Dissolution of a private foundation carries with it certain tax consequences, if the dissolution is in connection with a reorganization to which section 507(b) applies (transfer of the assets to a public charity, reconstituting the private foundation as a public charity, or transfer of assets to another private foundation). See the discussion of section 507(b) transfers in chapter 15. Section 507(a) applies to other transfers of assets in dissolution.

Section 507(a)(1) provides that private foundation status is voluntarily terminated when the foundation gives the requisite notice to the appropriate district director to terminate and the foundation pays the tax imposed by section 507(c) or that part of the tax which is not abated under section 507(g).[2]

The mere transfer of all the assets of a private foundation does not necessarily cause a termination of its private foundation status. Termination of status is an election. Thus, if a private foundation transfers all its assets but does not elect to terminate its private foundation status, it continues as a private foundation, and any subsequent gift or bequest made to it is deemed to be made to a private foundation unless the termination resulted from willful repeated acts (or failures to act) or a willful and flagrant act (or failure to act) giving rise to tax liability under chapter 42.[3]

Termination of private foundation status under section 507(a)(1) does not relieve a private foundation or disqualified person of tax liability imposed under chapter 42 with respect to acts or failures to act prior to termination or for any additional taxes imposed for failure to correct such acts or failures to act.[4]

Involuntary termination is provided in section 507(a)(2) for willful repeated acts (or failure to act) or a willful and flagrant act (or failure to act) giving rise to tax liability under chapter 42. Violations of chapter 42 are discussed in other chapters dealing with private foundations.

For purposes of section 507(a)(2), willful repeated acts (or failures to act) means that at least two acts or failures to act are voluntary, conscious, and intentional.[5] A willful and flagrant act (or failure to act) is one which is voluntarily, consciously, and knowingly committed in violation of chapter 42 (other than section 4940 or 4948(a)) and which appears to a reasonable man to be a gross violation of such provision.[6] Failure to correct the act (or failure to act) which gives rise to tax liability under chapter 42 may be a willful and flagrant act.[7]

Acts (or failures to act) of a foundation manager may be attributed to the private foundation even if the chapter 42 tax is only imposed on the foundation manager and not the foundation.[8]

The section 507(c) tax imposed on either a voluntary or involuntary termination of private foundation status under section 507(a) is the lesser of (1) the aggregate tax benefit resulting from the section 501(c)(3) status of the private foundation or (2) the value of the net assets of the foundation.

The burden of establishing the aggregate tax benefit resulting from section 501(c)(3) status is on the private foundation.[9] The aggregate tax benefit is the sum of the following:

1. The aggregate increases in tax under chapters 1, 11, and 12 (or predecessor provisions) which would have been imposed with respect to all substantial contributors to the private foundation if the deductions for all contributions made by substantial contributors to the foundation after February 28, 1913, had been disallowed

2. The aggregate increases in tax under chapter 1 (or its predecessor provisions) which would have been imposed with respect to the income of the private foundation for taxable years beginning after December 31, 1912, if it had not been tax exempt under section 501(a) (or its predecessors) and in the case of a trust, deductions under section 642(c) (or its predecessors) had been limited to 20 percent of the taxable income of the trust (computed without benefit of section 642(c) but with the benefit of section 170(b)(1)(A))

3. Interest on the increases in tax determined above from the first date on which each increase would have been due and payable to the date on which the organization ceases to be a private foundation[10]

A substantial contributor is any person who contributed or bequeathed an aggregate amount of more than $5,000 to the foundation, provided that amount is more than 2 percent of the total contributions and bequests received by the foundation before the end of the foundation's taxable year in which the contribution or bequest is received by such person.[11] A person will not be treated as a substantial contributor of a private foundation as of the close of any taxable year, provided that (1) the person and all related persons have not made any contribution to the private foundation during the ten-year period ending at the close of the taxable year, (2) the person and all related persons were not the foundation's managers, and (3) the aggregate contributions made by the person and all related persons are found to be insignificant by the Internal Revenue Service when compared with the aggregate contributions made by one other person.[12] A related person is any person with respect to whom would be a disqualified person within the meaning of section 4946. Contributions and bequests by one spouse are attributed to the other spouse.[13] For private foundations in existence before October 9, 1969, all contributions and bequests received before said date are treated as having been received on said date except for evaluation purposes.[14]

In determining the net assets of the foundation, their value is the greater of the value on the first day on which the action is taken by the foundation which culminates in its ceasing to be a private foundation or the date on which it ceases to be a private foundation.[15] For purposes of section 507(a)(1) the first date on which action is taken is the day notice is given to the district director's office. In case of an involuntary termination under section 507(a)(2), the first date is the date of first occurrence of the willful and flagrant act (or failure to act) or the first date on which the series of willful repeated acts (or failures to act) occurs.[16] Net assets means the excess of the fair market value of the gross assets over the liabilities of the foundation, including appropriate estimated and contingent liabilities.[17] Such liabilities and appropriate estimated and contingent liabilities may include liability for taxes imposed under chapter 42.[18]

Unpaid tax imposed under section 507(c) may be abated, in whole or part, if (1) the private foundation distributes its assets to one or more section 170(b)(1)(A)(i)-(iv) organizations each of which has been in continuous existence for more than sixty months, or (2) the commissioner is given assurances by the appropriate state officer that corrective action has been taken so that the assets of the private foundation will be preserved for charitable purposes under section 501(c)(3) by approval or order of a court of competent jurisdiction.[19] Corrective action means vigorous enforcement of state laws to insure compliance with chapter 42.[20]

NOTES

1. *People ex rel. Seeman v. Greer College*, 302 Ill. 538, 135 N.E. 80 (1922); *Flemming v. Heffner & Flemming*, 263 Mich. 561, 248 N.W. 900 (1933).
2. Treas. Reg. § 1.507-1(b)(1).
3. Treas. Reg. § 1.507-1(b)(7).
4. Treas. Reg. § 1.507-1(b)(2).
5. Treas. Reg. § 1.507-1(c)(1).
6. Treas. Reg. § 1.507-1(c)(2).
7. Treas. Reg. § 1.507-1(c)(4).
8. Treas. Reg. § 1.507-1(c)(3).

9. I.R.C. § 507(c)(1).
10. I.R.C. § 507(d)(1).
11. I.R.C. § 507(d)(2).
12. I.R.C. § 507(d)(2)(C).
13. I.R.C. § 507(d)(2)(B)(iii).
14. I.R.C. § 507(d)(2)(B)(ii).
15. Treas. Reg. § 1.507-7(a).
16. Treas. Reg. § 1.507-7(b).
17. Treas. Reg. § 1.507-7(d).
18. *Id.*
19. I.R.C. § 507(g).
20. Treas. Reg. § 1.507-9(c).

17

Antitrust Exemptions

Section 1 of the Sherman Act[1] declares illegal every contract, combination in the form of trust or otherwise, or conspiracy in restraint of trade or commerce among the several states or with foreign nations.

Analysis of cases under section 1 of the Sherman Act proceeds under either the *per se* rule or the rule of reason. Under the *per se* rule, some types of agreements or practices are so consistently unreasonable that they are deemed to be illegal without consideration of effect except for measuring damages or the intent of the offending party.[2] Group boycotts and concerted refusals to deal are examples of *per se* violations of the Sherman Act.

The rule of reason was developed by the U.S. Supreme Court in *Standard Oil Co. v. U.S.*[3] The Court held that Congress did not intend to prohibit all agreements but only those agreements which "unreasonably" restrain trade. Under the rule of reason the Court must examine the effect of the practice and the intent of the party to determine whether the practice, viewed in its totality, is an unreasonable restraint of trade. Factors to be considered are these:

1. Market power (defined in terms of the relevant geographical and product market) and the relative abilities of the parties to affect competition in the market
2. Freedom of access to capital and skills
3. Economic justification in terms of such things as commercial confidentiality, preservation of goodwill, and avoidance of conflict of interest
4. Excessiveness of restraint

The rule of reason is a balancing test whereby the court weighs the procompetitive against the anticompetitive aspects of the alleged violation.

Nonprofit organizations are engaged in trade or commerce within the meaning of the Sherman Act.[4] Hence, nonprofit organizations are subject to the antitrust law.

Courts may be reluctant to apply the *per se* rule to nonprofit organizations. However, where a clear *per se* violation does appear, the fact that the defendant is a nonprofit organization does not rule out application of the *per se* rule.[5] The United States Supreme Court held that the minimum fee schedule published by the Virginia State Bar for lawyers was a *per se* violation of the Sherman Act. There was no applicable exemption from the coverage of the antitrust law.

EXEMPTIONS

Self-Regulatory Associations

The U.S. Supreme Court has provided an exemption from the *per se* rule for self-regulating associations.[6] This "antitrust-due process" approach has been followed in several subsequent cases. Under this approach a self-regulatory association is not subject to the *per se* rule but to the rule of reason if (1) there is a legislative mandate for self-regulation or otherwise (e.g., self-regulation required by the market's structure); (2) the collective action is intended to accomplish an end consistent with the policy justifying self-regulation, is reasonably related to that goal, and is no more extensive than necessary; and (3) the association provides procedural safeguards which assure that the restraint is not arbitrary and furnishes a basis for judicial review.

Sovereignty

Although the antitrust laws of the United States have been applied to private parties, in general they have not been applied against sovereign states.[7] The command of a sovereign is neither a contract nor an agreement nor a conspiracy entered into in restraint of trade.[8] Moreover, a sovereign acting in its sovereign capacity is not a person, corporation, or association existing under the laws of the United States or of a foreign nation[9] and thus is not explicitly an entity within the language of the United States antitrust laws. However, when a sovereign is engaging in a purely commercial activity, it divests itself of its immunity; therefore, the Sherman and Clayton Acts are applicable, as they are against a person or association.[10]

The applicability of the antitrust laws to nonprofit organizations depends, in part, on whether their actions are the result of the command, approval, encouragement, or appointment as agent or legislative aid of a sovereign. "[A] state does not give immunity to those who violate the Sherman Act by authorizing them to violate it."[11] Moreover, actual participation of a sovereign in the transaction is not sufficient to confer antitrust immunity upon the private person.[12] To be immune from antitrust liability, (1) the anticompetitive activity must be commanded by the sovereign acting as sovereign, (2) the activity must be supervised by the sovereign, and (3) the anticompetitive activity must be related to or necessary for the accomplishment of a legislative goal.[13]

Labor

After the decision in *Loewe v. Lawler*[14] which declared a boycott by labor organizations and their members to compel unionization to be a violation of the Sherman Act, Congress passed the statutory exemptions for labor unions from the antitrust law. In the Clayton Act Congress declared that labor was not a "commodity or article of commerce" and that the organization of labor is not a violation of the antitrust laws.[15] The Norris-LaGuardia Act expanded on the exemption by broadening the definition of a labor dispute and forbidding injunctions from being issued in a variety of labor union activities.[16]

In addition to the statutory exemptions for labor, there is the nonstatutory labor exemption, which is a judicial tool created to effect federal labor policy. Federal labor policy favoring collective bargaining is given preeminence over antitrust policy where the restraint on trade primarily affects only parties to the collective bargaining relationship, provided the restraint of trade affects a mandatory subject of collective bargaining and is the result of bona fide arm's-length negotiation.[17] A mandatory subject of collective bargaining includes wages, hours, and other terms and conditions of employment.

An agreement covering a mandatory subject of collective bargaining, which originates with labor, and primarily affects only the bargaining parties is exempt from the antitrust laws. However, management and labor cannot combine to provide a shield for management against the antitrust law without review by the courts.

NOTES

1. 15 U.S.C. § 1 (1976).
2. The *per se* rule developed through repeated applications of the rule of reason to the same activities. *See, The White Motor Co. v. U.S.*, 372 U.S. 253 (1963); *U.S. v. E.I. DuPont de Nemours & Co.*, 351 U.S. 377 (1955); *U.S. v. Parke, Davis & Co.*, 362 U.S. 29 (1960); *Klors v. Broadway-Hale Stores*, 359. U.S. 207 (1959).
3. 221 U.S. 1 (1911).
4. *Loewe v. Lawler*, 208 U.S. 274 (1908).
5. *Goldfarb v. Virginia State Bar*, 421 U.S. 773 (1975).
6. *Silver v. New York Stock Exchange*, 373 U.S. 341 (1963).
7. *See, e.g., Parker v. Brown*, 317 U.S. 341, 350-52 (1943). The Supreme Court found that there might have been a violation of the Sherman Act if the primary producers' cartel had entered into a contract, combination, or conspiracy in restraint of trade without

state involvement. The Court continued: "We find nothing in the language of the Sherman Act or in its history which suggests that its purpose was to restrain a state or its officers or agents from activities directed by its legislature." *Id.* at 350-51.

8. *See Id.* at 352.

9. The subjects of the Sherman and Clayton Acts are "persons" defined as including "corporations and associations existing under or authorized by the laws of either the United States . . . or . . . of any foreign country." 15 U.S.C. §§ 7, 12 (1976). In *Hunt v. Mobil Oil Corp.*, 550 F.2d 68 (2d Cir.), *cert. denied*, 434 U.S. 984 (1977), the court of appeals noted that the government of Libya could not be guilty of violating the Sherman Act for its role in an alleged conspiracy against Hunt's oil concern because Libya "is not a person or corporation within the terms of the Act but a sovereign state." *Id.* at 78 n.14.

10. *See Victory Transp., Inc. v. Comisaria General de Alastecimientos y Transportes,* 336 F.2d 354, 360 (2d Cir. 1964), *cert. denied*, 381 U.S. 934 (1965); Foreign Sovereign Immunities Act of 1976, § 4(a), 28 U.S.C. §§ 1602-1611 (1976).

11. *Parker v. Brown,* 317 U.S. 341, 351 (1943).

12. *Cantor v. Detroit Edison Co.,* 428 U.S. 579 (1976).

13. *Goldfarb v. Virginia State Bar,* 421 U.S. 773, 791 (1975).

14. 208 U.S. 274 (1908).

15. 15 U.S.C. § 17 (1976).

16. 29 U.S.C. §§ 104, 113(c) (1982).

17. *See, Flood v. Kuhn,* 407 U.S. 258, 293 (1972) (dissenting opinion of Marshall, J.); *Philadelphia World Hockey Club, Inc. v. Philadelphia Hockey Club,* 351 F.Supp. 462 (E.D. Pa. 1972).

18

Multistate Operations

Nonprofit organizations have multiplied and expanded tremendously since World War II. Nonprofit organizations are not limited geographically to the state in which they were organized. Like business corporations, nonprofit organizations have become national in scope and operate in more than one state. It follows then that states would treat foreign nonprofit organizations similar to the way they treat foreign business enterprises. Not surprisingly there is a great deal of uniformity in treatment among the states regarding foreign nonprofit corporations.

CORPORATION LAW

A foreign nonprofit corporation is defined as a nonprofit corporation organized under the laws of another state or sovereign.

For a foreign nonprofit corporation to conduct affairs in another state, it must register, reincorporate, or be domesticated. Reincorporation creates a new corporation under the laws of the incorporating state. Reincorporation means operating a separate corporation under the laws of the incorporating state with all the attendant redundancies for each separate corporation regarding such things as meetings, voting, and reports. Registration requires compliance with the new state's registration process but does not create a second corporation. Domestication procedures are fast dying out and are now required only in Oklahoma. Domestication involves an assimilation of the foreign corporation into a domestic corporation without formal reincorporation.

A foreign corporation may not conduct affairs in a state until authorized to do so under one of the forms of admission. The definition of "conduct of affairs" is

333

broad and variable. Most statutes exclude the following from the definition of conduct of affairs:

1. Maintaining or defending any action or suit or administrative or arbitration proceeding, or effecting the settlement of such actions or suits or settlement of claims or disputes
2. Holding meetings of directors or members
3. Maintaining bank accounts
4. Creating evidence of debt, mortgages, or liens on real or personal property
5. Securing or collecting debts due to the foreign corporation or enforcing any property rights securing the debts[1]

Admission is procedurally accomplished by filing an application for a certificate of authority with the appropriate state official, usually the secretary of state. The application form generally is prescribed by the state and asks for the following statements:

1. The name of the corporation and the jurisdiction under which it is incorporated
2. Date of incorporation and duration of existence
3. Address of the principal office in the state of incorporation
4. The name and address of the proposed registered agent in the new state
5. The purpose or purposes for which the corporation was formed
6. The names and addresses of directors and officers[2]

If the application for a certificate of authority is filed and is found to comply with the statute and the fee is paid, the state authority issues a certificate of authority. Upon issuance of the certificate, the newly admitted corporation is authorized to conduct affairs in that state.[3] An admitted foreign corporation is entitled to the same rights and privileges as a domestic corporation and is subject to the same duties, restrictions, penalties, and liabilities as a domestic corporation.[4]

As is the case with a domestic corporation, a foreign corporation must maintain a registered agent for service of process within the state who may be changed if proper notice is provided to the state.[5]

A foreign corporation may voluntarily withdraw from a state in which it is authorized to conduct its affairs.[6] Application is made in the same manner as for a certificate of authority on forms prescribed by the state.[7] A certificate of withdrawal will be issued by the appropriate state authority.[8] Upon issuance of the certificate of withdrawal, the corporation must cease to conduct affairs within that state.[9]

A state may revoke a certificate of authority for several reasons. A fairly broad sample of grounds for revocation is as follows:

1. Failure to file required annual reports

2. Failure to pay fees or penalties when due and payable

3. Failure to appoint or maintain a registered agent within the state

4. Failure to notify the state of a change in registered agent

5. Failure to file any amendment to its articles of incorporation or any articles of merger

6. Fraudulent procurement of a certificate of authority

7. Continued abuse of authority granted by the state

8. Misrepresentation of a material matter in any application, report, affidavit, or other document filed with the state[10]

Failure to obtain a certificate of authority, voluntary withdrawal, or involuntary revocation of authority mean that a foreign corporation is not allowed to conduct its affairs within the state. A corporation which conducts its affairs within the state without a certificate of authority is not permitted to maintain any action, suit, or proceeding in any of the state's courts until a certificate of authority is obtained.[11] Failure to obtain a certificate of authority does not impair the validity of any contract or act of the foreign corporation nor prevent the corporation from defending any action, suit, or proceeding in the state's courts.[12]

STATE TAX LAW

Foreign corporations are subject to the tax laws of all states in which they conduct their affairs. Since state tax laws are not uniform, nonprofit corporation management cannot be oblivious to the different systems. Exemption in one state is not necessarily going to be granted or available in another.

An area of great controversy is the unitary tax system employed by some states. A state may tax value earned within its territory. The due process clause and the commerce clause of the United States Constitution prohibit a state from imposing an income tax on value earned outside its borders.[13]

The most straightforward method of imposing a state income tax is to use a formal geographical or transactional accounting system. The tax is then imposed on value earned within its boundaries. The problem with this method is that it is subject to manipulation to attribute value to the geographic area which imposes the least tax. Moreover, even in the absence of manipulation it is often virtually impossible to attribute value to certain transactions within a particular jurisdiction when that transaction is but one of a series which results in the end value.

Several states have adopted a unitary approach which rejects geographical or transactional accounting. The Uniform Division of Income for Tax Purposes Act[14] has been adopted in at least twenty-six states. See Table 18 for a listing.

A unitary tax system is based on allocation of the total income of a unitary business between or among taxing jurisdictions based on a formula. What con-

Table 18

Uniform Division of Income for Tax Purposes Act

States Which Have Adopted The Uniform Division of Income for Tax
Purposes Act as of February 1984.

Alabama	§ 40-27-1
Alaska	§ 43.19.010
Arizona	§§ 43-1131--43- 1150
Arkansas	§§ 84-2055--84-2073
California	Cal. Rev. & T. Code §§ 25120-- 25139
Colorado	§ 24-60-1310
Hawaii	§ 235-21--235-39
Idaho	§§ 63-3027, 63-3027A
Kansas	§§ 79-3271--79-3293
Kentucky	§ 141.120
Maine	ch. 36 §§ 5210, 5211
Michigan	§ 205.581
Minnesota	§ 290.171
Missouri	§ 32.200
Montana	§§ 15-31-301--15-31-313
Nebraska	§ 77-2901
Nevada	§ 376.010
New Mexico	§§ 7-4-1--7-4-21
North Dakota	§§ 57-38.1-01--57-38.1-21
Oregon	§§ 314.605--314.670
South Carolina	§§ 12-7-1110--12-7-1200
South Dakota	§ 10-54-1
Texas	Tax Code § 141.001
Utah	§§ 59-13-78--59-13-97
Washington	§ 82.56.010

stitutes a unitary business has been the subject of considerable litigation. The
out-of-state activities must be related in some concrete way to the in-state activities.[15] This means that there must be some sharing or exchange of value that
is not capable of precise evaluation which makes the formula apportionment
reasonable.[16] For example, a vertically integrated business with operations in
several states is a unitary business.[17] Likewise, a series of similar enterprises
linked by common management or operational resources that produced economies of scale and transfers of value was held to be unitary business.[18]

The formula allocation is based on three factors: property, payroll, and sales.
The total business income of the unitary business is multiplied by a fraction of
which the numerator is the sum of the three factors and the denominator is 3.[19]
Each factor is a fraction: the numerator is the value of that factor within the state
and the denominator is the total value of the factor worldwide.[20]

Business income is defined to be income derived from transactions and activity in the regular course of business including income from tangible and

intangible property if the acquisition, management, and disposition of the property are integral parts of the regular trade or business operations.[21] Business income is allocated using the formula.

Other types of income are allocated under the statutes. Net rents and royalties from real property are allocated to the state in which the real property is located.[22] Net rents and royalties from tangible personal property are allocated on the basis of use within the state or totally to the taxing state if the state in which the property is used does not tax them or is not the state of incorporation.[23] Capital gains and losses on real property are allocated to the state in which the property is located.[24] Capital gains and losses on tangible personal property are allocated on the basis of situs of sale or, if the principal office is in the taxing state, nontaxation by the state in which the sale occurred.[25] The allocation for capital gains and losses of intangible personal property is to the state having the principal place of business.[26] Interest and dividend income are allocated to the state in which the principal office is located.[27] Allocation of patent and copyright royalties is based on use or nontaxation in the other state if the principal office is in the taxing state.[28]

The U.S. Supreme Court has upheld unitary tax systems based on the above allocations; however, no single allocation system is required.[29] The taxpayer has the burden of proof that the state tax is imposed on out-of-state tax generated values.[30] The burden of proof must be carried by clear and cogent evidence.[31]

To be constitutional under the due process and commerce clauses the apportionment formula must be fair.[32] Fairness has two components. First, the formula must have internal consistency—that is, if it were applied in all jurisdictions in which the corporation operated, all the income would be taxed but once.[33] Second, there must be external consistency—that is, the factors used must actually reflect a reasonable sense of how income is generated.[34] The three-factor apportionment formula of the Uniform Act has passed constitutional muster.[35]

The most vehement opposition to the unitary tax system has come from its application to international business transactions. Many foreign sovereigns are concerned about the potential impact of the unitary tax system on their economies. A unitary tax system applied to transnational business operations is constitutional. If the trend is to be reversed, it must be reversed by Congress. There is no constitutional barrier to applying a unitary system to nonprofit corporations.

NOTES

1. ABA-ALI Model Nonprofit Corp. Act, § 63.
2. *See,* ABA-ALI Model Nonprofit Corp. Act, § 67.
3. ABA-ALI Model Nonprofit Corp. Act, § 69.
4. ABA-ALI Model Nonprofit Corp. Act, § 64.

5. ABA-ALI Model Nonprofit Corp. Act, §§ 70, 71, 72.

6. ABA-ALI Model Nonprofit Corp. Act, § 76.

7. *Id.*

8. ABA-ALI Model Nonprofit Corp. Act, § 77.

9. *Id.*

10. ABA-ALI Model Nonprofit Corp. Act, § 78.

11. ABA-ALI Model Nonprofit Corp. Act, § 80.

12. *Id.*

13. *ASARCO, Inc. v. Idaho State Tax Comm.*, 458 U.S. 307, (1982).

14. 7A Uniform Laws Annotated 91 (1978).

15. *ASARCO, Inc. v. Idaho State Tax Comm.*, 458 U.S. at 327.

16. *Id.*

17. *Underwood Typewriter Co. v. Chamberlain*, 254 U.S. 113 (1920).

18. *Butler Bros. v. McColgan*, 315 U.S. 501 (1942).

19. Uniform Division of Income for Tax Purposes Act, § 9.

20. Uniform Division of Income for Tax Purposes Act, §§ 10, 13, 15.

21. Uniform Division of Income for Tax Purposes Act, § 1(a).

22. Uniform Division of Income for Tax Purposes Act, § 5.

23. *Id.*

24. Uniform Division of Income for Tax Purposes Act, § 6.

25. *Id.*

26. *Id.*

27. Uniform Division of Income for Tax Purposes Act, § 7.

28. Uniform Division of Income for Tax Purposes Act, § 8.

29. *Wisconsin v. J.C. Penney, Co.*, 311 U.S. 435 (1940).

30. *Exxon Corp. v. Wisconsin Dept. of Revenue*, 447 U.S. 207 (1980).

31. *Id.*

32. *Container Corp. of America v. Franchise Tax Bd.*, _____ U.S. _____, _____, 103 S.Ct. 2933, 2942 (1983).

33. *Id.*

34. *Id.*

35. *Container Corp. of America v. Franchise Tax Bd.*, _____ U.S. _____, 103 S.Ct. 2933 (1983); *Butler Bros. v. McColgan*, 315 U.S. 501 (1942).

19

International Organizations

INTERNATIONAL ORGANIZATIONS

Since the end of World War II, international organizations have proliferated. In 1975, at least eighty-three international organizations were operating throughout the world.[1] The rights, duties, and place of these organizations in international and municipal law are uncertain. Prior to the appearance of international organizations, international law as well as the domestic law of most states had not been forced to differentiate between the legal concepts of international personality and national sovereignty. Consequently, international usage has blended these two legal concepts without demarcation. A separation of the two concepts is now necessary, particularly with the advent of the economically motivated international organization,[2] as contrasted with the public welfare organization.[3] Many of the economically motivated international organizations, such as the Organization of Petroleum Exporting Countries (OPEC), are capable of exerting, and do in fact exert, tremendous economic pressure on the international community, even to the point of threatening sovereignty.

In the absence of an effective international forum, the only way to check the powers of these international organizations and adjudicate disputes is to resort to municipal courts and municipal law. But municipal law, like international law, is not prepared to deal with international organizations.[4] International organizations are not sovereign states, corporations, or persons. Whether an international organization is capable of litigating its disputes within a municipal forum depends on whether the laws of the applicable sovereign accord the international organization "legal capacity."

International Legal Personality

Two distinct approaches have been used to determine whether an organization created by states has legal personality.[5] These two approaches may be labeled the inductive approach and the objective approach. The inductive approach requires an inquiry into the intent of the forming states by examining the evidence surrounding the organization's formation. In practice, this approach primarily involves examining the governing documents of the organization.[6] Under the inductive approach, a search of the organization's governing documents is made for the attributes of international legal personality, expressed or implied in those documents. From this it can be determined whether an international organization possesses international legal personality. The objective approach does not inquire into the intent of the forming states as expressed in the governing documents. Rather, this approach requires an examination of the structure of the organization in light of the principles of international law.[7]

The objective approach to international personality was used by the International Court of Justice in its advisory opinion in *Reparation for Injuries Suffered in the Service of the United Nations*.[8] There the Court set out four necessary preconditions for the existence of international legal personality. First, the organization must be created as more than a mere center for the harmonization of states' actions in the attainment of common ends.[9] This precondition distinguishes between organizations such as the United Nations and the British Commonwealth. Second, the organization must be equipped with an infrastructure of its own.[10] A conference or congress of states would not satisfy this precondition. Third, special tasks must be assigned to the organization.[11] Fourth, the position of the organization vis-à-vis its members must be defined to give the organization a life of its own, detached from that of its members.[12] In other words, the organization must be capable of expressing a will of its own, either by a power of decision binding on members by majority vote or by the competence of the organization to exercise certain independent functions. Once these four essential preconditions are met, international legal personality will be established. Certain consequences will then follow as a result of this determination.

The primary consequence of establishing that an organization possesses international legal personality is that such an organization is deemed a subject of international law and capable of possessing international rights and duties.[13] The attributes of international legal personality are generally conceded to be (1) the power to make treaties, (2) the attribution of privileges and immunities, (3) the power to contract, and (4) the power to undertake legal proceedings.[14] Despite the significance of these attributes, possessing international legal personality does not place an international organization on the same legal plane as a sovereign.

The application of the inductive approach to organizations of lesser magnitude than the United Nations provides little more than a determination of legal personality for municipal law purposes of the forming states. The existence of legal personality in international law under the inductive approach depends on the acceptance of the legal personality of the organization by states that are not parties to the formation.[15] The acceptance of legal personality in the municipal law of substantially all states would certainly prove legal personality on the international plane. At the same time, the absence of acceptance or the acceptance by just a few states outside of the forming group would cast serious doubt on the existence of international personality of an organization. However, when an organization has international legal personality under the objective approach, it is an international person, and the recognition of that legal personality in the municipal law of each state is immaterial.[16]

Immunity from Suit

The existence of international legal personality, determined under the inductive approach, is dependent on the goodwill and recognition of third-party states outside the forming members. If international personality is not recognized by a third-party state, the organization has no rights or privileges within the municipal law of the third-party state since the organization is not recognized as a juridical person. Therefore, the organization cannot sue and be sued in the courts of the nonrecognizing third-party state.

On the other hand, if an organization has international legal personality under the objective approach, express recognition of the organization as an international person is not necessary. Therefore, the organization would be entitled to sue and be sued within the United States. It would also be entitled to all the privileges and immunities that are necessary for the independent exercise of the organization's functions. At the same time, however, an international organization does not possess all of the privileges and immunities accorded sovereigns, but only those necessary to the performance of its functions. If a sovereign would not be immune from suit, neither would an international organization performing the same function or activity.

A sovereign is immune from suit in the courts of the United States as far as any political (*jure imperii*) act is concerned.[17] However, if the activity is commercial in nature, the sovereign is not granted immunity.[18] An international organization may, however, be immune from suit if so provided by municipal ordinance.

International Organizations Immunities Act

The International Organizations Immunities Act[19] authorizes the President to accord international legal personality to certain international organizations by executive order.[20] For purposes of the act, an international organization is a public international organization in which the United States participates pursuant to any treaty or under authority of act of Congress authorizing an appropriation for such participation.

A designated international organization has the power to contract, acquire, and dispose of real and personal property and institute legal proceedings. Such an international organization has the same immunity from suit as a foreign sovereign except for contract actions.[21]

A designated international organization may be accorded the same privileges with respect to internal revenue taxes as a foreign sovereign. Such an organization may be tax exempt by executive order. Income of international organizations derived from investments in the United States in stocks, bonds, or other domestic securities owned by the international organization, or from interest on deposits of money in United States banks belonging to international organizations, or from any other source within the United States is exempt from taxation.[22] Moreover, the compensation paid to employees, who are not United States citizens, of international organizations is not subject to United States tax[23] or to social security (FICA) taxes.[24]

The following international organizations have been designated as tax exempt by order of the President:

1. Caribbean Organization
2. Coffee Study Group
3. European Space Research Organization
4. Food and Agricultural Organization
5. Great Lakes Fishery Commission
6. Inter-American Defense Board
7. Inter-American Development Bank
8. Inter-American Institute of Agricultural Sciences
9. Inter-American Statistical Institute
10. Inter-American Tropical Tuna Commission
11. Intergovernmental Committee for European Migration
12. Intergovernmental Maritime Consultative Organization
13. International Atomic Energy Agency
14. International Bank for Reconstruction and Development
15. International Civil Aviation Organization
16. International Cotton Advisory Committee
17. International Finance Corporation

18. International Food Policy Research Institute
19. International Hydrographic Bureau
20. The International Labor Organization
21. International Joint Commission—United States and Canada
22. International Monetary Fund
23. International Pacific Halibut Commission
24. International Secretariat for Volunteer Service
25. International Telecommunications Satellite Consortium
26. International Telecommunications Union
27. International Wheat Advisory Committee
28. Lake Ontario Claims Tribunal
29. Multinational Force and Observers
30. Organization of African Unity
31. Organization of American States
32. Organization for European Economic Cooperation
33. Pan American Sanitary Bureau
34. The Pan American Union
35. South Pacific Administration
36. The United Nations
37. United Nations Educational, Scientific and Cultural Organization
38. Universal Postal Union
39. World Health Organization
40. World Intellectual Property Organization
41. World Meteorological Organization

MULTINATIONAL ORGANIZATIONS

The truth of the matter is that there is no such thing as a multinational, transnational, supranational, or international for-profit or nonprofit corporation. At present, no apparatus exists to organize or control such an organization. Corporations, firms, societies, companies, and other organizations are organized under national laws. Any definition of what is termed a multinational corporation or organization must be made in terms of national laws even though the character of the organization's activities may be international or multinational.

Within each sovereign's jurisdiction the multinational organization is subject to the host sovereign's laws. Hence, a multinational organization may be subject to the laws of several sovereigns simultaneously.

Alien Corporations

Under United States law a corporation is a citizen of the state where it is incorporated. Likewise, the nationality of a corporation is determined by country of incorporation, and treaties of friendship, commerce, and navigation generally so provide.[25] An alien corporation operating in the United States does so pursuant to rights set out in the particular treaty between the United States and the country of incorporation. In 'general, an alien corporation is treated by the states the same as a foreign corporation of a sister state.[26] There are constitutional limits on the power of a state to exclude foreign corporations even though a state recognizes a foreign corporation as a matter of comity and not as a matter of right. An alien corporation may not be treated differently from all other foreign corporations allowed into a state. Moreover, an alien corporation may become a domestic corporation while still retaining its original incorporated status. Some states in fact provide for domestication.[27]

An alternative is for an alien corporation to establish a subsidiary in the United States under state law. Such a right is generally provided by treaty. Many states do not require citizenship for the incorporators or directors. Whatever obstacles exist in a particular state corporation act can be avoided by choosing a more convenient state for incorporation.

An alien organization may qualify for tax exempt status under section 501(a) if it otherwise meets the requirements for tax exemption.[28] The problem is that generally no charitable deduction is allowed under section 170 for contributions to foreign charitable organizations[29] unless so provided under a tax treaty or convention between the United States and the foreign charitable organization's home sovereign.

United States Charitable Organizations Operating Abroad

A United States charitable organization operating abroad must comply with the laws of the host sovereign. A U.S. charitable organization may collect funds in the United States and distribute them in foreign countries without detrimentally affecting the section 170 charitable deduction.[30] But donations to a foreign charitable organization in the United States are not deductible contributions under section 170.[31] Similarly, donations to U.S. charitable organizations which merely act as conduits for contributions to foreign charitable organizations are not deductible under section 170.[32] However, contributions solicited for a specific project of a foreign charitable organization are deductible if they are made to a U.S. charitable organization that has reviewed and approved the project as furthering its own exempt purpose and has control and discretion over the use of the contributions.[33]

NOTES

1. See D. Bowett, *The Law of International Institutions* xi–xiv (1975) for a list of these international organizations.

2. For example, the European Community, Organization for Economic Cooperation and Development, Andean Pact, and other free trade associations and common markets.

3. For example, the United Nations and its specialized agencies such as World Food Program (WFP), World Health Organization (WHO), United Nations Educational, Scientific and Cultural Organization (UNESCO), United Nations Children's Fund (UNICEF), and United Nations Relief and Rehabilitation Agency (UNRRA).

4. For example, suit was dismissed against OPEC for lack of jurisdiction in *Int'l Ass'n of Machinists and Aerospace Workers v. OPEC*, 477 F.Supp. 533 (D.C.Cal. 1979). Moreover, the court thought that it would be impossible to acquire jurisdiction over OPEC. *Id.* at 560.

5. *See, e.g.,* D. Bowett, *supra* note 1, at 299–304. *See* I. Brownlie, *Principles of Public International Law* 520 (1966), for a discussion of the inductive approach. *See* for example Seyersted, *Objective International Personality of International Organizations* (1963), for a discussion of the objective approach.

6. Rama-Montaldo, *International Legal Personality and Implied Powers of International Organizations*, 44 Brit. Y.B. Int'l. L. 111, 112 (1970).

7. *Id.*

8. 1949 I.C.J. 174.

9. *Id.* at 178.

10. *Id.*

11. *Id.*

12. *Id.* at 178–79.

13. *Id.* at 179.

14. D. Bowett, *supra* note 1, at 302.

15. *E.g.*, Agreement on Judicial Status, Mar. 10, 1955, Switzerland-World Meteorological Association (WMO), 211 U.N.T.S. 278.

16. The United Nations as an international person had the legal capacity to make an international claim for reparation for injuries even against a nonmember defendant state. 1949 I.C.J. 184–85.

17. *Victory Transport, Inc. v. Comisaria General de Abastecimientos y Tranportes*, 336 F.2d 354, 360 (2d Cir. 1964), *cert. den.*, 381 U.S. 934 (1965); Foreign Sovereign Immunities Act of 1976, § 4(a), 28 U.S.C. §§ 1602–1611 (1976).

18. Foreign Sovereign Immunities Act of 1976, 28 U.S.C. §§ 1602–1611 (1976) [hereinafter cited as FSIA]. Passage of the FSIA represents an adoption by Congress of the restrictive theory of sovereign immunity which was first stated as United States policy in the "Tate Letter," 26 Dep't State Bull. 984 (1952). Under the restrictive theory, sovereign immunity is recognized only with respect to sovereign or public (political) acts but not with respect to private (commercial) acts. *Id.* For a good commentary on the FSIA, see Brower, *The Foreign Sovereign Immunities Act of 1976 in Practice*, 73 Am. J. In't. L. 200 (1979).

19. 22 U.S.C. § 288a (1976).

20. 22 U.S.C. § 288 (1976).
21. 22 U.S.C. § 288a(b) (1976).
22. I.R.C. § 892.
23. I.R.C. § 893.
24. I.R.C. § 3121(b)(15).
25. Art. XIV, United States and France (1960) 11 U.S.T. 2398, 2416, TIAS 4625; Art. XXV(5), United States and Federal Republic of Germany (1956) 7 U.S.T. 1839, 1866, TIAS 3593; Art. XXII(3) United States and Japan (1953) 4 U.S.T. 2063, 2079–80, TIAS 2863.
26. *Contra,* Wash. Rev. Code Ann. §23A.36.101 (1969) distinguishes between a corporation of a sister state and alien ones.
27. Miss. Code Ann. §79-1-19 (1973); Okla. Stat. Ann., Title 18, §1.199(a) (1953).
28. Rev. Rul. 66-177, 1966-1 C.B. 132.
29. I.R.C. § 170(c)(2).
30. Rev. Rul. 63-252, 1963-2 C.B. 101, *amplified by* Rev. Rul. 66-79, 1966-1 C.B. 48.
31. *Id.*
32. *Id.*
33. *Id.;* Rev. Rul. 75-65, 1975-1 C.B. 79; Rev. Rul. 63-252, 1963-2 C.B. 101.

APPENDIX: IRC Section 501. Exemption from Tax on Corporations, Certain Trusts, Etc.

(a) Exemption From Taxation.—An organization described in subsection (c) or (d) or section 401(a) shall be exempt from taxation under this subtitle unless such exemption is denied under section 502 or 503.

(b) Tax on Unrelated Business Income and Certain Other Activities.—An organization exempt from taxation under subsection (a) shall be subject to tax to the extent provided in parts II, III, and VI of this subchapter, but (notwithstanding parts II, III, and VI of this subchapter) shall be considered an organization exempt from income taxes for the purpose of any law which refers to organizations exempt from income taxes.

(c) List of Exempt Organizations.—The following organizations are referred to in subsection (a):

(1) any corporation organized under Act of Congress which is an instrumentality of the United States but only if such corporation—

(A) is exempt from Federal income taxes—

(i) under such Act as amended and supplemented before the date of the enactment of the Tax Reform Act of 1984, or

(ii) under this title without regard to any provision of law which is not contained in this title and which is not contained in a revenue Act, or

(B) is described in subsection (1).

(2) Corporations organized for the exclusive purpose of holding title to property, collecting income therefrom, and turning over the entire amount thereof, less expenses, to an organization which itself is exempt under this section.

(3) Corporations, and any community chest, fund, or foundation, organized and operated exclusively for religious, charitable, scientific, testing for public safety, literary, or educational purposes, or to foster national or international amateur sports competition (but only if no part of its activities involve the provision of athletic facilities or equipment), or for the prevention of cruelty to children or animals, no part of the net earnings of which inures to the benefit of any private shareholder or individual, no substantial part of the activities of which is carrying on propaganda, or otherwise attempting to influence legislation (except as otherwise provided in subsection (h)), and which does not partici-

pate in, or intervene in (including the publishing or distributing of statements), any political campaign on behalf of any candidate for public office.

(4) Civic leagues or organizations not organized for profit but operated exclusively for the promotion of social welfare or local associations of employees, the membership of which is limited to the employees of a designated person or persons in a particular municipality and the net earnings of which are devoted exclusively to charitable, educational, or recreational purposes.

(5) Labor, agricultural, or horticultural organizations.

(6) Business leagues, chambers of commerce, real-estate boards, boards of trade, or professional football leagues (whether or not administering a pension fund for football players), not organized for profit and no part of the net earnings of which inures to the benefit of any private shareholder or individual.

(7) Clubs organized for pleasure, recreation, and other nonprofitable purposes, substantially all of the activities of which are for such purposes and no part of the net earnings of which inures to the benefit of any private shareholder.

(8) Fraternal beneficiary societies, orders, or associations—

(A) operating under the lodge system or for the exclusive benefit of the members of a fraternity itself operating under the lodge system, and

(B) providing for the payment of life, sick, accident, or other benefits to the members of such society, order, or association or their dependents.

(9) Voluntary employees' beneficiary associations providing for the payment of life, sick, accident, or other benefits to the members of such association or their dependents or designated beneficiaries, if no part of the net earnings of such association inures (other than through such payments) to the benefit of any private shareholder or individual.

(10) Domestic fraternal societies, orders, or associations, operating under the lodge system—

(A) the net earnings of which are devoted exclusively to religious, charitable, scientific, literary, educational, and fraternal purposes, and

(B) which do not provide for the payment of life, sick, accident, or other benefits.

(11) Teachers' retirement fund associations of a purely local character, if

(A) no part of their net earnings inures (other than through payment of retirement benefits) to the benefit of any private shareholder or individual, and

(B) the income consists solely of amounts received from public taxation, amounts received from assessments on the teaching salaries of members, and income in respect of investments.

(12) (A) Benevolent life insurance associations of a purely local character, mutual ditch or irrigation companies, mutual or cooperative telephone companies, or like organizations; but only if 85 percent or more of the income consists of amounts collected from members for the sole purpose of meeting losses and expenses.

(B) In the case of a mutual or cooperative telephone company, subparagraph (A) shall be applied without taking into account any income received or accrued—

(i) from a nonmember telephone company for the performance of communication services which involve members of the mutual or cooperative telephone company,

(ii) from qualified pole rentals, or

(iii) from the sale of display listings in a directory furnished to the members of the mutual or cooperative telephone company.

(C) In the case of a mutual or cooperative electric company, subparagraph (A) shall be applied without taking into account any income received or accrued from qualified pole rentals.

(D) For purposes of this paragraph, the term "qualified pole rental" means any rental of a pole (or other structure used to support wires) if such pole (or other structure)—

(i) is used by the telephone or electric company to support one or more wires which are used by such company in providing telephone or electric services to its members, and

(ii) is used pursuant to the rental to support one or more wires (in addition to the wires described in clause (i)) for use in connection with the transmission by wire of electricity or of telephone or other communications. For purposes of the preceding sentence, the term "rental" includes any sale of the right to use the pole (or other structure).

(13) Cemetery companies owned and operated exclusively for the benefit of their members or which are not operated for profit; and any corporation chartered solely for the purpose of the disposal of bodies by burial or cremation which is not permitted by its charter to engage in any business not necessarily incident to that purpose and no part of the net earnings of which inures to the benefit of any private shareholder or individual.

(14) (A) Credit unions without capital stock organized and operated for mutual purposes and without profit.

(B) Corporations or associations without capital stock organized before September 1, 1957, and operated for mutual purposes and without profit for the purpose of providing reserve funds for, and insurance of shares or deposits in—

(i) domestic building and loan associations,

(ii) cooperative banks without capital stock organized and operated for mutual purposes and without profit, or

(iii) mutual savings banks not having capital stock represented by shares.

(C) Corporations or associations organized before September 1, 1957, and operated for mutual purposes and without profit for the purpose of providing reserve funds for associations or banks described in clause (i), (ii), or (iii) of subparagraph (B); but only if 85 percent or more of the income is attributable to providing such reserve funds and to investments. This subparagraph shall not apply to any corporation or association entitled to exemption under subparagraph (B).

(15) Mutual insurance companies or associations other than life or marine (including interinsurers and reciprocal underwriters) if the gross amount received during the taxable year from the items described in section 822(b) (other than paragraph (1)(D) thereof) and premiums (including deposits and assessments) does not exceed $150,000.

(16) Corporations organized by an association subject to part IV of this subchapter or members thereof, for the purpose of financing the ordinary crop operations of such members or other producers, and operated in conjunction with such association. Exemption shall not be denied any such corporation because it has capital stock, if the dividend rate of such stock is fixed at not to exceed the legal rate of interest in the State of incorporation or 8 percent per annum, whichever is greater, on the value of the consideration for which the stock was issued, and if substantially all such stock (other than nonvoting preferred stock, the owners of which are not entitled or permitted to participate, directly or indirectly, in the profits of the corporation, or dissolution or otherwise, beyond the fixed dividends) is owned by such association, or members thereof; nor shall exemp-

tion be denied any such corporation because there is accumulated and maintained by it a reserve required by State law or a reasonable reserve for any necessary purpose.

(17) (A) A trust or trusts forming part of a plan providing for the payment of supplemental unemployment compensation benefits, if—

(i) under the plan, it is impossible, at any time prior to the satisfaction of all liabilities with respect to employees under the plan, for any part of the corpus or income to be (within the taxable year or thereafter) used for, or diverted to, any purpose other than the providing of supplemental unemployment compensation benefits.

(ii) such benefits are payable to employees under a classification which is set forth in the plan and which is found by the Secretary not to be discriminatory in favor of employees who are officers, shareholders, persons whose principal duties consist of supervising the work of other employees, or highly compensated employees, and

(iii) such benefits do not discriminate in favor of employees who are officers, shareholders, persons whose principal duties consist of supervising the work of other employees, or highly compensated employees. A plan shall not be considered discriminatory within the meaning of this clause merely because the benefits received under the plan bear a uniform relationship to the total compensation, or the basic or regular rate of compensation, of the employees covered by the plan.

(B) In determining whether a plan meets the requirements of subparagraph (A), any benefits provided under any other plan shall not be taken into consideration, except that a plan shall not be considered discriminatory—

(i) merely because the benefits under the plan which are first determined in a nondiscriminatory manner within the meaning of subparagraph (A) are then reduced by any sick, accident, or unemployment compensation benefits received under State or Federal law (or reduced by a portion of such benefits if determined in a nondiscriminatory manner), or

(ii) merely because the plan provides only for employees who are not eligible to receive sick, accident, or unemployment compensation benefits under State or Federal law the same benefits (or a portion of such benefits if determined in a nondiscriminatory manner) which such employees would receive under such laws if such employees were eligible for such benefits, or

(iii) merely because the plan provides only for employees who are not eligible under another plan (which meets the requirements of subparagraph (A)) of supplemental unemployment compensation benefits provided wholly by the employer the same benefits (or a portion of such benefits if determined in a nondiscriminatory manner) which such employees would receive under such other plan if such employees were eligible under such other plan, but only if the employees eligible under both plans would make a classification which would be nondiscriminatory within the meaning of subparagraph (A).

(C) A plan shall be considered to meet the requirements of subparagraph (A) during the whole of any year of the plan if on one day in each quarter it satisfies such requirements.

(D) The term "supplemental unemployment compensation benefits" means only—

(i) benefits which are paid to an employee because of his involuntary separation from the employment of the employer (whether or not such separation is temporary) resulting directly from a reduction in force, the discontinuance of a plan or operation, or other similar conditions, and

(ii) sick and accident benefits subordinate to the benefits described in clause (i).

(E) Exemption shall not be denied under subsection (a) to any organization entitled to such exemption as an association described in paragraph (9) of this subsection merely because such organization provides for the payment of supplemental unemployment benefits (as defined in subparagraph (D)(i)).

(18) A trust or trusts created before June 25, 1959, forming part of a plan providing for the payment of benefits under a pension plan funded only by contributions of employees, if—

(A) under the plan, it is impossible, at any time prior to the satisfaction of all liabilities with respect to employees under the plan, for any part of the corpus or income to be (within the taxable year or thereafter) used for, or diverted to, any purpose other than the providing of benefits under the plan,

(B) such benefits are payable to employees under a classification which is set forth in the plan and which is found by the Secretary not to be discriminatory in favor of employees who are officers, shareholders, persons whose principal duties consist of supervising the work of other employees, or highly compensated employees, and

(C) such benefits do not discriminate in favor of employees who are officers, shareholders, persons whose principal duties consist of supervising the work of other employees, or highly compensated employees. A plan shall not be considered discriminatory within the meaning of this subparagraph merely because the benefits received under the plan bear a uniform relationship to the total compensation, or the basic or regular rate of compensation, of the employees covered by the plan.

(19) A post or organization of past or present members of the Armed Forces of the United States or an auxiliary unit or society of, or a trust or foundation for, any such post or organization—

(A) organized in the United States or any of its possessions,

(B) at least 75 percent of the members of which are past or present members of the Armed Forces of the United States and substantially all of the other members of which are individuals who are cadets or are spouses, widows, or widowers of past or present members of the Armed Forces of the United States or of cadets and

(C) no part of the net earnings of which inures to the benefit of any private shareholder or individual.

(20) An organization or trust created or organized in the United States, the exclusive function of which is to form part of a qualified group legal services plan or plans, within the meaning of section 120. An organization or trust which receives contributions because of section 120(c)(5)(C) shall not be prevented from qualifying as an organization described in this paragraph merely because it provides legal services or indemnification against the cost of legal services unassociated with a qualified group legal services plan.

(21) A trust or trusts established in writing, created or organized in the United States, and contributed to by any person (except an insurance company) if—

(A) the purpose of such trust or trusts is exclusively—

(i) to satisfy, in whole or in part, the liability of such person for, or with respect to, claims for compensation for disability or death due to pneumoconiosis under Black Lung Acts;

(ii) to pay premiums for insurance exclusively covering such liability; and

(iii) to pay administrative and other incidental expenses of such trust (including legal, accounting, actuarial, and trustee expenses) in connection with the operation of the trust and the processing of claims against such person under Black Lung Acts; and

(B) no part of the assets of the trust may be used for, or diverted to, any purpose other than—

(i) the purposes described in subparagraph (A), or

(ii) investment (but only to the extent that the trustee determines that a portion of the assets is not currently needed for the purposes described in subparagraph (A)) in—

(I) public debt securities of the United States,

(II) obligations of a State or local government which are not in default as to principal or interest, or

(III) time or demand deposits in a bank (as defined in section 581) or an insured credit union (within the meaning of section 101(6) of the Federal Credit Union Act, 12 U.S.C. 1752(6)) located in the United States, or

(iii) payment into the Black Lung Disability Trust Fund established under section 9501, or into the general fund of the United States Treasury (other than in satisfaction of any tax or other civil or criminal liability of the person who established or contributed to the trust).

For purposes of this paragraph the term ''Black Lung Acts'' means part C of title IV of the Federal Mine Safety and Health Act of 1977, and any State law providing compensation for disability or death due to pneumoconiosis.

(22) A trust created or organized in the United States and established in writing by the plan sponsors of multiemployer plans if—

(A) the purpose of such trust is exclusively—

(i) to pay any amount described in section 4223(c) or (h) of the Employee Retirement Income Security Act of 1974, and

(ii) to pay reasonable and necessary administrative expenses in connection with the establishment and operation of the trust and the processing of claims against the trust,

(B) no part of the assets of the trust may be used for, or diverted to, any purpose other than—

(i) the purposes described in subparagraph (A), or

(ii) the investment in securities, obligations, or time or demand deposits described in clause (ii) of paragraph (21)(B).

(C) such trust meets the requirements of paragraphs (2), (3), and (4) of section 4223(b), 4223(h), or, if applicable, section 4223(c) of the Employee Retirement Income Security Act of 1974, and

(D) the trust instrument provides that, on dissolution of the trust, assets of the trust may not be paid other than to plans which have participated in the plan or, in the case of a trust established under section 4223(h) of such Act, to plans with respect to which employers have participated in the fund.

(23) any association organized before 1880 more than 75 percent of the members of which are present or past members of the Armed Forces and a principal purpose of which is to provide insurance and other benefits to veterans or their dependents.

(d) Religious and Apostolic Organizations.—The following organizations are referred to in subsection (a): Religious or apostolic associations or corporations, if such associations or corporations have a common treasury or community treasury, even if such associations or corporations engage in business for the common benefit of the members, but only if the members thereof include (at the time of filing their returns) in their gross income their entire pro rata shares, whether distributed or not, of the taxable income of the association or corporation for such year. Any amount so included in the gross income of a member shall be treated as a dividend received.

(e) Cooperative Hospital Service Organizations.—For purposes of this title, an organization shall be treated as an organization organized and operated exclusively for charitable purposes, if—

(1) such organization is organized and operated solely—

(A) to perform, on a centralized basis, one or more of the following services which, if performed on its own behalf by a hospital which is an organization described in subsection (c)(3) and exempt from taxation under subsection (a), would constitute activities in exercising or performing the purpose or function constituting the basis for its exemption: data processing, purchasing, warehousing, billing and collection, food, clinical, industrial engineering, laboratory, printing, communications, record center, and personnel (including selection, testing, training, and education of personnel) services; and

(B) to perform such services solely for two or more hospitals each of which is—

(i) an organization described in subsection (c)(3) which is exempt from taxation under subsection (a),

(ii) a constituent part of an organization described in subsection (c)(3) which is exempt from taxation under subsection (a) and which, if organized and operated as a separate entity, would constitute an organization described in subsection (c)(3), or

(iii) owned and operated by the United States, a State, the District of Columbia, or a possession of the United States, or a political subdivision or an agency or instrumentality of any of the foregoing;

(2) such organization is organized and operated on a cooperative basis and allocates or pays, within 8 1/2 months after the close of its taxable year, all net earnings to patrons on the basis of services performed for them; and

(3) if such organization has capital stock, all of such stock outstanding is owned by its patrons. For purposes of this title, any organization which, by reason of the preceding sentence, is an organization described in subsection (c)(3) and exempt from taxation under subsection (a), shall be treated as a hospital and as an organization referred to in section 170(b)(1)(A)(iii).

(f) Cooperative Service Organizations of Operating Educational Organizations.— For purposes of this title, if an organization is—

(1) organized and operated solely to hold, commingle, and collectively invest and reinvest (including arranging for and supervising the performance by independent contractors of investment services related thereto) in stocks and securities, the moneys contributed thereto by each of the members of such organization, and to collect income therefrom and turn over the entire amount thereof, less expenses, to such members,

(2) organized and controlled by one or more such members, and

(3) comprised solely of members that are organizations described in clause (ii) or (iv) of section 170(b)(1)(A)—

(A) which are exempt from taxation under subsection (a), or

(B) the income of which is excluded from taxation under section 115(a), then such organization shall be treated as an organization organized and operated exclusively for charitable purposes.

(g) Definition of Agricultural.—For purposes of subsection (c)(5), the term "agricultural" includes the art or science of cultivating land, harvesting crops or aquatic resources, or raising livestock.

(h) Expenditures by Public Charities to Influence Legislation.—

(1) General rule.—In the case of an organization to which this subsection applies, exemption from taxation under subsection (a) shall be denied because a substantial part of the activities of such organization consists of carrying on propaganda, or otherwise attempting, to influence legislation, but only if such organization normally—

(A) makes lobbying expenditures in excess of the lobbying ceiling amount for such organization for each taxable year, or

(B) makes grass roots expenditures in excess of the grass roots ceiling amount for such organization for each taxable year.

(2) Definitions.—For purposes of this subsection—

(A) Lobbying expenditures.—The term "lobbying expenditures" means expenditures for the purpose of influencing legislation (as defined in section 4911(d)).

(B) Lobbying ceiling amount.—The lobbying ceiling amount for any organization for any taxable year is 150 percent of the lobbying nontaxable amount for such organization for such taxable year, determined under section 4911.

(C) Grass roots expenditures.—The term "grass roots expenditures" means expenditures for the purpose of influencing legislation (as defined in section 4911(d) without regard to paragraph (1)(B) thereof).

(D) Grass roots ceiling amount.—The grass roots ceiling amount for any organization for any taxable year is 150 percent of the grass roots nontaxable amount for such organization for such taxable year, determined under section 4911.

(3) Organizations to which this subsection applies.—This subsection shall apply to any organization which has elected (in such manner and at such time as the Secretary may prescribe) to have the provisions of this subsection apply to such organization and which, for the taxable year which includes the date the election is made, is described in subsection (c)(3) and—

(A) is described in paragraph (4), and

(B) is not a disqualified organization under paragraph (5).

(4) Organizations permitted to elect to have this subsection apply.—An organization is described in this paragraph if it is described in—

(A) section 170(b)(1)(A)(ii) (relating to educational institutions).

(B) section 170(b)(1)(A)(iii) (relating to hospitals and medical research organizations).

(C) section 170(b)(1)(A)(iv) (relating to organizations supporting government schools),

(D) section 170(b)(1)(A)(vi) (relating to organizations publicly supported by charitable contributions),

(E) section 509(a)(2) (relating to organizations publicly supported by admissions, sales, etc.), or

(F) section 509(a)(3) (relating to organizations supporting certain types of public charities), except that for purposes of this subparagraph, section 509(a)(3) shall be applied without regard to the last sentence of section 509(a).

(5) Disqualified organizations.—For purposes of paragraph (3), an organization is a disqualified organization if it is—

(A) described in section 170(b)(1)(A)(i) (relating to churches),

(B) an integrated auxiliary of a church or of a convention or association of churches, or

(C) a member of an affiliated group of organizations (within the meaning of section 4911(f)(2)) if one or more members of such group is described in subparagraph (A) or (B).

(6) Years for which election is effective.—An election by an organization under this subsection shall be effective for all taxable years of such organization which—

(A) end after the date the election is made, and

(B) begin before the date the election is revoked by such organization (under regulations prescribed by the Secretary).

(7) No effect on certain organizations.—With respect to any organization for a taxable year which—

(A) such organization is a disqualified organization (within the meaning of paragraph (5)), or

(B) an election under this subsection is not in effect for such organization, nothing in this subsection or in section 4911 shall be construed to affect the interpretation of the phrase, "no substantial part of the activities of which is carrying on propaganda, or otherwise attempting, to influence legislation," under subsection (c)(3).

(8) Affiliated organizations.—

For rules regarding affiliated organizations, see section 4911(f).

(i) Prohibition of Discrimination by Certain Social Clubs.—Notwithstanding subsection (a), an organization which is described in subsection (c)(7) shall not be exempt from taxation under subsection (a) for any taxable year if, at any time during such taxable year, the charter, bylaws, or other governing instrument, of such organization or any written policy statement of such organization contains a provision which provides for discrimination against any person on the basis of race, color, or religion. The preceding sentence to the extent it relates to discrimination on the basis of religion shall not apply to—

(1) an auxiliary of a fraternal beneficiary society if such society—

(A) is described in subsection (c)(8) and exempt from tax under subsection (a), and

(B) limits its membership to the members of a particular religion, or

(2) a club which in good faith limits its membership to the members of a particular religion in order to further the teachings or principles of that religion, and not to exclude individuals of a particular race or color.

(j) Special Rules for Certain Amateur Sports Organizations.—

(1) In general.—In the case of a qualified amateur sports organization.—

(A) the requirement of subsection (c)(3) that no part of its activities involve the provision of athletic facilities or equipment shall not apply, and

(B) such organization shall not fail to meet the requirements of subsection (c)(3) merely because its membership is local or regional in nature.

(2) Qualified amateur sports organization defined.—For purposes of this subsection, the term "qualified amateur sports organization" means any organization organized and operated exclusively to foster national or international amateur sports competition if such organization is also organized and operated primarily to conduct national or international competition in sports or to support and develop amateur athletes for national or international competition in such sports.

(k) Treatment of Certain Organizations Providing Child Care.—For purposes of subsection (c)(3) of this section and sections 170(c)(2), 2055(a)(2), and 2522(a)(2), the term "educational purposes" includes the providing of care of children away from their homes if—

(1) substantially all of the care provided by the organization is for purposes of enabling individuals to be gainfully employed, and

(2) the services provided by the organization are available to the general public.

(l) Government Corporations Exempt Under Subsection (c)(1).—The organization described in this subsection is the Central Liquidity Facility established under title III of the Federal Credit Union Act (12 U.S.C. 1975 et seq.).

(m) Cross Reference.—

For nonexemption of Communist-controlled organizations, see section 11(b) of the Internal Security Act of 1950 (64 Stat. 997; 50 U.S.C. 790(b)).

Bibliography

Atkinson, Thomas E. *Handbook of the Law of Wills and Other Principles of Succession, Including Intestacy and Administration of Decedent's Estates*, 2d ed. West Publishing Co., 1953.

Bittker, *Churches, Taxes and the Constitution*, 78 Yale L.J. 1285 (1969).

Bittker & Rahdert, *The Exemption of Nonprofit Organizations from Federal Income Taxation*, 85 Yale L.J. 299 (1976).

Bowett, D. *The Law of International Institutions*. Stevens & Sons, 1975.

Brownlie, Ian. *Principles of Public International Law*. Clarendon Press, 1966.

Cary, William L., & Bright, Craig B. *The Law and the Lore of Endowment Funds*. Ford Foundation, 1969.

Ellman, *Another Theory of Nonprofit Corporations*, 80 Michigan L.R. 999 (1982).

Fessler, *Codification and the Nonprofit Corporation: The Philosophical Choices, Pragmatic Problems, and Drafting Difficulties Encountered in the Formulation of a New Alaska Code*, 33 Mercer L.R. 543 (1982).

Hansmann, *The Role of Nonprofit Enterprise*, 89 Yale L.J. 835 (1980).

Hansmann, *Reforming Nonprofit Corporation Law*, 129 U. Pa. L.R. 497 (1981).

Hansmann, *The Rationale for Exempting Nonprofit Organizations from Corporate Income Taxation*, 91 Yale L.J. 54 (1981).

Henn, Henry G., & Alexander, John R. *Laws of Corporations*, 3d ed. West, 1983.

Henn & Boyd, *Statutory Trends in the Law of Nonprofit Organizations: California, Here We Come!*, 66 Cornell L.R. 1103 (1981).

1983 World Almanac. Newspaper Enterprise Association, 1983.

Nossaman, Walter L., & Wyatt, Joseph L., Jr. *Trust Administration and Taxation*, 2d ed. rev. Matthew Bender and Company, 1982.

Oleck, Howard L. *Nonprofit Corporations, Organizations, and Associations*, 4th ed. Prentice-Hall, 1980.

Oleck, *The Nature of Nonprofit Organizations in 1979*, 10 U. Tol. L.R. 962 (1979).

Oleck, H., et al. *Parliamentary Law*. ABA-ALI Joint Committee, 1979.

Permut, *Consumer Perceptions of Nonprofit Enterprise: A Comment on Hansmann*, 90 Yale L.J. 1623 (1981).

Robert, Henry M. *Robert's Rules of Order.* William Morrow and Company, 1970.

Scott, Austin W. *The Law of Trusts,* 3d ed. Little, Brown and Company, 1967.

Seyersted, Finn. *Objective International Personality of International Organizations.* United Nations, 1963.

Sowards, Hugh L., & Hirsch, Neil H. *Business Organizations: Blue Sky Regulation,* Vol. 13C. Matthew Bender and Company, 1983.

Treusch, Paul E., & Sugarman, Norman A. *Tax-Exempt Charitable Organizations.* ALI-ABA, 1979.

Weithorn, Stanley S. *Tax Techniques for Foundations and Other Exempt Organizations.* Matthew Bender and Company, 1964.

Index

About the Author

E. C. LASHBROOKE, JR., is Professor and Chairman of the Department of General Business–Business Law Programs in the College of Business and Graduate School of Business Administration, Michigan State University. He has contributed articles to a number of law reviews and journals.